MW00427671

Taiwan's
Security Policy

Taiwan's Security Policy

EXTERNAL THREATS AND DOMESTIC POLITICS

Michael S. Chase

LYNNE
RIENNER
PUBLISHERS

BOULDER
LONDON

Published in the United States of America in 2008 by
Lynne Rienner Publishers, Inc.
1800 30th Street, Boulder, Colorado 80301
www.rienner.com

and in the United Kingdom by
Lynne Rienner Publishers, Inc.
3 Henrietta Street, Covent Garden, London WC2E 8LU

Library of Congress Cataloging-in-Publication Data
Chase, Michael.
Taiwan's security policy : external threats and domestic politics / Michael S. Chase.
   p. cm.
   Includes bibliographical references and index.
   ISBN 978-1-58826-566-1 (hardcover : alk. paper)
   1. National security—Taiwan. 2. Taiwan—Military policy. 3. Taiwan—
Military relations—United States. 4. United States—Military relations—Taiwan.
5. Taiwan—Military relations—China. 6. China—Military relations—Taiwan.
I. Title.
UA853.T28C38 2008
355'.033551249—dc22

2007048378

British Cataloguing in Publication Data
A Cataloguing in Publication record for this book
is available from the British Library.

Printed and bound in the United States of America

The paper used in this publication meets the requirements
of the American National Standard for Permanence of
Paper for Printed Library Materials Z39.48-1992.

5 4 3 2 1

Contents

CHAPTER 1

The Puzzle of Taiwan's Security Policy

Widely dismissed as a "junkyard army" twenty years ago, the Chinese People's Liberation Army (PLA) is now becoming an increasingly professional and capable fighting force. Substantial increases in Chinese defense spending since the late 1990s reflect the priority that Beijing attaches to this impressive transformation, which includes not only the accelerated acquisition and development of advanced weapons and equipment, but also more complex and sophisticated training and exercises and the implementation of a comprehensive program of organizational restructuring, doctrinal innovation, and personnel reforms.[1]

Because acquisition trends and training scenarios suggest that this modernization program is directed primarily at a Taiwan scenario, and given that political relations between China and Taiwan remain tense despite rapidly growing cross-Strait economic interaction, Taipei might reasonably be expected to respond to the growing threat with a sense of urgency. Indeed, standard approaches to the study of international relations predict that Taiwan would respond by increasing the level of resources devoted to its own defense or attempting to solidify its relations with potential security partners. Although Taipei has made substantial progress in some areas and continues to emphasize its commitment to strengthening its defense and deterrence capabilities, the steady decline in Taiwan's defense budget that lasted from the mid-1990s until the legislature finally approved a substantial spending increase in 2007 appeared to reflect a disturbing inability to respond more rapidly and comprehensively to a growing external security challenge.[2] Moreover, in recent years, Taiwan's leaders have taken a number of steps that have demonstrated a surprising willingness to risk provoking China and perhaps even undermining US political-military support.

There are at least three ways in which Taiwan's underactive response to PLA modernization could result in greater instability. First, the shifting cross-Strait military balance could increase the risk of conflict. One possibility is

1

that the changing cross-Strait military balance could result in miscalculation and misperception. Another possibility is that even in the absence of miscalculation, serious deficiencies in Taiwan's defense modernization efforts could leave the island so vulnerable that Chinese leaders would be convinced they could use force quickly and easily to bring Taiwan to the bargaining table on their terms. Simply put, as the PLA's military advantage increases, the use of force becomes at least a somewhat more realistic option for Chinese leaders. This is because the shifting cross-Strait military balance not only increases the odds of success should China attempt to use force against Taiwan, but also reduces the likely military and political costs. In short, if Chinese leaders believe their growing military advantage is large enough to achieve a quick and decisive victory at limited cost, they are more likely to consider using force to achieve their political objectives.

The potential implications of this changing cross-Strait military picture are especially worrisome when viewed in the context of an increasingly dynamic political environment in which two successive leaders in Taiwan have shown considerable willingness to take steps that risk precipitating a cross-Strait crisis by crossing one of Beijing's "red lines." Further complications arise because different actors have different conceptions of what constitutes the status quo in cross-Strait relations. All of these factors make it more challenging to prevent the China-Taiwan impasse from erupting into a military conflict, which should be a vital goal for all three of the major parties given that a cross-Strait war would be incredibly devastating for all involved and would likely bring two nuclear powers, the United States and China, to blows over an issue that the latter regards as vital to its national security and perhaps even regime survival.

Second, Taiwan's security policy has serious implications for the island's relationship with the United States, which remains Taiwan's chief political and military backer despite the termination of the US–Republic of China (ROC) defense alliance in 1980. Considerable tension resulted from Taiwan's prolonged failure to increase the level of resources devoted to its own military modernization and defense reform efforts. In particular, delays in the weapons procurement process have caused frustration in Washington, especially because leaders in Taipei have not only failed to marshal support for more rapidly and comprehensively enhancing the island's military capabilities, but also taken a number of steps that risk provoking China. Policymakers in Washington are concerned that Taiwan may drag the United States into a conflict through this combination of military vulnerability and potentially provocative political behavior. At the same time, Washington's tendency to question the seriousness of Taiwan's commitment to its own security has led to considerable consternation in Taipei, further complicating an already difficult relationship.

Third, Taiwan's response to PLA modernization has important domestic political implications, particularly in the area of civil-military relations. In recent years, for example, many military officers have complained that President Chen Shui-bian has risked endangering Taiwan's security by provoking the People's Republic of China (PRC), annoying the United States, and failing to provide enough funding to accelerate the development of the armed forces. This tension could exacerbate some of the civil-military difficulties inherent in Taiwan's remarkable transition from authoritarianism to democracy.

Given the importance of these issues, it is striking that relatively little has been written on Taiwan's security policy, especially in comparison to the substantial recent scholarship and policy analysis on Chinese military modernization and its potential implications for regional security. In short, there are only a handful of studies that focus on the Taiwanese side of the equation, and only a few of these have attempted to identify and explain the underlying causes of Taiwan's response to Chinese military modernization.[3] This imbalance underscores the need for a more thorough assessment of Taiwan's security policy.

This study attempts to explain the puzzle of Taiwan's response to the increasing security threat posed by Chinese military modernization since the middle to late 1990s. In doing so, it addresses the following questions: What explains Taiwan's underactive response to the accelerating pace of Chinese military modernization? Why did the level of resources devoted to Taiwan's own military modernization and defense reform programs decline for nearly a decade, despite the growing threat to its security posed by the accelerating enhancement of Chinese military capabilities? Why have Taiwan's leaders taken so many symbolic steps that risk provoking an increasingly influential and powerful potential adversary and alienating an increasingly distracted and overextended security partner? Is Taiwan "free-riding" on the US commitment to its defense, as is often asserted in policy debates in Washington? If so, how does this square with long-standing concerns about Taiwan's heavy reliance on the United States and actions that risk increasing the possibility of abandonment by an unofficial security partner that shares many common interests with China? Does Taiwan's behavior reflect misperception in the form of an underestimation of the threat to its security? Is Taiwan's underactive response to the expansion of Chinese military power a function of domestic political factors such as institutional arrangements and party politics?

To address these questions, the study draws on a variety of Chinese-language sources and dozens of interviews with officials and analysts in Taiwan, China, and the United States, and employs an eclectic analytic framework that incorporates insights from several theoretical approaches to the study of internal and external balancing.

Explaining Taiwan's Security Policy

Three main factors explain Taiwan's seemingly puzzling response to Chinese military modernization: security ties, threat perceptions, and domestic politics.

Security Ties and Taiwan's Security Policy

Many observers have suggested that Taiwan's response to Chinese military modernization is a classic case of "free-riding," with the island relying on the United States for its security rather than devoting greater resources to improving its own defense capabilities.[4] "Free-riding" is clearly a factor in Taiwan's response to Chinese military modernization, but it is certainly not the only explanation. Taiwan's confidence in the reliability of US security assurances has fluctuated over time. In the early 1980s, Taipei was concerned about the possibility of US abandonment following Washington's announcement that it was switching recognition to Beijing and withdrawing from the 1954 US-ROC mutual defense treaty. Despite the passage of the Taiwan Relations Act and strong support from influential members of the US Congress, Taipei was disappointed that the election of President Ronald Reagan did not result in a fundamental shift in US policy toward China and Taiwan. In particular, Taipei was disheartened by the 1982 US-China communiqué and some of the Reagan administration's decisions on arms sales, such as its refusal to sell advanced fighter aircraft to Taiwan.

Following the 1989 Tiananmen crackdown, the downturn in US-China relations and the sharp contrast between severe political repression in the PRC and Taiwan's democratic transition increased Taipei's confidence in US security assurances. President Bill Clinton's decision to send two aircraft carrier battle groups to the waters around Taiwan during the 1995–1996 crisis, closer security cooperation with the United States, and increasing support in the US Congress further strengthened Taipei's confidence. Indeed, Taiwan was very confident that the United States would intervene in a cross-Strait conflict following deployment of the two aircraft carrier battle groups. Moreover, throughout the 1980s and well into the 1990s, Taiwan had ample reason to believe that even limited US military involvement would have resulted in a decisive defeat for the PLA.

The Republican victory in the 2000 US presidential election provided another boost to Taipei's confidence in US security assurances, especially given that President George W. Bush and several of his most prominent foreign policy advisers had characterized China as a potential strategic competitor during the campaign. This gave leaders in Taiwan an opportunity to capitalize on the view of China as a potential future adversary, and to portray the island as an important asset to US policy in the Asia Pacific region.

Indeed, in 2001, President Bush stated that Washington would do "whatever it takes" to defend Taiwan in the event of a Chinese attack on the island. As US-Taiwan security cooperation increased, the Bush administration offered other indications of support, such as the April 2001 decision on arms sales. Since about 2003, however, the free-riding approach does not seem to fit very well, especially given Washington's growing frustration with Taipei and the mounting costs of the Iraq War, which suggest that US security assurances are neither nonexcludable nor nonrival, and are thus not a true public good for Taiwan. This has clearly intensified fears of abandonment in Taipei. For example, Premier Yu Shyi-kun warned in August 2004 that Taiwan needed to rely on its own resources to safeguard its national security. "How do we expect to safeguard the country if we're not well-armed?" Yu asked reporters. "We cannot solely rely on the United States to protect us once Beijing launches a military attack."[5]

Strains in relations with Washington appear to have diminished Taipei's confidence in US willingness to intervene in a cross-Strait conflict, and the continuing expansion of Chinese military power and the situation in Iraq seem to have given rise to concerns about US ability to intervene rapidly and decisively. For example, some analysts in Taiwan are concerned that ongoing improvements in China's nuclear forces and Beijing's development of antisatellite capabilities could deter the United States from intervening on Taiwan's behalf in the event of a conflict with China.[6] At the same time, however, Taiwan historically has had a number of reasons to believe the United States would likely intervene militarily in a cross-Strait crisis. The prospect of US intervention may be uncertain, but it does help deter China from choosing to use force to resolve the Taiwan issue on its terms. For politicians in Taiwan, this is probably enough to lower the perceived costs of domestic political strategies that risk provoking China or generating stalemates on issues such as defense spending. Accordingly, the free-riding approach is probably most useful when it is employed in combination with theories that focus on Taiwan's threat perceptions and domestic political considerations.

Threat Perceptions and Taiwan's Security Policy

Although measuring threat perceptions is an imprecise business at best, it appears that Taiwan's threat perceptions have contributed to the island's seemingly puzzling response to Chinese military modernization.[7] In the 1980s, officials and analysts in Taiwan assessed that the PLA lacked the capability to pose a serious threat to Taiwan's security, and that China was unlikely to use force against Taiwan. Serious initial concerns following the termination of the US-ROC defense treaty gave way to the assessment that the PLA lacked the ability to attack or even blockade Taiwan, and improvements in cross-Strait relations led many observers to conclude that conflict was unlikely. Despite increasing concerns in the wake of the 1995–1996 crisis, most observers still doubted that the PLA had the capability to invade Taiwan, and few believed a major cross-Strait conflict was imminent, though there was increasing concern about China's ability to inflict economic and psychological damage on Taiwan.

In recent years, Taiwan's official threat assessments have suggested a recognition of China's growing military capabilities and increasing options to attack or coerce the island. Taiwan's National Security Council has highlighted the growing threat posed by PLA modernization,[8] as has the Ministry of National Defense, which recently issued a detailed assessment listing three potential scenarios for Chinese military action: intimidation, "paralysis warfare," and invasion.[9] At the same time, however, Taiwan's leaders appear to believe that the chances of conflict over the next few years are slight, since Chinese leaders, even given the PLA's improved military capabilities, would want to exhaust all other options before accepting the tremendous risks and uncertainties that would be associated with using force against Taiwan. For example, Taiwan's Ministry of National Defense judges that intimidation is the most likely threat through 2008, and dismisses the paralysis and invasion scenarios as "highly unlikely," at least in the short term, given the current political and economic environment and the limitations of Chinese military power.[10] Most politicians and analysts in Taipei seem to agree with this assessment. Simply put, they doubt that China would use force anytime soon.[11] As Bernard Cole puts it, the island's leaders "may understand the power of the PLA, but not Beijing's willingness to employ it against Taiwan."[12] Indeed, although analysts in Taipei recognize that the PLA's capabilities are improving, and although the government's official threat assessments suggest some concern over the potential consequences of Chinese military modernization for the island's security, many observers doubt Beijing's willingness to use force against Taiwan, at least in the near to middle term. This mixed view often results in somewhat contradictory statements, sometimes even within the same official reports. For example, Taiwan's 2004 national defense report warned that China's military modernization threatened Taiwan's security, but concluded that "taking into consideration its economic growth and political stability, and barring unpredictable factors, the PRC is unlikely to pick up the fight against Taiwan in the near future."[13] This contradiction reflects a broader lack of consensus on the immediacy and severity of the threat to the island's security. Political elites in Taiwan are divided on the seriousness and urgency of the threat, and on how to cope with the challenges posed by PLA modernization. These differences stem from disagreements about fundamental issues, including the future of Taiwan's relationship with China.

Thus it appears that Taiwan's threat perceptions diminish the likelihood of a more comprehensive and energetic response to Chinese military modernization. Moreover, the perception that China is unlikely to use force also helps to explain why some politicians in Taiwan pursue domestic political strategies that risk crossing Beijing's "red lines," and why many others appear relatively unconcerned about the potential implications of prolonged stalemates over defense policy issues. In addition, politicians on both sides of the debate have disincentives to emphasize the seriousness of the Chinese military threat to Taiwan's national security. The Kuomintang and People's First Party cannot draw attention to the growing threat without calling into question the wisdom of their desire for greater economic and political engagement with China and the motives behind their opposition to the Chen administration's attempts to increase defense spending. On the other side of the political spectrum, even many pro-independence politicians in the Democratic Progressive Party and the Taiwan Solidarity Union appear reluctant to draw attention to the threat, perhaps because emphasizing the growing capabilities of the PLA would leave them vulnerable to Pan-Blue charges that their "localization" policies and unyielding stance on cross-Strait relations are unnecessarily provoking China, alienating the United States, and thus endangering Taiwan's security. In short, neither side is in a position to highlight the threat without undermining its own positions on other key issues and thus losing votes for its candidates in future elections.

Domestic Politics and Taiwan's Security Policy

Domestic political considerations have always played an important part in Taiwan's national security and defense policy decisions, but the salience of political institutions and policy disagreements has increased dramatically as a result of the island's democratization. Taiwan's political institutions are problematic, and the island's politicians are unwilling to compromise with their rivals. This combination of unresolved flaws in institutional design and a highly polarized domestic political environment exacerbates the problem of reaching a consensus on security policy.[14]

Under the authoritarian system in the 1980s, the formal separation of powers between the legislative and executive branches was of little importance in practice, because Taiwan had a one-party political system. The legislature exercised limited oversight in areas such as foreign policy and national defense, and the chief executive effectively dominated defense policy, though the ruling Kuomintang was facing mounting internal and external pressure to liberalize the political system as a result of the island's successful economic reforms, growing demands for democratization and political rights from the opposition movement, and the pressures of international isolation.

More recently, all of this has changed as a result of Taiwan's transition to democracy. The victory of Democratic Progressive Party candidate Chen Shui-bian in the 2000 presidential election marked a new phase in Taiwan's democratic transition, but the Kuomintang and its allies retained control of the increasingly influential Legislative Yuan, resulting in divided government in a political system that was designed during the authoritarian period and somewhat hastily and incompletely revised during the democratic transition phase. These unresolved institutional issues and sharp disagreements between the ruling and opposition camps have resulted in severe gridlock on many key issues and a highly contentious political atmosphere.

In particular, since 2000, when the Democratic Progressive Party won the presidential election but the Kuomintang retained control of the Legislative Yuan, it has become clear that unresolved institutional problems and a highly polarized political environment make divided government deeply problematic for Taiwan. The result has been stalemate in legislative-executive relations. According to Shelley Rigger, "Taiwan's governance problems are rooted in both institutional weaknesses and dysfunctional patterns of behavior, especially among politicians."[15] When the ROC was under Kuomintang domination, some of the flaws in Taiwan's constitution were less evident. ROC presidents of the dominant-party era, Chiang Kai-shek, Chiang Ching-kuo, and Lee Teng-hui, were also the chairmen of the party that controlled the legislature, dominated all other parts of the government, and exercised control over the military and even the mass media. This allowed the ROC to function as the approximate equivalent of a strong presidential system. After the May 2000 presidential election ended the Kuomintang's domination of the political system, however, these underlying systemic flaws bubbled to the surface, revealing the weaknesses inherent in Taiwan's semipresidential political system. As a result, after the Democratic Progressive Party won the May 2000 election, "the problematic relationships among the president, premier, and legislature suddenly became starkly evident."[16]

Intense political rivalry between and within the two major camps has compounded these institutional problems. The main political parties demonstrate an alarming tendency to cast their rivals in the opposing camp as threats to Taiwan's security and prosperity. As Mark Stokes writes, Pan-Blue politicians suggest that the Pan-Greens "could potentially destroy Taiwan through pursuit of *de jure* independence," while Pan-Green politicians cast the Pan-Blues as "'selling out' to Communist China."[17] Major institutional weaknesses and the intense acrimony between the Pan-Blue and Pan-Green camps have thus resulted in inaction on many critical domestic and foreign policy problems, including defense policy issues. Moreover, both camps appear to have concluded that blaming their rivals for the ensuing political gridlock serves their own electoral interests.[18]

Domestic politics and electoral considerations influence not only Taiwan's defense policy, but also its overall approach to cross-Strait relations. Specifically, domestic political considerations help to explain why Taiwan's leaders have taken a number of steps that risk destabilizing cross-Strait relations. Bringing domestic political concerns into the equation also helps to explain why they have often done so in defiance of US criticism, despite warnings that their actions risk creating friction in what is undoubtedly Taiwan's most important, albeit unofficial, bilateral relationship. Domestic politics and the dynamics of election campaigns have driven much of this potentially provocative behavior. In short, at least some Democratic Progressive Party politicians in Taiwan appear to have concluded that provoking China is a winning campaign strategy[19] that gives them three advantages over their political adversaries. First, it allows the Democratic Progressive Party to portray itself as the only party that is truly capable of standing up to Beijing. Second, it helps Democratic Progressive Party candidates consolidate their own political support and mobilize voters. Third, it enables them to cast their political adversaries as being weak on China and unwilling or unable to defend Taiwan's interests. When Beijing overreacts to the perceived provocation, such bullying simply multiplies the effects of this approach. Even if China's reaction is relatively moderate, the campaign strategy can still succeed.

* * *

Since the late 1990s, the interaction of security ties, threat perceptions, and domestic politics has resulted in a relatively modest response to Chinese military modernization, and has led Taiwan's leaders to take a number of steps that risk increasing tension with China. The combination of an underactive security response and an increasingly assertive stance on Taiwan's independence has troubling implications for the island's security and raises serious concerns for the United States.

Implications for the United States

In recent years, US policymakers have become increasingly concerned not only that the United States may have to carry a disproportionate share of the burden of deterring China, but also that Taiwan's deteriorating security position and its approach to cross-Strait relations risk sparking an otherwise avoidable cross-Strait conflict in which the island is unlikely to prevail without substantial US military assistance. Avoiding this outcome requires understanding the underlying causes of Taiwan's behavior, which are not as simple as they are often assumed to be in much of the US discourse on Taiwan's security policy. Taiwan's views of the US security commitment, its assessments of the Chinese threat to its security, and domestic political considerations have all played crucial roles in shaping Taiwan's national security and defense policy decisions in the period of democratization and democratic consolidation. Bringing domestic factors into the equation is essential not only to explaining Taiwan's response to Chinese military modernization during this period, but also to understanding why Taiwan's leaders have taken so many political steps that risk provoking China and undermining US political and military support.

These findings suggest a number of important policy implications for the United States. First, greater attention should be devoted to understanding the factors that shape Taiwan's defense and national security policy decisions. In short, understanding Taiwan's security policy is just as important as understanding China's security policy, and policymakers in Washington must recognize the importance of both domestic and international political factors in understanding Taiwan's security policy decisions. Second, given the central role of domestic politics in Taiwan, policymakers in Washington will have to speak clearly and consistently if they are to persuade leaders in Taipei to increase their commitment to improving the island's defenses and refrain from symbolic or substantive moves that may offer advantages in a highly partisan and intensely competitive domestic political environment, but that run the risk of unnecessarily provoking China. Sometimes Washington will have to speak loudly to make sure the message is heard, as was the case in December 2003 when President Bush stated publicly that the United States would oppose any attempt by either side to make unilateral changes to the status quo. At the same time, however, US policymakers must exercise due caution, lest their comments be perceived as intending to bully Taiwan or interfere in its domestic affairs. Indeed, publicly chastising Taiwan over its failure to approve funding for arms purchases from the United States has probably been counterproductive. Finally, US policymakers should try to find ways to make incentive structures in Taiwan work in favor of US interests, such as by offering industrial cooperation arrangements that would increase the probability of winning legislative approval for arms sales.

Research Approach and Sources

My research draws on a wide variety of published sources and dozens of interviews with policymakers and analysts in Taiwan, China, and the United States. Wherever possible, I have attempted to corroborate information obtained from one source, whether a publication or an interviewee, with information from other sources.

The availability of published primary and secondary sources on national security and defense policy issues in Taiwan is increasing along with the proliferation of research institutes and think tanks focusing on foreign and security policy issues. At the leading edge of this trend is the bilingual journal *Guofang zhengce pinglun* (Taiwan Defense Affairs), which was established in 2000 and is currently published by the Institute for Taiwan Defense and Strategic Studies, a Taipei-based think tank. The Ministry of National Defense and the ROC armed forces also publish numerous Chinese-language journals and periodicals, such as *Guofang zazhi* (Defense Journal), *Haijun xueshu yuekan* (Naval Science Monthly), *Kongjun xueshu yuekan* (Air Force Science Monthly), *Guofang tongzi banniankan* (Defense Communications), *Lianhe houqin jikan* (Combined Logistics Quarterly), and *Guofang guanli xuebao* (National Defense Management Journal). Additional official sources include the biannual national defense reports of the ROC Ministry of National Defense, press releases from the ministry as well as from the presidential office, and other official documents such as the first and only report of Taiwan's National Security Council, published in 2006. In addition, the study draws on monographs and policy papers published by think tanks in Taiwan, and on articles published by the island's numerous daily newspapers.

Interviews constitute another important source of data, particularly because they often fill in gaps left by the published sources and provide insight into the decisionmaking process. This study draws on numerous interviews conducted with participants in Taiwan's national security and defense policy process, including current and former ROC government officials, legislators, military officers, Pan-Green and Pan-Blue politicians, think tank researchers, and academic national security policy specialists. It also draws on interviews with current and former US officials and analysts.

Organization of the Study

Part 1 examines the cross-Strait security environment and Taiwan's security policy since 1979, when the United States established diplomatic relations with the PRC and announced its intention to withdraw from its mutual defense treaty with the ROC. Chapter 2 provides an overview of China's policy toward Taiwan from 1980 to 1999. Chapter 3 assesses Taiwan's security policy during this period, with an emphasis on its response to Chinese military modernization. Chapter 4 analyzes China's Taiwan strategy since 2000, when the victory of Democratic Progressive Party candidate Chen Shui-bian in Taiwan's second democratic presidential election ended more than fifty years of uninterrupted Kuomintang rule in Taiwan. Chapter 5 analyzes Taiwan's response to this growing challenge under President Chen Shui-bian.

Part 2 seeks to explain Taiwan's security policy as a function of security ties, threat perceptions, and domestic politics. Chapter 6 focuses on Taiwan's security relationship with the United States and the latter's role in shaping Taiwan's security policy. Chapter 7 examines Taiwan's perceptions of Chinese capabilities and intentions. Chapter 8 analyzes the influence of political institutions and domestic politics on Taiwan's security policy.

Part 3, Chapter 9, reviews the study's key findings and assesses their implications for Taiwan's national security, cross-Strait relations, and US foreign and defense policy.

PART 1
The Chronological Picture

CHAPTER 2

China's Approach to Taiwan: 1980–1999

U nderstanding Taiwan's security policy in the 1980s and 1990s requires placing it in the context of China's policy toward Taiwan at that time, during which China pursued a multifaceted strategy incorporating the diplomatic, economic, political, and military instruments of national power to promote reunification with the island. Although Chinese policy toward Taiwan emphasized political and economic carrots throughout much of this period, Beijing also saw the need to develop more powerful sticks as part of this broader strategy. Accordingly, China embarked on a military modernization program designed to transform the People's Liberation Army (PLA) into a more professional and operationally capable fighting force. By the end of the 1990s, when Beijing decided to accelerate its military modernization programs in response to growing concerns about US national security policy and domestic political trends in Taiwan, the PLA was already beginning to pose a much more serious threat to Taiwan's security. As the decade drew to a close, military power was becoming a more prominent—and more potent—element of China's overall policy toward Taiwan.

China's Taiwan Strategy in the 1980s and 1990s

Following the normalization of US-China relations, the PRC adopted a softer approach toward Taiwan. Beijing stopped shelling the offshore islands and made several policy statements indicating its desire to achieve "peaceful reunification" with Taiwan, the most important of which were the 1 January 1979 "Message to Compatriots in Taiwan" and the 30 September 1981 "Nine-Point Proposal." These relatively conciliatory messages emphasized China's desire to establish cross-Strait economic links and promised that Taiwan would enjoy a high level of autonomy following reunification with China. Although Beijing remained dissatisfied with Washington's refusal to terminate arms sales to Taiwan, and was frustrated that US-China normalization had not forced Taipei to the negotiating table, the Chinese Communist Party continued to promote cross-Strait political dialogue. In June 1983, Beijing unveiled what became known as its "one country, two systems" proposal for peaceful reunification with Taiwan. Paramount leader Deng Xiaoping promised that Taiwan would enjoy a high degree of autonomy following reunification and could even continue to maintain its own armed forces. Taiwan expressed little interest in this formulation, but the US-China-Taiwan relationship remained relatively stable throughout the mid-1980s.

Even though Taiwan's democratization was fundamentally altering the dynamics of the cross-Strait relationship by creating space for domestic political and social trends that alarmed Beijing, growing economic ties with Taiwan gave Chinese leaders reason for at least cautious optimism. Indeed, one of the most important developments in China-Taiwan relations in the 1980s and 1990s was the dramatic expansion of cross-Strait economic ties. In the early 1980s, economic interaction between China and Taiwan was extremely limited. In the middle to late 1980s, however, Taiwan began to relax many of its long-standing restrictions on cross-Strait trade, travel, and investment. Taiwanese companies in labor-intensive industries such as textiles were the first to invest in production facilities in China. Soon electronics firms opened their own factories in China to take advantage of lower wages. China offered a variety of incentives to encourage Taiwanese investment, but many in Taiwan became concerned about the potential political and economic implications of growing cross-Strait trade and investment.[1]

The scale and scope of cross-Strait economic interaction increased dramatically, despite Taipei's misgivings, but the two sides were unable to overcome their long-standing political estrangement. In the early 1990s, however, there were some signs of a potential thaw in the cross-Strait political climate. Most importantly, in November 1992, Wang Daohan from China's Association for Relations Across the Taiwan Strait, and Koo Chen-foo from Taiwan's Strait Exchange Foundation, engaged in unofficial talks in Hong Kong, during which they reportedly reached an important understanding on cross-Strait ties. This unofficial agreement, which later became known as the "1992 consensus," allowed both sides to accept the "one China" principle, subject to their own differing interpretations.[2] Nevertheless, China and Taiwan continued to battle over Taiwan's participation in the international community and to engage in a "bidding war" over the loyalties of the island's remaining diplomatic allies.[3]

The next major Chinese initiative was unveiled on 30 January 1995, when Chinese Communist Party general secretary and president Jiang Zemin delivered an important speech on Taiwan policy, known as the "Eight-Point Proposal." Although Jiang refused to renounce the use of force and insisted that cross-Strait negotiations should take place on the basis of the "one China" principle, the overall tone of the proposal was conciliatory. In his speech, Jiang pledged that Beijing would seek peaceful reunification and expand cross-Strait economic and cultural exchanges. He indicated that China would permit Taiwan to maintain unofficial relations with other countries and even stated that Beijing would conduct negotiations with Taiwan on an "equal footing." President Lee Teng-hui rebuffed Jiang's offer, however, presumably at least in part because Beijing's preconditions suggested that interaction would not really take place on an equal footing and seemed to predetermine the outcome of any future negotiations. As Taiwan's first-ever democratic presidential election approached, cross-Strait relations entered a state of political-military crisis.

The event that sparked the crisis was President Bill Clinton's May 1995 decision to grant a visa for President Lee Teng-hui to visit Cornell University, his alma mater, despite previous high-level assurances to Beijing that Washington would not permit Lee to visit the United States. The reversal on the visa issue, which was clearly a response to congressional pressure, infuriated Beijing, even though US officials stated repeatedly that Lee would visit in a private capacity and would not be permitted to engage in official activities while in the United States. China denounced the decision and recalled its ambassador to signal the depth of its displeasure. Beijing also canceled a second round of unofficial cross-Strait talks that had been scheduled for July. China's most demonstrative response, however, was a series of military exercises and missile tests carried out ahead of Taiwan's legislative elections in 1995 and the island's first-ever presidential election in 1996.

Concerned about US policy toward Taiwan and worried that the island was "drifting away" from reunification as a result of its ongoing democratization, Beijing decided to conduct a series of military exercises designed to send a message to Taiwan and Washington.[4] From 21 to 28 July 1995, China conducted live-fire military exercises, including six ballistic missile launches into the ocean, in an area about eighty nautical miles northeast of Taiwan. From 15 to 25 August, the PLA conducted another round of live-fire exercises and launched six more missiles. The US response was relatively muted, but in December, around the time of Taiwan's second democratic legislative elections, the US aircraft carrier *Nimitz* transited the Taiwan Strait.[5] Despite the aircraft carrier transit and other signals of Washington's insistence that the Taiwan issue should be resolved through peaceful means, including blunt warnings delivered to senior Chinese officials, China conducted an even larger round of military exercises in March 1996, beginning just weeks before Taiwan's first-ever democratic presidential election. The 8–25 March 1996 military demonstration, which was designated "Strait 961," involved four short-range ballistic missile tests and a major display of firepower involving all three military services and much of China's most technologically advanced military equipment.[6] This time, the missiles were fired into closure areas off two of Taiwan's major ports, Kaohsiung and Keelung. Inclement weather curtailed another phase of the exercise that was scheduled to coincide with the presidential election in Taiwan. Nevertheless, the March 1996 exercise was "the largest-ever multiservice exercise China has . . . conducted in the Taiwan Strait area."[7] The March 1996 exercises were "demonstrations" of China's resolve, clearly designed to send a political message to leaders in both Taipei and Washington.[8] Washington responded by dispatching two aircraft carrier battle groups to the area around Taiwan, to underscore the credibility of its commitment to the island.[9]

The crisis was resolved peacefully, but it would have major implications for US-China-Taiwan relations and security in the Asia Pacific region. Although Beijing's actions underscored its resolve, the show of force also backfired to some extent, in that it undermined China's efforts to make unification more appealing to the people of Taiwan and provided the motivation for Washington and Taipei to enhance US-Taiwan security cooperation. As a result of the US intervention in the crisis, Beijing appears to have concluded that it would almost certainly have to contend with US military intervention in the event of a cross-Strait conflict. This in turn contributed to China's decision to further enhance its military power and to develop capabilities that would allow it to deter, delay, or otherwise interfere with US military intervention in a conflict with Taiwan. Indeed, within a few years, deteriorating relations with the United States and growing concerns about domestic social and political trends in Taiwan led Beijing to accelerate its military modernization programs.

The US intervention in the Kosovo conflict, in particular, raised serious concerns in Beijing and ultimately sparked a major debate about China's external security environment and foreign policy.[10] The Kosovo conflict was also the backdrop for an incident that caused enormous damage to US-China relations. On 7 May 1999, the United States accidentally bombed the Chinese embassy in Belgrade. Beijing refused to accept the US explanation that the attack was the result of serious mistakes in the targeting process, and crowds of demonstrators besieged the US embassy in Beijing. Many in China were convinced that the bombing was intentional, even after Washington briefed senior Chinese officials on the results of its investigation into the series of errors that led to the incident. For some, the embassy bombing confirmed their suspicions that the United States was determined to prevent China's emergence as a great power.[11]

The US-China relationship was barely beginning to get back on an even footing when another crisis erupted over Taiwan. On 9 July 1999, President Lee Teng-hui declared in an interview with *Deutsche Welle* that the relationship between China and Taiwan was not one between a central government and a local government, but a "state-to-state, or at least special state-to-state" relationship. Washington quickly became concerned that Lee's comments would provoke a crisis in cross-Strait relations, and Beijing took the statement as evidence confirming its suspicion that Lee was a dangerous proindependence ideologue.[12] In addition to excoriating Lee in the official media, China responded to his "state-to-state" comments by conducting military exercises and increasing air activity over the Taiwan Strait.[13] The military deployed additional planes to a base opposite Taiwan, increased its sortie rate, and for the first time employed its most advanced aircraft over the Strait as part of an apparent "show of force" designed to demonstrate Beijing's determination to prevent President Lee from moving Taiwan closer to formal independence. In the wake of the embassy bombing and Lee's "state-to-state" comments, Beijing began devoting much greater resources to modernizing the PLA, making military power an increasingly prominent component of its approach toward dealing with Taiwan.

PLA Capabilities in the 1980s and 1990s

China's poor performance in the 1979 border war with Vietnam revealed the underlying weaknesses of the PLA and motivated civilian and military leaders to undertake a series of reforms. As a result, the Chinese military began to gradually improve its capabilities in the 1980s and early 1990s.[14] The 1991 Gulf War provided added impetus to modernize and professionalize the PLA, as did a growing focus on preparing for a Taiwan contingency. Nonetheless, at the time of the 1995–1996 Taiwan Strait crisis, the PLA had few if any credible options to use force against Taiwan. This began to change in the late 1990s, however, especially after the Chinese leadership decided to increase the level of resources devoted to national defense, and to accelerate modernization of the Chinese military. As a result, by 2000, it appeared that Taiwan's traditional qualitative edge over the PLA was eroding, and some observers assessed that the cross-Strait military balance was beginning to shift toward China.

Threat Perceptions and Lessons Learned

The PLA's poor performance in the border war with Vietnam sparked renewed efforts to modernize and professionalize the armed forces.[15] Indeed, following the PLA's ineffective performance in the 1979 conflict with Vietnam, China embarked on a "fairly comprehensive modernization and reform program."[16] As the PLA was beginning to implement these reforms, changes under way in the Soviet Union provided the occasion for a major reassessment of China's external security environment. In 1985, Deng Xiaoping discarded the policy of preparing for "an early war, an all-out war, and a nuclear war" in favor of a program of peacetime army-building designed to enable the PLA to fight and win limited wars along China's periphery, subject to the resource constraints imposed by the high priority attached to economic reform programs. In short, Chinese leaders surveyed the international situation and determined that a limited war with a regional power along China's periphery was much more likely than a major war with the Soviet Union.[17]

Although China considered a major war unlikely, Chinese analysts devoted considerable attention to studying conflicts involving major military powers, such as the 1982 Falklands War, and determined that major changes were taking place in modern warfare, with potentially serious implications for the PLA, especially if it failed to narrow the gap that separated it from the militaries of the major powers. In particular, the performance of the US military in the 1991 Gulf War shocked the PLA brass and convinced them that despite the changes they had already implemented, they would have to accelerate the modernization program if the PLA was to avoid falling even further behind the United States.[18] The lessons learned from the Gulf War reinforced what many in the PLA were already thinking. As Paul Godwin puts it, "While there can be no doubt that the devastating display of military technology during the 1991 Gulf War had a profound influence on the Chinese military leaders, it served primarily to underscore what they had known for many years: that the absence of modern armaments severely restricted the PLA's effectiveness, and could even endanger military success under the restraints provided by limited war's requirements for speed and lethality in combined arms warfare."[19] Consequently, the PLA embarked on an ambitious program of reform and modernization.

In 1995, Jiang Zemin articulated the concept of the "Two Transformations," the defense policy line that serves as high-level guidance for the current reform and modernization programs. The concept refers to transforming the basis of the PLA from quantity to quality, and shifting from preparing to fight local wars under ordinary conditions to preparing to fight "local wars under modern, high-tech conditions." Closely associated with this concept is a policy that focuses on shifting from a manpower-intensive army to a science and technology–intensive fighting force, with a strong emphasis on "informatization" of the PLA.

At about the same time, the 1995–1996 Taiwan Strait crisis made it clear that the PLA would likely have to deal with US military intervention in a cross-Strait conflict, thus adding an even greater sense of urgency to the PLA's already ongoing transformation efforts. Indeed, since the 1995–1996 crisis, the PLA's modernization program, which consists of changes in planning, training and exercises, weapons procurement, and force deployment, has focused largely on a Taiwan contingency involving US military intervention. Moreover, the US intervention in the 1999 Kosovo conflict hardened perceptions of the United States as a hegemonic power seeking to restrain China's rise and keep Taiwan permanently separate from the mainland. Although the military operation was impressive, it was the alarm over the political implications of the US intervention and Taiwanese president Lee Teng-hui's "state-to-state" comments that added an even greater sense of urgency to the PLA's modernization program. The accidental bombing of the Chinese embassy in Belgrade, in particular, deepened Beijing's suspicions that the United States was determined to prevent China's emergence as a great power. Chinese foreign and security policy analysts argued that "hegemonism and power politics" and "military interventionism" were on the rise, and that the United States posed an increasing threat to Chinese national security.[20] This conclusion led to calls for increasing the pace of military modernization.

As this debate was taking place in the late 1990s, the PLA still had serious shortcomings. Most importantly, the PLA had little experience with joint operations and lacked the command, control, communications, computers, intelligence, surveillance, and reconnaissance (C4ISR) and logistics capabilities required to conduct joint warfare. The PLA had made major improvements in several key areas, however, and further changes were clearly on the horizon. Thus at the end of the 1990s, the PLA was "just beginning to turn the corner in emerging from broad obsolescence in terms of equipment, doctrine, training, and logistics."[21]

Chinese Defense Spending in the 1980s and 1990s

From the beginning of the economic reform and opening era in 1978, Chinese leaders stated that military modernization was subordinate to the primary task of domestic economic development. The relatively low ranking of military modernization among China's national priorities limited the funding available for training and acquisition of new equipment. According to an official Chinese account, "After the Third Plenum of the 11th [Chinese Communist Party] Central Committee, the top priority which had once been given to the needs of defense and military building was given to economic construction."[22] Deng Xiaoping argued that it would be necessary to delay major increases in defense expenditure until China achieved a higher level of economic development.[23]

In line with this guidance, the PLA's share of the central government budget declined throughout the 1980s and 1990s, from about 17 percent in 1979 to about 9 percent in 1989. Moreover, inflation devoured most of the increases in the defense budget that the PLA finally began to receive in the late 1980s and early 1990s. In nominal terms, defense spending increased 159 percent from 1986 to 1994. When adjusted for inflation, however, this amounted to only a 4 percent real increase in defense expenditure. Much of the modest increase in real spending the PLA received in the early 1990s went to raising salaries and improving living standards for servicemen and their families.[24] The PLA finally began to receive major real increases in the defense budget in the late 1990s, when rapid economic growth began to make more resources available for defense spending and Beijing decided to accelerate PLA modernization in order to develop more credible options to employ force against Taiwan and limit US intervention in a cross-Strait conflict. Indeed, the PLA has received a double-digit real increase in defense spending in almost every year since 1998.

Hardware Modernization

Acquisition of advanced weapon systems and military equipment was one of the central elements of China's military modernization program.[25] The ground forces traditionally dominated the military, but the shift in strategy from countering a Soviet invasion to fighting limited, local wars required greater emphasis on naval and air capabilities, making the PLA navy and PLA air force the highest priorities throughout the 1990s.

Naval power. China's naval capabilities were decidedly lacking in the late 1980s. The PLA navy was very large, but its warships and submarines were "mostly outmoded."[26] Although the navy had about sixty diesel submarines and six nuclear-powered submarines, including five Han-class attack submarines and one Xia-class nuclear-powered ballistic missile submarine, its subsurface capabilities were seriously limited. Indeed, before the navy acquired Kilo-class submarines from Russia in the mid-1990s, its submarine force was a major weakness. Most Chinese submarines were "old, noisy, and slow."[27]

The navy's surface warfare capabilities were also limited. In the 1990s, it sought to remedy this problem by retiring about 300 older warships and introducing a series of indigenously developed destroyers and frigates. Even after China began deploying its new Luhu-class destroyers and Jiangwei-class frigates, however, antiair warfare remained a potentially critical weakness for the navy.[28] Amphibious lift was another serious area of weakness. Even in the late 1990s, China's sealift capability was only sufficient to transport approximately one division of troops.[29]

Nonetheless, the acquisition of new surface ships and Kilo-class submarines represented a substantial enhancement of Chinese naval power. By the mid-1990s, the navy was well on the way to transforming itself from a coastal defense force into a modern navy capable of posing a more serious threat to Taiwan. Yet much of this transformation depended on access to Russian ships and submarines. This was part of a broader problem the PLA faced well into the 1990s.[30]

Air power and air defense. In the 1980s, the PLA air force had nearly 5,000 combat aircraft, but most were seriously outdated. Modernization of the air force was thus another key priority for the Chinese military in the 1990s.[31] It acquired its first advanced combat aircraft in 1992, when China purchased 26 Su-27 fighters from Russia. Even after this acquisition, however, the air force was composed mainly of aging Soviet-designed aircraft, many from the 1950s and 1960s. The air force also lacked in-flight refueling and airborne command and control capabilities, which limited its range and diminished its ability to locate targets. Training deficiencies represented another serious problem for the air force in the 1980s and 1990s.[32] For the most part, pilot training was heavily scripted and unrealistic, often relying on strict ground-control intercept techniques that left pilots little or no opportunity to act on their own initiative. In addition, Chinese pilots lacked proficiency in a number of key areas, including flying over open water, flying at night, and flying in bad weather.

In all, the air force still lacked modern defensive counterair and offensive counterair capabilities, and China's air defense architecture was widely regarded as "antiquated."[33] To its credit, however, the air force recognized the importance of addressing many of these problems. In addition, China identified air defense as a key priority and began acquiring SA-10 surface-to-air missile systems from Russia.

Ground forces. Even after cutting more than 1 million troops during the 1980s, the ground forces were still far too large to modernize the equipment of all units at the same time. Therefore, instead of attempting to undertake an across-the-board modernization effort that would be watered down by the size of the army, the PLA in the 1990s focused on upgrading the capabilities and readiness of key units, which were designated "rapid-reaction units" or "fist units," such as the Fifteenth Airborne Army. These units were the first to receive new weapons and equipment, and enjoyed priority access to funds for training. In addition, the PLA acquired more modern tanks. Nevertheless, in general, upgrading of ground forces tended to receive a lower priority than modernization of China's air and naval forces.

Conventional missiles. China had no conventional ballistic missile capability in the 1980s. At that time, the Second Artillery's only mission was to survive an adversarial first strike and launch a retaliatory nuclear attack. The Second Artillery added a conventional-strike capability to its mission in the early 1990s.[34] At the time of the 1995–1996 Taiwan Strait crisis, the PLA reportedly had deployed about 30–50 short-range ballistic missiles. In the late 1990s, the number of such missiles deployed across from Taiwan had reached about 200, but they were not very accurate, which would have limited their utility against military targets such as ports, airfields, and command and control centers.[35] In the late 1990s, however, China began to deploy more short-range ballistic missiles and to improve their accuracy by employing satellite-aided navigation. In addition, the PLA was developing land-attack cruise missiles capable of precision strikes against Taiwan and other regional targets.

C4ISR capabilities. For many years, the PLA also faced major shortcomings in its command, control, communications, computers, intelligence, surveillance, and reconnaissance capabilities. The PLA had traditionally relied upon an outdated telecommunications infrastructure that "severely limited the military's ability to transmit and process large amounts of information or coordinate activities between the various Military Regions, thereby reducing military effectiveness."[36] In the 1990s, however, the PLA embarked on a massive effort to upgrade and expand its communications infrastructure. This ambitious project was bolstered by the rapid development of the civilian information technology and telecommunications industries in China. One of the key results of the communications upgrade was the construction of a national fiber-optic communications network that provided the PLA with much greater communications capacity, higher reliability, and improved communications security.

The PLA also faced challenges when it came to modernizing its ISR architecture. Although China was capable of launching photoreconnaissance satellites, Chinese imagery satellite technology was "outdated by Western standards."[37] In the late 1990s, China began an ambitious manned space program, started participating in a variety of international space partnerships, and started planning a more sophisticated military space program. Nonetheless, in the late 1990s, C4ISR remained an area of substantial weakness for the PLA. As a US Department of Defense report published in 2000 pointed out, China still lacked real-time ISR capabilities, and the PLA's command and control capabilities were not up to the task of effectively supporting joint service operations.[38]

Defense industries. To a considerable extent, the PLA's hardware shortcomings stemmed from the chronic problems of China's defense industries. Indeed, throughout the 1980s and well into the 1990s, PRC defense industries were unable to produce the weapons the PLA needed, leaving China heavily dependent on foreign suppliers to meet its military modernization requirements. Despite numerous attempts to reform the sprawling defense-industrial complex and convert parts of it to civilian production, most of the enterprises that composed China's defense industry suffered from bloated work forces, social welfare burdens, inefficiency, mismanagement, financial difficulties, technological and organizational backwardness, excessive stove-piping, lack of exposure to market forces, and other such problems. The quality of output varied across sectors, including a few emerging "pockets of excellence," but generally was insufficient to meet the PLA's needs. For example, the aircraft and shipbuilding industries faced a number of problems that left them with little ability to produce modern weapon systems.

Even in the late 1990s, the military-industrial complex in China was "a closed, protected, state-within-a-state with only limited incentives and few resources to reform."[39] Given these constraints, there were serious doubts about the ability of the Chinese defense industries to produce the arms and equipment required to transform the PLA into a modern, high-tech fighting force. In 1998, however, Beijing began implementing major defense-industrial reforms that ultimately improved the capability of the defense industries to produce advanced weapons and equipment for the PLA.[40]

Software Reforms and Professionalization

The "Two Transformations" policy drives reforms not only in weapons, but also in institutions, personnel, and doctrine. Indeed, the Chinese military also undertook major downsizing and reorganization initiatives, implemented reforms in logistics, personnel policy, and training, and revamped its strategy and doctrine.

Downsizing and reorganization. Among the central aspects of the reforms were downsizing and organizational restructuring. Deng Xiaoping was widely seen as the driving force behind the downsizing of the PLA in the 1980s. In several key speeches, Deng emphasized the importance of streamlining the military and trimming personnel from bloated and over-staffed headquarters departments. The motivations were both operational and economic. The reduction in the number of troops was designed to make the military leaner and meaner. Moreover, reducing personnel expenses would leave more money available for force modernization, which would contribute to enhancing the PLA's war-fighting capabilities.[41] The second motivation was economic. The troop cuts were intended to reduce the financial burden of supporting the world's most massive military, which in the early 1980s consisted of about 4.75 million soldiers.[42]

As part of this policy, between 1982 and 1984 the PLA cut about 650,000–750,000 troops, mainly by handing over to civilian control entire units that were responsible for public security, production and construction, and railways. The People's Armed Police, which was established as a paramilitary security force in 1983, also absorbed a very large number of demobilized soldiers. In 1985, China announced an even more radical downsizing plan that involved cutting 1 million troops. Further rounds of downsizing took place in 1989, 1992, and 1994. As a result of these troop cuts, by the end of 1994 the number of troops in the PLA had declined to about 2.93 million. The restructuring of the PLA also reflected China's increasing emphasis on transitioning from manpower-intensive ground forces designed to repel a Soviet invasion, to technology-intensive forces, especially air and naval capabilities, more suited to engaging in limited conflicts along China's periphery. In 1997, Beijing announced that it would demobilize another 500,000 troops. Constraints that likely inhibited even more radical downsizing included the leadership's concerns about social stability and the limited capacity of local governments and enterprises to absorb demobilized servicemen.

Beyond downsizing the PLA, China also implemented a series of organizational reforms designed to restructure the PLA and make it a more modern and responsive fighting force. The major defense reforms initiated in the mid-1980s not only reduced the size of the PLA by 1 million personnel, but also reduced the number of military regions and reorganized the ground forces. China reduced the number of military regions from eleven to seven as part of this restructuring program.[43] The PLA also began reorganizing its thirty-five field armies into twenty-four group armies *(jituan jun)*. The objective of this restructuring was to "integrate infantry, armor, and other ground force branches into a single command in order to provide a more effective organizational structure for combined arms warfare."[44]

Logistics. Supporting modern combat forces is an extraordinarily complex undertaking that encompasses a wide variety of activities, ranging from supplying petroleum, oil, lubricants, ammunition, and spare parts, to providing food and medical services. Throughout the 1980s and well into the 1990s, however, the PLA still had a logistics infrastructure that was designed for a large-scale ground conflict and was thus poorly suited to supporting the types of operations the PLA expected it would have to conduct in future "high-tech local wars." Many logistics procedures were military region–specific, a problem that made it difficult to develop military-wide standards and undermined China's ability to conduct operations across military regions. The PLA recognized these deficiencies, however, and in December 1998 began implementing a series of reforms designed to modernize and enhance its logistics and support capabilities, including integration of logistics functions for the three military services, standardization of logistics and supply work, outsourcing of many functions to civilian contractors, automation of inventory control processes, and centralization and streamlining of procurement procedures.[45]

Personnel policy. In the 1980s, the PLA faced serious challenges in the area of personnel policy. The PLA officer corps was not very well educated and lacked proficiency in many areas that were becoming key components of modern warfare. To make matters worse, the standard of living for military personnel declined in the late 1980s, intensifying the PLA's recruitment and retention problems. As a result of personnel reforms implemented in the 1980s and 1990s, however, the Chinese officer corps became younger, better educated, and more professional.[46] Underlying this transformation were several key professionalizing trends, including higher levels of education, greater functional specialization, and more widespread adherence to retirement norms. These changes resulted in improved expertise, more rational career patterns, and a greater sense of "corporateness." Some of the key changes involved reversing policies adopted during the tumultuous years of the Cultural Revolution. Perhaps most importantly, in 1988 the PLA reinstituted ranks, which had been abolished in 1965.[47] Other key changes involved institutionalizing the policies and procedures that governed career patterns. For example, the PLA introduced new regulations that set objective criteria for promotions, and reformed the officer accession process. Another important change was the establishment of a noncommissioned officer corps.

The PLA also recognized the need to overhaul its professional military education system,[48] which underwent significant reform starting in the late 1970s as the PLA began rebuilding an educational infrastructure that was largely destroyed during the Cultural Revolution. The reforms consisted of reopening academies, establishing the National Defense University, and creating graduate degree programs.[49] In addition, the PLA began sending more officers to study and travel abroad.[50]

Training and exercises. Increasing the realism of training and conducting more complex exercises were also key components of the PLA's software reforms in the 1980s and 1990s. In the late 1980s, PLA exercises began to include rapid-reaction units and focus on coordination among ground, air, and naval forces. Many of the PLA's training reforms followed a predictable pattern. The PLA selected specific units to conduct experimental exercises, officers analyzed the lessons learned from those exercises, and these lessons were subsequently applied to other units.[51] In addition, the General Staff Department emphasized standardization of training practices and the development of criteria for evaluating training and exercises. Among the areas the PLA emphasized were combined arms, joint operations, nighttime training, and opposing-force training.[52]

In the 1990s, major exercises—many of which simulated attacks against Taiwan—became more frequent, increasingly sophisticated, and larger in scale.[53] Nonetheless, some of the PLA's joint exercises actually involved little more than forces from multiple services training at the same time and in the same general location, but conducting separate exercise scenarios. As John Culver observed, "While training may be improving and growing in scale, there is little evidence of the kind of sophisticated training that conforms to US definitions of joint training. Chinese exercises largely involve forces operating in close regional proximity, over the same training areas, but they lack combined command centers. This type of training is more than coincidental military training but still falls far short of integrated military operations."[54] In all, however, the PLA improved its training and exercises considerably by the end of the 1990s. As the US Department of Defense reported, PLA training had become "more realistic and challenging, with an increased participation by opposition force units and greater emphasis on combined arms."[55] These changes increased the chances that the PLA would be able to employ its forces effectively in the event of a conflict with Taiwan.

Strategy and doctrine. China's military transformation also required corresponding adjustments in strategy and doctrine. Throughout much of the 1980s, Chinese strategy was narrowly focused on a single strategic problem: countering a Soviet invasion. By the late 1990s, China had adopted a much broader approach to military strategy that incorporated a variety of contingencies and a number of potential opponents, albeit with a very heavy focus on Taiwan scenarios.[56] Factors contributing to the reexamination of operational doctrine included the performance of the US military and other militaries in a variety of conflicts, such as the Falklands War, Gulf War, and the Kosovo conflict, and China's changing assessment of its overall external security environment.

From the late 1970s to the late 1990s, the PLA underwent several major changes in its analysis of the likely format of future war, and revised its doctrine accordingly on several occasions. In the late 1970s, the PLA shifted its approach from "people's war" to "people's war under modern conditions." The latter marked important changes in several areas, such as preparing for shorter wars instead of protracted struggles, and attempting to defeat an adversary closer to China's borders rather than luring enemy forces deeper into the country. By the late 1980s, China was instead concentrating on peacetime "army-building" with an eye toward preparing for "local wars" *(jubu zhanzheng)* that would be fought with conventional weapons and would be limited in scope and objectives.

Chinese military doctrine underwent even greater changes in the 1990s, culminating in the retirement of the "first-generation operation regulations" and the development of new concepts of operations for "local wars under modern high-tech conditions."[57] For Chinese strategists, local wars are limited in objectives, geography, and amount of force employed. In addition, high-tech local wars are characterized by their high intensity, mobility, and destructiveness.[58] Among the types of operations that may be involved are blockades, amphibious assaults, and precision strikes. Chinese writings on campaigns in high-tech local wars stressed the importance of gaining the initiative, preemptive strikes, surprise, mobility, deep strikes, and joint operations.[59] PLA authors also began to discuss information warfare and offensive and defensive computer network operations. For the PLA, information warfare appeared to represent an attractive asymmetric option that it could use to exploit the reliance of technologically superior adversaries like the United States on advanced information systems.[60] Chinese strategists argued that information warfare would play a key role in the struggle for information supremacy, which they saw as a central aspect of future conflicts.[61]

For the PLA, the 1991 Gulf War provided real-world confirmation of these evolving theoretical trends. It also provided further stimulus for doctrinal and organizational change and force modernization. Future wars would be fought in all battlespace dimensions, and would place heavy emphasis on speed, mobility, and lethality. This would require high-technology forces, advanced C4ISR capabilities, and precision deep-strike capabilities. The PLA thus began to focus on preparing to fight "local war under high-technology conditions" *(zai gao jishu tiaojian xia de jubu zhanzheng)*. Well into the 1990s, however, the PLA's capabilities fell short of what would have been required to implement its emerging doctrinal preferences. As Nan Li put it, the PLA faced "a large gap between doctrine and capability."[62] Nonetheless, by the end of the decade, it appeared that the PLA's emerging views on future warfare and the development of a new body of doctrine were serving as a guide to procurement of advanced weapons, improvements in training, and changes in force structure that would allow the PLA to begin narrowing this doctrine-capabilities gap.

Potential Chinese Courses of Action

By the middle to late 1990s, the PLA had made some important strides toward its long-standing goal of becoming a more modern, professional, and operationally capable military, but it still suffered from a number of deficiencies in key areas such as air power, amphibious lift, C4ISR, electronic warfare, and logistics. Given these deficiencies, most analysts assessed that its prospects for success in scenarios such as a naval blockade or an amphibious invasion were limited. Even those analysts who credited the PLA with the capability to conquer Taiwan believed that China could do so only barring US intervention and at great political, economic, and military cost. For example, the US Department of Defense assessed that, should China attempt an amphibious invasion of Taiwan, "success only would be achieved with a massive commitment of military and civilian assets over a long period of time and without third party intervention."[63]

Many military analysts questioned even this relatively guarded assessment of the PLA's prospects for success in a cross-Strait conflict. Indeed, in the middle to late 1990s, a number of analysts assessed that the PLA's chances of winning a cross-Strait conflict were actually very low. Many of these assessments turned on two key factors: China's inability to achieve and maintain air superiority, and its limited amphibious lift capabilities. For example, Michael O'Hanlon argued that China lacked the capability to conquer Taiwan, even barring US military intervention in a China-Taiwan conflict. Specifically, he found that the PLA would not have been able to achieve air superiority, overwhelm local defenders at the point of attack, or strengthen its initial lodgment faster than Taiwan could bring additional troops into the area.[64] Similarly, a RAND study found that the struggle for air superiority would be the critical factor in a cross-Strait conflict, and that the PLA's chances of winning the air campaign were low, especially assuming US military intervention. The study concluded that the PLA's inability to achieve air superiority would make any Chinese invasion of Taiwan "a very bloody affair with a significant probability of failure."[65] Indeed, in the middle to late 1990s, China would have had an extremely difficult time gaining air superiority in a cross-Strait conflict, which would have greatly reduced the prospects for a successful amphibious invasion. Moreover, although PLA ground force units began receiving more sophisticated training in amphibious operations in the early 1990s, severely constrained lift capabilities and deficiencies in air power would have limited China's ability to conduct an amphibious assault and establish a beachhead against a determined and well-equipped adversary.

Conclusion

In the 1980s and 1990s, China employed a strategy that emphasized economics and politics. At the same time, however, it also used coercive diplomacy to influence Taiwan and the United States, and began developing a more credible capability to employ force against Taiwan. China's multifaceted approach to cross-Strait relations presented Taiwan with a complex set of challenges and opportunities.

CHAPTER 3

Democratization and Security in Taiwan

Throughout the 1980s and 1990s, the cross-Strait military balance was only one part of a broader set of national security challenges confronting Taiwan. The island faced a great deal of uncertainty in its external security environment, especially given the ambiguity of the US commitment to its security following Washington's withdrawal from the 1954 US–Republic of China (ROC) mutual defense treaty, numerous ups and downs in US-China-Taiwan relations, and dramatic increases in cross-Strait trade and investment. Against this backdrop of uncertainty, Taiwan's own military modernization efforts were adequate to maintain a qualitative edge over China's armed forces throughout the 1980s and well into the 1990s, and the People's Liberation Army (PLA) had few if any credible options to use force against Taiwan. During this same period, however, Taiwan's democratization was driving major changes in the island's approach to cross-Strait relations. This sparked serious concerns in Beijing, which placed preparations for a potential cross-Strait conflict at the center of its expanding military modernization program. Moreover, in the middle to late 1990s, Taiwan's defense budget began to decline and some of its defense modernization efforts slowed, just as the PLA was beginning to receive major funding increases to accelerate its own modernization programs. Consequently, it appeared that the military balance was beginning to shift in favor of the PLA, and that a cross-Strait conflict was becoming a distinct possibility given the deepening political estrangement between China and Taiwan.

Taiwan's Approach to Cross-Strait Relations, 1980–2000

In 1979, the United States established diplomatic relations with the People's Republic of China (PRC). As a condition of normalization of its relationship with Beijing, Washington announced that it would withdraw from the 1954 US-ROC defense treaty. The United States officially terminated its military alliance with the ROC on 1 January 1980. Although this left Taiwan without any major diplomatic allies, the United States maintained an ambiguous commitment to the island's security.[1] The lack of an explicit US commitment to defend Taiwan, however, left the ROC leadership constantly concerned about the possibility that the United States would sacrifice Taiwan's interests in favor of improving its relationship with China, or perhaps even abandon the island to avoid war with the mainland if a cross-Strait conflict erupted. Taipei's concerns were heightened in 1982, when the United States and China reached an agreement on one of the most sensitive issues that had been left unresolved at the time of normalization: US arms sales to Taiwan. On 17 August 1982, Washington and Beijing issued a joint communiqué in which the United States pledged to reduce arms sales to Taiwan.[2]

During the negotiations over the 1982 communiqué, Washington also sought to ameliorate Taipei's concerns that the third US-China joint communiqué would gravely undermine its national security interests. On 14 July 1982, Washington informed Taipei that it would not set a date for ending arms sales to the island, would not consult with Beijing on arms sales to Taiwan, would not attempt to become a mediator in cross-Strait relations, would not put pressure on Taiwan to negotiate with the mainland, would not revise the Taiwan Relations Act, and would not change its position on the issue of Taiwan's sovereignty. On 18 August 1982, Assistant Secretary of State John Holdridge repeated these points, often referred to as the "Six Assurances," in testimony before the US Congress. Nevertheless, US arms sales to Taiwan declined in the 1980s, deepening Taiwan's concerns about its unofficial security relationship with the United States.

At the same time, major changes were under way in Taiwanese domestic politics, with potentially enormous implications for cross-Strait relations. Taiwan in the 1980s was undergoing a political transition from authoritarianism to democracy. Since the end of the Chinese Civil War, Chiang Kaishek and the Leninist Kuomintang (KMT) had dominated the island's authoritarian political system. The KMT suppressed dissent, and advocating independence was illegal. In the 1980s, however, Taiwan was in the process of becoming a multiparty democracy.[3] The opposition movement was gaining momentum with its calls for democratization and independence. In 1986, leading opposition figures established the Democratic Progressive Party.[4] In 1987, President Chiang Ching-kuo lifted martial law. Another important change came the following year, when the ROC government lifted longstanding restrictions on press and media freedom, which permitted the establishment of independent newspapers and television stations. After Chiang's death in 1988, Lee Teng-hui became the first ethnically Taiwanese president of the ROC. Within the next several years, the ROC also lifted its "temporary provisions for suppression of the communist rebellion," enacted a series of constitutional amendments, and held its first democratic legislative election.

The 1995–1996 Taiwan Strait crisis coincided with Taiwan's first democratic presidential election, underscoring the military threat to the island's security. At the same time, rapidly expanding cross-Strait trade and growing Taiwanese investment in the PRC highlighted what some observers in Taiwan viewed as a potential threat to the island's de facto political independence. These concerns prompted President Lee Teng-hui to urge Taiwanese companies to divert their investments from China to Southeast Asia and impose limits on Taiwanese investment in the mainland.[5] It quickly became clear, however, that Taipei's policies were lagging behind the economic realities of rapidly expanding cross-Strait trade and investment.[6]

Although cross-Strait trade and investment continued to expand, China and Taiwan appeared to be headed toward ever greater political estrangement. As discussed in Chapter 2, the prospects for further negotiations between quasi-official representatives of Taipei and Beijing were dealt a major blow on 9 July 1999, when President Lee Teng-hui declared that the relationship between China and Taiwan was a "state-to-state, or at least special state-to-state" relationship.[7] Beijing responded with military exercises and denunciations in the official media.[8] The heightened cross-Strait tension that lingered in the wake of these events underscored the extent to which many of the key understandings that had provided stability in US-China-Taiwan relations since the 1970s had unraveled.

Military Modernization and Defense Reform in Taiwan, 1980–2000

In the 1980s and 1990s, Taiwan engaged in a major military modernization effort that included domestic development of programs such as the Ching-kuo indigenous defense fighters and the Tien Kung air defense system, as well as a number of major foreign arms acquisitions, including the purchase of F-16 fighters from the United States and Mirage fighters and Lafayette frigates from France. In the 1990s, Taiwan also implemented a major restructuring program intended to reduce the military's size while increasing its mobility and firepower. As a result of these modernization and reform initiatives, the ratio of advanced weapon systems to older equipment in each of the military services increased dramatically, and the military became smaller and more capable.[9] Taiwan undertook these extensive efforts to upgrade its defense capabilities even though the Chinese military threat at the time was relatively modest. As Lin Chong-pin puts it, "Taiwan's efforts to upgrade its defense became noticeable in the late 1980s when most outside observers hardly realized such a need existed."[10]

Taiwan's Defense Budget During the 1980s and 1990s

In the 1980s and 1990s, Taiwan's political transformation had a dramatic impact on the defense budget process. In particular, democratization opened the defense budget to greater public and legislative scrutiny. Prior to democratization, the Legislative Yuan played a very minor role in defense policy and had little influence in the defense budget process. In the words of one observer:

> For most of Taiwan's modern history, the appropriation of the national defense budget was never a matter of public controversy. The public, in fact, had little knowledge or involvement in the process. Under the long one-party rule of the Kuomintang (KMT), measures proposed by the executive branch were invariably dutifully passed with little debate by the legislature. . . . Lawmakers rarely touched on national defense issues, which were determined by the president and the Ministry of National Defense.[11]

As the democratization process progressed, however, the Legislative Yuan became a much more important and influential player in the defense policy process, especially in the area of defense spending. Nonetheless, the KMT continued to control both the executive and legislative branches of government, allowing it to contain many of the opposition's challenges to its policies.

Throughout the 1980s and early 1990s, Taiwan's defense budget increased fairly steadily, allowing the island to acquire new military hardware such as fourth-generation fighter aircraft and modern naval vessels. In the mid-1990s, however, Taiwan's defense spending began to decline precipitously. After a slight rebound in spending around the time of the 1995–1996 Taiwan Strait crisis, the defense budget began to decline again in the late 1990s. The share of central government expenditure devoted to national defense also declined considerably, from about 53 percent in 1985 to 22.8 percent in 1996.[12]

As a result, the ROC military was tasked with "doing more with less."[13] By the late 1990s, the Ministry of National Defense was concerned that the island's defense budget was too low to meet Taiwan's defense requirements, especially given the increasing capabilities of the Chinese military and the rise in cross-Strait tensions that followed President Lee's enunciation of the "two states" theory in July 1999. Senior ministry officials began to call for increases in defense spending. In August 1999, for example, the ROC defense minister suggested increasing the defense budget to 3.0 to 3.5 percent of gross domestic product to keep pace with Chinese military modernization.[14]

Arms Purchases from the United States and Other Foreign Suppliers

Although defense spending was increasing in the early 1980s, Taiwan's armed forces were in a difficult position. The island's military equipment was aging, its indigenous defense industry was not capable of meeting many of the island's defense needs, and it appeared that it could no longer rely on acquisition of advanced weapon systems and equipment from the United States and other Western countries. The United States declined to sell advanced fighters to Taiwan, and Beijing's response to the Netherlands' decision to sell two submarines to Taiwan seemed likely to deter many countries from selling weapons to the island. As Dennis Van Vranken Hickey observes, "By the early 1980s, much of Taiwan's military arsenal was approaching obsolescence. Even more worrisome for Taiwan, the United States and numerous other arms-exporting nations had opted to reduce or terminate their arms sales to Taiwan rather than risk reprisals from Beijing."[15] Most importantly, US arms sales to Taiwan declined steadily in the years following the signing of the August 1982 US-China communiqué. Total US arms sales to Taiwan, including foreign military sales and commercial arms sales, fell from US$774 million in 1984 to about US$640 million in 1991.[16]

This downward trend was reversed in the 1990s, however, as Taiwan signed a series of deals that made the island one of the world's largest recipients of US weapon systems and military equipment, at a total value of at least US$16.9 billion for that decade. Given the high costs of some of the parts of the defense modernization program, the ROC government used its special budget mechanism to fund the procurement of several of the big-ticket items purchased in the 1990s, such as the F-16 fighters from the United States and the Mirage fighters and Lafayette frigates from France.[17] By far the largest of these arms deals was the 1992 purchase of 150 F-16 fighters from the United States. The George H. W. Bush administration's decision to sell the F-16s to Taiwan marked a major reversal of US policy on arms sales to Taiwan in two important respects. First, since refusing to sell the FX fighter to Taiwan in 1982, Washington had repeatedly turned down Taiwan's requests to purchase advanced fighters. Second, with a price tag of almost US$6 billion, it was by far the largest US arms sale to Taiwan since the signing of the 1982 arms sales communiqué. President Bush's motives for approving the change in policy apparently included both strategic considerations and domestic politics. However, most analysts assess that President Bush's election-year concerns were the driving force behind the change in policy.[18]

Although Taiwan managed to purchase a number of major weapon systems from the United States and France, several problems plagued the ROC in its attempts to procure advanced arms and equipment from foreign suppliers. Most importantly, the uncertainty surrounding the arms sales relationship with the United States made it very difficult for Taiwan to develop long-term force modernization plans. As Mark Stokes observes:

> Since the shift in diplomatic relations from Taipei to Beijing in 1979 and the 1982 Communiqué regarding arms sales, the Taiwan military had annually submitted to the U.S. government a list with an average of six to twelve requests for defense articles and services. After a few months of deliberation, the U.S. government would release a fraction of them. This uncertainty caused Taiwan's defense establishment to use a spaghetti-on-the wall approach: throw a list out and see what sticks.[19]

Another problem was that many of Taiwan's arms procurement decisions were based largely on political and institutional considerations rather than operational requirements.[20] Finally, the military and the KMT became embroiled in corruption scandals involving several domestic procurements and foreign arms purchases. Most notably, Taiwan's acquisition of Lafayette frigates from France created a tremendous domestic political scandal involving charges of kickbacks and corruption and the suspicious death of an ROC navy captain in 1993. Investigators believe that the French company Thomson CSF paid US$486 million to a local sales representative, and that about US$120 million of this commission was ultimately transferred to officials in Taiwan to win their support for the deal. Some reports indicate that bribes were also paid to government officials in France and China. Several ROC navy officers were prosecuted in the wake of the scandal, but allegations that senior KMT officials were involved remain unresolved. The Lafayette scandal symbolizes the widespread suspicion of impropriety that continues to hamper Taiwan's procurement of weapon systems and equipment from foreign suppliers.[21]

Hardware Modernization

Air power. One of the major elements of Taiwan's defense modernization program during this period of time was improving capabilities of the ROC air force by replacing many of its aging fighters with fourth-generation aircraft. In the 1990s, Taiwan replaced many of its aging F-104s and F-5s with modern fighter aircraft, including F-16s acquired from the United States, French Mirage 2000-5 fighters, and the domestically developed Ching-kuo indigenous defense fighters. In 1992, Taiwan purchased 150 F-16 fighters from the United States, including 120 single-seat F-16 "A" and 30 two-seat F-16 "B" aircraft. The planes were armed with upgraded air-to-air missiles. At a total cost of some US$5.8 billion, it was the largest US arms sale to

Taiwan since the 1982 US-China communiqué. Deliveries of the F-16s began in 1997 and were completed in the late 1990s.

Taiwan also purchased Mirage 2000-5s from France. When the aircraft were delivered in 1997–1998, the Mirage became the ROC air force's "most formidable air defense fighter."[22] In addition to acquiring advanced fighters from the United States and France, Taiwan also developed and produced the Ching-kuo indigenous defense fighters. Although this program faced a variety of developmental problems during the 1980s and 1990s, the Ching-kuo aircraft was widely considered to be superior to any aircraft China had developed and deployed at the time of its introduction. By 2000, Taiwan had produced about 130 Ching-kuo fighters, which were armed with the indigenously developed Tien-Chien II (Sky Sword II), a beyond-visual-range air-to-air missile.

The air force also improved its airborne warning and command and control capabilities by acquiring four E-2T aircraft from the United States. In addition, Taiwan sought to improve survivability by constructing a major underground facility capable of sheltering some 200 combat aircraft.[23]

Naval capabilities. Taiwan in the late 1980s also began updating and expanding its naval capabilities. The modernization of the island's navy was long overdue. As the US Department of Defense observed, "Despite the Navy's ability to refurbish and extend the service life of its vessels and equipment well beyond expectation, a large portion of the fleet consists of obsolescent World War II–era ships."[24] To address this problem, Taiwan began replacing its older surface combatants with more modern ships, as part of the "Kuang Hua" naval modernization program. In 1993, Taiwan began deploying domestically developed Cheng Kung–class frigates, which were modeled after the US Perry-class frigates. Taiwan also acquired six Lafayette-class (Kang Ting–class) frigates from France, and leased eight Knox-class frigates from the United States. The Knox-class frigates were armed with Harpoon antiship cruise missiles. The ROC navy also acquired 34 antisubmarine warfare–capable helicopters, and began deploying domestically developed Hsiung Feng–2E antiship cruise missiles on its Perry-class and Lafayette-class frigates.[25] In addition, Taiwan modestly improved its submarine capabilities, which in the 1980s consisted of two US World War II–era Guppy II submarines, by purchasing two Dutch-made Zvaardvis-class submarines, which many analysts regarded as superior to the Chinese navy's Ming-class submarines.

As a result of the modernization program, the balance of naval forces continued to favor Taiwan through the mid-1990s, at least in terms of quality. In the late 1990s, however, it became obvious that the island's naval forces were in need of further modernization if they were to keep pace with the growing challenge posed by the enhancement of Chinese naval capabilities.

Ground forces. Taiwan also upgraded its ground forces. An essential element of the reform program was downsizing the army. Between 1983 and 1986, about 56,000 troops were cut, reducing the size of the ground forces to about 312,000 troops. An even more ambitious restructuring program began in 1997, further reducing the size of the army and reorganizing its command structure to improve its rapid-reaction capabilities. The most important change was the creation of combined arms brigades. Taiwan also upgraded the army's weapons and equipment to improve its firepower and enhance its mobility. In the 1990s, the army acquired a number of new systems, including transport aircraft, armored personnel carriers, attack helicopters, scout helicopters, and domestically produced and imported tanks. The ground force modernization program included purchasing 12 C-130H transport aircraft, 42 AH-1W Cobra attack helicopters, and 26 OH-58D Kiowa scout helicopters. Among the tanks acquired during the 1990s were indigenously manufactured M48 tanks and US M60 A3 tanks.

C4ISR capabilities. Taiwan's military faced problems in its command, control, communications, computers, intelligence, surveillance, and reconnaissance (C4ISR) capabilities in the 1980s and 1990s. The armed forces lacked the advanced communication and data-link capabilities required for timely, efficient, and secure communications between and within the military services. According to one analyst, this technology problem precluded Taiwan from molding its air, sea, and ground capabilities into "an integrated and cohesive force."[26] Part of the problem was that army, navy, and air force systems and platforms came from so many different suppliers. Command and control challenges were not limited to problems with hardware and technology. The ROC armed forces also faced challenges in the areas of command style and organizational culture. In 1999, the US Department of Defense reported that Taiwan's military was "hampered by systemic problems of poor, antiquated management and a traditional military culture with very rigid command structures which discourages lower level risk-taking, decision-making, and innovation."[27]

Air and missile defense. Another important thrust of the modernization program was improving Taiwan's air defense capabilities. In 1992, Taiwan deployed the indigenously developed Tien Kung (Sky Bow) surface-to-air missile. It also sought to establish a capability to defend against the growing Chinese conventional missile threat. In the early 1990s, Taiwan agreed to purchase the "modified air defense system," an upgraded version of the Patriot missile defense system used in the Gulf War, from the United States. Taipei purchased three fire units at a cost of approximately US$1.3 billion. The units were delivered to the island in the late 1990s, and the military deployed the modified fire units around Taipei. In a 1999 report to Congress, however, the US Department of Defense noted that these active defense systems would not be enough to offset China's growing conventional missile capabilities. Indeed, the report identified Taiwan's limited ability to defense against China's growing arsenal of conventional short-range ballistic missiles as the island's "most significant vulnerability."[28] Accordingly, many defense analysts recommended that Taiwan increase its investment in passive defense measures such as hardening of key facilities.[29]

Defense Strategy and Software Reforms

National security strategy and defense policy. The ROC's national defense strategy has undergone several major changes since 1949. Under Chiang Kai-shek, the principal objective of ROC national security policy and defense strategy was "retaking the mainland." Subsequently, the strategy shifted to focusing on both offensive and defensive capabilities. Indeed, ROC government publications continued to discuss "recovering the mainland" well into late 1980s, even though this was obviously a rhetorical rather than a practical goal. Still another major change in strategy came when Taipei effectively renounced its claim to sovereignty over the mainland and shifted to a military strategy focused exclusively on the defense of Taiwanese-controlled territory. According to a government publication, this represented a shift from the strategic principle of "equal stress on offense and defense" to one of simply "assuring defense."[30] Accordingly, throughout the 1980s and 1990s, ROC defense policy was focused on deterring Beijing from using force, and defending against a Chinese attack on Taiwan if deterrence failed. This shift to an exclusively defensive posture reflected a change in the overall objective of Taiwan's defense policy, which became focused entirely on maintaining the security of Taiwan and the other areas under ROC control.[31]

The evolution of Taiwan's defense strategy also had important implications for resource allocation and the relative importance attached to the modernization of ground, air, and naval forces. In short, the shift to a strategy based on deterrence and defense made modernizing the air force and navy the ROC's highest priorities. As the aforementioned government report stated, "while ROC national defense strategy calls for a balanced development of the three armed forces, naval and air supremacy receive first priority."[32] This increased emphasis on air and naval modernization came at the expense of the traditionally dominant ground forces.[33] Not surprisingly, some army officers continued to insist that the ground forces should remain the cornerstone of Taiwan's defense strategy. As one army officer put it in a 2003 essay, "Land operations and the need to secure and hold ground remain the keys to a final victory."[34]

Beyond interservice rivalry and resource competition, another problem was that Taiwan's strategy was not sufficiently detailed to serve as a guide to setting priorities and making difficult policy choices. Although Taiwan's strategy underwent three relatively clearly demarcated phases, articulating a detailed and consistent national security strategy has been a problem, one that persisted even after the government abandoned all pretenses that the military would ever participate in an attempt to "retake the mainland." This difficulty derives at least in part from underlying bureaucratic and institutional problems. As Michael Swaine observed in a late-1990s study of Taiwan's national security and defense policy processes, Taiwan lacked a formal, institutionalized interagency process for the formulation and implementation of national security strategy and policy. Consequently, policy development was fragmentary and undertaken by individual agencies, or sometimes by the president and his closest advisers. Coordination between the defense and foreign policy arenas was lacking.[35] In addition, Taiwan's National Security Council did not have the influence of its US counterpart, nor did it play a strong coordinating role.

The legacy of authoritarian rule was another problem facing Taiwan's national security and defense policy establishment. The military dominated the defense policy arena and the weapons procurement process through the end of Lee Teng-hui's presidency. Personal clout, rather than authority inherent in positions, determined the influence of senior civilian defense policy officials.[36] The Ministry of National Defense was relatively weak as an institutional player. Given the lack of clear guidance for the setting of priorities, the fragmentation of the policy process, and the weak role of civilian policymakers, arms procurement decisions were especially problematic. Moreover, according to Swaine, President Lee was often more concerned about the political implications of arms acquisitions, which he viewed as important symbols of US support, than he was about acquiring weapons and equipment that would contribute to improving the military's war-fighting capabilities.[37]

Still another issue facing the island was the lack of a joint approach to the development of military strategy and the defense-planning process. In the 1980s and 1990s, Taiwan's defense strategy focused on maintaining air superiority, conducting counterblockade operations, and defeating an amphibious invasion, but these three tasks were generally treated as separate and distinct, with responsibility for air superiority going to the ROC air force, counterblockade operations to the ROC navy, and antilanding operations to the ROC army. Coordination among the services was limited. As a result, the military lacked the capability to plan for and conduct joint operations. This was a major shortcoming of Taiwan's defense strategy.

Professional military education. Taiwan also began restructuring and reforming its professional military education system to enhance its efficiency and improve the quality of instruction. The centerpiece of this effort was the merger of several existing schools to form the ROC's National Defense University, which was established on 8 May 2000. The overall objective of the reforms went beyond simply reorganizing the professional military education system to make it more efficient. The principal goal was to make the system more capable of training officers in areas such as international relations and security, information technology and high-tech warfare, joint operations, and crisis management. This involved closer integration with civilian universities, higher standards for military schools and academies, and a greater emphasis on continuing-education programs. At the end of the 1990s, however, the reform of the professional military education system remained a work in progress.[38]

Personnel policy. Taiwan's military faced a broad range of personnel problems in the 1980s and 1990s. Perhaps the most serious were recruitment and retention of highly skilled personnel, which were especially difficult challenges for the armed forces given the island's dynamic economy and the military's inability to compete with private sector employers, particularly in high-technology fields where much more lucrative opportunities were available in the island's thriving information technology industry. The resultant personnel shortages caused morale problems. This problem was especially serious in the ROC air force due to retention problems associated with the availability of job opportunities with much better pay and benefits in the civil aviation sector. In addition, the military faced a shortage of non-commissioned officers (NCOs) that stemmed from low retention rates. According to the ROC's 2001 yearbook, "NCOs are the backbone of the Armed Forces' smaller units, and are required to train troops and develop their combat performance. In recent years, however, most senior NCOs have retired, leaving the current proportion of career NCOs too low."[39] Another problem was the limited training provided to reservists: "Reservists are on active duty for a very limited period of time, making it difficult for them to keep up with changes in the operation and maintenance of sophisticated weapons and equipment."[40] The military was only partially successful in addressing these personnel problems.

Downsizing and restructuring. Downsizing the military was another key component of the ROC's software reforms. In 1994, the military began implementing a ten-year troop reduction project.[41] The main goal of the project was to reduce the number of troops from 468,000 in 1994 to fewer than 400,000 in 2003. This reduction was intended to result in an "increase in the ratio of combat troops to overall military manpower."[42] The project was also intended to restructure the military and streamline the chain of command by eliminating redundant staff units and consolidating headquarters units. Specifically, the downsizing plan was intended to "eliminate superfluous and over-lapping staff organizations in the three major services and consolidate the Ministry of National Defense's General Staff Headquarters and the general headquarters of the three services to facilitate operations and expedite command and control."[43]

Training and exercises. Beginning in the mid-1980s, Taiwan conducted a series of annual exercises designed to improve the military's capability to conduct joint operations. For example, the "Han Kuang 4" exercise, conducted from 9 to 15 June 1987, was intended to test joint training and combat capabilities.[44] In the 1980s and 1990s, however, Taiwan's military faced a number of problems with joint exercises and training. Major exercises showcased the island's modern military equipment, but they were generally brief and were often heavily scripted. For example, the US Department of Defense's 1999 report on the cross-Strait security situation assessed the mid-May 1998 "Han Kuang 14" exercise as follows: "Primarily a C4I [command, control, communications, computers, and intelligence] exercise, the training was of very short duration and the scenario allowed for only limited exercise play."[45]

Conclusion

In the early 1980s, the PLA was just beginning to implement reforms in the aftermath of its weak performance in the 1979 border war with Vietnam. Following a major reevaluation of China's external security environment and several rounds of downsizing, the PLA had made some progress. Nonetheless, in the late 1980s the PLA was still hamstrung by antiquated weaponry and inadequate training. Moreover, the PLA faced corruption problems stemming from its privileged status and widespread involvement in business activities. Although Taiwan's military was largely isolated and its access to foreign hardware was limited, its superior equipment and training allowed the island to maintain a qualitative advantage over the PLA well into the early 1990s.

The PLA of the mid-1990s represented a dramatic improvement over the PLA of the mid-1980s, but it still posed a relatively modest threat to Taiwan, and its ability to deal with US forces was limited. David Shambaugh characterized the PLA of the mid-1990s as "a military undergoing transformation from top to bottom, with 'pockets of excellence' and some qualitative advances emerging within an overall force structure that is changing relatively slowly and remains substantially antiquated."[46] The PLA was improving its professionalism and modernizing its hardware, but it still faced a number of serious problems and deficiencies in both hardware and software. In particular, the PLA remained about ten to fifteen years behind advanced technology levels in many areas. Moreover, the PLA was still "predominantly a land force with weak air and naval forces and minimal power projection capability."[47] Consequently, in the mid-1990s the PLA was capable of posing little more than a "nuisance threat" to modern militaries operating in the region. According to Dennis Blasko, Philip Klapakis, and John Corbett, this meant that the PLA could "kill people, sink a few ships, or shoot down a few aircraft in one or two short engagements."[48] However, the PLA lacked the capabilities required to project power beyond its borders and sustain even the relatively limited operations envisioned as part of the "local wars under high-tech conditions" construct.

Given the PLA's shortcomings, most analysts assessed that the cross-Strait military balance still favored Taiwan. Although the PLA was about seven times the size of Taiwan's armed forces, the island maintained a qualitative edge and had a better-trained and more professional military.[49] As a longtime PLA-watcher put it at the time, "The PLA today, despite the aspirations expressed in Chinese publications, is still largely the same force it was at the time the USSR collapsed. It is still overwhelmingly a ground army with an inventory that, in most cases, has been deployed with the same units for up to 30 years."[50] As a result, the PLA was still far from having achieved the kind of transformation that would tip the cross-Strait military balance in favor of China. In all, the PLA was still considered somewhat backward technologically and even observers who credited the Chinese military with some major improvements believed its ability to use force against Taiwan was "seriously lacking."[51]

The PLA was beginning to acquire modern weapons, mainly from Russia, but this still left open the question of how well it could use its new equipment. In particular, the PLA's lack of combat experience and its level of training left many analysts uncertain about its force employment capabilities. The US General Accounting Office summed up this view in a 1995 report on Chinese military capabilities: "There are doubts about China's ability to absorb, operate, and maintain the new technologies and weapons needed to modernize its armed forces. Further, the mere possession of modern weapons, platforms, and sensors . . . does not necessarily create combat effectiveness."[52] Consequently, even in the late 1990s, the PLA's ability to present credible military options to senior Chinese leaders was still limited. As Bates Gill and Michael O'Hanlon observed in a 1999 assessment of Chinese military capabilities, "An enormous gap separates China's military capabilities from its aspirations."[53] Indeed, in the late 1990s, even relatively limited US military intervention would likely have meant rapid and decisive defeat for the PLA.[54] Nonetheless, much was beginning to change. Importantly, the PLA at the end of the 1990s was focused on a concrete mission. As Culver put it:

From the collapse of the Soviet Union until approximately 1993, the Chinese focus was threat-diffuse. The Chinese military planned for regional warfare in a very general sense, which reflected an inability to predict either the nature or likely origin of the next threat to Chinese security. . . . PLA threat perceptions shifted when Taiwan reemerged as a salient issue in 1995. Today, Taiwan is the focus for the PLA as it defines its mission; it is the most likely challenge to Chinese security and defines the scenario in which the PLA would be most likely to be called upon to use large-scale force.[55]

Along with this increasing focus on a Taiwan scenario, the PLA was also implementing a wide-ranging series of reforms. As David Finkelstein observes, "The decade of the 1990s was a period of tremendous change for the PLA. On nearly every front, this massive defense establishment was engaged in a myriad of reforms aimed at making it a more professional force in a corporate and institutional sense as well as a more operationally capable force."[56] Moreover, the PLA was beginning to benefit from long-delayed major increases in defense spending and the acquisition of much more advanced hardware. As a result of these trends, the PLA was beginning to develop capabilities that would allow it to pose a credible threat to US forces intervening in a cross-Strait conflict, even without "catching up" to the US military in a traditional sense.[57]

The transformation of the PLA was beginning to outpace Taiwan's own military modernization efforts, and many analysts began to warn that the cross-Strait balance would eventually tilt toward China as a result of these trends. The US Department of Defense's 2000 report to Congress on Chinese military power assessed that the cross-Strait military balance would continue to favor Taiwan from 2000 to 2005, given the PLA's limited ability to conduct integrated operations against the island.[58] By 2010, however, the military balance would begin to tip in favor of China, even though the PLA's shortcomings would make any large-scale use of force against Taiwan a risky, and probably very costly, undertaking. By 2020, the PLA would likely enjoy a much greater qualitative edge over Taiwan and be in a position to present the Chinese Communist Party leadership with credible military options. The extent and speed of the shift in the cross-Strait military balance, however, would of course also depend at least in part on Taiwan's response to the growing challenge posed by the modernization of the PLA. As the Defense Department report concluded, "The change in the dynamic equilibrium of forces over the long term will depend largely on whether Taiwan is able to meet or exceed developments on the mainland with programs of its own. Its success in deterring potential Chinese aggression will be dependent on its continued acquisition of modern arms, technology, and equipment, and its ability to integrate and operate these systems effectively, and its ability to deal with a number of other systemic problems."[59]

CHAPTER 4

China's Taiwan Policy and Military Modernization Since 2000

China's approach to Taiwan has gone through several distinct phases in recent years. The strident rhetoric of the period preceding Taiwan's 2000 presidential election and the posturing exemplified by the March 2005 antisecession law have given way to a softer approach that emphasizes economic incentives and increasing cross-Strait interaction. This shift in tactics appears to reflect a reassessment of the previous emphasis on harsh rhetoric and military threats, which ultimately backfired by harming China's international image and alienating many people in Taiwan. Even as China accords greater prominence to carrots, however, it is developing the ability to wield an increasingly powerful stick should this softer approach fail to prevent Taiwan from continuing to move toward formal independence. Indeed, the modernization of the Chinese military is clearly intended to support China's overall policy toward Taiwan. The principal objective of that policy in the short term is to deter Taiwan from seeking formal independence. In the long term, Beijing seeks to leverage increasing economic interdependence and a "united front" strategy, backed by increasingly credible military options, to persuade Taiwan to enter into unification negotiations on terms favorable to China.[1]

China's Evolving Taiwan Policy

The evolution of China's Taiwan policy—from trying to coerce Taipei into immediate reunification, to a more balanced approach that emphasizes preventing independence and setting the stage for the eventual achievement of Chinese political objectives—reflects an apparent reconsideration of its earlier, counterproductive approach, as well as China's changing assessment of political, economic, and military trends in cross-Strait relations.

Following the US intervention in Kosovo, the May 1999 accidental bombing of the Chinese embassy in Belgrade, and President Lee Teng-hui's July 1999 comments on "state-to-state relations," Chinese analysts became increasingly concerned about what they perceived as worrisome trends in cross-Strait relations, and growing instability in China's external security environment more broadly. Chinese scholars and national security specialists engaged in a heated debate about the security challenges confronting China.[2] Against this backdrop of growing concern about US strategic intentions toward China and the potential implications of domestic political trends in Taiwan, Beijing in February 2000 released a white paper on its Taiwan policy. Previously, Beijing's official statements had underscored its determination to use force in response to a declaration of independence or foreign occupation of the island. The 2000 white paper, however, for the first time formally stated another condition under which Beijing might resort to the use of force against Taiwan, warning that indefinite refusal to engage in cross-Strait reunification talks might trigger an attack on Taiwan.[3] The warning that an indefinite delay in the resumption of negotiations might lead to the use of force, which became known as the "third if," had been articulated in the past, but the 2000 white paper marked the first time it was incorporated into an official policy document.[4] The white paper also included some fairly moderate language. For example, the document contained assurances that Taiwan would retain a "high degree of autonomy" even after reunification with the mainland.[5] It was the more bellicose language, however, that grabbed the headlines, and the warning about the potential consequences of indefinite delays in the resumption of talks left many observers concerned that China's growing pessimism about future trends in cross-Strait relations might lead to a potentially disastrous conflict.[6] Indeed, in early 2000, pessimism in Beijing was so deep that some Chinese scholars were expressing "fairly severe doubts that peace could be maintained across the Taiwan Strait over the long term," according to Thomas Christensen.[7]

Following the release of the white paper, Beijing further intensified its rhetoric in an apparent attempt to influence the outcome of the upcoming presidential election in Taiwan. At a 15 March 2000 press conference, just two days before the election, then-premier Zhu Rongji issued an implicit threat to voters in Taiwan: "Do not just act on impulse at this juncture which will decide the future course that China and Taiwan will follow. Otherwise I'm afraid you won't get another opportunity to regret!"[8] Despite Zhu's admonition to Taiwan's voters, Democratic Progressive Party (DPP) candidate Chen Shui-bian was elected president on 18 March, bringing to an end more than fifty years of Kuomintang (KMT) rule.[9] China's initial reaction to the election of Chen Shui-bian was relatively muted. Beijing indicated that it would listen to Chen's words and watch his actions.[10] Moreover, a few months after Chen's inauguration, Beijing indicated that it was willing to show greater flexibility in its approach toward Taiwan. Qian Qichen suggested in July 2000 that China had somewhat softened its interpretation of the "one China" principle, shifting from the long-standing insistence that "Taiwan is an inalienable part of China" to the more neutral formulation that "both the Mainland and Taiwan belong to one China." Qian also stated that negotiations on the "three links" could begin even before Taipei accepted the "one China" principle, so long as the negotiations were handled by private organizations. Later in the year, Qian went a step further, sidestepping a contentious issue by declaring that cross-Strait air and shipping links could be called "cross-Strait routes." This was a substantial retreat from Beijing's previous position that such cross-Strait links would be classified as "domestic" routes. Presumably, the purposes of these modifications were to redefine the "one China" principle in a way that would make it at least somewhat more palatable to Taiwan and to demonstrate some flexibility to international audiences, primarily the United States.

Despite the diplomatic fallout from the March 2001 incident involving a collision between a US reconnaissance plane and a Chinese fighter aircraft, the April 2001 arms sales decision, President George W. Bush's comments about defending Taiwan, and President Chen's US transit visit, Chinese analysts were actually relatively optimistic throughout much of 2001 about the long-term prospects for peaceful reunification on China's terms. The economic downturn in Taiwan and President Chen's domestic political problems created expectations that Chen would be a one-term president and that a candidate more favorably disposed toward Beijing would likely win the next presidential election.[11] Growing cross-Strait economic interdependence was another source of Beijing's increasing optimism. Moreover, improvements in US-China relations following the 11 September 2001 terrorist attacks likely bolstered Beijing's confidence that Washington would attempt to restrain Chen.[12] The KMT's disappointing performance and the strong showing of the Pan-Green parties in the December 2001 Legislative Yuan election, however, raised new concerns in Beijing. As a result, by January 2002 the pendulum was swinging back in the other direction and Chinese analysts were once again expressing pessimism about cross-Strait relations.[13]

What was most worrisome from Beijing's point of view was that the outcome of the December 2001 legislative election suggested that the Pan-Green camp might eventually gain a majority in the legislature, which Chinese analysts feared would enable President Chen to pursue much more assertive proindependence policies.[14] Although Chinese analysts were concerned about the potential ramifications of the DPP's strong performance in the 2001 elections and Chen's pursuit of what they termed "creeping independence," the continuing expansion of cross-Strait economic relations moderated their concerns to some extent.[15] Chinese analysts also recognized that Beijing could no longer afford to ignore the DPP, since Chen might win a second term after all, and since the DPP appeared to be gaining popularity. In a speech delivered on 24 January 2002, Qian Qichen stated that China would be willing to hold discussions with moderate members of the DPP, though he indicated that Beijing would continue to shun those DPP politicians who were determined to pursue independence. At the same time, however, China continued attempting to deepen Taiwan's diplomatic isolation by wooing the island's remaining diplomatic allies.

President Chen's 2002 "one country on each side" *(yi bian, yi guo)* declaration and his comments about a referendum law prompted a harsh rejoinder from China.[16] Beijing's Taiwan Affairs Office responded that the period of "listening and watching" was over, and that Chen could never be trusted, since he was a "stubborn" supporter of Taiwan independence. Even as the "one country on each side" episode increased tension in cross-Strait relations, Beijing indicated some flexibility in its Taiwan policy. For example, by late 2002 there were signs that China was willing to soften its position on negotiations to establish direct links.[17] In an October 2002 interview with the Taiwanese newspaper *United Daily News,* Chinese vice premier Qian Qichen said China viewed the establishment of three links as an economic rather than a political matter, and indicated Beijing's willingness to characterize the links as "cross-Strait" rather than "domestic." The comments were seen by many analysts as indicative of Beijing's willingness to adopt a more flexible approach toward Taiwan. To reinforce the intended message, the official English-language newspaper *China Daily,* on 18 October 2002, carried an article that characterized Qian's comments as "a goodwill gesture, aimed at de-politicizing the definition of direct transport links between Taiwan and the mainland." The article underscored that Qian's remarks represented "a major effort by Beijing" to promote the establishment of the three links.[18]

Some progress toward the establishment of the three links was made when China and Taiwan agreed on cross-Strait charter flights, which was widely seen as a positive development. Nonetheless, in 2003, Beijing was becoming increasingly concerned about the potential implications of the Chen administration's plans to make a variety of symbolic changes, such as the addition of the word "Taiwan" to the cover of the Republic of China (ROC) passport, which Chinese analysts saw as further evidence of Chen's determination to pursue a "de-Sinification" campaign that would move Taiwan further and further toward permanent separation from the mainland.[19] Even more problematic from Beijing's perspective was Taiwan's passage of a referendum law, which Taiwan Affairs Office spokesman Zhang Mingqing warned would elicit an unspecified "strong response" if it permitted an islandwide vote on independence or other controversial sovereignty-related issues.[20]

Despite these concerns about "de-Sinification" and the referendum law, China adopted a relatively cautious approach in the months leading up to

Taiwan's March 2004 presidential election, especially in comparison to the missile tests it used to try to influence the outcome of the 1996 election and the verbal threats that preceded the 2000 presidential contest. Beijing may have concluded that its previous heavy-handed approach had failed to achieve the desired results, or perhaps had even proven counterproductive. Nonetheless, on 17 May 2004, a few days before President Chen was to give his second inaugural address, the Taiwan Affairs Office issued a major statement on cross-Strait relations that appeared to reflect a pessimistic assessment of recent trends, declaring that Chen Shui-bian had violated his "five no's" promises. It decried Chen's record in office as "one of broken promises and bad faith," and underscored China's determination to prevent Taiwan from slipping further toward independence.[21] The statement also contained some conciliatory language, most notably an offer to resume dialogue on an equal footing with any Taiwanese leader who was willing to accept the "one China" principle and refrain from engaging in "separatist activities." In addition, it promised economic incentives such as greater market access for Taiwan's agricultural products and offered assurances that Taiwan would be permitted to enjoy "international living space . . . commensurate with its status." After offering these potential carrots, however, the statement concluded with a sharply worded warning to Taiwan's leaders.

The statement reflected growing concern in Beijing about the prospects for cross-Strait relations during Chen's second term, as well as more immediate worries about what President Chen would say in his second inaugural address. Indeed, throughout much of 2004, "There was an air of severe pessimism about cross-Strait relations in Beijing."[22] President Chen's controversial reelection and his determination to reengineer Taiwan's constitution left many Chinese analysts convinced that time was no longer on Beijing's side, and led some to conclude that another cross-Strait crisis was all but inevitable. President Chen's 10 October 2004 National Day address appeared to reinforce this deepening pessimism in Beijing.

The pendulum swung in the other direction yet again just a few months later when the DPP and its allies failed to win a majority in the December 2004 legislative elections. Indeed, the relatively poor showing of the Pan-Green parties in the December 2004 legislative elections was a relief to China, because it meant that a Pan-Blue majority in the Legislative Yuan would block any attempts to alter the most sensitive parts of the ROC constitution and constrain President Chen's ability to make major changes in Taiwan's policy toward China. Just as it seemed that China-Taiwan relations were becoming more stable, however, Beijing's promulgation of previously planned legislation on preventing Taiwanese independence introduced a new element of tension into the cross-Strait dynamic. On 14 March 2005, China's National People's Congress passed the Anti-Secession Law, in which Beijing declared:

In the event that the "Taiwan independence" secessionist forces should act under any name or by any means to cause the fact of Taiwan's secession from China, or that major incidents entailing Taiwan's secession from China should occur, or that possibilities for a peaceful reunification should be completely exhausted, the state shall employ non-peaceful means and other necessary measures to protect China's sovereignty and territorial integrity.[23]

The passage of the antisecession law seemed to represent a case of particularly bad timing on Beijing's part, especially given the outcome of the December 2004 Legislative Yuan election and the constraints the opposition majority in the legislature imposed on President Chen's agenda.

Perhaps recognizing that the antisecession law had produced a variety of counterproductive results, Beijing soon shifted its emphasis to economic carrots and "united front" political tactics, mainly by wooing prominent opposition politicians. Shortly after the antisecession law was passed, KMT vice chairman Chiang Pin-kung led a delegation of KMT politicians on a visit to China, marking the highest-level contact between the Chinese Communist Party (CCP) and the KMT since 1949. The KMT delegation's discussions with Chinese officials resulted in a symbolic agreement on the expansion of cross-Strait economic and cultural ties, and in an invitation to KMT chairman Lien Chan to visit the mainland, who did so in late April.[24] During the trip, he visited Nanjing, Xian, Shanghai, and Beijing, and held talks with President Hu Jintao. In May, People's First Party chairman James Soong followed suit with his own visit to the mainland. The high-profile visits were part of an evolving Chinese strategy that aimed to build relations with the Pan-Blue opposition parties and put pressure on President Chen and the DPP to refrain from provocative moves toward formal independence.[25]

These developments reflected a shift in China's strategy, which now focuses on promoting cross-Strait economic ties, developing relationships with Taiwan's opposition parties, and deterring Taiwan from moving toward formal independence.[26] Moreover, President Chen's weakened domestic position and the strong possibility of a KMT victory in the 2008 presidential election appear to have boosted Beijing confidence that increasing economic interdependence and growing cross-Strait exchanges will preclude a push toward independence in the short term and promote some form of unification in the long term. Nonetheless, Chinese analysts remain concerned about what President Chen may do in the remainder of his term, particularly with regard to the DPP's proposed referendum on applying for United Nations membership under the name "Taiwan."[27] The possibility of a cross-Strait crisis thus cannot be dismissed, especially since Beijing has made it clear that it is willing to use force to prevent any actions it views as likely to diminish the possibility of eventual unification or put the Communist Party leadership in an untenable domestic position.[28] Indeed, senior Chinese leaders have stated that China would "pay any price" to prevent

Taiwan's permanent separation from the mainland, and People's Liberation Army (PLA) officers have indicated that even the risk of heavy casualties, a temporary decline in foreign investment and economic performance, and a possible boycott of the 2008 Olympics would not dissuade China from using force if necessary.[29]

Rising Chinese nationalism, which has been fueled in part by Beijing, is a big part of the reason.[30] As Thomas Christensen puts it, Chinese nationalism is "potentially explosive" when it comes to sensitive issues like relations with Taiwan.[31] Leaders in Beijing are convinced that apparent weakness or outright failure in dealing with the Taiwan issue could leave them vulnerable to their rivals within the elite, or perhaps even threaten the Communist Party's hold on political power. It is thus entirely possible that Beijing would consider inaction an even riskier proposition than the use of force under certain circumstances. Given these concerns about domestic political developments in Taiwan and rising Chinese nationalism, China clearly views the modernization of its military capabilities as an essential component of its overall approach to the Taiwan issue, notwithstanding the recent shift that emphasizes a softer overall approach toward cross-Strait relations. According to a recent US Department of Defense assessment, "Beijing continues to see the threat and possible use of force as integral to its policy of dissuading Taiwan from pursuing independence and moving Taiwan ultimately to unite with the mainland."[32] Indeed, since the late 1990s, China has redoubled its efforts to develop more credible military options.

Chinese Military Modernization

Chinese military modernization has been under way for decades, but it has taken on a much greater sense of urgency in recent years. This more rapid pace of hardware and software improvements dates to 1999, when Beijing ordered the acceleration of the military modernization programs that had been under way since the Gulf War, and in some cases since the 1980s. This increased commitment to military modernization resulted from the bombing of the Chinese embassy in Yugoslavia, growing concern about the potential threat posed by the United States more generally, and deepening pessimism in Beijing about the future prospects for cross-Strait relations following Lee Teng-hui's declaration that these were effectively "state-to-state" relations. In the wake of those events, Chinese foreign and security policy analysts engaged in an intense debate about China's external security environment.[33] The debate resulted in a reaffirmation of "peace and development" as the "key themes" in China's security environment, but it also yielded more guarded conclusions, specifically that "hegemonism and power politics" and "military interventionism" were on the rise, and that China needed to devote greater attention to military modernization. According to one report following those events and the resulting policy debate, "Then-President Jiang Zemin concluded that China needed a more potent and up-to-date military if it was to compete seriously in the world arena and back up its policy on reuniting Taiwan with the mainland."[34] The objectives of the move to speed up the transformation of the PLA were to provide the Chinese leadership with more credible military options against Taiwan and to complicate a US decision to intervene militarily in the event of a China-Taiwan crisis. More concretely, the PLA was ordered to focus on building the capabilities needed to win a short-duration conflict with Taiwan and deter US intervention or at least delay the arrival of US air and naval forces.[35]

Beijing has backed up this commitment to accelerate the modernization of the PLA with substantial budgetary resources. Indeed, China has increased its defense budget by 10 percent or more in real terms almost every year since the leadership ordered the acceleration of military modernization programs in the late 1990s. Estimates of actual Chinese military spending range from about one and a half to three times the announced defense budget numbers, but even the official figures reflect Beijing's commitment to enhancing China's military capabilities.

Within this context of greater urgency and increasing resources, the overall thrust of PLA modernization is an unprecedented transformation from a mass army designed to fight a protracted war of attrition within China's own territory, to a leaner, more modern military designed to fight high-intensity, local wars against technologically advanced adversaries in the surrounding region.[36] This transformation encompasses a wide range of hardware and software reforms. Through acquisition of advanced weapons and equipment from foreign suppliers, and indigenous development and production of increasingly capable weapon systems, the PLA has made substantial improvements in areas such as ballistic missiles, advanced fighter aircraft, air defenses, submarines and surface ships, and ground forces. Although this new hardware garners much of the attention in policy debates, software programs are an equally important element of PLA modernization. China is implementing a series of large-scale military reforms—including revamping the PLA's doctrine, reorganizing its command structure, reforming its logistics system, modernizing its personnel policies and professional military education system, and reducing its overall numbers—that are designed to make the Chinese armed forces more capable of conducting joint operations and achieving victory in modern, information-centric, high-tech wars.

This ambitious transformation of the PLA into a more modern and capable military is giving Chinese leaders much more credible military options than they had in the mid-1990s, when the PLA could do little more than attempt to intimidate Taiwan with symbolic displays such as military exercises and missile tests. Moreover, because Taiwan's own defense modernization efforts are no longer keeping pace, the transformation of the PLA is shifting the cross-Strait military balance in China's favor, which raises concerns about Taiwan's ability to defend itself absent US military intervention, and perhaps even to hold out until the arrival of US forces.

China's Assessment of Its External Security Environment

PLA and civilian strategists assess that China faces serious threats to its sovereignty and security.[37] Chinese national security analysts argue that the United States constitutes the most serious of these security threats. For example, China's 2004 national defense white paper argues that "tendencies of hegemonism and unilateralism have gained new ground," an apparent reference to Beijing's concerns about the potential implications of the Bush administration's foreign and security policy.[38] Given these perceived threats to Chinese security, the importance of military power is growing. According to the 2004 defense white paper, "The role played by military power in safeguarding national security is assuming greater prominence."[39] This, too, appears to be a reference to Beijing's concerns about US military power and Washington's intentions toward China.[40] Moreover, Chinese analysts assert that US support for Taiwan emboldens the island's leaders to pursue permanent separation from China.

The statements of the PRC's senior leaders also reflect this concern about the possibility that the United States will exploit its power to take actions that impinge on Chinese interests in the Taiwan issue or other areas. In 2004, for example, Jiang Zemin declared that the military challenges facing China were increasing and that the PLA should respond by implementing reforms "with a sense of immediacy."[41] Chinese foreign and security policy analysts are often even more explicit in listing the United States as the primary threat to China's emergence as a major power.[42]

Chinese analysts are also casting a wary eye on Japan. China's 2004 defense white paper implies that Beijing is becoming more and more concerned about Japan's growing role in the Asia Pacific region. According to the white paper, "Japan is stepping up its constitutional overhaul, adjusting its military and security policies and developing the missile defense system for future deployment. It has also markedly increased military activities abroad."[43] Tokyo's increasingly active security policy, historical animosity toward Japan, and recent difficulties in the bilateral relationship between China and Japan appear to have exacerbated the concerns of Chinese foreign and security policy analysts. Indeed, many in Beijing see the expansion of Japan's role in the US-Japan alliance as threatening to Chinese interests. The collapse of the US-Japan alliance would also be seen as threatening, however, because it would herald Japan's emergence as a truly independent player on the East Asian security scene.[44]

China's concerns about the United States and Japan center in large part, though not exclusively, on the Taiwan issue. Although Chinese analysts recently have indicated that they view growing cross-Strait economic interaction, breakthroughs in China's relationship with the Pan-Blue parties, and President Chen's growing domestic isolation as trends that work in China's favor, they remain concerned about cross-Strait relations. Given Chinese concerns about Taiwan—and widespread views of the United States and Japan as potential threats to Chinese security—it is not surprising that Beijing views PLA modernization as absolutely necessary to protecting its core political interests. As Thomas Christensen puts it, "Even many defensively minded moderates in Beijing are loath to halt the PRC military buildup across from Taiwan, lest Beijing lose leverage over the government of President Chen Shui-bian."[45]

Chinese Defense Spending

The PLA has enjoyed double-digit budget increases in real terms in most years since the mid-1990s. Chinese defense spending has increased even more rapidly in recent years. As a result, in 2005, China's announced defense budget of roughly US$30.2 billion was about double the amount officially spent on national defense in 2000. This trend continued in 2006, when China announced a defense budget of about US$35.1 billion, representing an increase of 14.7 percent over the previous year.[46] Officials stated that the 2006 increase would cover raises for servicemen, the growing costs of oil products resulting from rising international oil prices, enhanced training, and acquisition of improved military equipment. In 2007, China announced a 17.8 percent increase in military spending, bringing its defense budget to almost US$45 billion.

As mentioned previously, estimates of actual Chinese defense spending vary from about one and a half to three times the officially announced defense budget figures. The US Department of Defense's 2006 report on Chinese military power provides an estimate from the Defense Intelligence Agency that places actual Chinese military spending in 2006 at somewhere between US$70 billion and US$105 billion, or about two to three times the announced defense budget.[47] The London-based International Institute for Strategic Studies estimates that in 2003, actual Chinese military spending was about 1.7 times the official defense budget.[48] Similarly, a recent RAND study concludes that China's actual defense spending in 2003 was about US$31–38 billion, approximately 1.4 to 1.7 times the officially announced number.[49] The sharp upward trend in defense spending that began in the late 1990s is clearly evident whether one considers the PRC's official defense budget numbers or any of these outside estimates of actual Chinese defense spending.

Some of the items that are not reflected in the officially announced defense budget include foreign weapons procurement, paramilitary expenses, state subsidies for the defense-industrial complex, and defense-related research and development. The number of funding sources and the involvement of multiple levels of government greatly complicate attempts to estimate actual Chinese defense spending. Indeed, according to the 2006 Department of Defense report on the Chinese military, "Real spending on the military . . . is so disaggregated that even the Chinese leadership may not know the actual top line."[50]

As difficult as it is to calculate the current Chinese defense budget, projecting future trends in Chinese military spending entails struggling with even greater uncertainties and complexities. Forecasts of Chinese military spending over the next ten to twenty years thus vary widely depending on the methods employed and on underlying assumptions about factors such as China's future economic performance and the trade-offs the country's leaders will face as they decide how to balance military modernization against other budgetary requirements.[51] The US Department of Defense predicts a possible threefold or greater increase in Chinese defense spending over the next twenty years.[52] This would place China's military budget at US$210–315 billion (in constant 2005 US dollars) or more in 2025. Using what appears to be a more sophisticated methodology, a recent RAND report concluded that slowing economic growth and rising pressures to increase social welfare spending would probably impose constraints on future defense expenditures.[53] Thus the RAND study projects that in 2025, Chinese defense spending will reach about US$185 billion (in constant 2005 US dollars), an impressive sum, but one that is considerably lower than the Department of Defense forecast cited above.

These divergent estimates reflect considerable uncertainty about how China's leaders will elect to allocate budgetary resources when faced with competing priorities. Military modernization is certainly a high priority, as indicated by the recent statements of senior leaders. For example, addressing members of the PLA delegation to the March 2006 National People's Congress meeting, President Hu said, "We should strive to improve the capability of the armed forces to deal with crisis, maintain peace, contain wars and win victory in possible wars."[54] Hu urged the PLA to intensify its efforts to equip itself with information technology, improve its combat readiness, and push forward organizational and administrative reforms. Hu also stressed the importance of developing a capability for rapid and effective national defense mobilization.

Interestingly, despite the increased priority accorded to military modernization since the late 1990s, which has been reflected by a decade of double-digit budget increases, some PLA officers and Chinese scholars assert that Beijing is still not devoting enough resources to national defense. The comments of PLA deputies to the 2006 sessions of the National People's Congress and the Chinese People's Political Consultative Conference perhaps suggested some dissatisfaction with the level of resources devoted to the military.[55] Several think tank analysts and scholars have also called for even greater increases in military spending. Hu Angang, an economist at Qinghua University, recently stated that China is not spending enough on defense, especially considering the country's rapid economic development and recent trends in China-Taiwan relations.[56] Similarly, Shen Dingli, executive vice president of the Institute of International Studies at Fudan University in Shanghai, has argued that China needs to devote even greater resources to military modernization to increase its ability to compete with the United States.[57]

These calls for still greater defense spending, however, are likely to be counterbalanced by growing demands for government spending to cope with a wide range of social problems that have arisen as unintended consequences of Beijing's economic reform strategy. Indeed, defense spending eventually may have to compete with domestic problems such as a growing income gap, rising social unrest, and worsening environmental degradation, especially if economic growth slows.[58] These social, political, and economic challenges have the potential to impose constraints on further increases in military spending.[59]

Defense-Industrial Reforms

Although China has acquired some of its most advanced military technology from foreign suppliers, most notably Russia, indigenous procurement and the reform of China's defense-industrial complex are equally critical drivers of the modernization of the Chinese military.[60] Once viewed as almost hopelessly backward and inefficient, China's defense industries have improved dramatically in recent years. These changes stem in large part from the implementation of major defense-industrial reforms in 1998. This most recent round of reforms appears to have set in motion much greater changes than did numerous previous attempts, and has sparked a major turnaround in Western assessments of the capabilities and limitations of China's defense industries.[61]

These improvements in defense-industrial capability have resulted from a combination of several factors, such as increased funds for weapon acquisition, commercialization of some defense enterprises, limited foreign technical assistance, and reorganization and reform of the procurement system and defense industries that Beijing implemented in 1998, which addressed problems at both the central and the enterprise level. At the central level, the reforms consisted of a reorganization intended to make the procurement process more responsive to the PLA's requirements. The government created a civilian entity subordinate to the State Council to replace the old Commission on Science, Technology, and Industry for National Defense, which had been dominated by the PLA. It also established the General Armaments Department under the PLA and gave this new organization responsibility for the procurement and full life-cycle management of PLA weapon systems. Importantly, these two changes "separated the builders (the manufacturers) from the buyers (the military)," which contributed to the rationalization of the procurement system by reducing corruption and conflicts of interest.[62] In addition, the government issued a series of regulations to standardize the procurement process and create a competitive-bidding system for defense contracts.

At the same time, the government also adopted a number of reforms at the enterprise level to enhance the efficiency of defense industry operations. These included exposing enterprises to market forces, lessening reliance on government subsidies, tightening budget constraints, implementing new quality assurance procedures, and reducing social welfare burdens on enterprises. One notable structural reform was the transformation of China's traditional defense companies into defense-industrial group corporations, which was intended to stimulate competition and increase enterprise accountability. Additional changes have included the expansion and upgrading of production facilities and a variety of partnerships with civilian universities.

These reforms at the central government and enterprise levels are contributing to considerable improvements in the capabilities of China's defense-industrial complex. Indeed, according to a recent RAND study, the increases in the quality of output of China's defense industries demonstrate that the reform package put into place in 1998 "has not only taken hold but even accelerated in the past several years."[63] Some of the areas in which progress has been most evident are the missile, shipbuilding, aviation, and information technology sectors. Although the rate of improvement varies across and within sectors, and the defense industries still face a number of obstacles and constraints, the reforms are transforming vital parts of a defense-industrial complex that was once known primarily for its inefficiency, corruption, and backwardness.

China is pushing forward with further defense industry reforms. For example, Beijing recently announced plans to permit private companies to engage in defense-related research and development as part of its efforts to further stimulate competition and innovation in the defense-industrial sector.[64] As part of this new approach, the PLA has launched a procurement website that publicizes requests for bids from private contractors in categories ranging from weapon systems to food services.[65] Even though many problems remain unresolved, these reforms have contributed greatly to PLA hardware modernization in recent years.

Hardware Modernization

Conventional ballistic and cruise missiles. China's growing conventionally armed ballistic and cruise missile capability is perhaps the most attention-grabbing aspect of Chinese military hardware modernization. In particular, the number of short-range ballistic missiles in China's inventory has increased dramatically in recent years, posing an increasingly potent threat to Taiwan and US forces in parts of the region. Publicly released US Department of Defense estimates indicate that the number of short-range ballistic missiles China deploys in the military regions opposite Taiwan more than doubled since 2003. According to the Department of Defense's 2007 report to Congress, China currently fields about 900 CSS-6 and CSS-7 short-range ballistic missiles. The report also indicates that the number of deployed missiles is increasing at a rate of about 100 per year.[66] Moreover, newer versions of these missiles feature "greater ranges and improved accuracy."[67] The improvements in accuracy are a result of satellite-aided guidance systems.[68] In addition, newer versions of the CSS-6 have the range to strike not only targets in Taiwan, but also US forces in Okinawa.

Taiwan's Ministry of National Defense has released similar numbers. Moreover, in a public briefing held in March 2006, Lieutenant Colonel Chen Chang-hua, a ministry official, stated that the circular error probability of the Chinese missiles deployed opposite Taiwan has decreased from about 600 meters to around 50 meters. The increasing accuracy of Chinese short-range ballistic missiles makes them more effective against a broader range of targets. Indeed, as a result of the rapid growth in numbers and improvements in accuracy, China could paralyze Taiwan's communications links, command centers, airbases, and ports with five waves of strikes in as little as ten hours, according to Chen.[69] In addition, China is developing conventionally armed medium-range ballistic missiles, which will allow the Second Artillery to "extend the range of its conventional missile strike force."[70]

China is exploring the use of ballistic missiles for antiaccess missions, such as precision strikes against airbases, ports, command and control facilities, air defense systems, ground-based command, control, communications, computers, intelligence, surveillance, and reconnaissance (C4ISR) nodes, and possibly surface ships such as aircraft carriers. According to a recent Congressional Research Service report, China could eventually employ ballistic missiles in combination with a broad-area maritime surveillance and targeting system to strike ships at sea.[71] This would form part of an emerging area-denial or antiaccess capability. Another area of emphasis in Chinese ballistic missile modernization is the development of "an increased variety of conventional warheads," according to the 2004 Department of Defense report on Chinese military power.[72]

China is also developing land-attack cruise missiles that can be fired from bases on the ground as well as from aircraft and submarines. According to *Jane's Missiles and Rockets,* China is developing a land-attack cruise missile known as the Dong Hai-10 (DH-10) and an air-launched cruise missile called the Yong Ji-63 (YJ-63) that is likely to be carried by a bomber aircraft.[73] Defense officials in Taiwan have stated that some of China's land-attack cruise missiles will be highly accurate, with a circular error probability of 10 meters or less.[74] The Department of Defense assesses that land-attack cruise missiles will allow "greater precision than historically available from ballistic missiles for hard target strikes, and increased standoff."[75] The Defense Intelligence Agency estimates that by 2015, "China will have hundreds of highly accurate air-and-ground-launched [land-attack cruise missiles]."[76] In addition, China has deployed close to 100 Harpy drones, according to defense officials in Taiwan. The Harpy is an Israeli-made antiradiation weapon that is capable of loitering over enemy territory for extended periods and then striking air defense sites when they turn on their radars.

The PLA navy and PLA air force are also acquiring a variety of antiship cruise missiles, such as the SS-N-22 Sunburn and the SS-N-27 Sizzler, from Russia.[77] The modernization of antiship cruise missile capabilities, however, is not limited to foreign procurement. Indeed, according to the 2005 Department of Defense report on Chinese military power, "The pace of indigenous [antiship cruise missile] research, development, and production . . . has accelerated over the past decade."[78] The foreign acquisitions and indigenous development programs will give China antiship cruise missiles with greater closure speed and longer standoff distance, as well as allowing launch from different platforms, such as submarines.

In all, the growth of China's arsenal of short-range ballistic missiles, land-attack cruise missiles, and antiship cruise missiles reflects a growing emphasis on deep-strike and antiaccess capabilities. These capabilities could be used to attack Taiwan's airfields, command and control centers, air defenses, and other critical targets. They also represent an increasing threat to US forces operating in parts of the Asia Pacific region, including US airbases, logistics and support facilities, and potentially naval-carrier strike groups.

Strategic and theater nuclear forces. China is also modernizing its strategic and theater nuclear forces to enhance their striking power and survivability.[79] According to the 2005 Department of Defense report on Chinese military power, "China is qualitatively and quantitatively improving its strategic missile force. This could provide a credible, survivable nuclear deterrent and counterstrike capability."[80] According to the same report, China currently has about twenty silo-based, liquid-propellant CSS-4 intercontinental ballistic missiles, which are capable of striking targets in the continental United States, and a number of older missiles that are more limited in range and serve primarily as a regional nuclear deterrent. As China's nuclear force modernization continues, its strategic nuclear forces will consist of CSS-4

Mod 2 intercontinental ballistic missiles (longer-range versions of the older, silo-based, liquid-fueled CSS-4 Mod 1s); road-mobile, solid-fueled DF-31 and DF-31A intercontinental ballistic missiles; and JL-2 submarine-launched ballistic missiles. The deployment of road-mobile intercontinental ballistic missiles will improve the survivability of China's nuclear forces by making them "more difficult to locate and neutralize."[81] The addition of submarine-launched ballistic missiles will provide another survivable nuclear capability.[82] China also has the capability to deploy a multiple independently targeted reentry vehicle system for the CSS-4 intercontinental ballistic missile.[83] In addition to upgrading its strategic nuclear forces, China will continue to maintain nuclear-armed CSS-5 medium-range ballistic missiles as the cornerstone of its regional deterrence capabilities.[84]

Air power and air defense capabilities. China is enhancing its air power through foreign procurement and indigenous production of modern fighters, transports, refueling planes, and other types of aircraft. The overall thrust of PLA air force modernization is a transition from a purely defensive mission to a combination of offensive and defensive missions.[85] In support of this transition, the air force continues to acquire advanced fighter aircraft from Russia. Recent purchases include Su-30MKK multirole aircraft, Su-30MK2 maritime strike aircraft, and more deliveries of Su-27 fighter aircraft. The PRC is also producing a version of the Su-27SK aircraft, known as the F-11, under a licensed coproduction agreement with Russia. According to the 2006 Department of Defense report on Chinese military power, China in 2005 renegotiated this agreement so that it could produce the multirole Su-27SMK for the rest of the production run.[86] China has signed a contract to purchase about forty IL-76 transport aircraft and eight IL-78/Midas air refueling aircraft from Russia. According to the 2006 Department of Defense report, "These aircraft will increase the PLA Air Force strategic lift capacity, in particular, the ability to airdrop troops and fighting vehicles. The refueling aircraft will extend the range and strike potential of China's bomber and fighter aircraft."[87]

The PLA air force is also fielding its own indigenous fourth-generation fighter, the F-10. China completed development of the F-10 in 2004. Newer versions of the F-10, known as the F-10A and Super-10, are currently under development. These upgraded versions of China's indigenous fourth-generation fighter reportedly feature enhanced engines, weapons, and radar systems. China is also upgrading older FB-7 fighters to perform nighttime maritime strike operations. In addition, China is developing the KJ-2000 airborne warning and control aircraft, which features an indigenously manufactured radar system mounted on a Russian IL-76 transport plane, and other airborne battlefield command and intelligence-collection planes. The KJ-2000 aircraft will allow the PLA air force to monitor airspace and control fighters and other aircraft, functions that would be critical factors in the contest for air superiority should China decide to use force against Taiwan.[88]

China is also acquiring advanced precision-strike munitions, cruise missiles, and air-to-air, air-to-surface, and antiradiation munitions, and may be converting some of its hundreds of retired fighters into unmanned combat aerial vehicles.[89] As a result of these foreign procurement and indigenous production programs, advanced aircraft account for an increasing percentage of the PLA air force's inventory.

China is also improving its air defense capabilities in ways that will create serious military challenges for the ROC and the United States should a conflict erupt in the Taiwan Strait. It has acquired SA-10 and SA-20 surface-to-air missiles from Russia, and Chinese acquisition of extended range systems is anticipated. China has also purchased the Russian S-300PMU-2, which has an advertised range of 200 kilometers. China is also working on the HQ-9 surface-to-air missile, a reverse-engineered domestic variant of the SA-10. These upgraded air defense capabilities will provide surface-to-air missile coverage over the entire Taiwan Strait.[90]

Naval capabilities. China has also devoted considerable emphasis to enhancing the capabilities of the PLA navy, which consists of about seventy-five major surface combatants, fifty medium and heavy amphibious lift vessels, forty-five coastal missile patrol craft, and fifty-five attack submarines. As a result of Chinese acquisition of Russian hardware and the Chinese shipbuilding industry's development of several new classes of modern surface ships and submarines, advanced surface combatants and submarines represent an increasing proportion of the PLA navy's inventory.

Several of the PLA navy's most formidable surface combatants are Russian imports. China has acquired Russian-made Sovremenny-class guided-missile destroyers, which are equipped with the SS-N-22 Sunburn antiship cruise missiles. Advanced antiship cruise missiles and naval air defense systems make the Sovremennys the navy's most formidable surface ships. However, the navy is no longer dependent exclusively on acquiring surface ships from Russia. Improvements in the Chinese shipbuilding industry have also permitted the navy to meet some of its needs with indigenously produced systems. Indeed, many of the navy's most modern ships are currently produced in Chinese shipyards.[91] Specifically, the Chinese navy has deployed eight new classes of indigenous destroyers and frigates.

Among the PLA navy's new surface ships are five indigenously built classes of destroyers. According to a Congressional Research Service report, "Compared to China's 16 older Luda (Type 051) class destroyers, which entered service between 1971 and 1991, these five new destroyer classes are substantially more modern in terms of their hull designs, propulsion systems, sensors, weapons, and electronics."[92] One of the most important areas of improvement is antiair warfare technology. For example, the Luyang I–class destroyers feature the Russian SA-N-7B Grizzly surface-to-air missile system. The Luyang II–class destroyers also appear to have a capable antiair warfare system, the HQ-9 surface-to-air missile, which offers greater range, a vertical launch system, and a phased array radar system that appears at least somewhat similar to the Spy-1 radar, which is the centerpiece of the Aegis naval combat system for the United States. Moreover, in 2005, the PLA navy launched the Luzhou-class destroyer. According to the 2006 Department of Defense report on Chinese military power, "Designed for anti-air warfare, it is equipped with the Russian SA-N-20 [surface-to-air missile] system, controlled by the TOMB-STONE phased-array radar. The SA-N-20 more than doubles the range of current [PLA navy] systems."[93] Advances in this area are of particular significance because antiair warfare had been a shortcoming for the PLA navy historically. These antiair warfare improvements could give the navy the capability to acquire "local air superiority during maritime operations."[94]

China has also introduced three new classes of frigates that represent significant advances over its older Jianghu (Type 053)–class frigates. The three new classes—the Jiangwei I, Jiangwei II, and Jiangkai—also feature improved antiair warfare capabilities. In addition to its new destroyers and frigates, China has deployed "a new fast attack craft that uses a stealthy catamaran hull design."[95] The PLA navy is also building a new class of mine countermeasure ships. In all, the Congressional Research Service report on Chinese naval modernization concludes that these new ships "demonstrate a significant modernization of PLA Navy surface combatant technology."[96]

China is also making major strides in improving the capabilities of its submarine force. Indeed, US analysts have concluded that the PLA navy's submarine force is emerging as "the centerpiece" of Chinese naval modernization.[97] As with the navy's surface ships, some of the most capable submarines were purchased from Russia. China has twelve Kilo-class diesel electric submarines, which it acquired from Russia. The newest Kilo-class submarines carry the advanced SS-N-27 antiship cruise missile along with wire-guided and wake-homing torpedoes.

As well, China's domestic shipbuilding industry is turning out four new classes of submarines. China's Song-class diesel electric submarines, which carry the YJ-82 antiship cruise missile, are in serial production. In 2004, China launched the first of its new Yuan-class diesel submarines. China's next-generation nuclear-powered attack submarine, the Type 093, or Shang-class SSN, is now entering service. According to the 2006 Department of Defense report on Chinese military power, the Song-class diesel electric submarine features the YJ-82, "an encapsulated [antiship cruise missile] capable of submerged launch."[98] Also under development is the Type 094 nuclear-powered ballistic missile submarine. According to a Congressional Research Service report on PLA navy modernization, these new classes of submarines "are expected to be much more modern and capable than China's aging older-generation submarines."[99]

Many of China's submarines are still older models, but even these less-capable boats may have a role to play in a cross-Strait conflict. According to the Congressional Research Service, "Although China's aging Ming- and Romeo-class submarines are based on old technology and are much less capable than the PLA Navy's newer-design submarines, China may decide that these older boats have continued value as minelayers or as bait or decoy submarines that can be used to draw out enemy submarines (such as U.S. SSNs) that can then be attacked by more modern PLA Navy submarines."[100] Chinese submarines are also beginning to operate in more distant locations. In November 2004, a Han-class SSN was detected in Japanese territorial waters. The submarine also operated in other parts of the western Pacific Ocean during the same deployment.[101]

Overall, the PLA navy is becoming much more capable and now represents a serious threat not only to Taiwan's naval forces, but also to more modern navies operating in the region. At the same time, however, the PLA navy continues to face some major limitations. According to the Congressional Research Service, there is still room for PLA naval improvement in areas such as sustaining operations in distant waters, conducting joint operations, C4ISR and long-range surveillance and targeting systems for detecting and tracking ships at sea, antisubmarine warfare, mine countermeasures, and logistics.[102]

Ground forces. Although the main focus of Chinese military hardware modernization is increasing the capabilities of the PLA navy, PLA air force, and Second Artillery, China is also strengthening its ground forces, particularly units that would play a role in a Taiwan scenario.[103] China currently has 400,000 ground force personnel in the Nanjing, Guangzhou, and Jinan military regions, the three such regions opposite Taiwan. This represents an increase of about 25,000 personnel over the number deployed to those three regions in 2005, according to the 2006 Department of Defense report on Chinese military power.[104] In addition, China is upgrading the ground force units in those three military regions facing Taiwan, including increases in the number of tanks and artillery pieces, as well as qualitative improvements in tanks, armored personnel carriers, and artillery pieces. China is also addressing a traditional area of weakness by increasing its amphibious lift capabilities. In 2003, it began building three new classes of amphibious ships and landing craft.[105] In addition, in recent years, China has built at least nineteen amphibious ships and eight amphibious landing craft as part of this effort to improve the PLA's ability to conduct amphibious operations.[106]

Electronic warfare and information operations. Chinese military strategists view information and electronic warfare as critical elements of "informationized" war.[107] Chinese writings on information warfare suggest that computer network operations are required to support attempts to gain the initiative early in a conflict and to seize and maintain information superiority. Computer network attacks would form part of an integrated approach that would also include electronic warfare and possibly limited air, missile, or special operations attacks against key C4ISR nodes. According to the 2006 Department of Defense report on the Chinese military, "The PLA has increased the role of [computer network operations] in its military exercises. For example, exercises in 2005 began to incorporate offensive operations, primarily in first strikes against enemy networks."[108]

Space and C4ISR. Chinese military strategists view space operations as vital components of joint campaigns and high-tech local wars. For the PLA, space is "as vital a battlefield as any on earth."[109] Consequently, according to the US Department of Defense, "China has accorded building a modern ISR architecture a high priority in its comprehensive military modernization, in particular the development of advanced space-based C4ISR and targeting capabilities."[110] China is developing space-based ISR satellite systems for uses such as remote sensing, advanced imagery, and electronic intelligence and signal interception.[111] China may also purchase commercial imagery products to supplement its current reconnaissance capabilities. In addition, China has deployed its own Beidou navigation and positioning satellites. These three satellites provide navigation coverage accurate to within about twenty meters.[112] China also uses the global positioning system and the global navigation system, and is working with the European Union on the Galileo navigation satellite system.

The PLA is leveraging the PRC's dynamic commercial information technology sector to accelerate the modernization of its C4ISR capabilities. According to a recent RAND study, China's information technology (IT) sector is likely "the most organizationally innovative and economically dynamic producer of equipment for China's military." Even though Chinese IT companies are oriented mainly toward domestic and international commercial IT markets, "the PLA has been able to effectively leverage certain IT products to improve the military's command, control, communications, computers, and intelligence (C4I) capabilities—a critical element of the PLA's modernization efforts."[113]

Counterspace weapons. China is also working on counterspace capabilities. Chinese writers view dependence on space as a major vulnerability for technologically advanced militaries like the United States. Military space operations constitute a key element of information dominance, and may involve "gaining mastery by striking first."[114] The 2006 Department of Defense report on Chinese military capabilities indicates that China is pursuing the development of antisatellite weapons including laser antisatellite weapons capable of blinding or damaging imagery satellites. In January 2007, China successfully tested a kinetic-kill-vehicle antisatellite weapon by destroying an aging Chinese meteorological satellite, an action that raised considerable international concerns not only about China's growing counter-space capabilities, but also about the potential for damage to other satellites from debris created by the test. In addition, China is also enhancing its space situational awareness, a capability that is required to track, identify, and engage adversary spacecraft.[115]

Software Reforms and Professionalization

Doctrinal innovation. The PLA is revamping its doctrine to meet the challenges of the types of wars it expects it may have to fight in the future.[116] Based on assessments of recent conflicts, the PLA expects that future military conflicts will be "local wars under informationized conditions."[117] This formulation updates "local wars under modern, high-tech conditions," the type of wars that PLA strategists previously assessed as the most likely form of future military conflict. The defining features of contemporary warfare, as viewed by the PLA, are summarized in a number of books and journal articles by PLA authors.[118] First, such wars are information-intensive and heavily dependent on high-tech C4ISR. Second, like "high-tech local wars," "local wars under informationized conditions" are fought for limited political objectives and are limited in geographic scope. Third, they are short in duration, perhaps so short that a single campaign may decide the outcome of the conflict.[119] Fourth, they are high-intensity and high-lethality conflicts that place a premium on mobility, speed, logistics, sustainability, deep strikes, joint operations, and high-tech weapons. Fifth, they involve conflict in all dimensions of battle, including space and the electromagnetic spectrum.[120] This conception of future warfare necessitated a comprehensive overhaul of PLA doctrine at the operational level.

The watershed event in the PLA's effort to update its doctrine in accordance with its vision of future warfare came in January 1999, when the PLA issued revised doctrinal guidance for training and conducting warfare at the campaign and tactical levels. This new doctrinal guidance, known as the "new-generation operation regulations" *(xin yidai zuozhan tiaoling),* comprised a series of publications referred to as *gangyao,* which provide top-level guidance for ground, naval, air, and artillery campaigns, logistics and support, and joint campaigns.[121] The document on joint campaigns reportedly was the first joint *gangyao* ever issued. Western analysts assess that these documents are likely similar to US military field manuals and doctrinal publications.[122]

The PLA has not publicized the specific content of these documents, but some insights into the general focus can be gleaned from the careful reading of authoritative teaching materials that are used in professional military educational institutions, because the *gangyao* are supposed to serve as the basis for the development of new teaching materials. Those publications are available to students of Chinese military affairs.[123]

The new body of doctrine embodied in these documents, which was nearly a decade in the making, provides guidance for the conduct of campaign-level operations. As such, it also has implications for reforms in the areas of training, professional military education, force structure, weapons development, organization, command and control, and personnel. Studying the PLA's evolving doctrine is thus important because it reveals much about how the PLA will organize, train, and equip its forces, and also provides insight into how it may employ its new capabilities in the event of a regional conflict.

As for the content of the PLA's emerging doctrine, the new guidance appears to represent a strong focus on the operational level of warfare, and emphasizes the importance of joint operations. Furthermore, according to David Finkelstein: "Emerging PLA doctrine has shifted from a traditional emphasis on 'campaigns of annihilation' (a traditional PLA expression) that focused on force-on-force attrition, to campaigns of paralysis . . . in which offensive and preemptive strikes at the operational level of war deny the technologically superior (and technologically dependent) enemy the ability to conduct its campaign. Disrupting the enemy's campaign is acceptable if defeating the enemy's campaign head-on is not possible."[124]

Chinese military writings emphasize several key principles for planning and conducting future wars along these lines.[125] First, they emphasize the importance of coordinating military, political, and diplomatic actions. They also suggest that the PLA must seize the initiative early in a conflict. This is especially vital because the decisive stage may come very early in a war that may consist of only one campaign. Moreover, in future conflicts, the PLA would conduct "integrated operations and key point strikes" *(zhengti zuo-zhan, zhongdian daji),* which involves employing the most advanced portion of China's armed forces against an adversary and concentrating on attacking the opponent's key vulnerabilities. Chinese writings also suggest that the PLA would strive for rapid achievement of strategic objectives, often referred to as "rapid war, rapid resolution" *(suzhan sujue).* China would expect an adversary to launch precision deep strikes against targets such as its command and control centers, air defense network, and air and missile bases, so there is also considerable attention devoted to protecting strategic points from enemy long-range attacks. Finally, "unified leadership, centralized command" *(tongyi lingdao, jizhong zhihui)* is seen as important because of the complexity and rapid pace of high-tech local wars.[126]

Organizational change. The modernization of PLA command and control extends beyond the impressive communications buildout, encompassing a series of reforms in organizational structure and command relationships.[127] In 2004, the PLA added the commanders of its air force, navy, and strategic missile force (the Second Artillery) to the Central Military Commission (CMC), which previously had been dominated by senior officers from the ground forces. The addition of these officers to the CMC was intended to "bring the status of the Navy, Air Force, and the strategic missile force in line with that of the Army," according to a report carried in a Hong Kong newspaper with close ties to Beijing.[128] Another important development that took place in 2004 was the installation of two senior officers from the PLA air force and navy as deputy chiefs of the General Staff, which also was previously the preserve of ground force officers. The purpose of promoting the naval and air force officers was to demonstrate the "determination of the CMC in raising the strategic position of the Navy and the Air Force."[129] China-watchers in the United States also assessed that these expansions of the CMC and the General Staff were key developments reflecting China's emphasis on promoting interservice coordination and improving joint operations capabilities.

Joint operations. The PLA's reorganization of command structure, logistics reforms, and improvements in communications are all intended to better enable it to conduct joint operations. Numerous recent PLA publications emphasize the importance of joint campaigns and joint operations.[130] In *The Science of Campaigns,* for example, the authors describe joint campaigns as an important form of future military operations.[131] Chinese military authors define joint campaigns as campaigns that involve the participation of two or more services, and in which all participating forces operate under the direction of a joint campaign command. The writings on joint campaigns imply the equivalence of all of the participating services. This is potentially controversial in a military traditionally dominated by the ground forces. In Dean Cheng's words, this emphasis on the equality of the services in joint campaigns marks a "fundamental and major shift in PLA culture."[132]

Joint campaigns require joint campaign command structures, which are responsible for coordinating service activities in pursuit of the overall campaign objectives. According to Cheng, the chief roles of the joint campaign command are "resolving issues of timing, phasing, and various other aspects of coordination."[133]

The PLA is clearly striving to develop the capability to plan and conduct joint campaigns, and has already made considerable progress, but Chinese authors suggest that it is still in the preliminary stages of "jointness." Cheng highlights a 2002 *PLA Daily* article in which the author characterizes the achievement of a true joint operations capability as a three-stage process. In the first stage, considered preliminary joint training, there are three unbroken eggs in a bowl. In the second stage, which is characterized as limited joint training, the three eggs are broken. It is only in the third stage, however, that the eggs are mixed together and all-around joint training is achieved. The article implies that the PLA is still relatively early in this process, though it aspires to move forward so that it will ultimately be able to conduct the more sophisticated types of joint training and operations.[134]

The PLA still faces several potential problems, many of them bureaucratic and institutional. Perhaps the most important of these is a highly centralized and hierarchical command structure and organizational culture that is averse to delegating decisionmaking authority to lower levels, much less to junior officers and noncommissioned officers. Another potential roadblock is institutional resistance and bureaucratic opposition resulting from the tendency of joint campaigns to emphasize the importance of the navy, air force, and missile force, and to downplay the traditional dominance of the army. Developing a *gangyao* for joint operations, an accomplishment almost ten years in the making, was just the beginning of what will probably be a long and difficult process of reorganization and institutional change.

Still another challenge is the PLA's almost total lack of real experience in conducting joint operations (the only historical example being the relatively small-scale Yijiangshan campaign in 1955; the rest of the PLA's warfighting experiences were at most combined arms campaigns).[135] As the 2006 Department of Defense report on Chinese military power points out, "Although the PLA has devoted considerable effort to developing joint capabilities, it faces a persistent lack of inter-service cooperation and a lack of actual experience in joint operations."[136] Finally, the PLA faces the challenge of undertaking so many major changes simultaneously as it seeks to further improve its joint operations capabilities.[137]

Logistics and mobilization. Logistics reform is an important but often overlooked aspect of Chinese military modernization. The PLA is reforming its logistics system, placing increasing emphasis on joint logistics.[138] China's first "joint logistical unit" was deployed in 2004. The PLA is also outsourcing many tasks to civilian companies. Indeed, the logistics reforms devote particular attention to the "socialization" of logistics, which entails outsourcing functions that civilian providers can perform at lower cost compared to the PLA.

China is also devoting considerable attention to improving its ability to mobilize the civilian economy to support military operations. According to the 2006 Department of Defense report on Chinese military modernization,

"The PLA is placing greater emphasis on the mobilization of the civilian economy, both in peacetime and in war, to support national defense requirements."[139] This includes a wide variety of activities, such as preparing to use the civil merchant fleet to augment amphibious lift capabilities. The concept of mobilization, however, is a much broader one that encompasses a number of activities.

The *China War Mobilization Encyclopedia* defines war mobilization as a series of measures that a state implements "to shift from a peacetime situation to a wartime situation, and to unify and muster manpower, materiel, and finances to serve the war effort."[140] This is a broad definition that encompasses mobilization of the armed forces, the civilian economy, and the nation's science and technology resources, as well as more specialized undertakings such as political mobilization and people's air defense mobilization. According to that encyclopedia, successful mobilization depends not only on factors such as resource endowments, economic production, and level of science and technology development, but also on having an appropriate organizational structure and effective procedures.[141] Consequently, improving the organizational structure of the mobilization system is identified as one of the "key links" in terms of peacetime mobilization preparations.[142]

Downsizing the PLA. Another important factor in the professionalization and modernization of China's armed forces is the further streamlining of the PLA, which follows the implementation of several rounds of demobilization that reduced the size of the PLA from roughly 4 million personnel in 1985 to about 2.5 million before the latest round of downsizing, which began in 2003. This most recent demobilization, which was completed in December 2005, trimmed another 200,000 troops, reducing the total size of the PLA to about 2.3 million. Cutting the number of troops yields cost savings that can be applied to other requirements, such as improving hardware and raising salaries. According to Major-General Peng Guangqian, another objective of the latest round of troop reductions was streamlining the command structure by reducing the number of headquarters personnel: "It reflects the need to trim commanding personnel and make the chain of decision-making swifter and more rational."[143]

Although downsizing of the military is an important part of making the PLA a more modern and operationally capable fighting force, the process is not without social and economic costs. Indeed, social-stability concerns and economic burdens placed on local governments as a result of demobilization probably prevent Beijing from reducing the size of the PLA even more rapidly. The CCP does not want to see demobilized troops demonstrating in the streets. David Finkelstein assesses that this consideration "is likely the greatest factor that inhibits the PLA from scaling down to a much leaner military—one that can be evenly trained and equipped for excellence across the board."[144]

Personnel policy. The PLA is implementing a variety of personnel reforms as part of its broader effort to create a more professional and technically competent fighting force. These reforms include changes in the conscription system, the creation of a professional noncommissioned officer corps, and improvements in officer recruitment. The 1999 amendment to the military service law reduced the period of conscription to two years (previously, army personnel served three years, and air force and navy personnel served four years).[145] The amendment also represented the PLA's first serious attempt to develop a functioning noncommissioned officer corps, though a more limited system was adopted in 1978 to retain technically skilled enlisted personnel in select career fields for up to sixteen years. Noncommissioned officers can now serve for up to thirty years or until they reach age fifty-five. This allows for greater retention of technical skills and expertise, and for more continuity, but the system still faces problems, especially housing, pay, benefits, and party membership. The expansion of the noncommissioned officer corps is perhaps especially important given changes in conscription policies.

The PLA is also implementing reforms in officer accession. It has established several programs designed to broaden the pool of potential officers and attract more candidates with backgrounds in areas such as engineering, advanced technology, and social sciences. Among these programs are efforts to expand officer recruitment at civilian universities, and establish a national defense scholarship program. Since 2000, the PLA has established reserve officer training corps–type programs. Today, about 80 percent of PLA officers have college-level education, up from around 42 percent in the 1980s.

Professional military education. The PLA is also in the process of reforming its professional military education system to provide training that will enable officers to more effectively plan and conduct operations in a joint service environment.[146] At the core of the PLA's evolving approach to professional military education is a consciousness among China's military leaders of the importance and ramifications of steadily improving civilian and military technology. China's assessments of the relative quality of its own military personnel compared to the personnel of other world military powers, however, suggest alarming deficiencies in both general and specialized technical educational background. This awareness has led to new reform efforts to overhaul the education system in the PLA. The common thread that runs throughout the reform program is the transformation of the PLA into a high-technology fighting force. Officers are expected not only to develop the capability to command, but also to expand their knowledge of science and technology. PLA officers argue that the academies, in addition to developing programs of study for information technology specialists, must also incorporate the study of high-tech subjects into the curriculum for all military personnel, to give them a solid background in modern technology.[147]

The major components of the latest round of reforms include a new set of regulations governing the professional military education system, a series of structural reforms and reorganizations, changes to course content and academy curricula, changes in requirements for instructors, reforms in teaching style, upgrading of campus information technology networks, facility upgrades, increased emphasis on interservice educational exchanges and study-abroad programs, enhanced continuing-education and distance-learning programs, and a pronounced shift in emphasis from two- and three-year technical and specialized courses to four-year courses and postgraduate education.

Since the late 1990s, the PLA has recognized the serious flaws in the organizational structure of the military academy system. In keeping with this assessment, the most prominent aspect of the PLA's effort to enhance professional military education has been a wholesale reorganization of this system, which has taken place mainly through the merger and consolidation of existing schools and academies. Among the goals of the restructuring are improving the quality of education, reducing redundancy, and taking advantage of economies of scale by creating a system composed of a smaller number of more organizationally efficient institutions. Military schools have been consolidated to rationalize the structure of the professional military education system. In 1999, the PLA implemented an important reform of the academy system, merging numerous smaller schools to create five major universities: the National University of Defense Technology, the PLA Information Engineering University, the PLA Polytechnic University, the Naval Engineering University, and the Air Force Engineering University. According to one recent PLA publication, "This was a significant step toward establishing a comprehensive academy education organization system."[148] Beyond reorganizing the system to improve efficiency, the PLA has also taken steps to improve the quality of education, such as increasing the availability of computers, simulation technologies, and multimedia equipment at military schools.[149]

Improving PLA training and exercises. As discussed above, the Chinese military is shifting to a doctrine that focuses on "high-tech local wars," and continues to refine and elaborate that doctrine on the basis of lessons learned from its analysis of US military operations in Afghanistan and Iraq.[150] Accompanying this doctrinal change is an increasing emphasis on training and exercises that will help prepare the PLA for modern, high-intensity, information-centric conflicts. Indeed, parts of the PLA are engaging in more frequent, realistic, and challenging exercises and training. The PLA has established a national training center and is conducting more opposing-force exercises, though military newspapers still report numerous shortcomings.

In July 2001, the General Staff Department issued a set of documents titled "Outline of Military Training and Evaluation," which provide revised training guidance for the PLA. The navy issued its own such document in January 2002, and the air force followed suit in April 2002. China has not made these documents publicly available, but it is believed that their general content is reflected in various publicly available sources. The main themes include making training more realistic, emphasizing opposing-force training, strictly enforcing discipline, and using science and technology as the basis for improved military training.

Recent reports on Chinese military training suggest growing realism and complexity. For example, the Second Artillery has practiced a variety of techniques to counter enemy ISR, precision strikes, and electronic warfare attacks.[151] The air force in recent years has conducted night training, alternate base training, and more sophisticated exercises involving multiple types of aircraft.[152] Many PLA exercises now incorporate opposing forces and emphasize joint operations under realistic combat conditions. Exercises sometimes force participating units to deviate from their prepared plans. In addition, exercises often feature simulated electronic warfare and jamming conditions.

The PLA is also conducting more joint service exercises as part of the training reforms. Since 2000, it has conducted sixteen multiservice exercises, providing considerable opportunities to improve its experience with the conduct of joint operations and joint command and control, according to the US Department of Defense.[153]

Much of this improved training is focused on a Taiwan scenario. Ground force units in coastal provinces have conducted drills focused on landing operations in Taiwan scenarios. Some of the joint landing exercises employ integrated command procedures and feature full-scale mockups of key targets in Taiwan.[154] For example, Vice President Annette Lu said in March 2006 that China had established special training facilities at bases in several provinces at which its forces practiced assaulting Taiwan's airports and other important military targets.[155]

The Department of Defense's 2005 report on Chinese military power stated that the PLA held at least ten amphibious exercises in the preceding five years. It held two large-scale (division- to group-army level) amphibious exercises in 2004, and one of these focused explicitly on a Taiwan scenario.[156] According to the 2006 Department of Defense report, "PLA amphibious exercises and training in 2005 focused on Taiwan. In September 2005 the PLA held one large-scale, multi-service exercise that dealt explicitly with a Taiwan invasion. China has conducted 11 amphibious exercises featuring a Taiwan scenario in the past 6 years."[157]

Taiwan also figured prominently in August 2005 when China and Russia held a combined forces exercise called "Peace Mission 2005." The announced scenario involved UN-approved intervention to restore order following ethnic conflict in a fictitious country, but the exercise activities were more consistent with a scenario in which the PLA was ordered to attack Taiwan. According to the 2006 Department of Defense report on Chinese military power, "Participants conducted off-shore blockades, paradrops, airfield seizures, and amphibious landings—all components of a Taiwan invasion plan."[158]

The official CCP newspaper *People's Daily* has also publicized some Chinese military exercises that focused on Taiwan-related scenarios, demonstrating that such exercises serve not only to improve the PLA's capabilities, but also to send political messages to Taiwan and the United States. For example, in 2004 the newspaper ran a feature article on the PLA's series of Dongshan Island exercises. The article noted that the drills have focused mainly on amphibious operations against Taiwan, with the largest in the series up to that point being the "Liberation No. 1" exercise, conducted in 2001, which involved close to 100,000 troops from the army, navy, and air force and showcased the PLA's most advanced equipment.[159]

Potential Courses of Action

China's military modernization program is providing Beijing with much more credible potential military options than it had at the time of the 1995–1996 Taiwan Strait crisis. Despite this increased leverage, any use of force against Taiwan would still carry considerable risks. According to the most recent Department of Defense report on Chinese military power, potential courses of action available to the Chinese leadership include various forms of persuasion and coercion, limited use of force, an air and missile campaign, a blockade, and an amphibious invasion.[160]

Persuasion and coercion. This category includes options ranging from economic coercion and diplomatic pressure to various "show of force" actions undertaken to support deterrence or coercive diplomacy. On a fairly routine basis, China seeks to employ economic leverage and court the opposition parties to put pressure on proindependence politicians in Taipei. Beijing also tries to restrict Taiwan's diplomatic space by diminishing the support it receives from countries that still have diplomatic relations with the island.

In a situation of heightened political tension, "show of force" actions could include military exercises directed at Taiwan or perhaps missile launches toward closure areas off of Taiwan's principal ports like those the PLA conducted in 1995–1996. Indeed, the 1999 edition of *The Science of Strategy,* published by China's National Defense University, highlights the

1995–1996 military exercises as an effective demonstration of China's "re-solve in protecting the unity of the motherland" and concludes that they "served as a warning to Taiwan independence forces."[161] The purpose of such actions presumably would be to convince Taipei to refrain from any moves that Beijing would regard as a departure from the cross-Strait status quo, as defined by China, and to influence United States policy toward Taiwan. Persuasive or coercive courses of action probably entail the lowest risks from Beijing's point of view, but also might fail to achieve the desired re-sults, leaving Chinese leaders to face a decision between backing down without achieving their aims or escalation to higher levels of force.

Limited use of force. Limited-force options occupy an area on the conflict spectrum between persuasion/coercion and the higher levels of violence that would be characteristic of a major military action. One option would be to seize a lightly defended Taiwanese claim in the Spratly or Pratas Islands. This would probably be relatively easy, since Taiwan reportedly has with-drawn its marines from its possessions in those islands, leaving them pro-tected only by the ROC coast guard. Another oft-cited limited-force option is seizing one or both of the large ROC-held offshore islands, Kinmen and Matsu. Still another potential limited-force option is a decapitation strike against the civilian military leadership.[162] As part of a decapitation strike, analysts in Taiwan have speculated that the PLA would launch missile strikes or carry out special operations attacks against the presidential palace in Taipei and other important national-level command and control facilities to eliminate proindependence leaders and paralyze the armed forces. Limited-force options carry much greater risks than persuasion and coercion, but the rewards would be equally uncertain. The decapitation strike is a particularly high-risk course of action.

Air and missile campaign. Another potential course of action is an air and missile campaign, which would entail greater use of force than the limited-force options, but would not involve a large number of "boots on the ground." Mark Stokes argues that the PLA is developing the capability to execute a "joint aerospace campaign" of this type.[163] Such a campaign would include missile and air strikes, information operations, electronic warfare, and psychological operations.[164] The campaign would be designed to coerce Taipei into accepting Beijing's political demands as an alternative to attempting to use ground troops to seize and control territory. PLA writ-ings refer to this type of campaign as "noncontact warfare" *(fei jiechu zhan),* because it involves various types of beyond-visual-range indirect strikes, such as precision deep strikes and information and electronic attacks, rather than large-scale employment of ground forces.[165] Stokes assesses that a high-intensity coercive campaign of this type is the most likely course of action should China decide to use force against Taiwan, especially if China aims to achieve relatively limited political objectives. Some Chinese analysts believe that a coercive approach might reduce the odds of US intervention and limit the international repercussions of the use of force in the Taiwan Strait.[166]

PLA scholars note that lower levels of force may be sufficient to achieve modest objectives. More expansive objectives, however, are likely to require greater amounts of force. At least three types of coercive strategies—punishment, denial, and strategic paralysis—have featured prominently in the writings of Chinese strategists, though there is no general agreement about which approach is most likely to prove effective. Stokes assesses that the PLA is most disposed toward a denial strategy with a particular focus on achieving operational paralysis to compel an adversary to accede to Beijing's will.[167] The most important mission for the PLA's Second Artillery and air force in such a campaign would be the suppression of Taiwan's air defenses. The PLA is pursuing this capability through increased numbers of missiles, greater accuracy, and development of specialized warheads, as well as improved air power. The key target sets for PLA air, missile, information warfare, and electronic attack would include military command and control centers, early-warning facilities, communications facilities, air defenses, air bases, and surface-to-surface missile sites.

Stokes argues that this strategy would hinge on breaking the will of Taiwan's leadership so that it "sees no alternative but to accept Beijing's strategic aims." This is possible because "aerospace power makes it possible to compress the fury of the initial stages of conflict into a few hours. The hope is for termination of hostilities before a period of even greater conflict." This course of action would also be very risky. The PRC would need to be prepared to escalate the conflict if coercion fails. In fact, "successful coercion may depend largely upon Beijing's ability to credibly escalate the conflict and inflict a greater price of defiance," as Stokes puts it. "Ultimately, Taiwan may not fold without a credible threat to physically seize the island."[168] Consequently, PLA planners most likely assume they must be prepared to escalate to higher levels of violence, and perhaps even to invade and occupy Taiwan if coercion fails to achieve the desired political objectives. Consequently, notwithstanding China's emphasis on the development of its air, naval, and missile forces, the capabilities of the ground forces would be one of the key factors in determining the success or failure of a Chinese attempt to coerce Taiwan, even if the ground forces were never employed in the conflict. Having a credible threat to escalate to an invasion would probably make it more likely that the air, missile, special operations, information operations, and electronic warfare campaign envisioned by some PLA strategists would compel Taiwan to accept China's terms. At the very least, having a credible threat to escalate to higher levels of violence and ultimately to invade and occupy Taiwan would change Taipei's decision calculus and give Beijing greater bargaining leverage.

Naval blockade. Another option for Beijing is a naval blockade of Taiwan. Even just the threat of such a blockade could have considerable adverse effects on the island's economy. One advantage of such a "virtual blockade" is that it might allow China to put pressure on the island's leaders without immediately drawing a large-scale US response. An actual naval blockade would involve using submarines, surface ships, mines, and air assets to restrict maritime traffic into and out of Taiwan's main ports. This approach would have advantages in terms of applying greater pressure to Taiwan, but it would also involve running greater risks of escalation and possibly third-party intervention. According to the 2006 Defense Department report on Chinese military power, "More traditional methods of blockade would increase the impact on Taiwan, but would also tax PLA Navy capabilities and raise the potential for direct military confrontation."[169]

Amphibious invasion. At the highest end of the spectrum is an amphibious invasion of Taiwan.[170] This could take the form of a short-warning invasion with limited mobilization or a full-scale invasion that would be preceded by months of large-scale preparations, escalating rhetorical threats, and possibly even limited uses of force intended to increase pressure on Taipei and underscore Beijing's seriousness of purpose. In a short-warning scenario, the PLA would launch massive surprise air and missile strikes, followed by amphibious and airborne assaults against key targets.[171] The PLA could conceivably use a routine exercise to provide cover for the preparations that would be required to launch a short-warning attack.[172] In addition, China's most advanced military hardware is deployed to the military regions directly across from Taiwan, which could facilitate a rapid strike.[173]

Chinese planners would have to assume that the US military would intervene following such an attack on Taiwan. To deal with US military intervention, China could employ what US military analysts call an "antiaccess" strategy.[174] As a recent Congressional Research Service report puts it, "Consistent with the goal of a short-duration conflict and a *fait accompli* . . . China wants its modernized military to be capable of acting as a so-called anti-access force—a force that can deter U.S. intervention, or failing that, delay the arrival or reduce the effectiveness of U.S. intervention forces."[175] The 2006 Department of Defense report on the Chinese military also notes that the PLA air force appears to be preparing for antiaccess missions and that China could employ land-attack cruise missiles such as the

DH-10, which is now in development, and special operations forces to attack air bases and other ground targets.[176] In addition, Chinese analysts have concluded that logistics, transportation, and communications networks are potential key vulnerabilities. Options for exploiting these potential targets would include special operations, air and missile strikes, and computer network attacks.

In the short-warning invasion scenario, the PLA's chances of success would hinge on whether it could compel Taiwan to accede to Beijing's demands before the United States could intervene decisively, and on the extent to which it could deter, delay, or otherwise complicate US military intervention. While the outcome of any such roll of the dice would be far from certain, this scenario could present the United States and Taiwan with considerable operational challenges.[177]

Whether China opted for a short-warning invasion or a full-scale assault following large-scale mobilization, an amphibious invasion would be by far the most complex, demanding, and politically and operationally risky of the potential courses of action. Recent reports suggest that the PLA is making preparations for this scenario despite the associated risks. The 2006 Department of Defense report notes that China has increased its production of amphibious ships to address long-standing deficiencies in amphibious lift capacity.[178] Specifically, the report states that China increased its amphibious lift capabilities by more than 14 percent in 2005. However, the Department of Defense assesses that these increases in amphibious lift still fall short of what would be needed to meet the PLA's operational requirements for a large-scale amphibious attack on Taiwan.[179] Similarly, press reports indicate that the PLA is capable of lifting only a single armored division—about 12,000 personnel with their vehicles and equipment.[180] Moreover, China would likely have considerable difficulty sustaining an attack if its forces encountered determined resistance. According to the 2006 Department of Defense report:

> Amphibious operations are logistics-intensive and rely for success upon air and sea superiority in the vicinity of the operation, the rapid buildup of supplies and sustainment on shore, and an uninterrupted flow of support thereafter. The Joint Island Landing Campaign would tax the lift capacities of China's armed forces and maritime militia, posing challenges to those charged with providing sustainment for . . . this campaign. Add to these strains the combat attrition of China's forces, and an amphibious invasion of Taiwan would be a significant political and military risk for China's leaders. The PLA's prospects in an invasion of Taiwan would hinge on establishing persistent air superiority over the Strait and Taiwan, the availability of amphibious and air lift, attrition rates, interoperability of PLA forces, the ability of China's logistics system to support the necessarily high tempo of operations, Taiwan's will to resist, and the speed and scale of international intervention.[181]

Given the tremendous risks entailed in attempting a full-scale amphibious invasion, it thus seems likely that the Chinese leadership would choose this option only if all other measures at its disposal had failed.

* * *

As illustrated by this review of potential PRC courses of action, the modernization of the PLA has given Chinese leaders several options should they decide to use force against Taiwan. All of the potential courses of action would run the risk of conflict with the United States, and none would guarantee success. In addition, in many of the potential scenarios, Beijing would have to deal with the tension between the perceived need to strike hard early in a conflict to seize the initiative, and the desire to control escalation by limiting US and potentially Japanese involvement as well as the geographic scope of the conflict.[182] Nonetheless, several of these courses of action would place Taiwan and the United States in a very difficult political and military situation.

Conclusion

China is developing a more nuanced and sophisticated approach to Taiwan that is less reliant on bellicose statements and bullying. At the same time, however, China is also increasing the level of resources devoted to making the PLA much more operationally capable. The principal near-term objective of this ambitious military modernization program is developing capabilities that would allow the PLA to pose a credible threat to Taiwan, and to deter, delay, or otherwise complicate US intervention in a cross-Strait conflict. To support the achievement of these objectives, the PLA is making important advances in areas such as modernization of weapons and equipment, development of doctrine for joint operations, professional military education and training, logistics reform, and conducting more realistic exercises. Ongoing improvements in C4ISR and institutional reforms are enhancing the PLA's potential joint operations capabilities. It will likely take a number of years, however, for the PLA to realize the full benefits of such improvements. Moreover, lack of operational experience remains a concern for the PLA. The Chinese military has not had direct experience in major combat since the 1979 border war with Vietnam. As the 2006 Department of Defense report on Chinese military modernization notes, "In practice, the PLA remains untested."[183]

Although the PLA still faces considerable challenges, it has made major strides in a number of important areas over the past decade.[184] The PLA is continuing to enhance the professionalism of its soldiers, upgrade its military hardware and related equipment, and strengthen its operational capabilities as part of this ongoing transformation. The result is a dramatic change in the military options available to Chinese leaders. According to one account, "A decade ago, American military planners dismissed the threat of a Chinese attack against Taiwan as a 100-mile infantry swim."[185] After ten years of rising defense spending, military hardware modernization, and "software" reforms, however, the PLA now poses a much more serious threat to Taiwan's security. Moreover, it is increasingly capable of challenging US forces in the region should Washington decide to intervene in a China-Taiwan conflict. As a result of these developments, the challenge to Taiwan's security has increased dramatically since the late 1990s and will likely continue to grow over the next decade.

CHAPTER 5

Current Defense Policy in Taiwan

Taiwan's national security policy is concerned with a variety of issues, including the Chinese military threat, cross-Strait relations, raising the island's international profile, relations with the United States and Japan, and the implications of increasing cross-Strait economic interaction. The island faces serious challenges in all of these areas. In particular, modernization of the People's Liberation Army (PLA) has accelerated since the late 1990s, as reflected by sustained increases in defense spending, a series of major hardware modernization programs, and an impressive effort to transform the PLA into a more professional and capable fighting force. As a result, Beijing has much more credible military options than it had a decade ago, when all it could do was intimidate Taiwan with symbolic displays of force. Although Taiwan has made progress in several key aspects of its defense reform program, it is clearly falling behind the transformation of the PLA. Consequently, the cross-Strait military balance is shifting in favor of China. This change in the cross-Strait balance raises serious questions not only about Taiwan's ability to defend itself against a Chinese assault on its own, but also about its ability to hold out long enough to allow decisive third-party intervention. Moreover, President Chen Shui-bian's tendency to make pronouncements and pursue policy changes that risk provoking Beijing and undermining US support for Taiwan compound these growing concerns about the implications of the shifting cross-Strait military balance.

Taiwan's Security Policy, 2000–2007

Understanding Taiwan's response to Chinese military modernization requires placing it in the broader context of Taiwan's overall security environment. Indeed, Taiwan's national security strategy is concerned with more than the cross-Strait balance of military power. The Chen administration's

81

national security strategy document, for example, identifies a number of other objectives, including seeking broader international recognition, enhancing ties with unofficial allies such as the United States and Japan, gaining a foothold in international organizations, and upgrading the island's economy as critical elements of national strength.[1]

Taiwan's overall approach to cross-Strait relations has gone through a series of changes closely linked to the vicissitudes of the island's rough and tumble domestic politics. When President Chen entered office in 2000, he initially adopted a relatively moderate approach in the area of cross-Strait relations. Within about two years, however, the Chen administration had shifted to a more assertive stance that angered Beijing and led to concerns in Washington about Taipei's willingness to alter the cross-Strait status quo in ways that risked provoking another China-Taiwan crisis. President Chen's second-term agenda also featured several highly controversial policy initiatives.

Although President Chen was widely seen as a strong supporter of independence, he began his first term with a moderate statement on cross-Strait relations. In his 2000 inaugural address, Chen made a series of pledges that have come to be known as the "five no's." With an eye toward reassuring Washington and Beijing that a Democratic Progressive Party (DPP) administration could be trusted to maintain stability in cross-Strait relations, Chen stated:

> I fully understand that, as the popularly elected 10th-term president of the Republic of China, I must abide by the Constitution, maintain the sovereignty, dignity and security of our country, and ensure the well being of all citizens. Therefore, as long as the CCP [Chinese Communist Party] regime has no intention to use military force against Taiwan, I pledge that during my term in office, I will not declare independence, I will not change the national title, I will not push forth the inclusion of the so-called "state-to-state" description in the Constitution, and I will not promote a referendum to change the status quo in regard to the question of independence or unification. Furthermore, there is no question of abolishing the Guidelines for National Unification and the National Unification Council.[2]

Taipei also enacted a number of policies that relaxed restrictions on cross-Strait trade and investment. Although resisting demands to permit establishment of the full "three links," the Chen administration agreed to the "mini–three links," permitting direct shipping and passenger travel between the Taiwanese-held offshore islands of Kinmen and Matsu and the mainland cities of Xiamen and Fuzhou. The Chen administration also relaxed some restrictions on Taiwanese investment in China. In particular, the government replaced the "no haste, be patient" policy with one of "active opening, effective management." The new policy eliminated the long-standing US$50 million cap on individual investment projects in China and instituted a simplified review process for mainland-bound investments of less than US$20 million. Taipei also changed other long-standing policies that blocked certain types of high-tech investments in the People's Republic of China (PRC). The most important and controversial of these changes came in early 2002, when the Chen administration relaxed a long-standing ban on investments in semiconductor facilities on the mainland. The new policy permitted investment in previous generation fabrication facilities in China, provided that the companies complied with a host of conditions, including opening new cutting-edge facilities in Taiwan.

This moderate stance emphasizing political restraint and economic opening was relatively short-lived. President Chen subsequently adopted a more assertive stance, which was driven by a variety of factors, including domestic political considerations and China's attempts to put pressure on him by wooing Taiwan's remaining official diplomatic partners. Beijing's attempts to "squeeze Taiwan's international space" were perhaps particularly important in Chen's calculations. In July 2002, for example, Beijing persuaded Nauru, a tiny island nation in the South Pacific, to break its official ties with Taiwan and establish diplomatic relations with China.[3] That the incident coincided with President Chen's inauguration as chairman of the DPP was a further source of embarrassment. Indeed, officials in Taipei viewed the timing as a deliberate insult to the Chen administration and the DPP, and President Chen was swift to respond with a new formulation on cross-Strait relations that infuriated Beijing and raised serious concerns in Washington. In an address to the twenty-ninth annual meeting of the World Federation of Taiwanese Associations on 3 August 2002, Chen made some of the most controversial remarks of his presidency. Delivering the address via videoconference from the presidential office in Taipei, Chen declared:

> Taiwan is our country, and our country cannot be bullied, downgraded, marginalized, nor treated as a local government. Taiwan is not a part of any other country, nor is it a local government or province of another country. Taiwan can never be another Hong Kong or Macau, because Taiwan has always been a sovereign state. In short, Taiwan and China standing on opposite sides of the Strait, there is one country on each side. This should be clear.[4]

Importantly, Chen also used the occasion of the speech to call for the passage of a referendum law, which was anathema to Beijing. Chen's "one country on each side" *(yi bian, yi guo)* declaration and his comments about a referendum law prompted a predictably harsh rejoinder from China.[5]

Although the referendum law that ultimately made it through the Legislative Yuan did not include many of the potentially provocative provisions Chen had originally sought, and set a high bar for proposed amendments to the constitution, requiring the support of three-quarters of the legislature to submit a potential amendment to an islandwide vote, it also contained a clause that permitted the president to call a "defensive referendum" if Taiwan faced an imminent national security threat. President Chen subsequently announced that he was determined to hold such a referendum alongside Taiwan's March 2004 presidential election.

President Chen's plans to hold the referendum also raised concerns in Washington, where policymakers worried that his provocative policies might eventually draw the United States into an otherwise avoidable confrontation with China, and privately urged him to exercise restraint. At the same time, however, Taipei was receiving mixed signals from Washington, and some officials in Taipei appear to have taken the more favorable of these contradictory messages as evidence of implicit US support for their initiatives. In any event, because the Chen administration was not particularly responsive to Washington's initial expressions of concern, the George W. Bush administration decided to deliver its message at the highest level. In December 2003, during a joint press conference with Chinese premier Wen Jiabao, President Bush rebuked Chen for his insistence on proceeding with a referendum on cross-Strait issues and arms purchases: "We oppose any unilateral decision by either China or Taiwan to change the status quo," he said, "and the comments and actions made by the leader of Taiwan indicate that he may be willing to make decisions unilaterally to change the status quo, which we oppose."[6] This admonishment was clearly intended to underscore the depth of Washington's frustration with Taipei. It was all the more striking given President Bush's earlier pledge that the United States would do "whatever it takes" to defend Taiwan and his previous characterization of China as a potential strategic rival in the Asia Pacific region. In response to pressure from Washington, the Chen administration toned down the language of the two referendum questions.[7] Following an extremely narrow victory in the controversial March 2004 presidential election, President Chen delivered his second inaugural address on 20 May. The difficulty for President Chen was to craft a speech that would "appease a hostile Beijing, reassure a worried Washington, and unite a society split by March's hotly disputed presidential election."[8] It was clear that the relatively moderate speech he delivered was designed to respond to pressure from all sides.

Although President Chen's second inaugural speech seemed to foreshadow a fairly moderate approach to dealing with China, his second term was punctuated by a number of controversial pronouncements and policy adjustments that threatened to create renewed tension in cross-Strait relations. Much of President Chen's second term was spent fending off corruption allegations, and many of his policy initiatives were stymied by a recalcitrant opposition-controlled legislature, leaving him with few options other than pursuing symbolic policy moves, many of which were apparently intended to rally his proindependence political base and subtly reshape the political environment he would leave to his successors. Most notably, on 27 February 2006, President Chen announced that the National Unification Council would "cease to function" and the national unification guidelines would "cease to apply."[9] The move had little practical impact, since the National Unification Council was already essentially nonfunctional, but it was of great symbolic importance because of the political message it conveyed.

Following this episode, the Chen administration took several other steps that angered Chinese leaders and irritated US policymakers. In February 2007, the Chen administration renamed several state-owned companies, replacing the term for "China" in their titles with the word "Taiwan."[10] Although the changes seemed trivial to some observers, Chinese analysts interpreted it as additional evidence of President Chen's desire to sever Taiwan's remaining symbolic linkages with the mainland. The move also drew a rebuke from Washington, which expressed annoyance that Chen was ignoring previous warnings to refrain from altering the cross-Strait status quo. The next month, President Chen enunciated a new policy formulation, dubbed the "four wants and one without."[11] In a speech to an organization known for its strong proindependence views, Chen stated that Taiwan wanted independence, a new national title, and a new constitution; he also asserted that the primary political issue facing Taiwan was a struggle between supporters of independence and advocates of unification. Although the new formulation probably reflected domestic political calculations, at least in part, it drew a predictably petulant response from Beijing and led to further consternation in Washington.

Later in 2007, President Chen unveiled what would become his most controversial second-term initiative when he announced his decision to hold a referendum alongside the 2008 presidential election on the question of whether the island should seek admission to the United Nations under the name "Taiwan." The Kuomintang (KMT) countered with its own referendum proposal, which asked voters to support an attempt to return to the United Nations under the name "Republic of China," or any other practical and suitable title. President Chen contrasted the competing proposals, suggesting on at least one occasion that the choosing between the DPP and KMT referendum proposals was really equivalent to casting a vote on the larger question of Taiwan's future status: "If you think Taiwan is an independent state and not part of the PRC, please support the referendum proposed by the DPP," he said in September 2007 while campaigning for the DPP's version of the referendum. "If you think Taiwan is part of China or the PRC, or believe there is 'one China' and that Taiwan should ultimately unify with China or that the ROC includes China and Mongolia, please vote for the KMT's referendum proposal."[12] The DPP's referendum proposal infuriated Beijing. China released an official statement reiterating its determination to prevent Taiwan's permanent separation from the mainland and vowing to "undertake necessary preparations for a serious situation."[13] Underscoring the depth of the Chinese Communist Party leadership's displeasure, some Chinese scholars suggested to their US counterparts that the DPP's version of the referendum might lead Beijing to consider some sort of military demonstration or perhaps even result in limited use of force against Taiwan.[14] The United States was also highly critical of the DPP's referendum proposal, which several senior Department of State officials described as an unnecessarily provocative attempt to alter the status quo in a manner that Washington viewed as inconsistent with President Chen's previous assurances that he would not attempt to change the island's official title. The most extensive elaboration of US views was delivered by Thomas Christensen, deputy assistant secretary of state for East Asian and Pacific affairs, in a September 2007 speech to an audience that included senior officials from Taiwan:

> What worries us, very specifically, is the issue of name change. This draft referendum raises the question of what Taiwan should be called in the international community. Moreover, it does so in what could be interpreted by many to be a legally-binding popular vote. . . . The simple reality is that, in the world of cross-Strait relations, political symbolism matters, and disagreements over it could be the source of major tensions or even conflict.[15]

President Chen dismissed US criticism as well-meaning but misguided, and indicated that he would move forward with his plans to hold the referendum on seeking admission to the UN under the name "Taiwan."[16]

The Chen administration's second-term China strategy also featured a more circumspect approach toward the management of cross-Strait economic relations. In particular, it centered on a renewed effort to restrict the growing flow of trade and investment across the Taiwan Strait. Notably, the government reversed the rhetorical emphasis of the "active opening, effective management" policy it had put into place during President Chen's first term. In 2006, Chen announced that the earlier formulation would be scrapped in favor of a new policy of "active management, effective opening," as part of an effort to limit Taiwan's economic dependence on China. Under the new policy, the government urged Taiwanese companies to slow their investments in the Chinese market and increase their investments in other, emerging markets.

Military Modernization and Defense Reform in Taiwan, 2000–2007

The growing threat posed by the modernization of the Chinese military has highlighted the importance and urgency of military modernization and defense reform in Taiwan. Analysts in the United States assess that the modernization of China's PLA is increasingly giving Beijing credible, if potentially costly, options to use force against Taiwan. Moreover, officials in Washington are concerned that the military balance of power is shifting in favor of the PRC, and that the PLA is preparing to compel Taiwan to capitulate before US forces can intervene in a cross-Strait conflict. According to a recent US Department of Defense report, "Chinese air, naval, and missile force modernization is making it increasingly critical that Taiwan strengthen its defenses with a sense of urgency."[17] Specifically, Washington is urging Taiwan to acquire capabilities sufficient to make any attack costly and to buy time for US intervention. To date, however, Taiwan's response has failed to meet Washington's expectations, and many policymakers charge the island's leadership with complacency in the face of a growing threat to its security. As one former Department of Defense official put it, "There is already an arms race in the Taiwan Strait . . . but only one side is racing, and it is not Taiwan."[18]

Although US policymakers are frustrated with the pace and scope of Taiwan's response to the modernization of the PLA, a careful review of the evidence shows that in recent years Taiwan has made some important achievements in advancing its military modernization and defense reform programs. Officials in Taiwan have identified many of the key problems facing the military and are attempting to develop approaches to address many of these issues. The progress they have made is impressive, especially considering that Taiwan's defense establishment is simultaneously, among other things, enhancing civilian control over the armed forces, streamlining the military, improving joint operations capability, and modernizing to meet the challenge of an increasingly capable Chinese military, each one of which, by itself, presents formidable challenges. Moreover, the defense establishment is attempting to do all of this while facing serious budget constraints, adapting to work within the context of increasingly active legislative oversight, and contending with a highly charged partisan political atmosphere in which the ruling and opposition parties are at loggerheads on many key policy issues. The progress Taiwan has made thus far, however, falls short of what would be required to ensure the island's ability to hold out against a major Chinese attack until US forces could arrive in the region.

Declining Defense Expenditures

In a domestic political and economic environment where scarcity of budgetary resources requires trade-offs, defense spending increasingly must compete with other economic and social priorities. In the mid-1990s, democratization and electoral competition gave politicians strong incentives to promote tax breaks and increased spending on social welfare and infrastructure projects.[19] Although the Chen administration frequently draws criticism over

Taiwan's declining defense spending, the problem predates Chen's first-term election in March 2000. Indeed, Taiwan's defense budget has actually been shrinking steadily since the mid-1990s, when Lee Teng-hui was president. In 1995, Taiwan's defense budget was about 4.3 percent of the island's gross domestic product (GDP), and defense spending accounted for approximately 25.0 percent of central government expenditure. By 2002, Taiwan's defense budget had decreased to about 2.5 percent of GDP, and defense spending as a share of government expenditure had fallen to about 16.4 percent. In 2006, the defense budget was only about 2.2 percent of GDP, and defense accounted for approximately 16.0 percent of the overall government budget.[20] As a consequence, according to the Ministry of National Defense, defense spending was falling well short of what was needed to meet the island's security needs.[21] The Chen administration subsequently requested a major increase in the annual defense budget for 2007 and 2008. Although the defense budget the legislature belatedly approved for 2007 fell short of the amount the Chen administration requested, it still accounted for about 2.7 percent of GDP, a substantial increase over the previous year's budget. Moreover, the share of the total government budget allocated to defense spending increased to 18.0 percent, according to Taiwan's Directorate-General of Budget, Accounting, and Statistics.[22] Even though the 2007 defense budget was welcomed by many observers as a important step in the right direction, the prolonged period of shrinking defense budgets in Taiwan is still striking when compared to the dramatic increases in Chinese military expenditure that have been fueling the modernization of the PLA, especially since the late 1990s.

The decade of declining defense budgets for the Republic of China (ROC) should be considered against the backdrop of prolonged budget deficit problems in Taiwan. Since the early 1990s, a combination of declining tax revenues and increasing fiscal expenditures has fueled growing budget deficits. Indeed, since 1989, Taiwan has achieved a balanced budget only once (under President Lee, in 1998).[23] Electoral competition has resulted in a series of tax breaks as well as dramatic increases in spending on infrastructure development and social welfare programs. In a January 2002 amendment, public debt was capped at 15 percent of total government expenditure. Greater defense spending would thus have to be offset by cuts in other government programs, but politicians are reluctant to scale back infrastructure and social welfare spending for fear of losing votes to their rivals.[24] Thus defense spending has declined and the share of government expenditure devoted to social welfare programs has increased since the island's democratization.

In part as a result of the budget deficit problem and the accompanying defense-spending crunch, some major foreign arms acquisitions remained at a standstill for years. Most notably, it took Taiwan about six years to reach a decision on the purchase of the antisubmarine warfare aircraft, Patriot missile defense batteries, and diesel submarines that the Bush administration agreed to sell to the island in April 2001.[25] Indeed, the Chen administration's request for approval of a special budget to fund these acquisitions came only after a long delay, and quickly became bogged down in the Procedure Committee of the opposition-controlled Legislative Yuan, where it languished for several years (discussed in greater detail in the next section).[26]

Even as the defense budget declined, the level of Legislative Yuan scrutiny of budget requests increased dramatically, partly as a result of increasing openness of the defense budget to public review. Indeed, Taiwan's defense expenditures, which were extraordinarily opaque even in the early to middle 1990s, have become increasingly transparent in recent years. The proportion of the defense budget that is classified declined from about 37 percent in 1995 to about 19 percent in 2004.[27] This push for greater transparency in defense and national security affairs is also a result of the partisan political fights that have dominated Taiwan politics in recent years. Since defeating the KMT in the 2000 presidential election, Chen and the DPP administration have faced an uncooperative, opposition-controlled legislature. As a result of this confrontation between the DPP administration and the legislature, in which the opposition Pan-Blue camp—composed of the KMT and the People's First Party (PFP)—holds the largest number of seats, many important reforms have been delayed. At the same time, the role of the Legislative Yuan in defense policy has been increasing. All defense policy issues, especially procurement policy and the acquisition of weapons and equipment from the United States, are often subject to highly charged partisan debates. The Legislative Yuan is becoming "more assertive, even arrogant," in the words of one knowledgeable US-based observer.[28]

The Legislative Yuan's National Defense Committee reviews the entire defense budget, but it is the investment portion of the budget, covering acquisitions of new weapons and equipment, that generates the most intense debates. Major acquisitions must conform to a highly structured, twenty-four-month process that requires the drafting, submission, and approval of a series of formal planning documents. This enhanced scrutiny and involvement on the part of the Legislative Yuan has "greatly extended the time required to complete the procurement process."[29] Indeed, the increasing assertiveness of the Legislative Yuan on procurement issues has resulted in prolonged indecision on purchases of arms from the United States. The Ministry of National Defense has established the Office of Legislative Affairs to improve coordination with the Legislative Yuan, and each of the services also has its own legislative relations office or working group.

The composition of the defense budget is another problem. Like many other countries, Taiwan divides its defense budget into three categories: personnel expenses *(renyuan weichi fei)*, operations and maintenance *(zuoye weichi fei),* and military investment *(junshi touzi).* Personnel expenses include salaries, insurance and other benefits, retirement and pensions, and subsidies for military dependents. Operations and maintenance expenditures are devoted mainly to "maintaining basic combat capability related items," including weapons and equipment, fuel, and ammunition supplies. Military investment includes acquisitions and force modernization programs.

Many defense analysts in Taiwan assess that the distribution of resources across these three categories is suboptimal. For example, personnel expenditures accounted for 54.5 percent of the 2003 defense budget, while operations and maintenance accounted for only 19.6 percent and military investment only 21.8 percent.[30] This reflects a trend in recent years in which the share of the defense budget dedicated to purchasing new weapons and equipment has declined as the proportion of defense expenditure allocated to personnel expenses has increased. With more than half of the defense budget allocated to covering personnel costs, relatively little remains for purchasing new weapons or conducting operations and maintenance. This has drawn fire from a number of prominent Legislative Yuan members. For example, in a critique of the Ministry of National Defense's 2002 report, Ku Chung-lien, a member of the Legislative Yuan's Defense Committee, wrote: "The percentage represented by personnel maintenance costs remains rather high, crowding out funds for weapons research and development and military investment in the defense budget."[31] Ministry of National Defense officials and other analysts in Taiwan are well aware of this problem, and the ministry has been trying to reduce personnel costs to free up a larger share of the defense budget for increased investment in new equipment.[32] The personnel cutbacks were expected to yield savings that the Ministry of National Defense could redirect to increase the force modernization portion of the defense budget, but the need to raise salaries as part of Taiwan's effort to recruit and retain highly qualified volunteer military personnel (with the ultimate goal being an all-volunteer force) may at least partially cancel out some of the expected savings.

The force modernization budget in 2005 was about US$1.9 billion, down slightly from US$2.0 billion in 2004. Although the amount of funding Taiwan is allocating to military investment is too low to meet its defense requirements, the military is moving forward with a number of important programs. The 2005 defense budget, for example, included funding for modernization of command, control, communications, computers, intelligence, surveillance, and reconnaissance (C4ISR) through the "Posheng" (Broad Victory) program, Kidd-class destroyers, amphibious vehicles, airborne early-warning aircraft, and an ultra-high-frequency radar system. The 2005 defense budget also included funding to support a number of new and ongoing research and development programs, including cruise missiles and missile defense systems.

Even if the Ministry of National Defense is ultimately successful in reducing overall personnel costs enough to shift more money into the military investment and operations and maintenance categories, the Chen administration and the ministry appear to have recognized that further defense budget increases will still be required. In 2005, the Chen administration announced plans to increase defense spending to 2.85 percent of GDP in 2007 and 3 percent of GDP in 2008. Taiwan's May 2006 national security report reiterated the Chen administration's commitment to boosting military spending to 3 percent of GDP:

> Whilst China's military spending has grown at a double-digit rate for 17 consecutive years and it has continually strengthened its capability to militarily intimidate Taiwan, Taiwan's national defense has steadily declined from 3.8 percent of GDP in 1994 to 2.54 percent at present. To prevent the balance in the cross-Strait military situation from tipping further in China's favor, Taiwan must strive to raise the defense budget to 3 percent of GDP by 2008. . . . Furthermore, Taiwan must also comprehensively review the allocation and utilization of its national defense resources in order to maximize efficient utilization of national defense resources.[33]

In the run-up to Taiwan's 2008 presidential election, both major parties also indicated that Taiwan's defense budget should be raised to about 3 percent of GDP. It remains unclear, however, if even this proposed increase would be enough, given the acceleration of Chinese military modernization since the late 1990s. The bottom line, in the words of one Taipei-based analyst, is that "the price of maintaining the status quo is getting higher and higher."[34] Furthermore, the defense budget has often failed to reflect Taiwan's strategic priorities. According to Luor Ching-jyuhn, Wang Huei-huang, and Yeh Jun-hsiu, "Defense budgets and military resource allocation . . . have not followed the guidelines laid down by our defense policies, strategic framework, and military buildup principles."[35] Interservice rivalry is one reason for this problem. Another is a lack of clarity in the national security policy and defense strategy pronouncements that are supposed to serve as guides to decisions about the allocation of Taiwan's limited resources.

Arms Purchases from the United States and the Special Budget Proposal

When the United States approved an enormous arms sales package in April 2001, Taiwan was surprised and slow to respond. Three years passed before the Chen administration finally made a decision, and it was only after Washington engaged Taipei in a dialogue about procurement priorities that the Chen administration submitted a special budget request to the Legislative Yuan in June 2004. The Chen administration probably chose to use the special budget mechanism to avoid politically unpopular trade-offs with social welfare spending that would have been required had the items been included in the regular annual defense budget. The Pan-Blue parties strongly opposed the proposal and kept it bottled up in the Legislative Yuan's Procedure Committee, preventing it from being considered. Pan-Blue legislators argued that the weapons were outdated and overpriced, but denying President Chen a political victory was probably an equally important motive for Pan-Blue opposition to the special budget.

In response to the vehement Pan-Blue opposition and the repeated refusal to place the bill on the legislative agenda, the Chen administration reconfigured the proposal and cut the budget twice, first from US$18.97 billion to US$14.91 billion, then down to US$10.56 billion. The opposition-dominated Legislative Yuan, however, continued to block consideration of the bill. The Chen administration finally gave up in 2006, after the Procedure Committee had refused to place the bill on the legislative agenda more than fifty times. After dropping the special budget request, the Chen administration announced, as discussed previously, that it planned to raise the regular annual defense budget to 2.85 percent of GDP in 2007 and 3 percent in 2008 to cover the arms purchases. The seemingly interminable struggle over the US arms sales proposal was finally resolved in June 2007, when the legislature approved the purchase of the P-3C maritime patrol aircraft, but voted to upgrade Taiwan's existing missile defense systems instead of buying the PAC-3 batteries and radically slashed funding for further evaluation of the submarine procurement program.

Importantly, the prolonged debate over the special budget became a major point of contention between the United States and Taiwan. It led many in the United States—including some of Taiwan's strongest supporters in the US Congress—to question Taiwan's commitment to its own defense, diverted attention from equally pressing national security and defense reform issues in Taiwan, and may very well have decreased Washington's willingness to approve further arms sales requests from Taipei.

The April 2001 arms sales decision and Taipei's sluggish response. In April 2001, the United States offered to sell Taiwan an arms package that was unprecedented in size and content. The total cost of the items offered was over US$15 billion, and the package was to include a number of items that had never before been approved for sale to the island's military. Among the highlights were eight diesel electric submarines, twelve P-3C maritime patrol aircraft, and an integrated undersea surveillance system. Washington also offered to sell the island four decommissioned Kidd-class destroyers, but deferred Taiwan's request for Aegis-equipped destroyers. In addition, Washington agreed to provide Taipei a classified briefing on the capabilities of the PAC-3 missile defense system. Later the same year, the Bush administration agreed to release several additional items, including tanks, helicopters, and PAC-3 missile defense systems.

The approval of the arms package represented a major departure from previous US policy in several respects, most notably the approval of diesel electric submarines, which previous US administrations had been unwilling to offer to Taiwan. According to Mark Stokes, a former US Department of Defense official who was responsible for China-Taiwan affairs at the time, "The objective was to reverse twenty years of relative neglect and frontload the systems that Taiwan had asked to be made available as the Clinton administration drew to a close."[36] Although Washington's intention was to emphasize the importance of assisting Taiwan in its efforts to strengthen its defensive capabilities, Taipei was apparently caught off-guard. From the Chen administration's point of view, as Stokes puts it, "the Bush administration's approval of the largest arms package in history was a surprise."[37] The scale of the package offered to Taiwan was so large it overwhelmed Taiwan's defense establishment, especially given its limited expertise in the analysis of operational requirements, cost effectiveness, and budget planning. Taipei was simply unprepared to deal with the simultaneous approval of so many major systems. Analysts in Taipei argued that the government was caught off-guard because Washington traditionally had declined many of Taiwan's arms procurement requests, leading the island's military to expect that only a fraction of what it requested would actually be approved in any given year. Loh I-cheng, a researcher at the KMT-affiliated National Policy Foundation, summarizes the views of policymakers in Taipei as follows:

> During the 80's and 90's, Taiwan was on a short leash; most of its arms requests were simply ignored by Washington or put on hold, so as not to antagonize Beijing. The island would be thrown a few crumbs in those annual bilateral consultations, just enough to keep it on a starvation diet, except for the one-time F-16 sale under George H. W. Bush. . . . Understandably, a hungry man tends to beg for more, in the hope that his meager ration of just bread and water could include a piece of meat once in a while. When George W. Bush became president, he extended the leash by a good length, and approved in one stroke a long list of [foreign military sales]. It has been compared to the sudden appearance of a king's banquet at the wave of a magic wand, which the poor beggar cannot possibly digest in one sitting, and does not even know how to react to such good fortune.[38]

As one US researcher put it, Taiwan was accustomed to a "spaghetti-on-the-wall" approach to the annual arms sales process, given the uncertainty about which requests Washington would approve in a given year. Consequently, in 2001 the island's defense establishment found itself surprised that so much of the spaghetti "stuck."[39] Beyond Taiwan's apparent surprise, a number of other factors—including a tendency to discount China's repeated admonitions that it would "pay any price" to prevent Taiwan from moving further toward formal independence, tension between the new civilian leadership and senior military officers, and interservice rivalry among the ROC army, navy, and air force—also contributed to the three-year delay in the Chen administration's response to the April 2001 arms sales, according to interviews with analysts and observers in Washington and Taipei.

Despite these problems, some progress was made in May 2003, when Taiwan agreed to purchase the four Kidd-class destroyers from the United States to replace its World War II–era Gearing-class destroyers. Taiwan received two of the Kidd-class destroyers in December 2005; the two remaining destroyers were delivered in 2006. The Kidd-class destroyers' antiair, antisubmarine, and antisurface warfare capabilities will make them the ROC navy's most powerful surface ships. In particular, ROC navy officers emphasize that the ships will greatly improve Taiwan's naval air defense and battlefield management capabilities.[40]

Although the purchase of the Kidd-class destroyers represented an important step forward, Taipei's sluggishness in moving forward with the rest of the items approved as part of the April 2001 arms package frustrated policymakers in the United States, who began pressuring the Chen administration to accelerate the procurement process. Indeed, policymakers in Washington began to complain openly that Taiwan was not moving quickly enough to take advantage of the George W. Bush administration's unprecedented arms sales offers. Some expressed that their frustration was amplified because Taipei was slow to act, even though Washington had already paid the diplomatic price of offending China after announcing the approval of the arms package.

Although the United States did not suggest that the Chen administration employ the special budget mechanism, which is sometimes used in Taiwan to pay for expensive programs such as major arms purchases and large-scale public infrastructure projects outside the regular annual government budget channels, Washington did emphasize the importance that Taiwan move quickly to find a way to purchase the arms approved in April 2001. The US approach also appears to have influenced Taiwan's decision to focus on the submarines, antisubmarine warfare aircraft, and missile defense batteries in the special budget proposal. Specifically, in early 2003, the Bush administration provided several suggestions on what it regarded as the top priorities for Taiwan's defense. The three areas Washington highlighted as crucial for Taiwan's military modernization program were command, control, and communications (C3) systems, missile defense, and antisubmarine warfare. According to Mark Stokes: "These suggestions were intended to start a dialogue on priorities and break the paralysis that has plagued Taiwan's defense establishment since the Bush administration's approval of the 2001 arms package. During the summer of 2003, Taiwanese officials relayed to the US that it intended to pursue submarines, PAC-3, and P-3Cs through a special budget request."[41]

Despite the pressure from Washington, almost another year passed before the Chen administration finally acted. Thus it was not until 2 June 2004 that President Chen and his cabinet submitted a special budget request to the Legislative Yuan for about US$18.2 billion to purchase the three big-ticket items from the United States. This original version of the special budget proposal included requests for PAC-3 missiles, P-3C antisubmarine warfare planes, and diesel electric submarines. According to the proposed schedule, the arms were to be delivered over a fifteen-year period beginning in 2005.

Why did the Chen administration choose to use a special budget proposal instead of incorporating the systems into the annual defense budget? One reason was that including them in the regular annual defense budget would have crowded out other defense modernization programs, absent a substantial increase in the defense budget. More importantly, however, given Taiwan's budget and debt laws, a substantial increase in defense spending would have necessitated reducing the budgets of other government agencies. The Chen administration thus chose the special budget mechanism to avoid having to make trade-offs between defense spending and domestic social welfare spending. Cutting spending on popular domestic programs to buy arms from the United States would not have been a good electoral strategy. The comments of senior government officials suggest that this was a major consideration that motivated the decision to propose using the special budget mechanism to fund the procurement of the weapons from the United States. For example, in August 2005, then–deputy minister of national defense Michael Tsai explained the government's preference for the special budget by stating that it would not force the government to cut other parts of its budget. Referring to the use of the special budget, Tsai said, "This way, no government agencies need to worry about a crowding-out effect."[42] A few months later, Tsai described the special budget as "bigger than an elephant" and lamented that including the three major items in the regular budget would "squeeze out" the budgets of the other government agencies.[43]

Pan-Blue opposition to the special budget. The Pan-Blue parties strongly opposed the special budget request from the beginning, and their control of the legislature allowed them to foil the Chen administration's arms procurement plans. The Pan-Blue–dominated Procedure Committee blocked the bill more than fifty times, as mentioned previously, which prevented it from even being considered in the Legislative Yuan, and this ultimately forced the DPP to abandon the special budget. The debate represented a strange turn of events in that Chen and the DPP, which had frequently opposed greater military spending when the KMT was in power, were now pushing for a major investment in military hardware. Moreover, the KMT, which had traditionally supported arms purchases from the United States when in power, was now strongly opposed to the DPP's request for a special budget to pay for some of the very hardware that KMT officials had previously sought to acquire from Washington.[44] As one observer pointed out, "The DPP questions why the blue camp now objects to the same national defense policy that it initiated during its own days in power. If the KMT were still the ruling party, ask DPP representatives, would it have a different attitude?"[45]

Yet the KMT and the PFP were adamantly opposed to the special budget, for a number of reasons, and opposition lawmakers raised several different objections to the government's proposal to use the special budget mechanism to procure military equipment from the United States. The broadest set of arguments held that the approval of the special budget would not really enhance Taiwan's national defense, and that Taiwan's national security could not be ensured through defense modernization alone. The most concise summary of this argument was provided by KMT legislator and former Mainland Affairs Council chief Su Chi, who wrote in a January 2006 op-ed, "Arms procurement does not amount to national defense, and national defense does not amount to national security."[46] Instead, Su argued, Taiwan should focus on a strategy that would combine major improvements in cross-Strait relations with the acquisition of "more economical, pragmatic, and effective" defense capabilities.

Beyond this broader debate, the main Pan-Blue arguments focused on the high price of the weapons and Taiwan's fiscal policy situation. Many Pan-Blue members of the Legislative Yuan asserted that the items were overpriced, and some suggested that the United States was inflating the threat posed by PLA modernization as part of its effort to persuade Taipei to purchase expensive US weapons. Some claimed that the weapons were simply unaffordable given Taiwan's budgetary circumstances, and would worsen the government's financial situation. Another set of arguments centered on the military value of the items included in the arms sales package. Some Pan-Blue politicians argued that the items would not meet Taiwan's defense needs. Some also said that the items would not be enough to keep pace with PLA modernization. Other opposition politicians suggested that the arms would arrive too late to make a difference. Finally, some suggested that it would make more sense to devote more funding to enhancing maintenance and operations instead of spending such a large amount of money on arms procurement.

Another major argument centered on the appropriateness of the use of the special budget mechanism. The Pan-Blue camp argued that the use of the special budget was an inappropriate attempt to circumvent restrictions imposed by Taiwan's budget laws. At the same time, however, KMT and PFP members differed over whether they would support the programs if the Chen administration would incorporate them into the regular defense budget instead of using the special budget mechanism. Some opposition politicians indicated that they opposed the use of a special budget to pay for the items, but would not oppose the purchases if they were financed through the regular defense budget. For example, in July 2005, KMT legislator Chen Chieh said, "The KMT is not against buying new weapons. As long as the DPP government is willing to use the regular annual budget for that purpose, and not to leave the debt to our children and grandchildren, then we can discuss it."[47] Many in the KMT were apparently willing to support raising the defense budget to 3 percent of GDP instead of using a special budget to buy weapons from the United States.[48] Members of the PFP, however, tended to take a harder line on the question of shifting the arms purchases to the regular budget. Lin Yu-fang, a PFP member of the National Defense Committee, said that his Pan-Blue colleagues were "stupid" to support funding the purchases through the regular budget, since it would be a waste of taxpayers' money no matter how the purchase was funded.[49]

In late 2005, the KMT and PFP also began emphasizing that they objected to the proposed PAC-3 procurement on the grounds that the outcome of the 2004 referendum precluded the purchase of missile defense systems for three years. Outlining this element of the Pan-Blue camp's argument, PFP legislator Lee Yung-ping said, "The referendum held in tandem with the presidential election . . . vetoed the question that the nation should beef up its missile defense in the face of Chinese ballistic missile deployments."[50] Although the overwhelming majority of voters who cast ballots opted in favor of boosting missile defense capabilities, the question was declared invalid because less than half of eligible voters participated in the referendum.[51] The failure to achieve the required threshold was the result of a boycott of the referendum by some voters, which implied their opposition either to the issue at hand, the Chen administration's decision to hold a referendum, or perhaps both.[52] As for the Pan-Green position, prior to the referendum, President Chen had stated that the government would go ahead with the planned purchase of the PAC-3 systems regardless of the outcome of the vote, since the question addressed the broader policy issue rather than any specific procurement proposal that was already in process. After the KMT and PFP raised the issue of the referendum, Deputy Defense Minister Michael Tsai reiterated the government's position that the procurement of the PAC-3 batteries could proceed as planned regardless of the result of the referendum.[53] The Pan-Blue camp rejected this position, however, and insisted that the PAC-3 batteries be taken off the table as a result of the referendum. It seems likely that this argument emerged because a new justification was needed to oppose the PAC-3 procurement once it appeared likely that the Chen administration would shift it to the regular annual defense budget.

The final reason that Pan-Blue legislators put forward to explain their opposition to the special budget was that spending an enormous amount of money on weapons from the United States would do little to benefit Taiwan's economy or create jobs at home. They pointed to Taiwan's recent economic slump and called for replacing at least a portion of the proposed arms imports with indigenous production. Proponents of this course of action argued that it would provide a boost to companies in the sagging defense and shipbuilding industries, some of which were and remain major employers.

Some Legislative Yuan members insisted that they would only support the submarine purchase proposal if the United States would allow Taiwanese shipbuilders to produce at least some of the submarines. Similarly, some legislators have argued that the Chungshan Institute of Science and Technology, the military's main research and development institution, should be given the opportunity to design and build the island's missile defense system. In May 2002, the Legislative Yuan asked the Executive Yuan to negotiate a deal with Washington that would allow six of the eight diesel submarines to be built domestically. The Chen administration responded by establishing an interdepartmental task force to examine the possibility of domestic submarine construction. The task force was charged with evaluating the China Shipbuilding Corporation's capability to produce submarines, and establishing mechanisms for negotiations with the United States.[54]

The task force was unable to win US support, effectively scuttling the plan to build submarines domestically. According to a Ministry of National Defense press release, Washington indicated that it would not support the proposal to manufacture some of the submarines in Taiwan, largely because doing so would likely have resulted in increased costs and program delays.[55] Given the negative response from the United States, the Ministry of National Defense reached the conclusion that "the obstacles to fulfilling the policy of domestic submarine-building are too hard to overcome" and requested that the Legislative Yuan "reassess the feasibility of promoting domestic submarine-building at this stage."[56] Anticipating further criticism from the opposition parties, the ministry pointed out that industrial cooperation would still yield considerable benefits for Taiwanese companies.[57] This argument left the opposition unconvinced, however, and many legislators continued to complain that the Chen administration's arms procurement plan would not do enough to support Taiwan's economy, upgrade its defense-industrial capabilities, or create jobs in their districts.

As the example of the submarines demonstrates, without a larger role for Taiwanese companies, the legislators probably saw little if any electoral advantage in supporting the special budget. Indigenous production of some of the submarines would have allowed at least some legislators to take credit for obtaining business for major companies like the China Shipbuilding Corporation, creating employment opportunities in their districts, and boosting the local economy, which presumably would improve their reelection prospects.

These potential electoral advantages would have made it in their interest to support the special budget. With only a modest role for Taiwanese companies, however, many legislators apparently concluded that supporting the special budget would not translate into votes.

Another very important though usually unstated reason for opposition to the special budget was that the Pan-Blue leadership simply wanted to deny President Chen any sort of political victory that would boost his sagging popularity, increase the DPP's chances of winning additional seats in the Legislative Yuan, or boost the DPP's prospects in the 2008 presidential election. Indeed, the Pan-Blue opposition blocked a considerable number of the Chen administration's proposals in addition to the special budget, suggesting that the refusal to allow the special budget to leave the Procedure Committee was part of a broader political strategy. As one KMT heavyweight put it when asked to explain his party's approach to dealing with the Chen administration, "Whatever Chen Shui-bian supports, we shall oppose."[58] Such an approach is not unique to Taiwan. Indeed, it is not uncommon in other countries and often leads to stalemate, particularly under conditions of divided government. Importantly, however, in this case it also appears to have reflected a judgment on the part of the opposition parties that giving Chen what he wanted would simply have emboldened him to take further steps toward formal independence.[59] Finally, the Pan-Blue camp probably calculated that forcing the Chen administration to fund the acquisitions through the annual budget would squeeze out spending on more popular programs and cost the Pan-Green camp votes in future elections.

The risks the Pan-Blue camp was running by thwarting the Chen administration's attempts to win approval for the special budget as part of this broader political strategy were twofold. First, it left them open to criticism on the grounds that they were engaging in politically motivated obstructionism. Second, the approach also left the Pan-Blue camp vulnerable to charges that it was not serious about improving Taiwan's defense capabilities and safeguarding the island's national security. Eager to deflect domestic and US charges of obstructionism, the Pan-Blue camp sought to blame the Chen administration for the special budget debacle. The opposition noted that the Chen administration had waited three years to submit the special budget request, and continued to argue that the special budget was an inappropriate way to fund the purchases and that it was their responsibility to ensure that Taiwan did not purchase the wrong weapons at an exorbitantly high price. To deflect charges that they were weak on national security issues, the KMT and PFP also insisted that they were in fact concerned about improving Taiwan's national defense capabilities. Some Pan-Blue legislators indicated that they would support some alternative proposal to improve the island's defense capabilities, and the Pan-Blue leadership insisted that they would not oppose an arms procurement plan that they considered reasonably priced and appropriate to Taiwan's circumstances.[60] Moreover, the KMT leadership pledged in early 2006 that it would release its own arms procurement proposal within a few months. The KMT ultimately backed away from that timeline, however, apparently due to differences with the PFP.

The Chen administration's response. The Chen administration's counterargument to the Pan-Blue camp's criticism of the special budget consisted of three main strands. First, the Ministry of National Defense stated that it had performed a considerable amount of analysis to validate the operational requirements and suitability of the weapons. Second, defense and national security officials emphasized the importance of acquiring the weapons to help prevent a further deterioration of the cross-Strait military balance. Third, President Chen and other officials indicated that proceeding with the arms procurement was essential to demonstrating Taiwan's resolve and maintaining good relations with the United States.

The Ministry of National Defense has countered the Pan-Blue camp's opposition to the special budget by releasing a number of assessments detailing the operational requirements for the PAC-3 missile defense systems, antisubmarine warfare aircraft, and submarines. The ministry's assessments indicated that these systems would address weaknesses in antisubmarine warfare and missile defense, which the ministry had identified as key areas for improvement given its analysis that missile attack and naval blockade were the most likely Chinese threats.[61] In a February 2005 speech, Defense Minister Lee Jye said, "I have to emphasize that there is no cheap way to ensure national defense," and stated that the PAC-3 missile defense systems, P-3C Orion antisubmarine warfare planes, and diesel electric submarines were all "necessary for homeland security."[62] Lee and other senior Ministry of National Defense officials met personally with numerous legislators as part of the lobbying effort, and the ministry produced a variety of materials urging greater support for the special budget, including a publicity campaign that called on Taiwanese citizens to forgo one cup of milk tea each week so the government would have enough money to buy the weapons.[63]

The Ministry of National Defense defended the utility of each of the components of the special budget. The director of the ministry's Integrated Assessment Office stated publicly that detailed computer simulations bolstered the case for procurement of the Patriot missile defense systems. He said that the ministry spent nine days running four different scenarios more than 10,000 times and concluded that the Patriots would have a success rate of 83 percent against Chinese short-range ballistic missiles if two Patriot missiles were used to attempt to intercept each Chinese missile launched at Taiwan.[64] In response to Pan-Blue charges that the P-3C antisubmarine warfare planes were outdated and overpriced, the Ministry of National Defense stated that more-modern multimission maritime aircraft would not be available from the United States for another fifteen years and would cost more than twice as much as the P-3C aircraft offered for sale in April 2001. Moreover, the ministry noted that the unit cost of the P-3C planes (US$2.7 billion per aircraft) was actually lower than the unit cost of the less capable P-3B aircraft that South Korea was planning to purchase.[65] Perhaps anticipating suggestions that Taiwan should consider purchasing a smaller number of antisubmarine warfare aircraft, the Ministry of National Defense stated that it would need to have at least eight available at all times, and that this would require acquisition of twelve aircraft, since some planes would be unavailable at any given time due to regular maintenance and training requirements. "This is the minimum that can meet our combat needs," the ministry concluded.[66] In addition, the ministry stated that submarines were required to counter a Chinese blockade and threaten Chinese surface ships in an invasion scenario.

In response to Pan-Blue Legislative Yuan members' demands that the government should drop the special budget and add the items to the regular annual defense budget, the Ministry of National Defense stated that including the items in the regular defense budget would squeeze out other important projects. According to a March 2005 ministry press release:

> The annual budget is already covering 204 projects to increase military strength (including the Kidd-class destroyer, the Posheng projects, the Kuanghwa 6 project, and reconnaissance and surveillance radar). The annual budget for 2005 was 260 billion NTD, with only 60 billion NTD for military investment. . . . [I]f the funding of one or two parts of the three-part procurement were supplied through the annual budget, this would displace existing projects.[67]

The only way to accommodate the addition of the three big-ticket items without squeezing out other projects would be to raise the annual defense budget to at least 3 percent of GDP, but the ministry warned that such an approach "would have an impact on other government spending."[68]

Beyond emphasizing the suitability of the weapons to meet Taiwan's defense requirements and the desirability of using the special budget to avoid painful trade-offs, the government argued that failure to approve the special budget would cause further deterioration in the cross-Strait military balance, increase the likelihood of war, undermine US support for Taiwan, and diminish Taipei's leverage with Washington. High-ranking military officers and senior government officials emphasized that allowing the cross-Strait military balance to continue shifting in China's favor would make military action a more tempting option for Beijing. In June 2005, Hu Chen-pu, director-general of the Ministry of National Defense's General Political Warfare Bureau, warned that "failure to pass the arms purchase bill means our fighting power cannot be improved at a time when Communist China's defense spending is growing at double-digit percentage points every year. . . . [A]s the gap grows wider and wider, we are in fact encouraging them to attack."[69] Similarly, in a December 2005 speech to newly promoted generals, President Chen suggested that failure to maintain sufficient defense capabilities might increase the risk of war, despite growing cross-Strait economic interaction.[70] Pan-Green think tank analysts echoed these concerns in their assessments. In addition, Pan-Green analysts argued that failure to pass the special budget would diminish Taiwan's ability to expand its international space. Lai I-chung, an analyst at the Taiwan Think Tank, wrote, "There is no realistic foundation to fight for . . . autonomous diplomatic space without self-defense capability."[71]

The government also pointed out that failure to pass the special budget risked damaging US-Taiwan relations and undermining US support for Taiwan by creating the impression that the island was not serious about improving its own defense capabilities. As Hu Chen-pu, chief of the General Political Warfare Bureau, put it, "If we don't buy the weapons we need, other people will think we don't have the determination to defend ourselves. . . . If we are too weak to fight, they will give up on us. Will the Americans risk its soldiers being killed because of Taiwan?"[72] During a March 2006 military promotion ceremony at the presidential office, Chen suggested that failure to devote greater resources to defense would lead Taiwan's friends and allies to question the island's willingness to take responsibility for an appropriate share of its own security. Chen criticized the Pan-Blue parties for blocking the special budget and asked, "How can we have our international allies convinced that Taiwan is a 'responsible partner' if we leave our national security aside and breach our promise to defend ourselves only because of our partisan animosity resulted from past elections?"[73] Another variant of the argument that the arms procurement delay was problematic in terms of US-Taiwan relations was that failure to modernize the military would lead to excessive reliance on the United States, which in turn would leave Taipei with minimal leverage in its relationship with Washington. In comments reflecting this concern, Premier Yu Shyi-kun cautioned, "If we completely depend on the United States in defense affairs, we'll fall to U.S. control."[74]

These arguments failed to persuade Pan-Blue politicians, however, and the Chen administration was forced to make major concessions to try to win approval of the special budget, including reducing the total cost of the package and transferring two of the three items to the regular annual defense budget. On 16 March 2005, the government submitted a new version of the special budget, which lowered the total price of the arms package to US$14.91 billion, mainly by transferring some of the expenses to the annual budget and dropping the original proposal for cooperative production of the submarines. This concession failed to break the logjam in the Legislative

Yuan. On 2 September 2005, the government reduced the special budget again, this time to about US$10.56 billion, mainly by agreeing to drop the PAC-3 missiles from the proposal and place them in the annual defense budget instead, which left only the submarines and the P-3C Orion antisubmarine warfare aircraft in the special budget.[75] Defense Minister Lee Jye called this move to placate critics of the special budget a "grueling" decision, and said that the transfer of the missile defense systems to the regular defense budget would compel the Ministry of National Defense to cancel or delay some fifty-three other investment projects that it had previously planned to fund.[76] The Executive Yuan spokesperson emphasized that the Chen administration felt it was necessary to make the change anyway, to try to win the support of opposition lawmakers. Eventually, the P-3C antisubmarine warfare planes were also moved into the regular annual defense budget. This concession lowered the price tag to about US$9.32 billion, by leaving only the submarines in the special budget. This was basically the end of the bill, since the submarines were the most controversial and problematic of the three items.

In short, by the end of 2005, the government had reduced the cost of the proposed acquisitions dramatically, and had agreed to include all of the items except for the submarines in the regular budget instead of seeking approval for a special budget. To do this, it planned to increase the annual defense budget to about 3 percent of GDP. Despite these concessions, however, the opposition parties still refused to approve the package.

The demise of the special budget. In February 2006, the government finally announced that it would abandon the special budget. The Ministry of National Defense continued to maintain that the PAC-3 missile defense batteries, P-3C antisubmarine warfare planes, and submarines were required to protect Taiwan's security and respond to China's rapid military buildup and the changing cross-Strait military balance, but acknowledged that it would be unable to overcome the resistance of the opposition-controlled legislature, where the Pan-Blue parties had used their majority in the Procedure Committee to block consideration of the bill an astounding fifty-six times since it was introduced in June 2004.[77] Consequently, the Chen administration decided that it would attempt to finance the purchase of the P-3C antisubmarine warfare planes and submarines through the island's annual defense budget.[78] The Chen administration also agreed to defer the planned purchase of the PAC-3 missiles until March 2007, bowing to the Pan-Blue camp's insistence that the government's failure to gain enough votes to validate the referendum question on missile defense required a three-year delay in the acquisition of missile defense systems.

The Chen administration's abandonment of the special budget initially seemed to offer some hope that the procurement of the arms sales package

Washington had approved in April 2001 would finally move forward. During a March 2006 visit to Washington, KMT chairman Ma Ying-jeou stated that the KMT was working to build a consensus in the Legislative Yuan that would allow the passage of a scaled-down version of the arms procurement package. At the same time, however, Ma said that the Pan-Blue parties were unable to move forward immediately because passing the bill following President Chen's decision to scrap the National Unification Council would suggest that the opposition endorsed Chen's decision: "If we let it go, people would get a wrong signal from us and think that we support President Chen's scrapping of unification guidelines."[79] Other KMT officials indicated, however, that Pan-Blue legislators still remained divided over the US arms purchase deal: "It is true that lawmakers are still divided. We are trying to find a consensus," a KMT spokeswoman said. "We also need time to consult with other opposition parties," she added, suggesting that disagreements between the KMT and the PFP still needed to be taken into account.[80]

The KMT's decision to defer further negotiations on the arms purchases infuriated Defense Minister Lee Jye: "Damn it. I want to quit my job," he told legislators during a March 2006 Legislative Yuan hearing. "We are making no progress and I am wasting my time here."[81] In a speech later that month, President Chen warned that further delays threatened to exacerbate US concerns about Taiwan's willingness to invest in its own defense.[82]

The saga of the special budget came to a formal close in May 2006, almost two years after the Chen administration proposed the bill and more than five years after Washington approved the sale of the items to Taiwan. In late May, the cabinet indicated that it would officially withdraw the special arms procurement bill and replace it with a new plan to add about US$193 million to the Ministry of National Defense's regular annual budget. In June 2007, the Legislative Yuan finally voted on the long-delayed arms sales package as part of the regular annual defense budget. The legislature voted to approve funding for the twelve P-3C maritime patrol aircraft, but it chose to upgrade the military's older PAC-2 missile defense systems in lieu of purchasing the PAC-3 batteries from the United States, and slashed funding for further consideration of the submarine procurement program to a mere US$6 million.

Implications. The prolonged haggling over the special budget had important domestic and international implications for Taiwan. The heated debate over the special budget not only intensified the standoff between the Chen administration and the Pan-Blue–controlled Legislative Yuan, but also created potentially serious problems in US-Taiwan relations. The United States maintained that the items included in the special budget were needed "to correct growing imbalances in the critical areas of missile and air defense and anti-submarine warfare."[83] The failure to build a consensus in support of key components of the procurement plan for more than six years following the April 2001 arms sales decision led to charges that Taiwan was not serious about its defense and blunt warnings that Taiwan could not count on the United States to defend it in a crisis if it was not willing to shoulder at least part of the burden of protecting its own security. This was particularly striking in that the George W. Bush administration came into office very favorably disposed toward Taiwan and determined to increase security cooperation with the island's military. Perhaps of greatest concern to Taiwan, however, was that these warnings came not only from US Defense Department and State Department officials, but also from some of the island's longtime supporters in the US Congress. In response, prominent opposition politicians asserted that Washington was attempting to bully Taipei into purchasing weapons it did not need and could not afford. Opposition lawmakers accused the United States of demanding "protection money" from Taiwan. PFP leader James Soong stated that Taiwan should determine what it needed for its own defense and would not bow to pressure from Washington. In a more memorable episode, Li Ao, an independent legislator with a flair for the dramatic, pulled out a leash in the middle of a March 2005 appearance by Defense Minister Lee Jye before the National Defense Committee and railed against the United States for "treating us like its watchdog."[84]

The special budget debacle also diverted attention from equally pressing national security and defense reform issues in Taiwan, such as the ongoing efforts to civilianize the defense bureaucracy, enhance training and exercises, improve the military's ability to conduct joint operations, upgrade the military's communications networks, harden critical infrastructure to withstand a Chinese attack, address recruitment and retention challenges associated with the movement toward an all-volunteer military, and complete the reform of the island's professional military education system. Moreover, the failure to follow through on a substantial portion of the April 2001 arms sales package may have long-term implications for US-Taiwan relations, especially in the areas of arms sales and security cooperation. In particular, it seems likely that the United States would be reluctant to approve further major arms sales requests from Taiwan, at least for some time, given Washington's frustration with the protracted struggle over the arms procurement proposal.

Defense Research and Development

Taiwan's heavy dependence on the United States as its principal supplier of advanced military technology, and the political and military uncertainties this dependence entails, are the motives underlying another objective of Taiwan's defense modernization program: enhancing indigenous defense research and development capabilities. By improving its domestic defense research and development capabilities, Taipei hopes to lessen the island's reliance on the procurement of foreign weapon systems. The goal of greater self-sufficiency in defense production is mentioned in several major laws and policy documents. Article 22 of Taiwan's National Defense Act stipulates that the government must give priority consideration to acquisition of domestically produced weapons and equipment. The same article also stipulates that when arms are acquired from foreign suppliers, the government should pursue technology transfers that would benefit Taiwan's defense industry. In addition, Taiwan's 2006 national security report proposes enhancing Taiwan's indigenous defense research and development capabilities: "The National Security Council and Executive Yuan should promptly develop effective mechanisms through which the nation's independent development of defense technologies can be strengthened."[85]

Greater self-sufficiency in defense production is a long-standing goal, and Taiwan's defense industry has made some fairly impressive achievements in certain areas, such as combat aircraft and missile systems, but the island remains heavily reliant on the United States for acquisition of modern weapon systems and other types of advanced military technologies.[86] This heavy reliance on the United States is in large part a result of the structural shortcomings of Taiwan's defense industry. Some of the main problems include funding limitations, excess capacity, excessively large work forces, lack of economies of scale, limited exposure of state-owned firms to market competition, and a shortage of systems integration skills.

Hardware Modernization

Counterstrike capabilities. As policymakers and analysts in Taipei continue to debate the merits of a counterstrike strategy, Taiwan is moving forward with the development of several missile systems capable of reaching targets on the mainland. Senior officials from the Ministry of National Defense stated in early 2006 that Taiwan began developing missiles capable of striking targets on the mainland following the PLA's 1995–1996 missile exercises, as part of an effort to develop capabilities to deter China.[87] As part of this program, Taiwan's Chungshan Institute of Science and Technology is developing several different types of missiles, including ground-launched and air-launched cruise missiles.

One of the missiles Taiwan is developing is the Hsiung Feng–2E land-attack cruise missile, which reportedly has a range of up to 1,000 kilometers. According to a report published in *Apple Daily,* about 100 Hsiung Feng–2E ground-launched cruise missiles have been produced and are in the process of deployment.[88] Another report claims that the military will deploy three batteries consisting of a total of 24 mobile launchers and 48 missiles within the next two years.[89] Still another press report indicates that Taiwan may eventually deploy as many as 500 Hsiung Feng–2E missiles and that the Chungshan Institute of Science and Technology is designing an extended-range version of the cruise missile.[90] In addition, Taiwan reportedly is developing a supersonic ground-launched cruise missile as part of the "Ch'ing T'ien" project.[91]

Another Chungshan Institute of Science and Technology program is focused on the development of an air-launched cruise missile. In March 2006, Taiwan successfully flight-tested the Wan Chien air-launched cruise missile, which was designed to target PLA airfields and missile bases in the military regions opposite Taiwan.[92] The Wan Chien reportedly has a maximum range of more than 600 kilometers, which would be sufficient to allow the ROC air force's F-16s and Ching-kuo indigenous defense fighters to launch it from Taiwan's side of the Strait centerline, reducing the exposure of the fighters to PRC air defenses and thus improving their survivability. In addition, the Wan Chien air-launched cruise missile reportedly carries a submunition warhead designed to crater runways, and can be configured so that the explosion of some of the bomblets is delayed, a technique that would complicate attempts to quickly repair damaged runways.[93] In March 2006, Defense Minister Lee Jye confirmed publicly that the Wan Chien missile was designed to enable the air force to launch long-range attacks against Chinese air bases, specifically by using cluster bombs to crater the taxiways and runways.[94] Beyond the land-attack cruise missile and air-launched cruise missile programs, press reports indicate that Taiwan's Chungshan Institute of Science and Technology is also working on a short-range ballistic missile system based on the Tien Kung surface-to-air missile system, but the press reports provide little information on the status of this program.[95]

The deployment of these and perhaps other missile systems will eventually give Taiwan at least a modest capability to launch precision deep strikes against a limited number of military targets in China. This will provide Taiwan with some previously unavailable military options, especially if it refrains from striking population centers and economic targets and instead focuses its limited counterstrike capabilities against targets critical to China's ability to sustain military operations against Taiwan, such as staging areas, fuel and ammunition storage facilities, and the PLA's logistics network. Nevertheless, even this approach would probably have a limited impact on the PLA's combat capabilities. Indeed, China would clearly be able to absorb far more punishment than Taiwan could inflict with conventional weapons. Beyond uncertainty about the effectiveness of a limited number of missiles against the large number of military targets on the mainland, Taiwan's possession of counterstrike capabilities could complicate US efforts to control escalation in the event of a cross-Strait crisis or conflict.

Air and missile defense systems. Enhancing air and missile defense capabilities is a particularly important issue for Taiwan, and it is becoming an increasingly challenging problem as China deploys greater numbers of more sophisticated aircraft and cruise and ballistic missiles in the military regions opposite Taiwan.[96] The air and missile defense systems Taiwan currently fields, which include three Patriot "modified air defense system" batteries, the indigenously developed Sky Bow II surface-to-air missile system, and a variety of short-range and vehicle-mounted air defense missile systems, fall well short of what would be required to meet this growing challenge.[97]

The acquisition of more advanced air and missile defense systems has thus become an area of particular concern in US-Taiwan relations. Washington is concerned that Taipei is moving too slowly in expanding and upgrading its air and missile defenses, especially given the pace of the short-range ballistic missile buildup on the mainland. Indeed, US Department of Defense officials have warned that these missiles constitute the PLA's most potent coercive threat, and have strongly encouraged Taipei to purchase PAC-3 missile defense systems.[98] However, the PAC-3 procurement was sidelined by the controversy over the special budget and the Pan-Blue camp's insistence that the outcome of the 2004 referendum precluded consideration of purchasing missile defense systems until 2007, as discussed previously. Interservice rivalry is another complicating factor, according to some reports.

Even the acquisition of six additional PAC-3 batteries, however, would not be sufficient to defend all of Taiwan against China's large and growing arsenal of increasingly capable short-range ballistic missiles. According to a recent report by the Center for Strategic and International Studies, "Taiwan is in a singularly unenviable position when it comes to missile defense." Indeed, Chinese missiles would outnumber Taiwan's interceptor missiles by six or seven to one, greatly complicating attempts to defend against a full-scale missile attack.[99] Accordingly, many defense analysts in Taiwan have concluded that Taiwan has few realistic options to defend itself against Chinese short-range ballistic missiles. According to a recent study by the Foundation on International and Cross-Strait Studies, the increasing quantity and growing capability of the Second Artillery's short-range ballistic missiles has made it "impossible for Taiwan to put up an effective defense" against Chinese missiles.[100]

For these reasons, opposition legislators have expressed considerable skepticism about the cost-effectiveness of missile defense systems such as the PAC-3. For example, as KMT Legislative Yuan member and retired army lieutenant-general Shuai Hua-min put it during an April 2006 press conference: "If China has 700 ballistic missiles, and two missiles are theoretically required to intercept one offensive missile, then 1400 Patriot missiles would be needed. Taiwan can't afford to buy that many missiles."[101] Although defending against a full-scale Chinese short-range ballistic missile attack is probably unrealistic from an economic standpoint and perhaps from an operational perspective as well, many analysts have argued that improved missile defenses would at least allow Taiwan to defend against smaller-scale, coercive missile strikes. For example, Mark Stokes argues that the acquisition of PAC-3 missile defense systems "would undercut the limited, coercive use of ballistic missiles."[102] In particular, the combination of advanced active missile defense systems and enhanced passive defenses could help in the protection of key military targets such as airbases and command and control facilities.

Although the acquisition of additional PAC-3 batteries has been bogged down in the politically charged debate over active missile defenses, Taiwan is making some progress in improving its passive defense measures, such as rapid runway repair and the hardening of important facilities. In a July 2004 journal article, Chen Pi-chao, a former senior Ministry of National Defense official, stressed the importance of enhancing passive defense measures, such as hardened shelters or underground facilities to protect combat aircraft, reserve and alternate runways, rapid runway repair capabilities, and redundant communications systems. According to Chen, a combination of active and passive missile defense measures would strengthen deterrence by denying China the opportunity to neutralize Taiwan's airpower with cruise and ballistic missile strikes.[103] Taiwan also appears to be moving toward acquisition of long-range early-warning radar systems, which the United States has identified as a key priority for Taiwan's development of advanced air and missile defenses.[104]

Air power. Taiwan's air force consists of about 320 modern fighter aircraft, including 146 F-16 A/B fighters purchased from the United States in the 1990s, 128 Ching-kuo indigenous defense fighters, and 56 French-made Mirage 2000-5 fighters. Military analysts classify all of these aircraft as "fourth-generation" fighters.[105] In addition to its modern fighter force, the ROC air force also has about 60 Northrup F-5 fighters, but these aircraft are more than three decades old and the air force uses them mainly for training purposes.

The bulk of Taiwan's fighter aircraft were imported from the United States and France. The 146 F-16 A/B fighters Taiwan purchased from the United States in 1992 are the Block-20 versions, which are considered excellent fighters for air-to-air combat missions. Taiwan's F-16s are also capable of other missions such as launching Harpoon antiship missiles at surface targets in a maritime strike role. Their utility for attacks against ground targets, however, is very limited, especially given the difficulties they would encounter in trying to penetrate Chinese air defenses. Taiwan's 56 Mirage 2000-5s, produced by Marcel Dassault Breguet Aviation, were purchased from France in 1992, and were delivered to the ROC air force in 1997 and 1998. They are equipped with Mica beyond-visual-range air-to-air missiles.

Several of the Mirage 2000-5s, however, were lost in training accidents.[106] The F-5s, which have been part of the ROC air force for about thirty years, are obsolete and will most likely be removed from service over the next several years. In the wake of a recent training crash that killed one ROC air force officer and left another seriously injured, legislators began pressing the Ministry of National Defense to retire the remaining planes as soon as possible.[107]

In addition to the US F-16s, French Mirage fighters, and aging F-5s, Taiwan has also developed its own modern fighter aircraft, known as the Ching-kuo indigenous defense fighter. Taiwan's Aerospace Industrial Development Corporation built 130 Ching-kuo indigenous defense aircraft during the 1980s to replace the ROC air force's aging F-104 Starfighters and F-5 Tigers. The decision to proceed with an indigenous development program was made at a time when the United States and other potential suppliers were unwilling to sell advanced fighter aircraft to Taiwan for fear of disrupting their relations with the PRC. The ROC air force originally planned to order 250 Ching-kuo indigenous defense fighters, but cut the number to 130 in the early 1990s when it became possible to purchase high-performance fighters from the United States and France. The last Ching-kuo was delivered to the ROC air force in January 2000. The indigenous defense fighters are equipped with TC-2 beyond-visual-range air-to-air missiles. The indigenous defense program has faced a number of developmental difficulties and operational problems. In 2000, a Western media report described the Ching-kuo as "a symbol of the deep-seated problems faced by Taiwan's armed forces." According to the report, "The plane is no match for the Russian-built SU-27s and 30s, which are rapidly becoming the core of the Chinese air force. Also, its systems are virtually incompatible with the other fighters in Taiwan's own armory, the French Mirage and the U.S.-built F-16."[108] Nonetheless, the Aerospace Industrial Development Corporation is working on an upgraded version of the Ching-kuo with improved range and enhanced avionics, firepower, and electronic warfare capabilities, according to media reports.[109] The upgraded fighters will be able to carry the Tien Chien 2A antiradiation missile and the Wan Chien air-launched cruise missile, which has a submunition payload. In addition to its fighter aircraft, the ROC air force also has a variety of other types of aircraft. In 2006, Taiwan acquired E-2K Hawkeye airborne early-warning airplanes to improve its air defense capabilities. The air force's inventory also includes a number of reconnaissance and patrol aircraft, transports, and trainers.

Despite this fairly impressive inventory of aircraft and the high quality of Taiwan's pilots, the island's air force faces several critical challenges. First, the air force reportedly suffers from a "serious shortage of air-to-air missiles."[110] Although the air force's air-to-air missile inventory appears to be insufficient for most projected cross-Strait conflict scenarios, the missiles the air force does have include beyond-visual-range AIM-120 advanced medium-range air-to-air missiles purchased from the United States.[111] Second, the ROC air force has little capability to strike targets in China without suffering prohibitive losses. The F-16 A/B fighters currently in Taiwan's inventory are not well suited to conducting ground attack missions.[112] According to a media report, "During the Hankuang war games in 2002, the Air Force, after surviving initial PLA air and missile strikes, deployed 90 percent of its F-16 fleet in a major air campaign against key targets in China. But the military lost 70 percent of the fighters to PLA air defenses, unable to neutralize the PLA's missile batteries."[113] Third, because Taiwan does not have enough pilots, "The ratio of pilots to aircraft is dangerously low for sustained combat operations."[114] Fourth, Taiwan's air bases are vulnerable to disruption or destruction by Chinese air and missile strikes, and perhaps to attacks by special operations forces. Taiwan is taking some steps to mitigate this risk. The ROC air force is working to improve its rapid runway repair capabilities, which would be critical to its ability to continue to conduct air operations following a PRC attack. In addition, during the annual Han Kuang military exercise in July 2004, two ROC air force Mirage fighters practiced using a highway as an emergency runway in a televised drill that was probably intended to signal that the air force could continue to generate sorties even if the PLA damaged or destroyed key air bases. Finally, according to a press report, the ROC air force is also considering procurement of vertical/short takeoff and landing fighter aircraft that would be able to continue operating from other locations if Taiwan's air bases were shut down by a Chinese missile attack.[115]

Fifth, the air force may face a gap in fighter aircraft capability in the coming years as it retires the obsolete F-5s and gradually phases out the Ching-kuo indigenous defense fighters. This has led to consideration of the requirements for new-generation fighters.[116] In January 2006, Defense Minister Lee Jye told journalists, "Because of the gradual decommissioning of the aging F-5Es and Taiwanese [Ching-kuo fighters] over the coming years, the air force is expected to be short by more than 40 fighters in 2015 and needs to build a new fighter fleet to fill the vacuum."[117] Lee has expressed interest in purchasing US-made joint-strike fighters when they become available, but is concerned that US reluctance to offer Taiwan its newest and most advanced aircraft means Taiwan would not be able to acquire the fighters before 2020. Consequently, Taiwan wants to purchase sixty F-16 C/D fighters from the United States to replace some of its aging fighter aircraft. Washington has not yet reached a decision on this request; in any case, the new planes would not enter service in the ROC air force until 2011–2012. According to another report, Taiwan is also considering procuring at least forty US F-15s to fill the gap between the retirement of some of its current fighters and the deployment of its next-generation fighter force.[118]

In sum, Taiwan has a very professional and capable air force, but its capabilities are not keeping pace with the modernization of the PLA air force, especially given the increasing percentage of advanced aircraft in the latter's inventory and improvements in the latter's training. Consequently, the qualitative advantage that ROC air force traditionally enjoyed over the PLA air force in terms of pilot skill and aircraft performance is eroding.[119] Moreover, Taiwan's airbases are vulnerable to a potentially disabling air and missile attack, raising questions about the ability of the ROC air force to sustain operations for more than a short time in the event of a cross-Strait conflict.[120]

Naval power. The modernization of the PLA navy presents a considerable set of challenges to the ROC navy.[121] Today, the ROC navy consists of two destroyers, twenty-two frigates, twelve tank landing ships, four medium landing ships, four diesel submarines, and about fifty coastal patrol craft. In 2002, Taiwan purchased four Kidd-class destroyers from the United States to replace its World War II–era Gearing-class destroyers. Two were delivered in December 2005, and the remaining two were delivered in 2006. The Kidd-class destroyers' antiair, antisubmarine, and antisurface warfare capabilities will make them the ROC navy's most powerful surface ships. In particular, ROC navy officers emphasize that the ships will greatly improve Taiwan's naval air defense and battlefield management capabilities.[122]

Taiwan also has six Kang Ding–class (French Lafayette–design) frigates. Recent media reports indicate that Taiwan is upgrading the air defense capabilities of these frigates. In addition, the ROC navy has seven Cheng Kung–class frigates, which are based on the US Perry-class design, and eight Chi Yang–class frigates, which were formerly US Knox-class frigates. The ROC navy is looking for replacements for the Knox-class frigates, however, due to their age and associated maintenance problems.[123]

The ROC navy also has more than fifty fast-attack missile craft, and is in the process of procuring thirty new fast-attack boats armed with advanced antiship cruise missiles. This acquisition program, however, has encountered obstacles related to a dispute between the China Shipbuilding Corporation, which was awarded the contract, and the Jong Shyn Shipbuilding Corporation, which lost the competition and is challenging the results. The ROC navy also deploys several types of small patrol craft, mine warfare vessels, and amphibious ships.

Beyond its surface warfare capabilities, the ROC navy has four diesel submarines, including two Hai Lung–class submarines (Zwaardvis design) acquired from the Netherlands in the 1980s, and two World War II–era Hai Shih–class (previously US Guppy II–class) submarines. The two Hai Lung–class submarines, the SS 793 Hai Lung (Sea Dragon) and the SS 794 Hai Hu (Sea Tiger), are modern and reasonably capable diesel electric submarines.

These could potentially be used in a counterblockade scenario, though they would likely have little if any capability to counter the PLA navy's submarines. The Guppy-class submarines are training platforms with little operational capability: "The Guppy-class diesel submarines, the SS-791 Hai Shih (Sea Lion) and SS-792 Hai Bao (Sea Leopard), were built in the late 1940s based on World War II technology. They remain the oldest active military submarines in the world. The ships, which were sold to Taiwan in 1973, are now used only for training purposes and cannot dive below periscope depth."[124] The potential acquisition of advanced diesel submarines from the United States to upgrade Taiwan's subsurface capability is the subject of considerable controversy on the island, as discussed previously.[125]

Taiwan's naval air capabilities consist of a few dozen ship-based and shore-based antisubmarine warfare helicopters and twenty-one S-2T antisubmarine warfare planes. Airborne antisubmarine warfare is another area of weakness for the ROC navy, given that the S-2T planes have been in service for about forty years, and only eleven of them are still operational. Moreover, even the remaining operational aircraft suffer from age and maintenance problems.[126] The ROC navy's S-2T antisubmarine warfare planes are practically obsolete, according to a Ministry of National Defense report to the Legislative Yuan.[127] Another ministry statement laments that the planes are "unfit for combat."[128]

Also part of the ROC navy is the ROC marine corps, which fields a variety of ground combat vehicles and amphibious personnel carriers. Some members of the Legislative Yuan have argued that the ROC marine corps lacks a mission, given that Taiwan no longer aspires to "retake the mainland."[129] Many strategists, however, still see a need for the military to maintain the capability to conduct amphibious operations. Chai Wen-chung and Mei Fu-shin argue that the ROC marine corps still has a number of important missions, including playing the opposing force in counter-landing exercises, providing security for naval bases, reinforcing the offshore islands, and serving as a rapid-reaction force capable of conducting counterattacks against Chinese forces attempting to invade Taiwan. They support strengthening the ROC marine corps to enhance its ability to undertake these missions. According to Chai and Mei:

> For operations in the Taiwan theater, a rapid-reaction force organized from [ROC marine corps] assets that are capable of seaborne mobility and combining the advanced amphibious platforms (such as high-speed amphibious assault vehicles and hovercraft), helicopters, and air/naval fire support, would be the only fighting force that is completely unhampered by geographical obstacles and capable of force projection missions against PLA forces that have already landed on Taiwan-controlled territory. A suitably transformed [ROC marine corps] would, therefore, be able to undertake the counter-landing mission.[130]

In addition, they argue, enhancing the combat power of the ROC marine corps would complicate PLA operational planning and strengthen deterrence.[131]

In sum, the ROC navy is no longer superior to the PLA navy. Notwithstanding the recent acquisition of the highly capable Kidd-class destroyers, the ROC navy's long-standing qualitative edge over the PLA navy has been eroding over the past decade, as China has deployed advanced Russian-made and indigenously developed destroyers, frigates, and submarines. Consequently, the balance of naval power in the Taiwan Strait area has shifted toward China.

Ground forces. Taiwan's army traditionally dominated the defense establishment. As Taiwan's strategy has shifted to emphasize naval and air power, however, the army's influence has declined to some extent. Nevertheless, with nearly 200,000 troops, the army is still the largest of the island's armed services. Moreover, the army continues to emphasize that ground forces remain the "last line of defense" in the event of a Chinese invasion of Taiwan, and should maintain a central role in the defense of the island.

The army has a considerable number of tanks, including about 375 M60-A3 main battle tanks. It also has more than 1,000 armored personnel carriers, including about 650 M113s, and a large number of artillery pieces. The army has considered purchasing M1-A1 tanks from the United States, but many defense analysts argue that light-armored vehicles are a better alternative given Taiwan's defense requirements.

Indeed, the army is purchasing indigenously built "Yun Pao" armored vehicles to improve its maneuverability. It is also buying new multiple-launch rocket systems. In addition, the army is considering purchasing advanced attack helicopters from the United States, though some analysts assess that medium-lift helicopters capable of transporting rapid-reaction troops are better suited to the army's most likely missions in the event of a cross-Strait war. Over the next several years, the army is likely to undergo a transition designed to make it into "a lighter, more maneuverable force with a greater capability both to repel a PRC assault before it reaches Taiwan's shores and to react quickly to sudden landings by PLA amphibious and paratroop/[special operations] units."[132]

Electronic warfare and information operations. ROC military authors emphasize the importance of electronic warfare in modern military operations. According to an article by Lieutenant Colonel Wan Jiren of the ROC air force, for example, "Electronic warfare has already become a decisive factor in determining victory and defeat in modern warfare and whoever gains dominance in electronic warfare will be able to seize the initiative on the battlefield, get the jump on the enemy, and vanquish the enemy."[133] Similarly, senior ROC military officers have stated that information and electronic warfare would play a key role in a cross-Strait conflict. For example, Lieutenant General Abe Lin, former director of the Ministry of National Defense's Communications, Electronics, and Information Bureau, has stated that computer network operations would determine the outcome of the struggle to seize "intelligence dominance" in future wars.[134] Taiwan is thus placing a considerable amount of emphasis on the development of information operations and electronic warfare capabilities. It is also working to improve its computer network defense and information security measures to reduce the vulnerability of its critical military and civilian networks. Taiwan's military has created a special information warfare unit and incorporated offensive and defensive computer network operations into major joint service exercises.[135] In addition, the island's dynamic civilian information technology and electronics industries provide a solid foundation for the development of advanced capabilities in all of these areas.[136]

Space and C4ISR. Another crucial defense modernization program where funding represents a crucial problem is the upgrading of Taiwan's command, control, communications, computers, intelligence, surveillance, and reconnaissance system. Taiwan's "Posheng" modernization program, which was initiated in 1997 to dramatically upgrade the military's C4ISR systems and improve its joint operations capabilities, reportedly has been scaled down as a result of concerns about the cost of the project as it was originally proposed. Developing an integrated, survivable C4ISR system to support joint operations, however, remains a high-priority need for Taiwan.[137]

Taiwan is also attempting to improve its space-based ISR capabilities. The 21 May 2004 launch of ROCSAT-2, an imagery satellite that produces photos with two-meter resolution, substantially upgraded Taiwan's space-based remote-sensing capabilities. According to Taiwan's National Space Program Office, imagery from the satellite will be used mainly for civil applications, including disaster prevention, geological surveys, and environmental research. The satellite will also enable Taiwan to collect imagery intelligence on military developments on the mainland. Although ROC officials generally do not stress this mission in their public statements, President Chen has indicated that the satellite will advance Taiwan's national defense capabilities.[138]

Software Reforms

Strategy and doctrine. For Taiwan, acquiring high-tech weapon systems and related hardware, and enlisting US support, usually have been seen as the main counters to the growing Chinese military threat. In recent years, however, it has become increasingly clear that some of the most serious challenges facing Taiwan's armed forces have more to do with software issues, such as strategy and doctrine, establishing civilian control over the armed forces, reorganizing the defense bureaucracy, recruitment and training of qualified personnel, and the capability to conduct joint operations.[139] It has also become clear that purchasing advanced military equipment and seeking firmer backing from Washington will not be enough unless Taipei manages to deal with these underlying problems. Consequently, Taiwan has embarked on a series of major defense reforms designed to address these challenges and has made impressive strides in several key areas. In others, however, Taiwan still faces considerable challenges.

The hardware modernization programs and software reforms that are currently under way are taking place against the background of ongoing debate over Taiwan's military strategy and doctrine. Indeed, defining and articulating a national security strategy and a corresponding framework for defense policy is recognized as a central part of the defense reform and reorganization process in Taiwan. As Michael Swaine and James Mulvenon point out, the ultimate objectives of Taiwan's strategy are threefold: deterring China from using force against the island, seeking increased support from the United States, and reassuring the Taiwan public that the government is doing everything possible to ensure the island's security.[140] Yet Taiwan has encountered considerable difficulty in its effort to translate these broad national security objectives into a coherent national security strategy and a concrete framework for national defense policymaking.

As Taiwan has struggled with these problems over the past decade, there have been important changes in the island's declared military strategy. In the early 1990s, Taiwan's strategy shifted from emphasizing both offensive and defensive operations *(gongshou yiti)* to focusing exclusively on defense of the territory under the island's control *(shoushi fangyu)*. This shift came as the ROC government formally abandoned all pretensions that it intended to retake the mainland. Taiwan's military strategy is now centered on the concepts of "effective deterrence" *(youxiao hezu)* and "resolute defense" *(fangwei gushou)*. When President Lee Teng-hui first enunciated this strategy in the mid-1990s, "resolute defense" took precedence over "effective deterrence." The order was subsequently reversed to place increased emphasis on deterring the mainland from using force against Taiwan, and this change was reflected in the ROC's 2000 defense white paper.[141] Another key element of ROC strategy is "preserving fighting capability and sustaining strategic endeavor," which entails maintaining the capability to conduct defensive operations after the enemy's initial attack.[142]

The ROC's 2004 national defense report reaffirmed the policy of "effective deterrence, resolute defense."[143] The first part of the construct, "effective deterrence," refers to deterrence through threat of retaliation as well as deterrence through denial of enemy objectives. According to the 2004 report, "By establishing effective deterrent counterstrike and defense capabilities and by deploying forces capable of effectively neutralizing or delaying enemy attacks, the enemy will be persuaded to give up any military ambition after rationally assessing the outcome."[144] The second part, "resolute defense," refers to defeating invading forces if deterrence fails. As the 2004 report puts it, "Once deterrence fails and the enemy launches a military invasion against us, we will combine comprehensive all-out defense capabilities and joint operations capabilities to firmly defend our homeland and stop, defeat, and destroy the invading enemy."[145]

Some defense analysts in Taiwan argue that this reformulation of the island's defense strategy makes it necessary to develop the capability to strike targets on the mainland, and Taiwan is developing land-attack cruise missiles, and possibly ballistic missiles, that would allow it at least a limited counterstrike capability against mainland targets, as discussed previously. Many of these debates date back to the Li Teng-hui years. However, it is Taiwan's current president, Chen Shui-bian, together with his Democratic Progressive Party administration, who has been responsible most recently for injecting these more offensive-oriented elements into Taiwan's military strategy. In 2000, during the presidential election campaign, the DPP introduced the concept of fighting a "decisive battle offshore" (jingwai juezhan) as part of a defense policy that emphasized shifting from a purely defensive policy to a posture of "offensive defense." The key objective of the "decisive battle offshore" concept is to defeat a Chinese invasion attempt at the greatest possible distance from the island itself in order to minimize the costs that Taiwan would bear in terms of casualties and destruction of infrastructure. The policy places a strong emphasis on "paralyzing the enemy's warfighting capability." To achieve this objective, Taiwan's military would have to "actively build up capabilities that can strike against the source of the threat."[146] More concretely, this new policy would involve seizing the initiative as quickly as possible in response to a Chinese attack, destroying Chinese forces at sea and in the air before they reach the beaches, and possibly launching precision deep strikes at command and control centers, logistics and support nodes, airbases, and other targets on the mainland.[147] According to the 2004 national defense report, counterstrikes would include information operations, electronic warfare, long-range precision weapons, air and naval forces, and special operations. The objective of the counterstrikes would be to "rapidly paralyze the enemy's critical nodes and delay its invading operation tempo, so as to disrupt its ambition of winning a decisive victory in the first battle and swiftly ending the war."[148]

The DPP's "decisive offshore battle" concept received increased attention following Chen's victory in the presidential election. In his 16 June 2000 speech at the Army Academy's seventy-sixth-anniversary celebration,

President Chen once again raised the issue of fighting the decisive battle in a conflict with China as far from the beaches as possible. President Chen said that Taiwan's military must develop precision deep-strike, information warfare, and early-warning capabilities to enable it to fight and win a "decisive battle offshore" against the PLA. The mention of this concept in the address sparked a renewed debate over several related issues, especially whether the island's military should prepare to take the fight to the mainland in the event of a conflict with China. Although Chen's 16 June speech reignited the debate over the "decisive battle offshore" strategy, the concept itself was not the main focus of the speech. In fact, the term was not even mentioned until near the end of the address, and only briefly:

> Since my election as the 10th President of the ROC, I have continuously displayed my good intentions concerning the tense relations across the Taiwan Strait, so as to ensure that the people on both sides will be able to avert the disaster of war. But the CCP has never promised to renounce the use of force against Taiwan. Moreover, China has increased its military budget and strengthened its war preparations. Although we have no intention of engaging in an arms race with China, we are facing the threat of the CCP's formidable military strength. To ensure national survival and guarantee the security of the people's lives and property, we must strengthen the construction of our national defense forces, according to the "effective deterrence, resolute defense" policy. We must energetically prepare to build a high-quality, modernized, professional military. Moreover, the air-control, sea-control, counterlanding operational procedures, and the operational concepts of improving our precision deep-strike, early-warning, and information superiority capabilities and fighting a decisive battle offshore should be regarded as the direction of future military modernization and preparations for war. In addition, we should integrate civilian science and technology, improve the standards of the national defense industry, establish self-sufficiency in national defense, and build deterrence fighting capacity in order to guarantee peace and stability in the Taiwan Strait.[149]

Chen's comments apparently reflected fairly broad agreement on the desirability of developing capabilities to engage Chinese forces farther away from Taiwan, both to enhance deterrence and to reduce the extent of damage the island would suffer in a confrontation with China should deterrence fail, but the possibility of carrying out operations against targets on the mainland—especially the timing and purpose of any such counterstrike—remains extremely controversial in Taiwan's defense and national security policy community.[150] According to Chang Li-the, a senior editor at Taiwan's *Defense Technology Monthly,* "The idea was very controversial because people thought it would provoke China and alarm the nation's allies."[151]

Defense policy specialists associated with President Chen and the DPP are among the most vocal proponents of the "decisive battle offshore" concept. Some prominent think tank analysts have also stated their support for the policy. For example, the authors of one recent report concluded, "Traditional ideas of decisive battles against communist forces on the coastlines should be changed, with 'paralysis warfare' replacing the traditional 'war of attrition.'"[152] Former president Lee Teng-hui also favors acquisition of "some kind of long-range missiles" capable of striking targets in China.[153] For some proponents of the counterstrike strategy, the option is attractive at least in part because it would be much less expensive than acquisition of active defense systems like PAC-3. At a conference held in Taipei in January 2003, for example, Lieutenant General Fu Wei-ku, deputy commander of the ROC air force at that time, argued that Taiwan should develop a counterstrike capability due to the extremely high cost of defensive systems such as early-warning radars and missile defense interceptors.[154] Many military officers have publicly indicated their support for the counterstrike strategy as well, but the policy also has a number of detractors. Some critics argue that Taiwan's armed forces are incapable of carrying it out, and others assert that the development of offensive capabilities to strike targets on the mainland is potentially destabilizing.[155] In addition, interservice rivalry may generate opposition within the army, where some officers may have reservations about the strategy because of concerns that it would enhance the influence of the navy and air force and increase their share of the defense budget at the expense of the traditionally dominant ground forces.

Another object of contention is the selection of appropriate targets for possible counterstrike operations. The comments of some officials seem to suggest that they favor adopting a countervalue targeting strategy that would threaten major economic and population centers on the mainland. For example, in September 2004, Premier Yu said, "If you [mainland China] fire 100 missiles at us, we should be able to fire at least 50 at you. If you launch an attack on Taipei and Kaohsiung, we should be able to launch a counterattack on Shanghai."[156] Most civilian and military officials, however, seem to prefer refraining from attacks against civilian targets. Instead, they advocate a counterforce strategy that would involve strikes against military targets in the military regions opposite Taiwan. For instance, the 2004 national defense report states that the military will launch counterstrikes against military targets; it explicitly rules out strikes against civil infrastructure and civilian targets.[157] Similarly, Defense Minister Lee Jye told the Legislative Yuan's National Defense Committee in September 2004 that in the event of a conflict, Taiwan would strike military targets in China, but would not launch attacks against civilian population centers.[158] In addition, other senior military officers have stated publicly that the ROC armed forces would launch retaliatory attacks against military targets on the mainland, but would not attack civilian targets like Shanghai or the Three Gorges Dam.[159]

One reason that most strategists oppose striking civilian targets is that it would likely lead to rapid escalation. Indeed, some Kuomintang politicians see this offensive strategy as potentially destabilizing. Another reason for opposition to this approach is that it would risk seriously undermining US support for Taiwan at a time when such support would be badly needed. Indeed, KMT politicians also point out that it could jeopardize relations with the United States and cost Taiwan the moral high ground in a cross-Strait conflict. Still another reason for opposition to the strategy is that conventional attacks against most of the proposed countervalue targets would probably be little more than symbolic, pinprick attacks, and the threat of such strikes would thus have little or no ability to deter China. Among the handful of commentators and think tank analysts who have advocated countervalue targeting, a few have suggested that the only way to make countervalue targeting a credible deterrent strategy would be to develop nuclear weapons or other weapons of mass destruction.[160] However, senior Taiwanese officials have explicitly ruled out such development. For example, in November 2004, President Chen pledged that Taiwan would never develop such weapons.[161] Similarly, in May 2006, Michael Tsai, deputy secretary-general of Taiwan's National Security Council, said, "Any kind of countermeasures would be for defense. We're not pursuing preemptive capabilities, and we will not develop nuclear weapons or weapons of mass destruction."[162]

Other analysts in Taiwan have argued that neither countervalue nor counterforce deterrence strategies are realistic options for Taiwan. Indeed, they argue that the only reasonable approach for Taiwan is deterrence by denial. Chen Pi-chao summarizes this argument as follows:

> There are three types of deterrence strategy: deterrence by massive retaliation; counterforce deterrence; and deterrence by denial. The first two are not practical in view of the asymmetry in population size and territorial expanse. Deterrence by massive retaliation is not credible without nuclear warheads. Even if we had nuclear warheads, parity would still be a problem. Nor is counterforce deterrence feasible thanks to the vast difference in the number of strategic targets that have to be neutralized. Deterrence by denial is the only practical deterrence strategy available to Taiwan. The PRC aims to coerce Taiwan into accepting its terms. It hopes to achieve this with the threat of force, and failing that, to use as little force as possible at a bearable cost. To deter them from ever resorting to the use of force and deny them what they want must be the goal of Taiwan's deterrence posture. Ideally our goal should be to deter the PRC from taking the plunge and, failing that, to prevail over them initially and prolong the fighting until a third party intervenes and puts an end to the armed conflict.[163]

Still others doubt that Taiwan has any reasonable counterstrike options. For example, as one KMT politician put it, developing capabilities to strike targets in China may be "psychologically satisfying and symbolically important, but it is ultimately unrealistic."[164]

Perhaps attempting to dampen the controversy in Taipei and reassure policymakers in Washington, President Chen said in a March 2004 interview that Taiwan would not develop "offensive capabilities." In the same inter-view, however, he also said that Taiwan would strengthen its "counterstrike capabilities," making them "very effective."[165] Opinion among US think tank analysts and scholars is divided. Some support Taiwan's plans to de-velop a limited offensive capability, pointing out that cruise missiles would replace the capability Taiwan had to conduct air strikes against targets on the mainland with its F-16s before improvements in PLA air defense capa-bilities made such an approach virtually impossible, but others argue that the deployment of ballistic and cruise missiles capable of striking targets on the mainland would be destabilizing and make it very difficult to control escalation in the event of a crisis in the Taiwan Strait.

The revelation that the command-post portion of Taiwan's April 2007 "Han Kuang 23" exercise featured the use of "tactical shore-based missiles for fire suppression" to attack military targets on the mainland reignited this long-standing debate over Taiwan's development of offensive military ca-pabilities and prompted US officials to state their opposition to the deploy-ment of long-range offensive weapons. The Bush administration finally weighed in on the debate publicly a few weeks later when Dennis Wilder, US National Security Council senior director for East Asian affairs, re-sponded to a journalist's question about Taiwan's development of offensive missile capabilities with the following statement: "We think that developing defensive capabilities is the right thing to do. We think that offensive capa-bilities on either side of the Strait are destabilizing and therefore not in the interest of peace and security. So when you ask me whether I am for offen-sive missiles, I am not for offensive missiles on the Chinese side of the Strait and I am not for offensive missiles on the Taiwan side of the Strait. But appropriate defense capabilities are certainly the right of the people of Taiwan."[166] Given the ambiguity of the US commitment to Taiwan's de-fense, however, it seems likely that Taiwan will continue to develop mis-siles capable of striking targets in coastal China, despite US concerns.

Civilian control and reorganization. Establishing civilian control over the military and reorganizing the defense bureaucracy are crucial compo-nents of Taiwan's defense reform program. Taiwanese researchers empha-size that this process is a necessary condition for the implementation of the rest of the defense reforms and the further improvement of Taiwan's de-fense capabilities.[167] Historically, these efforts are also closely associated with Taiwan's democratization and democratic consolidation. Indeed, civil-ian control of the military is a crucial requirement in a democratic society. As Richard Kohn observes, "For democracy, civilian control—that is, con-trol of the military by civilian officials elected by the people—is fundamen-tal. Civilian control allows a nation to base its values and purposes, its in-stitutions and practices, on the popular will rather than on the choices of military leaders, whose outlook by definition focuses on the need for internal order and external security."[168]

The nationalization of the armed forces and establishment of civilian control represented a major transformation for Taiwan. During the 1949–1987 martial law period, the military was loyal not to the state, but to the ruling party, the Kuomintang. The ruling party and the military were effectively one and the same. The military participated actively in efforts to mobilize voters, and was heavily involved in the suppression of opposition to the KMT regime. Military officers held seats on the most powerful KMT bodies and filled numerous government positions, the officer corps was composed primarily of mainlanders, and the military was permeated by a political commissar system that ensured its loyalty to the ruling party. The chief of the General Staff reported directly to the president, bypassing Taiwan's cabinet and the Executive Yuan, and minimizing legislative oversight of defense affairs. In addition, there were no civilian defense policy experts. In the words of one Taipei-based analyst, under Chiang Kai-shek and Chiang Ching-kuo, the armed forces were the "military arm of the KMT instead of the nation. The military was infused with KMT ideology to implement the KMT's policy."[169] The process of democratization in Taiwan, marked by the lifting of martial law in 1987 and the end of the "period of mobilization to suppress the communist rebellion" in 1991, opened the way for the nationalization of the armed forces and the establishment of civilian control.[170]

Restructuring the defense bureaucracy is a central part of the broader effort to enhance civilian control over the military. Two pieces of legislation, the National Defense Act *(Guofang fa)* and the Ministry of National Defense's Organization Act *(Guofangbu zuzhi fa),* sometimes referred to collectively as the "two defense laws," are particularly crucial in this regard. After a lengthy process of drafting and debate that began in the early 1990s, the two defense laws were passed in January 2000 and took effect on 1 March 2002.[171] They carry far-reaching implications for the modernization of Taiwan's military. Indeed, Mark Stokes describes the potential consequences of the two laws as equal to those of the 1947 US National Defense Act and 1986 Goldwater-Nichols Act combined.[172]

The primary purpose of the laws is to lay the groundwork for the reorganization of the defense bureaucracy, which is intended not only to consolidate civilian control and nationalization of the armed forces, but also to quicken the pace of the overall defense reform and military transformation efforts. According to Taiwan's 2002 national defense report, the reforms and reorganization mandated by the laws have several major policy objectives, including enhancing civilian control and promoting the "thorough nationalization of the ROC armed forces"; rationalizing the defense bureaucracy; increasing the capability of armed forces to support the mission of "effective deterrence, resolute defense"; developing the capability to conduct joint operations; and improving procurement procedures and optimizing the allocation of resources.[173]

To promote the achievement of these objectives, the laws codify the political neutrality of the armed forces. Article 6 of the National Defense Act states, "The ROC Armed Forces shall remain neutral from individual, regional and party affiliations." The laws also establish a new chain of command. Article 8 of the National Defense Act states, "The President shall assume the supreme command of army, navy, and air force of the ROC, and is the commander-in-chief of the ROC Armed Forces. He exerts executive authority over the Minister of National Defense, and the Chief of the General Staff follows the command of the Minister to lead the ROC Armed Forces." This means that the chief of the General Staff, who previously reported directly to the president, is now subordinate to the civilian defense minister. The two defense laws increase the power of the defense minister by placing both the ministry staff and the armed forces under his direct authority.

Under the new laws, the Ministry of National Defense is thus effectively put in charge of all major aspects national defense affairs. Specifically, the Organization Act declares, "The Ministry of National Defense . . . is in charge of the overall national defense affairs of the Republic of China." Accordingly, the law grants the ministry authority over a number of areas that were previously the exclusive preserve of the General Staff headquarters and the military services. Specifically, the law stipulates that the ministry is in charge of defense policy; military strategy; budgetary plans; development of military forces; national defense technology and weapons system research and development; armament production and national defense infrastructure; human resources matters, including commissioning, decommissioning, promotion, and transfer of military personnel; national defense resources; national defense codes and regulations; military justice; political warfare; reserve affairs; military assessments; military history and translation; national defense education; and "other national defense related affairs."

The laws thus give the defense minister control of both military administration and military command, for the first time placing these two functions under the jurisdiction of a single official.[174] Moreover, Article 12 of the National Defense Act stipulates that the defense minister must be a civilian. The laws thus stipulate that a civilian defense minister is in charge of administration, command, and armament, and is responsible for developing military strategy and defense policy, and for making decisions concerning resource allocation. Another important change resulting from the two defense laws is that the Ministry of National Defense now has the power to make important personnel decisions, a function that was previously dominated by the General Staff headquarters.[175]

The laws also reorganized the Ministry of National Defense and established new departments and offices within it to assist the defense minister in carrying out his new duties. The most important are the Strategic Planning Department *(Zhanlue guihua si)* and the Integrated Assessment Office *(Zhenghe pinggu shi)*. The former is responsible for outlining the Ministry of National Defense's vision, coordinating the organizational adjustment of the armed forces, analyzing the overall strategic environment, and planning a "forward-looking and comprehensive national defense policy." Another of the Strategic Planning Department's responsibilities is promoting security cooperation and exchanges with foreign militaries. The Integrated Assessment Office is charged with supporting strategic planning and ensuring efficient resource allocation. Its main responsibilities are to analyze and assess military strategy, plans, force structure, military capabilities, and resource allocation. It is also responsible for military modeling and simulation.

The ministry's Bureau of Armaments and Acquisition was also established as a result of implementation of the new defense laws.[176] Its responsibilities include developing defense procurement policies, strategies for procurement of weapons and equipment, and plans for the development of defense-related technologies. It is to provide "rapid, efficient, and high-quality support" for weapons acquisition by the services.[177] The primary reasons for the establishment of the bureau were twofold. First, officials in Taiwan recognized that procurement policy was often irrational, in part because interservice rivalries tended to "distort the allocation of military resources."[178] They concluded that there was a need to rationalize and improve the efficiency of the acquisition system. The second important motivation was stamping out the corruption that plagued the arms procurement process under the KMT, which was symbolized by the scandal surrounding Taiwan's purchase of six Lafayette-class frigates from France in 1991.[179]

Although Taiwan has made admirable progress in depoliticizing the military and civilianizing the defense bureaucracy, several major challenges still lie ahead. Perhaps the most important is completing the "civilianization" of the defense bureaucracy. Prior to the implementation of the two defense laws, the Ministry of National Defense had a total of 224 personnel, of whom a mere 28 were civilians. The new laws increased the authorized number of personnel to 570 and mandated that civilians must fill at least one-third of the total positions in ministry headquarters. The ministry has experienced some difficulties in meeting this goal. As of 1 November 2004, the number of civilian employees stood at 167.[180] The ministry has since made some progress, mainly by filling the designated civilian positions with retired military personnel. The primary problem is the limited pool of civilians with backgrounds in defense analysis and national security affairs. It will take a considerable amount of time to develop a community of civilian defense experts in Taiwan.[181] According to former ministry officials, another problem is that the defense minister and vice minister are not permitted to bring sufficient numbers of civilian staff with them when they assume their positions, nor are they given the opportunity to appoint civilian officials to many key mid-level positions, most of which are filled by career military officers. These personnel issues contribute to the difficulty the senior officials face in controlling the military and implementing bold initiatives and major policy changes.

Another issue is that since the passage of the "two defense laws," all of the civilians who have served as defense minister have actually been senior military officers who retired to take the position. The appointment of a civilian defense minister with little or no prior military experience, which some observers expect to take place within the next few years, would thus represent an important milestone on the road to completing civilianization of the defense bureaucracy. In sum, Taiwan has made considerable progress, but the establishment of a truly civilian defense ministry may take as long as another ten years, according to knowledgeable observers.

Downsizing and personnel policy. Decreasing the overall size of the military and improving the personnel system are also key aspects of Taiwan's defense reforms. Through a series of downsizing programs, Taiwan is trying to streamline the personnel and organizational structure of its armed forces. The "Jing Shi" streamlining and consolidation program, which was put into effect in July 1997, reduced the number of military personnel to about 385,000 within three years. The ground forces faced the heaviest cuts, though the army, with almost 200,000 personnel, still constitutes about 52 percent of the island's armed forces.[182] Beyond a reduction in the total number of military personnel, other elements of the program included reducing the number of levels in the chain of command, merging or consolidating military educational institutions, streamlining high-level staff units, increasing the number of noncommissioned officers, and reducing the number of general officers, especially in the ground forces.

The Ministry of National Defense is now implementing the "Jing Jin" force consolidation program, which will result in further manpower reductions over the next several years. In the first stage of the program, the total manpower of the armed forces was cut from 385,000 to about 340,000. In the second stage, the ministry plans to further reduce the size of the military to 275,000 troops. The goal of the troop reductions is "to create a smaller army with more mobility and firepower."[183] In a March 2003 report, several DPP Legislative Yuan members proposed even deeper cuts that would reduce the total size of the armed forces to about 256,000, largely by trimming more personnel from the ground forces.[184] DPP legislators have also proposed dramatic reductions in the size of Taiwan's reserve forces and extended and improved reserve training.[185]

Taiwan is also reorganizing several parts of its armed forces to make the military more flexible and responsive, mainly by flattening the command structure.[186] Moreover, Taiwan is restructuring its ground force units by transforming the ROC army's traditional infantry and mechanized divisions into smaller combined arms brigades, to improve the army's mobility and firepower. The Ministry of National Defense is also creating new commands and reorganizing some existing commands. For example, a combined logistics command was created as part of the reorganization and restructuring of the logistics system. The military is also creating a missile command that will be in charge of air defense missiles, sea dominance missiles, and "stand-off precision-strike capabilities."[187] In addition, Taiwan has reorganized its reserve command.

Closely related to the streamlining programs and reorganizations are a series of personnel policy reforms.[188] Among their key aspects are several initiatives intended to reform the conscription system and address chronic recruitment and retention problems. The traditional conscription system has been criticized for failing to provide the military with highly motivated, technically capable personnel. Defense analysts and politicians have also pointed out that low salaries for conscripts have resulted in morale problems and resulted in many young men trying to avoid military service. There have been reports of conscripts faking health problems and even feigning mental illness to avoid compulsory military service.[189] For its part, Taiwan's military has acknowledged that it faces manpower problems. One of the most critical personnel problems is maintaining a sufficient number of qualified fighter pilots in the ROC air force.[190] Another major priority is strengthening the military's corps of noncommissioned officers. Indeed, the recruitment of larger numbers of career noncommissioned officers is seen as an important prerequisite for the longer-term objectives of decreasing the term of mandatory military service and ultimately moving toward the establishment of a voluntary enrollment system and a more professional fighting force. Premier Yu Shyi-kun recently outlined these objectives, telling members of the Legislative Yuan that the technological demands of modern warfare require career soldiers with professional training, making an all-volunteer military "the wave of the future" for Taiwan.[191] In addition, during the most recent presidential election campaign, KMT leaders stated their support for transitioning away from compulsory military service.

Although senior politicians have highlighted the importance of improving the recruitment system and adjusting the balance between voluntary recruitment and conscription, this remains a challenge for Taiwan, especially given the current composition of the military. Indeed, in 2004, the ROC military consisted of roughly 40 percent volunteers and 60 percent conscripts. The Ministry of National Defense's goal is to reverse that ratio by 2008.[192]

As part of its gradual effort to move toward this ambitious goal, the Taiwan military has begun to experiment with alternatives to its long-standing reliance on conscription. In May 2002, the Ministry of National Defense attempted to implement a trial voluntary enlistment program in which recruits who had higher levels of education and better technical skills were offered higher salaries if they agreed to serve for three years.[193] The plan called for recruiting several hundred volunteers by the end of 2003, with further expansions in subsequent years. According to recent Taiwan media reports, however, the experiment failed to attract the desired number of recruits. Reform in this area clearly remains a crucial long-term issue for Taiwan's armed forces. Indeed, defense officials assess that it may not be possible to achieve a military that comprises 60 percent volunteers and 40 percent conscripts until at least 2012.[194] Moreover, the Ministry of National Defense is likely to confront several additional problems as it attempts to complete the transition to an all-volunteer force. First, the higher salaries it will need to offer to attract and retain qualified personnel may put upward pressure on the personnel portion of the defense budget, possibly canceling out the savings realized by reducing the overall number of troops in the military. Second, further reductions in the term of mandatory military service will leave little time to train new conscripts. The conscription period has already been reduced to such an extent that this has become a serious problem, according to some ROC military officers. For example, army colonel Wan Ch'uan-chao writes, "The service period for the military's enlisted personnel cannot satisfy the requirements of high-tech operational training."[195]

Joint operations. Taiwan appears to be making considerable progress in its drive to improve the military's joint operations capabilities. Military officers and civilian policymakers alike emphasize the importance of this enhancement.[196] According to an article that appeared in the July 2006 issue of *Air Force Science Monthly,* a journal published by the ROC air force, the ability to conduct joint operations has taken on greater importance along with the advent of advanced C4ISR and long-range precision-strike technology.[197] Traditionally, however, Taiwan's defense strategy did not call for much cooperation between the army, navy, and air force. As Michael Swaine and Roy Kamphausen point out, "Taiwan's military force were given three largely independent missions: (1) air superiority *(zhikong)* for the air force; (2) sea denial *(zhihai)* for the navy; and (3) antilanding warfare *(fan denglu)* for the army. Each of these missions was generally viewed by each service as constituting a relatively separate and distinct task."[198] Similarly, Taipei-based defense analyst Andrew Yang has lamented the lack of communication between Taiwan's army, navy, and air force, which has limited the Taiwan military's ability to plan for and conduct joint operations: "With regard to conducting joint warfare, the army doesn't talk to the air force. The navy doesn't talk to the army."[199] Given this history of limited interaction between the services, it is not surprising that Taiwan's military still faces considerable shortcomings in the area of joint operations.[200]

Nonetheless, Taiwan has made some progress in this key area in recent years, stemming from the increased importance attached to joint operations capabilities. Notably, Taiwan's 2004 national defense report strongly emphasizes the need to improve the capability of the ROC armed forces to conduct joint operations.[201] In this respect, it highlights the "Posheng" C4ISR program, which is intended to "facilitate the coordination and integration of the ROC Armed Forces' joint capabilities."[202] The report notes that the Hengshan Combined Operations Center has been restructured with the aim of turning it into a "network centric modern joint operations command center."[203] It also states that the military is formulating a joint operational doctrine and drafting plans for joint operations.[204] In addition, the military is upgrading its joint training centers, procuring new training simulators, and improving its joint exercises to better synchronize ground, air, and naval operations.

In recent years, the Taiwan military has used its annual "Han Kuang" exercises to test its ability to conduct joint operations in high-tech conflict scenarios. The twentieth annual Han Kuang exercise, for example, conducted in summer 2004, focused on readiness and joint command and control. The first phase consisted of joint planning, the second consisted of computer simulations and war-gaming, and the third involved actual exercises and training and a thorough evaluation of joint operational capabilities. In addition, during another recent major joint exercise, the air force and navy worked together to coordinate a simulated antisurface warfare battle in which air force F-16s launched Harpoon antiship missiles against targets representing Chinese surface ships.[205]

These changes are yielding some real improvements in Taiwan's ability to conduct joint operations, according to US personnel who have observed recent joint exercises. After observing the twenty-second annual Han Kuang military exercise in April 2006, for example, retired US admiral Dennis Blair, former Commander of US Pacific Command, said that Taiwan had made considerable progress in its joint operations capabilities.[206] Blair noted, however, that there was room for further improvement in the areas of equipment, procedures, and training. Military officers in Taiwan recognize that realistic and rigorous joint exercises and training are required to improve the ROC military's ability to conduct joint operations in a high-intensity, network-centric conflict.[207] According to one author, however, the ROC military still suffers from a number of shortcomings that limit its ability to conduct realistic and challenging joint training and exercises.[208] In addition to addressing these problems, overcoming service departmentalism is seen as a key element of the military's effort to improve its joint war-fighting capabilities. To address departmentalism and other shortcomings, legislators from both the Kuomintang and the Democratic Progressive Party are calling for measures that would further enhance the military's ability to plan and conduct joint operations. Several members of the Legislative Yuan's National Defense Committee, including Lee Wen-chung, Lin Yu-fang, Shuai Hua-min, and Ku Chung-lien, reportedly are preparing to propose a national defense reform law modeled on the US Goldwater-Nichols Act, to promote the transformation of Taiwan's armed forces and development of joint combat capabilities. The proposed law would accelerate the pace of reform in areas such as professional military education, personnel policy, training, organization, and force modernization.[209]

Professional military education. Enhancing the professional military education system is another important component of Taiwan's defense software reforms.[210] One of the major parts of this reform program involves merging and consolidating military educational institutions to make more efficient use of resources. Another involves establishing educational exchanges between military and civilian educational institutions. As part of this initiative, the National Defense University, the Naval Academy, the Air Force Aviation Technology College, and Fu Hsing Kang College have established exchange programs with civilian universities. In addition, the military is placing greater emphasis on distance learning and continuing education.

Although Taiwan is making progress, it has also encountered challenges in its attempts to reform and reorganize the professional military education system. Some of the problems are the result of institutional resistance from the services, particularly the traditionally dominant army, which reportedly opposes President Chen's attempts to merge the three service colleges into a single joint service military educational academy.

Training and exercises. The ROC military is reforming its training programs to support the development of joint operational capabilities, improve Taiwan's homeland defense posture, and verify the suitability of operational plans. According to Taiwan's 2004 national defense report, the Ministry of National Defense is trying to make Taiwan's military exercises more realistic and "battle-focused." It is also implementing more rigorous evaluations and making greater use of computer simulations in its training and exercises.[211] Recent iterations of the ROC military's annual "Han Kuang" exercises, which have featured various cross-Strait conflict scenarios, reflect the ROC military's efforts to improve the quality and utility of its training and exercises.

The live-fire phase of Taiwan's twenty-third annual Han Kuang military exercise took place in May 2007. Perhaps the most dramatic portion of the exercise involved six fighter aircraft—two F-16s, two Mirage fighters, and two Ching-kuo indigenous defense fighters—conducting simulated emergency landings on a major highway. This was the second time that the Han Kuang exercise featured the use of major roadways as alternate landing strips. The drill was intended to demonstrate the ability to continue to conduct air operations in the event that Chinese missile and air strikes shut down Taiwan's air bases during a cross-Strait conflict. The four-day live-fire portion of the exercise also featured counterlanding drills and tested the military's ability to respond to Chinese airborne and special operations attacks. The field-training portion of the Han Kuang exercise was preceded by a five-day computer-simulated war-game phase, which was held from 16 to 20 April. The scenario involved a Chinese surprise attack carried out in 2012 and simulated Taiwan's plan to respond by implementing a three-phase plan involving "joint preservation of fighting capacity" *(lianhe zhanli baocun)*, "joint interception operations" *(lianhe jieji zuozhan)*, and "joint territorial defense operations" *(lianhe guotu fangwei zuozhan)*. Although the live-fire exercises are normally the primary focus of media attention, in 2007, as discussed previously, it was the command-post portion of the exercise that drew the most notice from observers and analysts in Taiwan and the United States. During the computer-simulation phase of the exercise, the scenario involved the PLA launching a surprise missile, air, and special operations attack that caused heavy damage to air bases, radar stations, and other military facilities in Taiwan. In this simulation, the PLA then attempted to seize an offshore island to try to compel Taiwan to negotiate on China's terms, to which Taiwan's armed forces responded by launching a series of long-range missile strikes against military targets in coastal China.[212] This was reportedly the first Han Kuang exercise to employ long-range missiles in a counterstrike capacity.

The previous year's Han Kuang exercise was less controversial, but equally important as an example of Taiwan's determination to make training and exercises more challenging and realistic. The computer-simulated war-game phase of the 2006 exercise simulated a cross-Strait war set in 2008. According to the Ministry of National Defense spokesman, the scenario featured the PLA launching a full-scale missile and air attack on Taiwan and then landing troops on the island. In the simulation, Taiwan responded by mobilizing more than 3 million active duty and reserve service members to counter the PLA invasion, resulting in a high-intensity ground battle for control over Taipei. The spokesman said the purpose of the computer simulation was to determine how long the ROC military would be able to hold out against a Chinese assault. An unnamed official said the Ministry of National Defense believed the military would be able to maintain effective resistance for about two to four weeks, assuming the military and the people of Taiwan maintained the determination to fight. If they lost the will to fight, however, resistance could collapse in as little as three days.[213]

The 2005 Han Kuang exercise focused on improving "anti-terrorism and anti-unrestricted warfare" response capabilities and enhancing joint operations capabilities.[214] In keeping with these areas of emphasis, the exercise featured a simulated defense of major air and naval bases from attacks by Chinese airborne troops and special operations forces.[215] Another important feature of the 2005 Han Kuang exercise was a renewed emphasis on psychological warfare training. In addition, Defense Minister Lee Jye said ahead of the 2005 exercise that it would include a simulated Chinese decapitation strike.[216] Other areas of emphasis in the 2005 training program included urban warfare and disaster relief operations.[217]

Beyond the use of more realistic scenarios in recent joint exercises, Taiwan appears to be making some advances in terms of implementing more sophisticated evaluations as well as improvements based on lessons learned. For example, the military's recent annual training plans have highlighted the use of quantitative testing standards and more rigorous evaluations of combat readiness. As well, the Ministry of National Defense reportedly strengthened defenses at key air force facilities after concluding during the computer-simulation phase of the 2005 Han Kuang exercise that security forces were too weak to defeat a Chinese airborne assault and that air bases were vulnerable to enemy infiltration.[218] In addition, the 2004 Han Kuang exercise was designed to validate joint operations command and control procedures and interagency coordination mechanisms, which were developed on the basis of the lessons learned from the previous two Han Kuang exercises, and to address readiness problems, according to the Ministry of National Defense's 2004 national defense report.[219]

Although Taiwan has made some progress in training and exercises for its active duty forces, training for the island's reserve forces is still in need of improvement. The military conducts an annual mobilization exercise, but it is typically the only training that reservists receive during the course of the year. Among the proposed improvements is the adoption of a reserve training system more like that of the US military's, including institution of weekend drills and a longer annual training period. Another problem is that Taiwan simply lacks the space required to conduct some types of live-fire training, according to defense experts in Taiwan and the United States.

Progress and Problems

Taiwan's military modernization and defense reform programs have yielded considerable progress in some areas, but problems persist in others. Researchers who are involved in the military modernization and defense restructuring process acknowledge that it has been extremely difficult to implement, in part due to the scope of the changes under way. Given the internal and external challenges Taiwan faces, it is clearly a process that will require a number of years to complete.

Despite these challenges, Taiwan's progress in implementing some of the central elements of the reform and restructuring programs has been considerable, especially in terms of nationalizing the armed forces and establishing civilian control over military affairs. Although much remains to be accomplished, Taiwan has made impressive strides in each of the three pillars of civilian supremacy since the lifting of martial law in 1987, moving toward the political neutrality, democratic control, and social impartiality of the armed forces.[220]

The transformation of the armed forces from a party-army to a national army, and the civilianization of the defense establishment, though still works in progress in some respects, are important and impressive achievements. The DPP's victory in the 2000 presidential election represented a crucial test of the military's role in Taiwan's democratization, one that Taiwan passed despite considerable friction in civil-military relations. As Mark Stokes notes, "Many in the military were alarmed by the ascendance of a political organization that represented ideals previously viewed as dangerous to national security. Despite the legacy of mistrust between the ruling party and the military, the latter's support for Taiwan's democratic transition is perhaps its greatest achievement in the past six years."[221] President Chen underscored the importance of this accomplishment for democratic consolidation and political stability in a November 2006 interview:

> Building a truly nationalized armed forces that is not controlled by any individual or political party is not a matter of writing it into the Constitution to make it so. Over the past six-plus years, we have implemented nationalization of the military, and it is no longer just an article in the Constitution. Rather, it is a true nationalization of the military. Therefore, I often say that we needn't be afraid of chaos in the Legislature or worry about a wild media; what we worry most about, and feel is most frightening, is a military that is not truly nationalized. If the military doesn't get out of hand, then regardless of how chaotic the Legislature or media is, the country will not fall into chaos. Therefore, during the protests in front of the Office of the President after the March 20, 2004 election, and the sit-in demonstrations staged by the "Red-Shirt Army," we saw the results of the nationalization of the military. This is the most important stabilizing force the nation has. It is different from what is seen in many countries in Southeast Asia, Latin America, and Africa. This is one of Taiwan's success stories and it is the pride of a democratic Taiwan. Taiwan's military is no longer a so-called party army or private army, but truly belongs to the people and the country. Its loyalty is to the Constitution, to this nation, and to this land. This is what is right.[222]

This is a particularly impressive accomplishment in light of the considerable tension between the DPP civilian leadership and some elements of the military, which dates back to the period of martial law and was exacerbated by President Chen's accusation that senior military officers had attempted to conduct a "soft coup" to overturn the results of the 2004 presidential election, in which Chen and Vice President Annette Lu won by a razor-thin margin following a bizarre shooting incident. Despite this continuing tension, the military appears to be well on its way toward internalizing its new role as a professional army that serves the civilian leadership and refrains from interfering in party politics. Indeed, as of late 2006, political analysts in Taipei generally dismissed any possibility of military involvement in the partisan political battle surrounding the presidential-office corruption scandal, reflecting Taiwan's progress in nationalizing the military and establishing civilian control.

Taiwan has also made at least some progress in other important areas, according to US officials and analysts. As noted previously, some of Taiwan's military exercises are becoming more realistic and devoting increasing emphasis to joint operations. Taiwan has also made some improvements in logistics and C4ISR. In addition, US officials and analysts point out that Taiwan's military has made improvements in several areas that are critical to airbase recovery after attack, including rapid runway repair, firefighting, and airbase security.

Despite these advances, however, Taiwan still faces serious shortcomings in several key areas, most notably national security strategy, defense policy, and defense spending. First, the details of national security strategy and defense policy remain vague, limiting their utility to guide planning and procurement. According to Steven Kosiak and Andrew Krepinevich, "Strategy is about setting priorities (and thus, making choices) in an environment of limited resources."[223] In an ideal situation, as Denny Roy writes, "a rational debate conducted in public by defense experts would establish a set of basic strategic principles. Subsequent decisions and policies on doctrine, procurement, and the size, shape, and posture of Taiwan's armed forces would then flow logically from these principles."[224] When strategy is overly vague, however, it cannot perform this critical prioritization function or serve as a guide to decisionmakers, who must necessarily make trade-offs when it comes to resource allocation.

Taiwan is still searching for a consensus on a reasonable defense strategy and thus lacks a meaningful guide to doctrine, procurement, and related defense policy issues. Some policymakers in Taiwan believe that the island's current strategy is "too passive." They favor a strategy focused on "active defense," one incorporating submarines, land-attack cruise missiles, and possibly short- and medium-range ballistic missiles, so that Taiwan will have at least a limited capability to inflict damage on China, which would allow it to complicate Chinese military planning and influence Beijing's decision calculus. Others, including many Pan-Blue politicians, see "offensive defense" as "potentially destabilizing."[225] According to some KMT politicians, developing capabilities to strike targets in China may be "psychologically satisfying and symbolically important, but it is ultimately unrealistic."[226] Moreover, they argue that launching strikes against targets on the mainland could jeopardize relations with the United States and cost Taiwan the moral high ground in a cross-Strait conflict. Consequently, as Denny Roy puts it, "Taiwan's defense strategy exhibits parts of different approaches rather than a coherent, underlying logic linking bedrock assumptions with principles, doctrine, and force structure."[227] This remains one of Taiwan's fundamental defense policy problems.

Second, Taiwan's defense budget has declined in most years since the mid-1990s and remained relatively flat in recent years even as China's defense spending has increased sharply. As the US Department of Defense's 2006 report on Chinese military capabilities points out, "Taiwan's defense spending has steadily declined in real terms over the past decade, even as Chinese air, naval, and missile force modernization has increased the need for defense measures that would enable Taiwan to maintain a credible self-defense."[228] As noted previously, Taiwan's 2007 defense budget increase was a step in the right direction, and there appears to be an emerging consensus on increasing Taiwan's annual defense spending to about 3 percent of gross domestic product, but even this may not be enough to fulfill the island's defense requirements.

The Taiwan military faces a number of other problems as well. Although the island is making some progress in improving its ability to conduct joint operations, many officers in Taiwan argue that jointness exists "more on paper than in practice."[229] In particular, military officers point to weaknesses in the planning process. Another problem is that Taiwan's professional military education system "remains in a state of uncertainty."[230] Its consolidation and organizational restructuring program was suspended in 2004 due to bureaucratic resistance, and civilian students have not yet been integrated into the ROC's National Defense University, even though the corresponding curriculum has already been developed.

Conclusion

In the 1980s and throughout much of the 1990s, the PLA's numerous shortcomings left Chinese leaders with few if any credible options to use force against Taiwan. The accelerated pace of PLA modernization since the late 1990s, however, has given Beijing a variety of increasingly credible military options. Although standard realist and neorealist theories of international relations predict vigorous balancing under these circumstances, Taiwan's response to this growing security challenge has been less rapid and comprehensive than might be expected given the scope of the growing security threat. For example, the 2006 Department of Defense report on Chinese military power characterizes Taiwan's defense modernization efforts as "modest," and warns that they are insufficient given continuing improvements in Chinese military capabilities.[231] Consequently, the cross-Strait military balance is tilting toward China. According to the same report, "The cross-Strait military balance is shifting in the mainland's favor as a result of Beijing's sustained economic growth, increased diplomatic leverage, and improvements in military capabilities based within striking range of Taiwan."[232]

The shift in the cross-Strait military balance means that Taiwan probably would be unable to successfully defend itself against a major Chinese use of force without significant US military intervention. That said, however, the most appropriate yardstick for Taiwan's military modernization and defense reform efforts is not the ability to defeat a major Chinese attack without US assistance, a task that is most likely becoming impossible given the vast power asymmetries between Taiwan and China. Instead, Taiwan needs to develop capabilities sufficient to maintain resistance against a determined Chinese attack until US forces could intervene decisively, within one to two weeks. Even though Taiwan cannot realistically hope to compete with China in an arms race, it should strive to raise the costs of Chinese military action and sustain its defense for long enough to allow third-party intervention. Even by this standard, however, Taiwan's position has eroded considerably in recent years. According to Mark Stokes, "Taiwan's ability to sustain a resistance used to be measured in terms of months or weeks. Now it is measured in terms of days."[233] The implications for Taiwan's national security are extremely troubling. Even if China never uses force to attempt to resolve the Taiwan issue on its terms, the shift in the cross-Strait balance of military power is likely to further erode Taiwan's bargaining leverage in any future cross-Strait negotiations.

Even more worrisome from Washington's perspective is Taiwan's tendency to risk taking potentially provocative steps toward formal independence even as the cross-Strait military balance shifts toward China. Indeed, the combination of President Chen's apparent willingness to test China's limits and the legislature's reluctance to support the large-scale investments required to prevent a further deterioration of the island's military position has serious implications for US-Taiwan relations. After the George W. Bush administration came into office, public pledges to defend Taiwan and approval of an unprecedented arms sales package reflected a strengthened US commitment to the island's security. By late 2003, however, Washington felt increasingly compelled to persuade President Chen to moderate his proindependence rhetoric and refrain from taking any steps toward formal independence that would run the risk of provoking a conflict with China. Moreover, the Bush administration repeatedly encouraged Taiwan to increase its defense spending and to approve funding to complete the long-delayed arms purchase. Taiwan's approach to dealing with China, and the seemingly sluggish pace of its defense modernization initiatives, created a considerable amount of friction in US-Taiwan relations. To better understand Taiwan's security policy, we must focus on three key factors—security ties, threat perceptions, and domestic politics—and the roles they play in shaping the island's seemingly puzzling response to a growing external security threat.

PART 2

Focusing on Key Factors

CHAPTER 6

Security Ties

Taiwan's informal security relationship with the United States has played an important role in shaping the island's national security and defense policy decisions, influencing its response to Chinese military modernization since the early 1980s. More than a few observers in the United States and elsewhere have characterized Taiwan's response to Chinese military modernization as a classic case of "free-riding." Indeed, this is perhaps the predominant view in Washington policy circles, with many analysts arguing that Taiwan is underspending on defense and pushing the envelope in terms of its pursuit of formal independence because its leaders believe the United States will continue to protect the island from China no matter what they do. According to this line of analysis, leaders in Taipei are convinced that US security assurances are essentially a "blank check," which allows them to dismiss US warnings about the potential consequences of failing to devote adequate resources to their own defense or unnecessarily provoking China as nothing more than hollow threats.

It is certainly true that great powers' threats to abandon smaller allies are sometimes found lacking in credibility, and free-riding is clearly part of the explanation for Taiwan's response to Chinese military modernization. At the same time, however, the full story is far more complicated than popular portrayals of Taiwan's defense policy, which tend to suggest the island is simply free-riding by shifting the burden of its defense onto the shoulders of the United States because it believes the US military would intervene on its behalf under virtually all imaginable circumstances. Indeed, Taiwan's perceptions of the US security commitment have changed over time, and different actors in Taiwan have held different views about the nature of the US commitment to Taiwan's defense, largely because Taipei has simultaneously had reasons for both confidence in the US security commitment and concern about the possibility of abandonment.

Taiwan's Changing Views

From the time that Washington shifted recognition to Beijing and announced that it would withdraw from the US–Republic of China (ROC) defense treaty, Taiwan could no longer count on US military support. As Yang Chih-heng puts it, "Chiang Ching-kuo and Taiwan had to face communist China by themselves. In terms of military strategy, Taiwan had to consider how to defend itself with no guaranteed support from the USA."[1] To be sure, Taipei in the 1980s and 1990s had a number of reasons to fear the possibility of abandonment, such as the 1982 US-China arms sales communiqué, Washington's decision to refrain from selling the FX fighter to Taiwan, and improvements in US-China relations, which even included a number of security cooperation programs and arrangements. At the same time, however, Taiwan also had several reasons for confidence in implicit US security guarantees, such as the 1979 Taiwan Relations Act, continued arms sales, strong congressional backing for Taiwan, and the sharp contrast between the communist regime in China and the emerging democratic system in Taiwan, which became especially pronounced after the 4 June 1989 Tiananmen crackdown. The Bill Clinton administration's decision to dispatch two aircraft carrier battle groups to the area around the island during the 1995–1996 Taiwan Strait crisis underscored the importance the United States attached to Taiwan's security and suggested that Taipei had strong reason to believe that the United States would become involved in a future cross-Strait crisis.

On balance, Taipei seemed to believe that the United States was likely to provide military support if a war broke out in the Taiwan Strait. Indeed, in the late 1990s, senior officials in Taiwan were generally confident that the United States would intervene in a cross-Strait conflict and that the prospect of US intervention was sufficient to deter China.[2] For example, former president Lee Teng-hui stated that it would be "impossible" for China to attack Taiwan, arguing that the mainland would not dare attack the island as long as it was under the protection of the United States.[3] Moreover, Lee suggested that the purchase of US weapons was needed to maintain US-Taiwan relations and avoid charges that Taipei was free-riding on US security assurances. "You can't take a bus without paying for it," Lee said.[4] The implication was that arms purchases from the United States served to strengthen ties with Washington and symbolized US support.

This confidence carried over after the Democratic Progressive Party (DPP) won the 2000 presidential election. Indeed, for at least the first three years of President Chen Shui-bian's first term, policymakers in Taiwan seemed to remain confident that the United States had the capability and the will to act quickly and decisively if China ever attempted to use force against Taiwan. Taipei had a number of good reasons for this high level of confidence, such as growing security cooperation with the United States and President George W. Bush's statement that the United States would do "whatever it takes" to help Taiwan defend itself. Consequently, as many foreign observers noted, the Chen administration appeared highly confident that the United States would help defend Taiwan in the event of a cross-Strait conflict. Taiwan's high level of confidence in the early part of President Bush's first term, however, stands in stark contrast to its mounting anxiety since Bush's December 2003 statement that Washington would oppose unilateral changes in the status quo by Taiwan and repeated admonitions by administration officials and prominent members of Congress about Taiwan's failure to approve funding for the April 2001 arms sales package. According to one observer, "The apparent decline in positive U.S. feeling toward Taiwan sent political shock waves through the island."[5]

The recent comments of senior officials appear to reflect these growing concerns. For example, in a September 2004 speech to military personnel, President Chen said, "Taiwan's national security is held in our own hands. . . . [W]e cannot afford to engage in any wishful thinking that enemies will show us goodwill or that friends will come to our aid."[6] In addition, in a speech at a National Day rally on 10 October 2005, Chen said, "We cannot expect to rely on others for Taiwan's own self-defense. We must shoulder the responsibilities to build up sufficient national defense, psychological defense, and civil defense."[7]

For its part, the military leadership also appears to harbor serious concerns that the United States might not come to the rescue in the event of a war with China. Indeed, some senior military officers are quite skeptical about the reliability of the US commitment to Taiwan's defense. Some of this could be attributed to the tendency toward worst-case planning and the requirement to prepare for a cross-Strait conflict under circumstances in which third-party intervention is at least somewhat less than certain, but the skepticism of senior military officers is also rooted in concerns that Washington might sacrifice Taiwan in the interests of maintaining stability in US-China relations, especially given China's growing strength and increasing international influence. Given this uncertainty, Taiwan cannot assume US involvement as the basis for military planning. Indeed, Hu Chen-pu, director of the Ministry of National Defense's General Political Warfare Bureau, stated in February 2006 that the island's defense plans do not assume that the United States or other countries will provide assistance to Taiwan: "The U.S. has never promised to come to Taiwan's aid in the event of cross-Strait hostilities. Nor has Taiwan anticipated such aid from the U.S., for we can never be sure if it would render us assistance."[8]

Some politicians in Taiwan have also stated that they believe the United States would be less likely to come to the island's aid if the ROC military was unable to sustain at least somewhat effective resistance in the face of a

Chinese attack. For example, in late 2005, David Lee, Taiwan's top representative in Washington, told Legislative Yuan members he was concerned that Washington would not intervene on Taiwan's behalf if the island's defense collapsed rapidly under the pressure of Chinese coercion: "If Taiwan is in ruins, the United States will not come to the island's aid."[9] ROC military officers have also warned that the United States would be far less likely to intervene if doing so meant "liberating" a defeated Taiwan by driving Chinese occupation forces from the island. They argue that Taiwan's importance to the United States is not great enough to justify the commitment that would be required to reverse a successful Chinese invasion and occupation of Taiwan. In the words of retired rear admiral Ting Chien-ching of the ROC navy:

> In all fairness, Taiwan's strategic position cannot be overlooked, but compared to Kuwait, if Taiwan had already fallen into enemy hands, would the United States lead a multi-national force to recover Taiwan? So we must be able to go on long enough, until the United States can mobilize the force to intervene. . . . If Taiwan is still holding out, the United States will send troops to the rescue, possibly. If Taiwan has already fallen, it would not be important enough to lead a multi-national force to counter-attack.[10]

Beyond Taipei's long-standing concerns about whether it is truly possible to rely on Washington's ambiguous security assurances, some leaders in Taiwan appear to have concluded that free-riding would have some potentially serious disadvantages, even if they could get away with it. In particular, some policymakers in Taipei are concerned that depending on the United States would undermine Taiwan's interests by reducing its bargaining leverage in US-Taiwan relations. For example, Premier Yu Shyi-kun in September 2004 cautioned that excessive reliance on the United States would leave Taiwan with little bargaining leverage: "If we completely depend on the United States in defense affairs, we'll fall to U.S. control."[11]

Concerns about the reliability of US security assurances are widespread in Taipei, but they are by no means universal. Indeed, some politicians and policymakers in Taiwan continue to believe that the United States would come to the rescue under almost any imaginable circumstances, and seem unconcerned about the potential downside of relying on the United States to provide security for Taiwan. For example, Parris Chang, a presidential adviser and former legislator known for his controversial comments, has stated that he believes the United States would definitely intervene if China attacked Taiwan. Chang has also asserted that Japan would almost surely become involved, citing the February 2005 US-Japan joint statement that identified stability in the Taiwan Strait as a common security objective.[12] Similarly, DPP legislator Chian Chau-yi said in April 2005, following a visit to Washington by a delegation of DPP politicians, that the United States would defend Taiwan if China attempted to use force to upset the status quo in cross-Strait relations.[13] The broad range of views on this topic likely derives at least in part from the fact that Taiwan has both reasons for confidence in the US security commitment and causes for concern about the possibility that Washington would abandon the island rather than risk a war with China.

Reasons for Confidence

Notwithstanding public comments of senior Taipei officials about the need for independent defense capabilities, these leaders may still have several good reasons to be fairly confident that Washington would come to the island's aid in the event of a cross-Strait crisis or conflict. First, the Taiwan Relations Act of 1979 remains the cornerstone of US policy toward Taiwan. Although the act does not obligate the United States to intervene militarily in a cross-Strait conflict, it does indicate that any Chinese attempt to use force against Taiwan would be a grave concern for Washington. Second, the dispatch of the two aircraft carrier battle groups in response to Chinese exercises and missile launches in 1996 underscored the importance the United States attaches to maintaining peace and stability in the region and protecting Taiwan's freedom and democracy. As Bernard Cole points out, following the 1995–1996 crisis, Beijing was not the only party that concluded that a China-Taiwan conflict would almost certainly lead to US military intervention. The US decision to deploy the aircraft carriers most likely led Taipei to the same conclusion.[14]

Third, the April 2001 arms sales decision and President Bush's statement that the United States would do "whatever it takes" to defend Taiwan suggested to some observers in Taiwan that Washington was discarding its traditional policy of "strategic ambiguity" in favor of a new approach based on greater clarity. US officials have generally refrained from making similarly categorical statements since President Bush's comments. In May 2006, however, Deputy Secretary of State Robert Zoellick suggested that the United States would defend Taiwan even if the island declared independence. In a question and answer session following testimony before the House International Relations Committee, Zoellick said, "We have to be very careful. . . . [T]he balance is that we want to be supportive of Taiwan while we're not encouraging those that try to move towards independence. Because let me be very clear: independence means war, and that means American soldiers."[15] Although Zoellick's comments were not intended to convey the message that the United States was giving Taiwan a blank check, the wording appeared to suggest a belief on the part of senior officials that the United States would likely end up intervening in a cross-Strait war even if it was a provocative action on Taiwan's part that sparked the conflict. Presumably, this statement reinforced Taipei's belief that the United States would likely become involved in any cross-Strait crisis or conflict, despite subsequent clarifications.

Fourth, Taiwan has historically enjoyed very strong support in the US Congress, in part as a result of its world-class lobbying and public relations skills. Democratization in Taiwan has further enhanced the island's appeal, especially when the democratic reforms in Taiwan are contrasted with continuing one-party rule and repression of dissent on the mainland. At the same time, however, some members of Congress are becoming increasingly irritated with the island's failure to purchase the weapons that Washington agreed to sell it in April 2001 (discussed in greater detail below), and with Taiwan's sometimes provocative actions that have the potential to further roil cross-Strait relations.

Fifth, the defense of Taiwan is linked to the credibility of other US security commitments in the region and to broader US strategic interests. Playing up this theme, Pan-Green politicians in Taiwan have tried to persuade US officials that China's growing power is a threat not only to Taiwan, but also to US predominance in the Asia Pacific more broadly. In a June 2005 interview, for example, Foreign Minister Chen Tan-sun warned, "China is trying to push away American influence in Asia."[16] Similarly, in a November 2006 speech, Mainland Affairs Council chairman Joseph Wu asserted that Chinese acquisition of midair refueling aircraft suggests a desire on Beijing's part to project military power throughout Asia; Wu also stated that Taiwan represents a "stumbling block" that the People's Liberation Army (PLA) must overcome if China is to mount a broader challenge to US interests in the region.[17] Moreover, some analysts in Taiwan have suggested that the island will likely benefit from concerns in the United States about China's potential to challenge US strategic dominance in Asia. For example, Ou Si-fu, an analyst at the Institute for National Policy Research, has argued that the United States is highly unlikely to abandon its commitment to Taiwan's defense, even if Taiwan does little to boost its own capabilities, in large part because its commitment to Taiwan's security is part of a broader policy that supports US strategic interests in East Asia.[18]

Given the above factors, some US analysts argue that leaders in Taipei are probably correct to believe that the United States would defend Taiwan against a Chinese attack under virtually any conceivable circumstances, even if the conflict resulted from Taiwan crossing one of Beijing's "red lines." Taiwan's leaders, they argue, can be reasonably confident that the United States would defend the island under virtually any circumstances, and this greatly limits Washington's influence. Similarly, in a recent book, Ted Galen Carpenter argues that mixed messages from the United States encourage proindependence politicians to push the envelope, "because they are so confident that the US will defend them under any circumstances."[19] Even if this confidence is misplaced, the perception that US support is virtually unconditional clearly influences Taipei's foreign policy and national security decisionmaking process.

Some US policy decisions and public statements during the early part of President Bush's first term, such as the statement about doing "whatever it takes" to defend Taiwan, may have inadvertently exacerbated this problem. These decisions and statements may very well have unintentionally increased Taiwan's willingness to undertake potentially provocative action and diminished its incentives to devote greater resources to its own defense. According to a February 2006 article, for example, the April 2001 arms sales decision and the "whatever it takes" comment emboldened proindependence politicians in Taiwan, leaving them confident that they could provoke Beijing while relying on US military support: "The concern that is growing . . . is that Taiwan is being politically provocative to Beijing while declining to boost its own defenses, largely because President Chen seems convinced that American protection is guaranteed."[20] Moreover, Taipei sometimes received mixed messages from different people in the Bush administration. Most notably, during President Chen's late 2003 transit stop in New York, Therese Shaheen, at that time head of the Washington office of the American Institute in Taiwan, stated that President Bush was Taiwan's "secret guardian angel," a message that appeared to imply that US support for Taiwan was unconditional. Shaheen also voiced support for President Chen's plans to hold a referendum concurrently with Taiwan's 2004 presidential election even as other US officials were expressing serious concerns that the initiative was potentially destabilizing.[21] Interviews with Taiwanese officials suggest that Taipei tended to give more weight to the favorable messages than the unfavorable ones, and that some of President Chen's advisers may have interpreted certain comments as evidence of virtually unconditional US support for Taiwan. At the very least, these contradictory messages increased the possibility that Taiwan would misinterpret US policy, and they may even have led some in Taiwan to conclude that US support was basically ensured under any and all circumstances.

Finally, the likelihood that Taiwan would be unable to defeat a determined PLA attack absent third-party intervention seems to have led some ROC policymakers to the conclusion that Taiwan has few realistic options other than depending on the United States, and that Washington has few realistic options other than continuing to support Taiwan. Senior ROC officials indicate that Taiwan has neither the willingness nor the ability to engage in an all-out arms race with China. As one former ROC government official put it, "To be candid, we must rely on the US for security."[22] Paradoxically, this very weakness may reduce US leverage, since carrying out any threat to write off Taiwan would leave the island so vulnerable that the outcome would likely harm US interests as well. For example, if the US threatened to abandon Taiwan, the island's growing military vulnerability might tempt Beijing to behave more aggressively than it would if the prospect of US intervention were still on the table, since the possibility of US involvement in a cross-Strait conflict makes the potential risks and expected costs of using force considerably higher for China. Alternatively, if the United States indicated that it would no longer support Taiwan politically and militarily, Taiwan's leaders might elect to develop nuclear weapons to deter China from using force, potentially sparking an otherwise avoidable cross-Strait conflagration.

Causes for Concern

These factors notwithstanding, since 1980, Taipei has had serious causes for concern about the possibility the United States would not intervene on its behalf in the event of a cross-Strait crisis, especially if Taipei's actions were seen to have provoked the conflict. In addition, since about 2003, Taipei has had reason to question not only Washington's willingness to intervene, but also its capability to do so quickly and effectively.

US Willingness to Intervene in a Cross-Strait Conflict

Taiwan's concerns about the possibility of US abandonment intensified as US-China relations progressed toward normalization in the 1970s.[23] Taiwan's fear of US abandonment and the heavy costs of conventional defense even led to interest in developing nuclear weapons; the island's nuclear weapons program, however, was ultimately given up under US pressure.[24] By the end of the decade, anxiety was so high that many businesspeople and even some government officials were sending family members to the United States and making plans to flee the island in case the withdrawal of US support led to disaster. The very limited advance notice Washington provided to Taiwan ahead of President Jimmy Carter's announcement of the normalization of relations with Beijing sparked considerable resentment and deepened Taiwan's concerns about US intentions. In 1980, the ROC government increased the defense budget by 12.4 percent, even though military spending was already a considerable drain. Although President Ronald Reagan's victory in the 1980 presidential election seemed to augur well for Taiwan, relatively little changed in US policy toward China and Taiwan when he took office. Indeed, Reagan declined to sell the FX fighter to Taiwan and signed the August 1982 US-China communiqué, in which Washington indicated that the United States would reduce its arms sales to Taiwan. Human rights abuses under Kuomintang rule were another source of friction in the US-Taiwan relationship in the 1980s. This became much less of an issue after the 1989 Tiananmen crackdown, which demonstrated in dramatic fashion that China remained a repressive, one-party state even as communism was crumbling in Eastern Europe and Taiwan was becoming a vibrant democracy.

In recent years, however, concerns about the possibility of US abandonment have once again moved to the forefront in Taiwan. Many in Taiwan are becoming increasingly concerned about US willingness to intervene in a future cross-Strait crisis. Indeed, Taiwan's concerns about the strength of the US commitment seem to have increased since President George W. Bush's December 2003 statement that the United States would oppose any efforts to disrupt the status quo, whether they were undertaken by Beijing or Taipei. Most recently, at least some officials in Taiwan were concerned by US opposition to President Chen's decision to hold a referendum on seeking admission to the United Nations under the name "Taiwan." US officials stated that the wording of the referendum question contradicted President Chen's previous assurances that he would not attempt to officially change the island's name and threatened to destabilize the cross-Strait status quo. The Bush administration's concerns were underscored by Thomas Christensen, deputy assistant secretary of state for East Asian and Pacific affairs, in a September 2007 speech at the US-Taiwan Business Council's annual defense industry conference: "Taiwan's security is inextricably linked to the avoidance of needlessly provocative behavior. This does not mean that Taipei should or can be passive in the face of PRC pressure. But it means that responsible leadership in Taipei has to anticipate potential Chinese red lines and reactions and avoid unnecessary and unproductive provocations."[25] These comments, which one seasoned observer described as a "tough love" message to Taiwan, emphasized that the United States opposes assertions of independence that are potentially destabilizing and not in the interests of Taiwan or the United States. The growing bluntness of US statements to this effect in recent years appears to have led some in Taiwan to consider the possibility that US intervention in a cross-Strait conflict is not a given, especially if Washington were to conclude that Taiwan's leaders had sparked the crisis.

The Bush administration has criticized Taipei not only for undertaking political actions that run the risk of provoking China, by creating the impression that it is intent on changing the cross-Strait status quo, but also for failing to spend more money on its own defense. In particular, several high-level US defense and foreign policy officials have publicly expressed the Bush administration's frustration over Taiwan's inability to move forward, for more than six years, with the arms sales approved in April 2001. This irritation with the weapons procurement delay became increasingly evident, and US criticism of Taiwan became increasingly strident, as the domestic political debate in Taiwan deepened.

Some of the strongest rebukes came from senior Defense Department and State Department officials, including several officials who entered office very favorably disposed toward Taiwan. For example, in a speech at the 2004 US-Taiwan Business Council's defense industry conference, Richard Lawless, deputy undersecretary of defense for Asian and Pacific affairs, warned that failure to pass the special budget would have potentially serious consequences for US-Taiwan relations: "If the budget fails to pass . . . that failure will have repercussions in the United States, will have repercussions for Taiwan's friends, and it will be regarded as a signal . . . as to the attitude of the legislature toward national defense for Taiwan."[26] The Bush administration delivered an even more sharply worded message at the next annual defense industry conference of the US-Taiwan Business Council. In September 2005, Edward Ross, a senior Defense Security Cooperation Agency official, said, "As the lone superpower, our interests are plentiful and our attention short . . . we cannot help defend you if you cannot defend yourself." Ross also delivered a blunt message suggesting that Washington would not tolerate free-riding: "It is time that the people of Taiwan and their elected officials understand that when it comes to defense, they, and not the United States nor any third party, are in the first instance accountable."[27] That same month, State Department official James Keith, at a congressional hearing, expressed Washington's growing frustration with Taipei's failure to pass the special budget: "Our position is that we need to see a response. This is an issue that requires results and we would like to see Taipei do whatever it takes to get it done."[28]

Perhaps most important, given Taiwan's long-standing support in Congress, recent criticism of Taiwan has not been limited to the executive branch. Congress has also expressed a great deal of frustration about Taiwan's apparent unwillingness to increase its defense spending. Indeed, what is most worrisome from Taiwan's perspective is this growing chorus of frustration among many of the island's traditional supporters in Congress. Statements by several prominent members of Congress suggest that even some of the island's staunchest backers are losing patience with Taiwan. In September 2005, for example, Representative Rob Simmons, a Connecticut Republican, said that, given the island's failure to approve the special budget, the United States should conclude that "Taiwan's leadership is not serious about the security of its people or its freedom." Consequently, Simmons warned that the United States might not be willing to defend Taiwan if the island was unwilling to pay the costs of improving its own defense posture. As Simmons put it, "The American People have come to the aid of foreign countries in the name of freedom many times in our history; but Americans will not in good conscious support countries that are unwilling to defend themselves."[29] Similarly, Richard D'Amato, chairman of the US-China Economic and Security Review Commission, chastised Taiwan for "demonstrating a remarkable lack of urgency in approving the arms sale." D'Amato complained that the delays raised questions about Taiwan's willingness to "foot the bill" for its own defense.[30] And Ohio Republican Steve Chabot, cochair of the House Taiwan Caucus, warned that the Legislative Yuan's unwillingness to pass the special budget would undermine congressional support for Taiwan: "I believe that many members of Congress who have long supported Taiwan, including myself, will re-evaluate the degree of their support for the island if Taiwan does not pass the bill."[31]

Most recently, in March 2006, Republican senator John Warner, chairman of the Senate Armed Services Committee, delivered what was perhaps one of the bluntest warnings Washington has ever delivered to Taipei: "If a conflict with China were to be aided by inappropriate and wrongful politics generated by the Taiwanese elected officials, I am not entirely sure this nation would come full force to their rescue."[32] Newspapers in Taiwan were quick to pick up on Warner's statement, and many interpreted it as a serious warning, particularly coming from an influential figure known for his record of strong support for Taiwan.

Comments such as these are clearly intended to send a message to Taipei. According to Mark Stokes, a former Department of Defense official who was responsible for security cooperation with Taiwan, "There is an implicit threat contained in messages emanating from Washington: American support for Taiwan will diminish if Taiwan is not willing to invest the proper resources in self-defense."[33] Although the extent to which that message will produce the intended results remains uncertain, Washington's frustration with the Chen administration's approach to cross-Strait relations, and its inability to win support for the special budget clearly, have left some analysts in Taipei concerned about the potential implications for US-Taiwan relations and the US commitment to the island's security. According to Lai I-chung, a researcher at the Taiwan Think Tank, "Taiwan-US relations appear to have changed in the past four years. Compared to President Bush's statement when he was first inaugurated that the US would assist Taiwan in defending itself, his current stance reflects much more doubt."[34] Similarly, a number of Pan-Green politicians have expressed concern that failure to pass the special budget would lead Washington to question whether Taiwan is serious about its own defense: "We don't want our friends to have second guesses about our determination to defend Taiwan," Foreign Minister Chen Tan-sun told a US reporter in June 2005.[35] In addition, some DPP-affiliated analysts argue that the failure to pass the special budget may lead the United States to consider Taiwan a "lost cause," and speculate that Washington may abandon its commitment to the island's security.[36]

Another potential consideration for officials in Washington and Taipei is US public opinion. The traditional reluctance of the American people to commit troops to conflicts that seem to involve anything less than vital national security interests, and widespread dissatisfaction with the mounting costs of the Iraq War, would seem to cast doubt on public support for military intervention in a cross-Strait conflict. Indeed, recent polls suggest that there is little appetite for involvement in a war between China and Taiwan. For example, a 2006 public opinion survey conducted by the Chicago Council on Global Affairs found that less than one-third of Americans would favor the use of US troops if China attacked Taiwan.[37] The same study noted that only about 18 percent of Americans view the possibility of a cross-Strait conflict as a "critical threat" to US national security interests.[38]

Finally, some policymakers in Taiwan are becoming increasingly concerned about the possibility that the modernization of Chinese nuclear forces may diminish Washington's willingness to intervene in a cross-Strait conflict.[39] ROC military officers have also expressed concerns about the potential implications of the modernization of PRC strategic forces.[40]

US Ability to Intervene Quickly and Decisively in a Cross-Strait Conflict

During the 1980s and 1990s, the United States had more than enough capability to intervene decisively in the event of a cross-Strait conflict. Indeed, the involvement of US forces would almost certainly have resulted in a Chinese defeat. Moreover, as of the late 1990s, even relatively limited US intervention—perhaps two aircraft carrier battle groups, a single land-based fighter wing, and a dozen bombers—would have been more than enough to repulse a Chinese invasion attempt, according to RAND modeling.[41] Leaders in Taipei may have had reasons to doubt Washington's willingness to defend the island, but they had little reason to doubt that the United States had the capability to turn the tide should it decide to become involved militarily in a cross-Strait war.

In recent years, however, the capability of the United States to intervene rapidly and decisively in the event of a China-Taiwan conflict has been questioned. From Taiwan's point of view, the picture is mixed. Although the US military is developing and deploying a number of new high-tech weapon systems, strengthening its presence in the Asia Pacific, and enhancing cooperation with key partners like Japan, it has also stretched itself thin because of ongoing commitments to the global "war on terror" and major deployments to Afghanistan and Iraq, which have diminished its ability to respond to crises in other parts of the world. In particular, the Iraq War has created severe readiness and training problems for US ground forces.[42]

The US Department of Defense is preparing to field a series of advanced air and naval capabilities. Over the next several decades, the military is to deploy an impressive array of advanced hardware, including the F-22A "Raptor" fighter, the joint-strike fighter, the Virginia-class attack submarine, the littoral combat system, and the next-generation DD(X) destroyer. The Defense Department is also accelerating plans to develop and deploy a new long-range strike capability, enhancing its unmanned aerial vehicle capabilities, developing a joint unmanned-combat air system, and preparing to place precision-guided conventional warheads on some Trident submarine-launched ballistic missiles. In addition, the United States is continuing to improve its intelligence, surveillance, and reconnaissance (ISR) capabilities. China's growing military power is certainly not the only factor driving US procurement plans, but is still among the key justifications for many of these new systems.

The Pentagon is also strengthening the US military presence in the Asia Pacific, shifting considerable resources to the region as part of a strategy designed at least in part to hedge against China's emergence as a major regional military power.[43] As part of the Pentagon's increased focus on the Asia Pacific, the US military is deploying additional aircraft to Guam and additional attack submarines to the Pacific theater. The United States is also planning to deploy Patriot PAC-3 missile defense batteries to protect US air bases and other key facilities in Japan. In addition, the US Pacific Command (PACOM) has conducted several major exercises in the region in recent years, the most recent of which, "Valiant Shield," was conducted in June 2006 and involved an impressive display of US air and naval power. Of particular note, a Chinese delegation observed this exercise at the invitation of Admiral William J. Fallon, commander of PACOM.

The United States is also strengthening its security ties with Japan and other key countries in the region. Most importantly, in February 2005, the United States and Japan identified Taiwan's security as a "common strategic objective." In May 2006, senior officials from the United States and Japan reaffirmed their mutual interest in Taiwan's security during high-level security cooperation meetings held in Washington. Moreover, recent US Department of Defense publications reflect this increasing emphasis on the Asia Pacific region. The 2006 *Quadrennial Defense Review*, for example, identifies China as one of the greatest potential security challenges facing the United States: "Of the major and emerging powers, China has the greatest potential to compete militarily with the United States and field disruptive military technologies that could over time off set traditional U.S. military advantages absent U.S. counter strategies."[44] To be sure, all of these developments should give Taiwan greater confidence in the ability of the United States to help protect the island's security. For example, ROC military officers note that the growing US military presence on Guam will strengthen Washington's ability to intervene in a cross-Strait conflict.[45]

Despite the growing US presence in the Asia Pacific and the strengthening of US-Japan security ties, US military intervention in a Taiwan Strait crisis would face several potentially serious operational and diplomatic constraints. First, improvements in Chinese military capabilities would make US intervention a much more costly proposition than it was at the time of the 1995–1996 Taiwan Strait crisis. In March 2006 congressional testimony, Assistant Secretary of Defense Peter Rodman indicated that Washington would face a much more difficult decision today than it did it 1996 when it dispatched two aircraft carrier strike groups to the area in response to Chinese military exercises and missile tests. As Rodman put it, "There's a here and now problem, given how much China has advanced since say ten years ago. . . . [A]n American president facing a similar situation would have a different calculus given the extraordinary improvement in China's capabilities."[46] Some observers in Taiwan are becoming increasingly concerned about these developments. For example, in January 2007, several ROC observers expressed concerns about the implications of China's successful test of a kinetic-kill-vehicle antisatellite weapon.[47] Lin Chong-pin, former vice minister of national defense and now a professor at Tamkang University, assessed that the PRC's demonstration of an antisatellite capability would have an "indirect impact on Taiwan's security." According to Lin, as a result of the PRC's development of this new capability, the United States "may no longer be as effective as in 1996 when it comes to rendering military aid to the island."[48]

Second, the distance many forces would need to travel from their home bases to the area surrounding Taiwan would delay the bulk of US intervention, perhaps by as long as several weeks, unless those forces were already deployed in the area around Taiwan in response to heightened tensions. Although US military aircraft stationed in Japan, South Korea, and Guam would be able to intervene much more quickly, the distances they would need to cover to reach the Taiwan Strait area would reduce their effectiveness, especially in the case of fighters based on Guam.[49] Finally, the extent to which key allied countries such as Japan, South Korea, Australia, and the Philippines would support US military operations in the event of a cross-Strait conflict is uncertain at best. Indeed, there is ample reason to doubt that these countries would want to become involved at all. China's growing regional economic power and diplomatic clout would make regional leaders very reluctant to choose sides. Moreover, recent public opinion polling indicates that few people in the region see a China-Taiwan conflict as a major threat to vital national security interests in their countries. For example, according to a recent survey by the Chicago Council on Global Affairs, only about 33 percent of Australians see a China-Taiwan conflict as a critical threat.[50] In South Korea, the percentage is even lower, suggesting that leaders in Seoul would face strong domestic political constraints if a cross-Strait conflict erupted and the United States requested military assistance.

Perhaps most important, Washington's focus on the global "war on terror" and the mounting costs of the Iraq War suggest that Taiwan's leaders should doubt not only whether the United States would be willing to come to the rescue in the event of a war with China, but also whether it is truly capable of intervening decisively. In particular, the deployment of large numbers of US ground troops in Iraq and Afghanistan is constraining the US military's ability to provide such forces for other contingencies and ensure adequate training for war-fighting and stability operations, according to a recent RAND study. The large-scale deployments also create considerable manpower and personnel policy challenges. According to the RAND report, US ground forces are "stretched thin," and there are no easy fixes barring a substantial decrease in current deployment requirements.[51] Although the US military's ground forces have probably paid the heaviest price, other branches have been heavily taxed as well. Indeed, as Bernard Cole points out:

> Washington's post–September 11, 2001 "Global War on Terrorism" . . . continues in 2005 to place very heavy demands on US military resources in areas far from the Taiwan theater. While the commitments in Afghanistan, Iraq, and elsewhere are most heavily impacting the Army and Marine Corps, the Navy and Air Force are also stretched thin. Significant U.S. military intervention in a Taiwan scenario will require the transfer of forces from other commitments around the world. Furthermore, the costs of these conflicts will extend well beyond actual combat, as the United States will require significant time and money to restore its military weapons, supplies, and manpower from the ravages of the Iraqi commitment.[52]

This should concern military planners and civilian policymakers in Taipei, because the deployment of US forces in Iraq, Afghanistan, and elsewhere may very well reduce the US capability to defend Taiwan. Still, it remains unclear how leaders in Taiwan view the potential implications of these developments.

Conclusion

Taiwan's security relationship with the United States is clearly a major factor in the island's security policy decisions. Although Taiwan has not been able to count on US military support since 1979, when Washington recognized Beijing and announced that it would withdraw from the US-ROC defense treaty, it has still retained some confidence that the United States would likely intervene in the event of a cross-Strait conflict. Its confidence was particularly bolstered in 2001 when President George W. Bush stated that the United States would do "whatever it takes" to defend Taiwan, and Washington approved an unprecedented arms sale package to the island. Since about 2003, however, Taiwan's confidence in the United States has diminished, given Washington's repeatedly expressed frustration with the Chen administration's tendency to risk provoking China and its failure to win approval for the 2001 arms sales package. Moreover, even if policymakers in

Taiwan remained convinced that the United States would defend the island from Chinese attack, they should still be concerned about US capabilities to intervene rapidly and decisively, especially given improvements in Chinese military capabilities and the rising costs of the US commitment in Iraq and the potential implications for the US military in areas such as manpower, training, readiness, and force modernization. Although free-riding may very well be part of the explanation for Taiwan's security policy, doubts about whether US support is truly a public good suggest that this is not the whole story.

CHAPTER 7

Threat Perceptions

Analysts often cite threat perceptions as a potential explanation for Taiwan's security policy, including its response to Chinese military modernization and its approach to cross-Strait relations. Many analysts in Washington argue that Taiwan simply does not take the Chinese military threat as seriously as it should. In particular, they argue that since the late 1990s, leaders in Taipei have consistently underestimated Beijing's willingness to use force to prevent or reverse any actions on Taiwan's part that Communist Party leaders see as a challenge to China's core national security interests, the party's grip on power, or their own political positions.

To be sure, Taiwan's perceptions of Chinese capabilities and intentions influence the island's security policy decisions, and it appears that Taiwan's threat perceptions interact with other factors, such as US security assurances and Taiwan's domestic political environment, in a way that helps explain Taiwan's security policy, including within the cross-Strait arena. One difficulty with this approach, however, is determining whose threat perceptions matter the most. This is especially problematic when there are differing opinions among key policymakers, politicians, and analysts, as is the case in Taiwan today. It is also important to note that Taiwan's transition to democracy resulted in broader participation in the policy process, which in turn increased the number of people whose views and perceptions matter. To address this difficult but vital issue requires understanding not only Taiwanese assessments of Chinese military capabilities, but also Taiwanese perceptions of Chinese intentions. The latter is particularly important, because decisionmakers consider not only military capabilities, but also perceived intentions, when evaluating the level of threat posed by a potential adversary.[1]

Taiwan's Threat Perceptions in the 1980s and 1990s

China's Military Capabilities

In the 1980s and 1990s, when Taiwan was undergoing a dramatic transformation from authoritarianism to democracy, most Republic of China (ROC) observers assessed that the Chinese military lacked the capability to invade the island. For example, the Legislative Yuan concluded in September 1994: "In the present stage the Communists do not have the capability to invade Taiwan."[2] At the time, most US analysts agreed with this assessment. Indeed, throughout the early to middle 1980s, most US observers judged that China was unlikely to attempt to invade Taiwan, given its limited military capability. The People's Liberation Army (PLA) had performed very poorly during the 1979 border conflict with Vietnam, demonstrating that it lacked the logistics, communications, and coordination capabilities required to conduct military operations against a moderately capable or advanced opponent. Moreover, because Sino-Soviet tension remained high, a considerable proportion of the Chinese military was dedicated to preparing to counter the massive Soviet military presence on the northern border of the People's Republic of China (PRC). In addition, the PLA simply lacked the amphibious lift capability that would have been required to move sufficient forces across the Taiwan Strait. All of these factors led to an assessment that whatever China's intentions, the PLA lacked the capability to use force against Taiwan, at least in the near to middle term.

Military analysts in Taiwan echoed this assessment. In particular, ROC military officers pointed out that, although the Chinese military was very large, its weak transport capabilities limited its ability to mount a successful amphibious invasion.[3] As one ROC military officer put it in a mid-1990s assessment of the PLA's ability to invade Taiwan:

> In estimating the capability for an armed invasion of Taiwan, the most important factor is transport capability. No matter how much manpower the Chinese Communists can muster, or how strong their troops are, if their transport strength cannot fully coordinate or is insufficient, then they cannot transport military forces to the battlefield, and they will not be able to fight the war. . . . [T]he Taiwan Strait is a military obstacle; if one wants to cross the Strait to invade Taiwan they must have adequate transport capability.[4]

The same ROC military officer also noted that, despite the PLA's numerical superiority, much of its equipment was woefully outdated: "At least half of the submarines, warships, aircraft, and tanks of the Communist armed forces are facing the need for replacement."[5] Given the PLA's numerous shortcomings, most analysts in Taiwan also assessed that China would have had a relatively slim chance of successfully undertaking a coercive campaign against the island. In particular, analysts in Taiwan generally doubted the Chinese military's capacity to enforce a blockade. For example, in the late 1980s, the ROC Ministry of National Defense assessed that China was "by no means able" to conduct a blockade against Taiwan, especially given the limitations of China's air power, the PLA air force's poor chances of gaining air superiority over the Taiwan Strait, and the PLA's logistics and supply weaknesses.[6] In addition, in the middle to late 1990s, the ROC assessed that China's conventional ballistic missile force was still fairly small, and that its missiles were relatively inaccurate, limiting their operational utility in a potential military campaign against Taiwan.

Despite these doubts about Chinese capabilities, by the middle to late 1990s many analysts had become concerned that the PLA was beginning to develop enough capability to undertake disruptive or coercive actions against Taiwan. In particular, China's military exercises and missile tests in 1995–1996 heightened concerns about the possibility that Beijing would use more saber-rattling, or perhaps even a limited use of force, to cause serious economic disruption. In addition, many analysts viewed even a failed Chinese invasion attempt as potentially disastrous for Taiwan. Indeed, some assessed that the PLA was likely capable of causing a tremendous amount of damage to the island, even if its invasion attempt produced military results that were less than fully satisfactory from a Chinese perspective. According to the same military officer cited above, for example, "If the Chinese Communists launch an invasion of Taiwan and take it into their heart to use arms to unify China, the end results, no matter whether they be 70 percent, or 90 percent, or even below 60 percent successful from the level of satisfaction of the Chinese Communists, will be catastrophic for Taiwan."[7]

China's Willingness to Employ Force

Beyond these military concerns, cross-Strait tensions seemed to be declining throughout much of the 1980s, as Beijing launched a series of new policy initiatives designed to woo Taiwan to the negotiating table and promote "peaceful reunification." Although the ROC spurned most of China's overtures, it seemed that the threat of military conflict was relatively remote. Indeed, throughout this period, most civilian and military leaders in Taiwan doubted that China would use force anytime soon. During the 1980s and early 1990s, this assessment was probably fairly accurate, but the 1995–1996 Taiwan Strait crisis caused Taiwan's stock market to plummet and left many observers in the United States concerned that China was increasingly likely to consider using force to resolve the Taiwan issue on its terms, or at least to prevent any changes in the situation that would diminish the long-term prospects for reunification. Many in Taiwan and the United States were also becoming increasingly worried about the potential economic and psychological impact of further Chinese saber-rattling. Nonetheless, within a few short years, it seemed that some officials and observers in Taiwan were once again beginning to doubt that Beijing was serious about using force against the island on a large scale, at least in the short term and absent a dramatic political provocation on Taiwan's part. Consequently, in the late 1990s, Taiwanese assessments of the possibility that China would use force began to diverge from those of many observers in the United States, who were becoming increasingly concerned that Beijing might resort to the military option, at least under certain circumstances.

Taiwan's Threat Perceptions Since 2000

The official threat assessments Taiwan has released since 2000 appear to reflect growing concern over the potential consequences of Chinese military modernization for the island's security. In its 2002 national defense report, for example, Taiwan's Ministry of National Defense warns that, as a result of improvements in Chinese military capabilities, "the PRC's threat against the ROC's security is ever increasing."[8] The report's analysis of Chinese military modernization highlights the PLA's increasing budget and growing military capability, which pose a "surging threat" to Taiwan's security.[9] Moreover, ROC defense officials assess that the modernization of the PLA is focused primarily on a Taiwan scenario. As one ROC military intelligence official stated in December 2004, "All their military equipment is completely directed against us."[10] Similarly, the ROC's 2006 national security report notes that the PLA has built mockups of some of Taiwan's major military bases and other critical facilities, and has conducted a number of military exercises simulating attacks on Taiwan.[11] At the same time, however, many ROC defense officials have suggested that the most dangerous period of time for Taiwan will not arrive until about 2010–2015, when they believe China will have developed an overwhelming military advantage. Perhaps more importantly, Taipei also seems to doubt Beijing's willingness to employ its growing military capability against the island. In addition, it is important to keep in mind that when policymakers in Taipei consider how to deal with China, they do not focus exclusively, or even primarily, on the military threat.

ROC officials and analysts regard the enhancement of Chinese military power as part of a much broader Chinese challenge to Taiwan's political, military, and economic security. Indeed, Taiwan's definition of national security encompasses much more than the cross-Strait military balance. According to Taiwan's 2006 national security report, the concept of national security includes military security, economic and financial security, information security, energy security, population and land conservation issues, epidemic prevention, and issues related to ethnicity and national identity.[12] Similarly, according to a recent article in *National Defense Magazine,* which is published by the ROC's National Defense University, China's growing power and influence threaten Taiwan's security in no fewer than six areas: politics, economics, psychology, information, military affairs, and science and technology.[13]

Taipei is particularly concerned about China's "united front" tactics and the potential long-term implications of increasing cross-Strait economic interaction. President Chen Shui-bian and his administration view Beijing's tactics, such as its recent courting of opposition leaders, as highly threatening to Taiwan's national security. Hu Chen-pu, head of the Ministry of National Defense's General Political Warfare Bureau, asserted that China's engagement of opposition leaders and Beijing's outwardly more relaxed attitude toward Taiwan were calculated to lessen the vigilance of Taiwan's people and undermine support for the procurement of arms from the United States.[14] Pan-Green politicians are also deeply concerned about China's growing economic power, increasing cross-Strait trade, and rising Taiwanese investment in China and technology transfer to the mainland. According to Foreign Minister Chen Tan-sun, for example, "If Taiwan depends too much on the Chinese market the Chinese could try to use the economic tie as a means to apply political pressure. This has already happened."[15]

Although policymakers in Taiwan define the threat to the island's national security rather broadly, and many tend to focus most heavily on the political and economic aspects of the threat, they certainly do not ignore military issues. Indeed, many view the military balance as an important part of the larger equation. Senior Democratic Progressive Party (DPP) officials have stated that they view China's increasing military muscle as a key element of a broader political, diplomatic, and economic threat to Taiwan's security. Indeed, senior ROC defense officials view the capabilities and readiness of the island's armed forces as important factors that help to maintain peace and stability. Moreover, politicians from both political camps state that if Taiwan is to protect its interests in any future dialogue with the PRC, it must be prepared to negotiate from a position of strength.[16]

China's Military Capabilities

In its public statements over the past few years, the ROC Ministry of National Defense has generally suggested that the military balance will soon begin tipping toward China, with trends worsening in the longer-term as China's military power continues to grow. For example, the ministry's 2004 national defense report stated that the cross-Strait military balance would begin to tilt in favor of China in 2006.[17] Furthermore, according to the report, "If the trend continues, the military balance between the two sides would tip against Taiwan after 2008, leaving Taiwan in an extremely unfavorable position."[18] Similarly, in April 2005, Vice Defense Minister Michael Tsai told reporters, "If Beijing keeps building up its strength, our analysis is that by 2008 to 2012, the balance of power will tip towards China."[19]

Beyond tracking trends in the cross-Strait military balance, ROC defense officials also highlight what they view as three possible Chinese courses of action: "intimidation warfare," "paralysis warfare," and "invasion warfare."[20] The first could involve anything from major military exercises to information operations, electronic warfare attacks, and air and naval provocations, or even a partial or full naval blockade. The second would likely involve cyber attacks, missile strikes, special operations attacks, and joint precision strikes. The third would involve a large-scale military takeover. According to Taiwan's National Security Council, in its 2006 report:

> In the event of an invasion of Taiwan, China will utilize all the political, economic, military, psychological, and diplomatic means at its disposal, use various high-tech weapons on a massive scale, launch conventional military attacks, and use unconventional approaches such as infiltration and sabotage to engage in a multidimensional, multilevel assault on Taiwan. It aims to quickly destroy or paralyze Taiwan's defensive capabilities through waging asymmetrical, nonlinear warfare.[21]

However, most official assessments indicate that ROC officials view a full-scale invasion of this type as the least likely potential Chinese course of action, at least in the near term, because the PLA does not yet have the capabilities required to successfully conduct such a campaign. For example, the National Security Council states that the PLA currently "does not have the capability to launch a large-scale invasion of Taiwan."[22]

Although officials in Taiwan assess that a full-scale Chinese invasion attempt is highly unlikely, at least in the near term, they express considerable concern about a variety of coercive use-of-force scenarios that would fall into the "intimidation" and "paralysis" categories. Taiwan's 2006 national security report states that the PLA has the capacity to conduct various types of coercive military operations, such as attacking the offshore islands, Kinmen and Matsu, and imposing a blockade on Taiwan. In addition, the report suggests that the PLA might attempt to launch a decapitation strike against Taiwan to paralyze its defenses. According to the report, "With its new command and control systems and weapons capabilities, the PLA is now able to . . . launch a quick decapitation strike against its opponents' command systems, and destroy its opponents' abilities to put up organized defenses, thus shortening wars and gaining quick victories."[23] Similarly, ROC defense officials have stated publicly that China might use its growing military capability, especially its growing arsenal of increasingly accurate missiles, to launch a decapitation strike against the island's civilian and military leadership.[24] In January 2003, for example, Vice Minister of Defense Lin Chong-pin said, "We are preparing for a scenario . . . a PLA with advanced weapons invading Taiwan in a very rapid manner . . . something like decapitation, as we saw in the war in Iraq."[25]

Taiwan's 2006 national security report assesses that China's goal, if it should decide to use force, would be to fight a "quick war with quick results." The same report further describes a possible course of action in which China would attempt to achieve this objective by launching a joint service attack against Taiwan that would combine precision strikes with limited use of ground forces to bring about a rapid collapse of Taiwanese military resistance:

In the event of a future Chinese invasion of Taiwan, it is highly likely that China will launch missiles to carry out precision strikes, combine its special operations forces with personnel it has in place in Taiwan, and coordinate airborne, heliborne, and amphibious assaults to conduct simultaneous multi-point, multi-level attacks on Taiwan's core political, economic, and other centers. This new type of warfare . . . is designed to allow the PLA to mount attacks from within and outside Taiwan, paralyze and control the core of Taiwan's government and economy, and quickly destroy the government's decision-making mechanisms and capabilities to respond, so that it may achieve decisive results on the battlefield.[26]

Similarly, ROC military officers assess that a PLA attack would likely involve multidimensional assaults, electronic warfare, and long-range precision strikes, in an attempt to achieve victory through "shock and awe."[27] In particular, ROC military officers assess that China would likely employ special operations forces in conjunction with air and missile strikes to degrade the island's command, control, communications, computers, intelligence, surveillance, and reconnaissance (C4ISR).[28] In addition, Ministry of National Defense officials have warned about the potential threat of "fifth-column" attacks that could be carried out by Chinese operatives, and ROC intelligence and security officials have reportedly assessed that some Chinese fifth-columnists are already living in Taiwan.[29]

Senior ROC officials have stated that Taiwan would have a difficult time responding to such multidimensional attacks, which could have a devastating impact on the island. In March 2005, for example, Defense Minister Lee Jye told reporters that China would have the capability to launch a potentially devastating series of attacks on military, political, and economic targets in Taiwan as soon as 2006. "With the defense capability we now have," Lee warned, "we may not be able to effectively repel such attacks."[30] Popular portrayals of Taiwan's ability to withstand a Chinese assault are even more pessimistic than the official assessments. The author of *Taiwan's Final 72 Hours,* a fictional account of a Chinese surprise attack on the island, predicts that the ROC military would surrender within three days.[31] The author of another book on the same topic argues that Taiwan's armed forces have little ability to repel a Chinese invasion attempt without rapid and substantial US assistance, which may or may not be forthcoming and is unlikely to arrive in time anyway, and that the government must be prepared to surrender within a few days.[32]

China's Willingness to Employ Force

Although government officials and think tank researchers in Taiwan clearly recognize that China is improving its military capabilities, many US observers are becoming concerned that these researchers may be underestimating China's willingness to use force, especially if Taipei crosses one of

Beijing's "red lines." Although it is difficult to say whether Taiwan truly underestimates China's willingness to use force, its analysis that China will not attack the island anytime soon certainly contrasts to that of US experts, who argue that China may very likely use force in the near term if Communist Party leaders felt such action was required to prevent Taiwan from moving provocatively toward formal independence. For example, Taiwan's Ministry of National Defense, in its 2004 report, painted a picture of an increasingly capable Chinese military, but cast doubt on Beijing's near-term willingness to use force: "Taking into consideration its economic growth and political stability, and barring unpredictable factors, the PRC is unlikely to pick up the fight against Taiwan in the near future."[33] Similarly, in a March 2006 report to the Legislative Yuan's National Defense Committee, Hsueh Shih-min, director of Taiwan's National Security Bureau, predicted that it was unlikely China would use force against Taiwan within the next two years, despite continuing tension in cross-Strait relations.[34] Hsueh told Legislative Yuan members that President Chen's decision to "cease the functioning" of the National Unification Council and the latter's guidelines could not be considered as crossing any of China's "red lines." He assessed that China would not start a war as long as Taiwan refrained from taking much more provocative steps toward formal independence. Although it appears that Hsueh's assessment turned out to be correct in this case, many analysts in the United States are becoming increasingly concerned that Taiwan's assessment of Chinese willingness to go to war risks sparking a crisis through miscalculation.[35]

Taiwan's analysis of China's willingness to employ force is based upon assessments of the PRC leadership's domestic and international political concerns. Indeed, analysts in Taiwan cite a number of factors that they believe would make China reluctant to seriously contemplate using force against Taiwan. One factor is Beijing's preoccupation with domestic politics and its unwillingness to take actions that run the risk of further undermining social stability. For example, in his March 2006 report to the Legislative Yuan, Hsueh said that Beijing would exercise restraint because of concerns about political stability and preparations for the seventeenth party congress in 2007.[36] Similarly, in August 2005, often-outspoken DPP official Parris Chang said that China would be reluctant to use force because of its domestic problems, such as a growing income gap and rising social unrest.[37]

Another Taiwanese argument is that Beijing would not want to risk derailing its plans to host the 2008 Olympics, an important event that the Chinese Communist Party leadership views as a reflection of China's emergence as an influential and respected global political and economic power. Still another argument is that China would seek to avoid becoming embroiled in a conflict with the potential to disrupt its continued domestic economic development, which has become one of the regime's primary sources of legitimacy and a key factor in the maintenance of social stability. For example, in a March 2006 interview with the *Taipei Times,* Koo Kuan-min, senior adviser to the president, said, "China will not attack Taiwan because it needs five to 10 years of peace to develop itself into an economic and military power so it can dominate the Asian region."[38] Some senior officials in the DPP reportedly calculate that the combination of these factors gives Taiwan a "window of opportunity" to make further progress toward formal independence.[39]

Analysts in Taiwan also maintain that, even though the military balance is shifting toward China, any use of force by the latter would still be a risky and probably costly endeavor. Consequently, they argue, China is unlikely to seriously contemplate using force until it has such an overwhelming military advantage that it would be ensured a rapid and decisive victory at relatively low cost. For example, in January 2003, Lin Chong-pin, vice minister of defense at that time, stated that the PLA would surpass Taiwan's capabilities between 2005 and 2008, but dismissed concerns that this shift in the cross-Strait military balance would embolden China enough to make a war likely in the near term: "The simple fact of a crossover is insufficient to make leaders in Beijing feel 100 percent confident in winning a war."[40] In the near term, according to Lin, Beijing would place economic development above national unification, relying on diplomatic isolation, increased cross-Strait economic ties, and "united front" tactics to prevent Taiwan from achieving de jure independence. "Beijing's leaders consider it unwise to resort to the military option right now," said Lin. The period of greatest danger would not arrive until 2010–2015, he argued, "when the PLA will have such a supremacy in both qualitative and quantitative comparison of forces that it may feel confident to move."[41] Similarly, in a report released in 2004, the Ministry of National Defense assessed that China would begin to assume a military advantage over Taiwan in 2006, and that by 2008 the continuation of this trend would result in an imbalance that would enable China to use force against Taiwan. The report contended, however, that China would not likely consider invading Taiwan until around 2012, by which time it would have achieved greater levels of economic development, military power, and regional influence.[42] Although this assessment may be correct, it appears to discount the possibility that China would seriously consider using force earlier, even with insufficient preparation, in response to an action that Communist Party leaders viewed as a provocative move toward formal independence. Many officials in Taiwan simply do not believe that China is willing to "pay any price" to prevent Taiwan's independence. Moreover, some state that they regard Chinese military threats as a ploy aimed at persuading Washington to use its leverage to help Beijing contain Taiwanese moves toward independence.[43]

Although many analysts in Taiwan tend to downplay the possibility of a cross-Strait conflict, some do argue that the combination of increasing internal unrest and growing nationalism in China could prompt Chinese leaders to attack Taiwan in an effort to shore up their legitimacy. Indeed, some officials and analysts in Taipei assess that serious domestic political problems in China would be the most likely cause of a cross-Strait conflict. They argue that in the event of a severe economic downturn or mounting social unrest, Beijing might be tempted to use a crisis over Taiwan to distract a disgruntled populace. For example, Mainland Affairs Council chairman Joseph Wu warned in a November 2004 speech that Beijing might exploit nationalism to unify the populace and distract attention from social unrest and domestic problems.[44] Taiwan's National Security Council, in its 2006 report, also warns that China might attempt to shift attention away from internal social crisis, "by inciting extreme nationalism and directing hostility toward foreign targets, or even initiating military aggression against Taiwan."[45] Another variant of this line of analysis suggests that serious divisions within the Chinese Communist Party leadership or an intense leadership succession struggle could result in leaders attempting to use the Taiwan issue to manipulate nationalist sentiment as a tactic to overcome their rivals.

Although politicians across the political spectrum in Taiwan tend to downplay the possibility that China would employ force against the island in the near term, at least absent a strong provocation on Taiwan's part, the Pan-Green and Pan-Blue camps appear to have somewhat different views on the nature and seriousness of the Chinese threat to Taiwan's national security. In particular, the two camps appear to disagree about what represents the most serious threat to Taiwan's security, as well as about Beijing's intentions and its willingness to use force against Taiwan.

In general, Pan-Green politicians often seem to be more concerned about PLA modernization than are their Pan-Blue counterparts, with the exception of some retired military officers and other defense experts within the Pan-Blue camp who express serious concerns about the Chinese military threat. Pan-Green threat assessments generally portray PLA modernization as a growing threat to Taiwan's security. According to the National Security Council's 2006 report, which presumably reflects the views of President Chen and his senior national security advisers, "China's growing military power poses a substantial and direct threat to Taiwan's national security."[46] Moreover, President Chen has highlighted various aspects of this threat, especially China's deployment of large numbers of missiles opposite Taiwan, on numerous occasions over the past several years. During an April 2006 debate with the Kuomintang's 2008 presidential candidate, Ma Ying-jeou, for example, President Chen emphasized the threat posed by China's growing arsenal of short-range ballistic missiles. Chen said that the number of ballistic missiles targeting Taiwan had reached 787, up from the 200 or so missiles the PLA had in 2000. Moreover, Chen warned that Beijing had embarked on a long-term plan to develop more credible options to use force against Taiwan: "They have come up with a three-stage timeframe for using force against Taiwan. They plan to beef up their emergency warfare capabilities by 2007, and large-scale warfare capabilities against Taiwan by 2010, and capabilities to have a military showdown with Taiwan by 2015, according to information we have collected."[47] Similarly, Mainland Affairs Council chairman Joseph Wu warned in his November 2004 speech that the likelihood of China using force against Taiwan was increasing, and that the people of Taiwan should not underestimate the possibility of a Chinese attack. Wu stated that PLA exercises were expanding in scale, and that most were aimed at Taiwan and took into consideration possible third-party intervention.[48]

Although members of the Pan-Green camp generally seem to be more concerned about the PLA threat than are their counterparts in the Kuomintang and People's First Party (PFP), there are some differences of opinion within the Pan-Green camp as well. In general, politicians from the Taiwan Solidarity Union (TSU) tend to have the darkest views about Chinese intentions. For example, in an August 2005 editorial, TSU chairman Shu Chin-chiang wrote, "China's influence in this region is gradually increasing due to its rapid economic and military growth. . . . [T]his is squeezing out Taiwan, making it more difficult for the nation to compete on the international stage. It threatens Taiwan by refusing to rule out military action, even as it engages in an all-encompassing, multi-faceted war of attrition, manipulating law, public opinion and psychology."[49] The TSU also asserts that China seeks to dominate East Asia, and that this makes a strong case for greater US and Japanese support. In addition, some in the Pan-Green camp appear to believe that the Pan-Blue camp's willingness to negotiate with the leadership of the Chinese Communist Party is an even more severe threat to Taiwan's security than China's military buildup. For instance, former president Lee Teng-hui, now the "spiritual leader" of the TSU, has suggested that his most serious concern is not China's military power, but the "pro-China" attitudes of the Kuomintang and PFP leaderships.

Pan-Blue politicians generally seem to be somewhat less concerned about Chinese intentions than their Pan-Green rivals. Indeed, some Pan-Blue politicians have suggested that China would never use force against Taiwan, absent dramatic provocation by a DPP president. Some Pan-Blue politicians seem to view cross-Strait relations as purely a political and economic contest, in which military power is useful largely as a source of bargaining leverage. In the words of PFP legislator Lin Yu-fang, "China deploying those missiles against Taiwan does not mean it will fire them at Taiwan." According to Lin, the true value of the missiles lies in their deterrent capabilities and "psychological impact" on the people of Taiwan.[50] At the same time, however, many Pan-Blue politicians who hold such views recognize that the PLA's growing strength enhances Beijing's bargaining leverage vis-à-vis Taipei, and express concerns that "reckless" behavior on the part of a DPP president could very well spark an otherwise avoidable cross-Strait conflict.

Beyond these differences of opinion between and within the Pan-Green and Pan-Blue camps, there are other domestic political factors that contribute to Taiwan's tendency to underestimate the possibility that China would use force against the island. Indeed, the dynamics of party politics give both political camps incentives to downplay the seriousness and immediacy of the threat to Taiwan's security. This comes at a time when many in the United States are becoming increasingly concerned about the possibility of a determined Chinese response, possibly including at least limited use of military force, to Taiwanese actions that could be perceived as altering the cross-Strait status quo.

Conclusion

After Washington announced that it was switching recognition to Beijing and withdrawing from the US-ROC defense treaty, many in Taiwan worried that China would be tempted to employ force to achieve reunification. Once the dust settled, however, it became clear that these initial fears were exaggerated. Indeed, throughout much of the 1980s and 1990s, most military and civilian leaders in Taiwan tended to downplay the Chinese threat to the island. They assessed that the PLA lacked the capabilities and training required to launch an amphibious invasion or conduct a naval blockade. Moreover, they believed that Beijing preferred an approach that emphasized the diplomatic and economic elements of national power, and was unlikely to attempt to use force to resolve the Taiwan issue on its terms. This analysis generally tracked with mainstream assessments in the United States.

Since the late 1990s, analysts and planners in Taiwan have become increasingly concerned about China's growing military power. Most policymakers and analysts in Taipei appear to recognize that China is developing increasingly credible options to use force against Taiwan, but many discount the possibility that China would actually use its growing military capabilities to attack the island, at least in the near term. Instead, they argue, Beijing is likely to continue employing a mix of "united front" political tactics, diplomatic pressure, and economic inducements, backed by the threat of force, to promote reunification. Nonetheless, some observers in Taipei argue that Beijing will become much more likely to consider the military option sometime after 2010, when it will have a far better chance of limiting the costs of using force by achieving a rapid victory over Taiwan's armed forces and deterring US military intervention.

Given this perspective, it would seem that Taiwan's threat perceptions, along with its views on US security assurances, contribute to a security policy that is at least somewhat underactive in terms of defense modernization. At the same time, Taiwan risks eliciting a sharp reaction from Beijing—and possibly undermining US political and military support—by taking symbolic steps toward independence.

CHAPTER 8

Domestic Politics

Domestic political factors sometimes constrain decisionmakers in ways that lead them to adopt ineffective half-measures in response to growing external security threats instead of seeking allies or building up their own military strength. Indeed, domestic political constraints often lead statesmen to respond slowly, ineffectively, haphazardly, or halfheartedly to external security threats.[1] In Taiwan, when the Kuomintang (KMT) controlled the executive and legislative branches of government, as well as the armed forces, the judiciary, and even the mass media, the specifics of separation of power did not play a major role in national security policy. Moreover, separation of purpose did not impair the ability of the Republic of China (ROC) to respond to the threat posed by the Chinese military in whatever way the president of the ROC and his advisers saw fit.[2] The process of democratization, however, greatly increased the salience of institutional and political factors in the defense and national security policy processes. At times, such factors have impeded Taiwan's ability to respond adequately to Chinese military modernization. For example, a January 2006 editorial bemoaning the failure of the Legislative Yuan and Executive Yuan to reach a compromise on the special arms budget asserted that national security had "taken a back seat to partisan maneuvering." To some political commentators in Taiwan, it seems like almost everything has taken a back seat to such short-term political calculations in the intense competition between the Pan-Blue and Pan-Green camps. For example, the same editorial surveyed the state of the political system in Taiwan more broadly, finding that "the pan-blue alliance is pathologically opposed to any measure that would give the Chen administration a legislative victory and the pan-green camp is powerless to implement any action on its own."[3] Indeed, the standoff over the special budget is but one example of political gridlock in Taiwan. As Democratic Progressive Party (DPP) legislator Hsiao Bi-khim observes, "The opposition has been stopping everything the DPP proposes, not just the arms deal."[4]

The opposition's unwillingness to compromise has frustrated many DPP politicians, including President Chen Shui-bian. In the 22 December

2005 edition of *A-Bian's E-Newsletter,* Chen lamented, "In the past five years, the confrontation between the Blue and Green camps has resulted in a political stalemate *(zhengzhi jiangju)* that has affected the functioning of the government and damaged the interests of all of the people of Taiwan."[5] It was no wonder that President Chen was ready to vent his frustration with the political gridlock that was causing legislative activity to grind to a standstill. The opposition-controlled Procedure Committee repeatedly refused to allow the full Legislative Yuan to even consider several major bills, most notably the arms procurement proposal and the nominations for the Control Yuan. Moreover, the first session of the Legislative Yuan in 2005 set a record for the lowest number of bills passed in a legislative session.

Many analysts and political commentators in Taiwan observed that this standstill reflected institutional weaknesses and "hypercompetitive" partisan politics.[6] In a November 2006 article, for example, one observer described Taiwanese politics as "critically divided along systemic and ideological lines."[7] These institutional and political divisions play a critical role not only in explaining Taiwan's response to People's Liberation Army (PLA) modernization, but also in accounting for its leaders' sometimes provocative policies and pronouncements.

Separation of Power

Taiwan's Political System

Taiwan has a semipresidential system that combines elements of presidential and parliamentary systems. The institutional tensions and ambiguities embedded in this system are among the key factors underlying many of the island's current political problems.[8] Many of these problems stem from decisions made during the democratization process. Key actors considered the decisions expedient at the time, but many of these compromises have subsequently proven problematic in practice. The KMT made decisions with an eye toward maintaining power as the transition progressed. According to Shelley Rigger, "As the hegemonic party, the KMT was able to manipulate reforms in ways that prolonged the party's influence at the expense of efficient, effective democratic institutions. Thus, the presidency was strengthened, but without regard for maintaining a workable relationship between executive and legislature, while the rubber-stamp legislature was given power without the resources to wield that power effectively."[9] For its part, the DPP accepted many of these flawed decisions, in large measure because many of the changes "seemed to offer a shortcut to power."[10] Indeed, many of the flaws in the current system resulted from a series of constitutional amendments enacted during the 1990s. According to political scientist Chu

Yun-han, these amendments were "governed by short-term calculations and improvised compromises," resulting in a political system that is a "makeshift contraption desperately lacking in balance and coherence."[11]

These institutional problems were buried beneath the surface when the ROC was a dominant-party state under the control of the KMT. As Rigger points out, "The most damaging feature of Taiwan's political system is the lack of institutional mechanisms to stabilize the balance of power between the legislative and executive branches. Until 2000, this failing was evident only to constitutional specialists because the unity of power between KMT presidents . . . and KMT legislative majorities prevented its manifestation in practice."[12] Prior to democratization, the constitutional separation of powers held little practical importance, because the ROC had a dominant-party system. Although the 1947 constitution gave a considerable amount of power to representative bodies, in practice the ROC government operated under the domination of very strong presidents. Moreover, the power of these strong presidents was derived not from the constitution, but from the president's position as head of the ruling party. According to Rigger, "For 50 years, Taiwan politics followed a pattern quite different from the one laid down in the ROC Constitution. . . . Dominant-party politics fused presidential and party leadership, short-circuiting constitutional arrangements so that the parliament became subordinate to the presidential office."[13]

In the 1990s, however, the transition from authoritarianism to democracy dramatically altered Taiwanese domestic politics, raising the salience of existing institutional shortcomings and introducing additional problems as part of the political jockeying over the reform process. Some elements of the political system appear to favor the legislature, while others grant greater authority to the presidency. Perhaps the most severe weakness is that the system does not provide adequate mechanisms for resolving impasses between the executive and legislative branches. Consequently, "a determined parliamentary majority can stymie the ROC president, who lacks constitutional tools to overrule the legislature."[14] Taiwan's current political problems—including its inability to resolve the debate over the appropriate response to Chinese military modernization—are linked to these institutional weaknesses, especially the lack of mechanisms to resolve disputes between the executive and legislative branches of Taiwan's government.

Taiwan's executive branch. On paper, the presidential office is not very powerful. The legislature holds the "lion's share of lawmaking authority" and "the powers reserved to the president are few."[15] Nonetheless, the president is popularly elected, which strengthens the president's legitimacy.[16] Moreover, the president gained the right to appoint the premier without legislative confirmation as the result of a 1997 constitutional amendment, which further strengthened the position of the executive branch.

The president exercises authority over the formulation of grand strategy and is extremely influential in the areas of cross-Strait relations and foreign, defense, and national security policy. The president, as the head of state and the commander in chief of the ROC armed forces, has the final word on key decisions in each of these policy areas. Nonetheless, the presidency is relatively weak in the Taiwanese political system, which is an especially important factor when government is divided and the opposition is uncooperative. The president lacks veto power, but can send a bill back to the Legislative Yuan if he deems it "difficult to execute." The Legislative Yuan may overrule such action with a simple majority vote, however, forcing the president to implement it as originally passed.

The premier of the ROC is appointed by the president without legislative confirmation and serves as head of the Executive Yuan, Taiwan's cabinet. As the head of the cabinet, the premier possesses formal line authority over the government ministries. Nonetheless, the premier exercises relatively little influence in the areas of foreign, defense, and national security policy. The Legislative Yuan can remove the premier through a vote of no-confidence with a simple majority, but such an action is rarely contemplated, because it entitles the president to dissolve the legislature and call for new elections.

Taiwan's legislative branch. As for the legislative branch, the process of democratization transformed the Legislative Yuan from a rubber-stamp body full of superannuated members elected on the mainland in the late 1940s, to a "roaring lion" that plays a major role in Taiwan's political system.[17] Nevertheless, because the Legislative Yuan was a rubber-stamp body until the early 1990s, it was never given the resources that a modern, democratic legislature requires to function efficiently and effectively. Many of the Legislative Yuan's current problems reflect this legacy.

Members of the Legislative Yuan elected on the mainland in 1948 were supposed to serve for three years, but after the nationalist government fled to Taiwan, their terms were extended indefinitely in accordance with the "temporary provisions for suppression of the communist rebellion." No additional members were elected until 1969, when eleven new legislators were added as a result of the increasing population of Taiwan. Additional elections were held in 1972, 1975, 1980, 1983, 1986, and 1989, introducing several hundred new members. It was not until 31 December 1991, however, that all of the remaining members who had been elected on the mainland finally retired, marking an important step forward in Taiwan's democratization process. The first election following the retirement of the superannuated mainland legislators took place in December 1992. Legislative elections are now held every four years.

The recently streamlined Legislative Yuan now has 113 members. Of these, 73 are elected in single-member districts and 34 are chosen according to the level of support for their political party. The remaining 6 seats are set aside for the representation of Taiwan's indigenous people.[18]

The Legislative Yuan has twelve standing committees. The National Defense Committee and the Budget and Final Accounts Committee are the two that are most relevant to defense and security policy issues. The Legislative Yuan also has four ad hoc committees, perhaps the most important of which is the Procedure Committee. All government bills are initially sent to the Procedure Committee, which decides whether and when a given bill will go before the rest of the Legislative Yuan. The Procedure Committee must list a bill on the agenda before it can be read and referred to the appropriate standing committee or committees.

The Legislative Yuan still faces several institutional challenges. Two that are particularly relevant to its growing role in defense and national security policy are a lack of sufficient professional staff support and a dearth of members with strong expertise in defense and national security policy issues. Although each member of the Legislative Yuan is permitted to recruit from six to ten personal staff members, the Legislative Yuan's committees still lack adequate professional staff support. As for the shortage of members with experience in defense affairs, this problem is at least in part a function of the institutional structure of the Legislative Yuan. Membership on the Defense Committee changes too frequently for legislators to develop deep expertise in defense affairs. It is also in part a consequence of the electoral system, which usually does not reward members who try to become more familiar with defense issues. As one observer puts it, "The result is that neither members nor conveners have an opportunity to develop a deep understanding of any subject, which is a particular liability for something as technical and complex as military affairs."[19] As Lee Wen-chung, a former DPP member of the Legislative Yuan's Defense Committee, puts it, "The level of defense expertise within the legislature remains extremely low, and there is little incentive to acquire such expertise because knowledge about national defense usually doesn't win votes."[20]

Separation of power and Taiwan's democratic consolidation since 2000. Although the DPP's victory in the March 2000 presidential election was a watershed event in Taiwan's transition to democracy, the island's democratization remains "unfinished business" because of unresolved institutional problems.[21] According to many exasperated observers of Taiwanese politics, the ruling party is mired in incompetence and the opposition is bent on obstructionism. Indeed, the Chen administration has bungled a number of important issues and the Pan-Blue parties seem obsessed with blocking the DPP's policy initiatives, but the roots of Taiwan's current political difficulties run much deeper than the Pan-Green camp's inexperience as a ruling party or the Pan-Blue camp's unwillingness to play the role of loyal opposition. The underlying problem is that the island's existing political institutions are unable "to balance and resolve the competing pressures that have emerged over the course of the island's democratization."[22]

Taiwan's democratic consolidation remains incomplete and the island has achieved mixed results in the three areas that Larry Diamond identifies as the essential elements of consolidation: democratic deepening, political institutionalization, and regime performance.[23] Taiwan has made considerable progress in the area of democratic deepening, which involves political liberalization, respect for civil and political rights, government accountability, and representation of public preferences and interests. Taiwan has liberalized its political system and guaranteed civil and political rights. Moreover, Taiwan's government institutions are accountable and the island's vibrant civil society, decentralization of power, and low barriers to political participation reflect the representativeness of its political system.[24]

Although Taiwan has made laudable progress in deepening its democracy, the island has not fared as well in the area of political institutionalization, which encompasses the establishment of "routinized, recurrent, and predictable patterns of political behavior" and growing commitment to these "rules of the game."[25] Taiwan faces problems and unresolved tensions in the areas of legislative-executive relations, the electoral system, and political parties. Politicians continue to attempt to achieve their objectives in ways suggesting that they "have not internalized a common notion of the boundaries of political competition."[26] Examples include the legislative-executive collision over the fourth nuclear power plant during President Chen's first term, the disputes and demonstrations that followed Chen's controversial March 2004 reelection, and more recent attempts to recall Chen over alleged corruption involving his family members. The lack of consensus on "rules of the game" that contribute to incidents of this type also limits the ability of politicians to make the compromises that are required to ensure the smooth functioning of a democratic political system. To make matters worse, Taiwan's political institutions reinforce the contentiousness that characterizes the island's "hypercompetitive" politics.[27]

Finally, Taiwan is also experiencing difficulties in the area of regime performance, which refers to the government's capacity to produce the desired public policy outcomes. In recent years, Taiwan has been beset by economic difficulties, legislative obstructionism, political gridlock, and corruption scandals. Taiwan's electoral system, in some respects, compounds the problems of the island's semipresidential political system and unfinished democratic consolidation.

Taiwan's Electoral System

In Taiwan, executive elections and legislative elections use very different systems. Executive elections use a first-past-the-post system, while legislative elections employ a single-member-district, two-vote system (prior to January 2008, legislative elections employed the single-nontransferable-vote [SNTV] system in multimember districts).

The DPP always felt that it had a better chance to win executive elections than legislative contests, because the first-past-the-post system would allow it to win executive elections with a plurality when the opposing camp was internally divided. Some analysts have criticized this system because it allows a candidate to win the presidency with a plurality of the vote rather than requiring a majority. When this happens, the president may lack a clear popular mandate. Nevertheless, most commentators in Taiwan appear reasonably satisfied with the executive election system as it currently stands, though some analysts have proposed alternatives such as a runoff system to ensure that the victorious candidate would have a stronger popular mandate.

More problematic was the island's old legislative electoral system, which many analysts blamed for a host of ills ranging from corruption to contentious politics. The SNTV, multimember-district system was used in legislative elections up to December 2004, but it was replaced prior to the January 2008 legislative election. The SNTV system features large, multimember electoral districts in which candidates must compete against members of their own parties as well as politicians from the opposing camp.[28] Because there is a negative relationship between the district magnitude (the number of seats in a district) and the percentage of votes required to win election under the SNTV voting method, this electoral system often allows candidates running in larger districts to win with a very small percentage of the votes cast. Indeed, in districts with numerous seats, candidates can sometimes win an election with a vote share lower than 10 percent. Moreover, very few candidates will receive very high vote shares, since another effect of the system is to discourage parties from "wasting" too many votes on any individual candidate.

Under the SNTV system, parties running more than one candidate per district must avoid the errors of "undernomination" and "overnomination." The former occurs when a party nominates fewer candidates than it can actually elect in a district given its vote share, thus wasting votes that could have been allocated to additional candidates. The latter error occurs when a party nominates more candidates than it can elect given the share of the vote it receives in a district, splitting the vote so that fewer candidates are elected; thus in this case the party would have been better off nominating a smaller number of candidates. In addition to the problem of choosing the optimal number of candidates, parties face the challenge of "allocating the vote among candidates so that the maximum number of seats is won for the party."[29]

The SNTV electoral system fostered a number of political problems in Taiwan. One if these was vote-buying, a practice in which KMT operatives distributed voting instructions and red envelopes *(hongbao)* full of cash to party supporters. This was a problem because candidate-centered voting tends to promote vote-buying. Another consequence of the SNTV system was the emergence of intraparty factions. Furthermore, the SNTV system contributed to extremist political positions and did not facilitate the types of compromises that are required to make democracy work. Given the mechanics of the SNTV system, "pleasing one's committed base (which, given Taiwan's multi-member districts, need not be very large) is more important that appealing to centrist voters, a calculus which further diminishes incentives to cooperate and compromise."[30] Because the SNTV electoral system promoted factionalism and candidate-centered voting, it also created strong incentives for legislators to focus on pork barrel politics at the expense of national-level policy issues. Given the incentive structure created by the system, "constituent service and pork barrel projects play a central role in proving a candidate's worth to voters."[31] Consequently, "National policy issues often get short shrift, as politicians cannot afford to focus so much effort on them that they become distracted from the local issues that matter most to voters."[32]

Another criticism sometimes leveled against SNTV systems is that they tend to favor large, well-organized political parties. Indeed, even after democratization, the SNTV electoral system continued to favor the KMT in legislative elections. The system gave the KMT an advantage because of its experience, organizational capabilities, and deep pockets. Although the DPP's ability to win seats under the SNTV system increased over the years, the KMT appears to have retained an edge in legislative elections, at least in part because of its ability to exploit the SNTV system. This was also the case in Japan, where the ruling Liberal Democratic Party skillfully exploited the SNTV system by avoiding overnomination (too many candidates dividing the vote) and undernomination (wasting too many votes on too few candidates). As in Taiwan, two of the results of the system in Japan were candidate-centered voting and factionalism within parties. In all, payoffs and personalities—rather than policy issues, candidate quality, and party identification—are usually the central factors in the SNTV system. For this reason, reform advocates in Japan argued that the SNTV system had many disadvantages and few benefits, and it was ultimately discarded.[33] Similarly, the numerous problems associated with the SNTV system in Taiwan gave rise to strong demands for electoral reform.

Finally, the scheduling of elections in Taiwan is also problematic, according to many observers. Legislative and presidential elections do not coincide, which tends to increase the likelihood of divided government. Holding legislative and executive elections simultaneously would be possible now that Legislative Yuan members serve four-year terms, and some in Taiwan have called for this change in the hope that it will increase the chances that the same party will control the presidency and the legislature. For example, the KMT has proposed holding legislative and presidential elections simultaneously. It is possible that such a change would reduce the likelihood of divided government, because holding executive and legislative elections at the same time sometimes results in a "coattail" effect, which provides a substantial boost to legislative candidates from the party that wins the presidency, and may be sufficient to allow that party to gain a legislative majority. Although simultaneous legislative and executive elections might very well reduce the frequency of divided government, they would not resolve the problems that make divided government in Taiwan so dysfunctional when it occurs. These problems are rooted not only in separation of power issues, but also in the intense acrimony between the Pan-Blue and Pan-Green camps.

Separation of Purpose

Party politics and policy issues in Taiwan, and the composition and platforms of the Pan-Blue and Pan-Green camps, reflect a serious lack of elite consensus. Although the major parties are in broad agreement in many areas, they differ on their interpretation of the Chinese threat to Taiwan's security and the appropriate strategy to respond to China's growing military power.

Party Politics and Policy Positions

The defining feature of Taiwan's current political landscape is the intense acrimony between the Pan-Green camp, which comprises the DPP and Taiwan Solidarity Union (TSU), and the Pan-Blue camp, which comprises the KMT and People's First Party (PFP). Despite the intense political rivalry between the Pan-Green and Pan-Blue camps, the major political parties are actually in broad agreement on the basic outlines of Taiwan's foreign policy and cross-Strait issues. Moreover, further convergence between the policy positions of the DPP and the KMT is likely as the island moves toward a two-party system and the power of smaller political parties declines. At the same time, however, the major parties still have sharp differences in several critical areas.

Foreign policy and cross-Strait relations are among the most controversial political issues in Taiwan. According to Shelley Rigger, with the exception of the TSU, all of the major parties subscribe to five fundamental foreign policy goals: preventing entrapment by China, avoiding an unnecessary cross-Strait conflict, maintaining a strong relationship with the United States, striving to maintain formal diplomatic ties with the handful of states willing to grant formal diplomatic recognition to the ROC, and strengthening unofficial international ties and seeking a greater role in some international organizations.[34] Although the major parties agree on these broad foreign policy goals, they disagree on the tactics the ROC should employ to achieve them. Disagreements center on how much Taiwan should give up to enter into negotiations with China, the appropriate pace and scope of cross-Strait economic interaction, the importance of Taiwanese nationalism, and the need for constitutional reform. The Pan-Green and Pan-Blue camps also have very different views on the appropriate response to the increasing security threat posed by PLA modernization.

The Pan-Blue camp is in fact an uneasy alliance between the Kuomintang, Taiwan's former ruling party, and the People First Party, which was founded by former provincial governor James Soong, whose decision to break with the KMT and run as an independent in the 2000 presidential election split the KMT vote and allowed the DPP to win the presidency. The Pan-Blue camp favors stable cross-Strait relations and closer economic cooperation with China, and regards President Chen's uncompromising proindependence stance as the greatest threat to cross-Strait stability. For example, PFP leader James Soong stated that a Pan-Green victory in the December 2004 Legislative Yuan election would result in a cross-Strait conflict.[35] In addition, KMT politicians have accused Chen of undermining Taiwan's security by mismanaging relations with the United States. The PFP typically has preferred a more confrontational stance toward the Chen administration than has the KMT, sometimes influencing the KMT's approach on issues such as arms sales, but the PFP's political influence has been fading and its standing will probably be further diminished as a result of the recent legislative and electoral reforms.

Many KMT officials emphasize differences in the grand strategies preferred by the DPP and the KMT. They argue that the DPP's grand strategy aims to promote de jure independence, and that this has troubling implications for defense policy and the defense budget. Because moving further toward independence could increase tension or cause war, this strategy means spending much more on defense to prepare for a future conflict with China. KMT politicians argue that Taiwan simply doesn't have the money needed to afford such a high level of defense spending. They argue that the DPP's grand strategy cannot deal with this contradiction between provocative behavior toward China and lack of resources to support high levels of military spending. Moreover, they assert that the DPP's grand strategy also causes problems in relations with the United States, which further diminishes Taiwan's security.

The KMT argues that economic growth and stable relations with the mainland should be Taiwan's top priorities, and that it is more capable than the DPP when it comes to delivering economic growth and maintaining a stable relationship with China. Moreover, some KMT officials suggest that stable cross-Strait relations would allow Taiwan to spend less on defense without diminishing its security.

The KMT favors negotiations with China and an interim agreement that would promote stable cross-Strait relations. In October 2006, Ma Ying-jeou, KMT chairman and 2008 presidential candidate, proposed a cross-Strait peace agreement under which Taiwan would pledge not to declare independence and China would promise not to use force. The proposed peace agreement does not address China's goal of unification, but many Pan-Green politicians have derided Ma's approach as tantamount to surrender on China's terms. According to KMT politicians, however, such an agreement is the best way to ensure Taiwan's security. In the words of Su Chi, a KMT legislator and former chairman of the Mainland Affairs Council, "The KMT-proposed 'Peace Accord' is a viable path out of Taiwan's present conundrum. . . . In the future, in order to maintain the 'no independence, no use of force' framework, it is imperative that some sort of 'peace accord' is to be established."[36] Such an agreement would constitute a cornerstone of what Su calls the KMT's "walk on two legs" approach to cross-Strait relations. According to Su, this approach consists of two parts: "moderate[d] cross-Strait relations based on exchanges and dialogue as well as political assurance that Taiwan would not pursue *de jure* independence"; and "survivable defense based on a strong political and military relationship with the US."[37]

Critics have noted that the "walk on two legs" formulation suggests that the KMT's approach to cross-Strait relations does not place a great deal of emphasis on Taiwan's own defense efforts. However, the Pan-Blue camp argues that improving cross-Strait relations is more important than arms procurement. According to Su Chi, for example, "Previous efforts toward mending cross-Strait relations such as the Koo-Wang meetings, the historic visits by Lien and Soong to China last year, and official negotiations between the two sides are probably more effective in improving national security than the procurement of advanced missiles and other weaponry."[38]

The Pan-Blue camp does not dismiss the need to improve Taiwan's defense capabilities, but appears to accord it a lower priority than maintaining stability in cross-Strait relations. It also advocates a somewhat different tack than that of the Chen administration. Su Chi, for example, has put forward a concept of "defensive defense," which entails improving Taiwan's capacity to withstand a sudden strike and deny Beijing the ability to occupy the island. The objective of the strategy is to deter Chinese leaders from risking an attack on Taiwan and reduce the chances of conflict by diminishing China's confidence in its ability to rapidly defeat Taiwan's armed forces. Some of the proposed methods include procurement of antiship missiles and mines, and hardening of military facilities such as air bases, command and control centers, and logistics infrastructure. Su and some other KMT officials argue that such methods would be less expensive and probably more effective than the Chen administration's proposal to procure submarines,

PAC-3 missile defense systems, and antisubmarine warfare aircraft from the United States. Indeed, the KMT and PFP have strongly opposed President Chen's proposal to acquire these systems from the United States for the past several years. More recently, Ma Ying-jeou, the KMT's 2008 presidential candidate, has proposed the "hard ROC" defense strategy, which aims to strengthen deterrence and buy more time for international intervention. The KMT's latest proposal suggests increasing the defense budget to 3 percent of gross domestic product, strengthening defense research and development, and moving toward an all-volunteer military.[39]

The KMT is also trying to appeal to moderate voters by moving away from its traditional image as a party that is dominated by mainlanders who favor reunification with China. Indeed, the KMT has deemphasized reunification, indicating that it is a possibility only in the long term, should China become more economically developed and democratic and develop greater respect for human rights. In a February 2006 speech, Ma said:

> The Kuomintang firmly supports the maintenance of the status quo across the Taiwan Strait for the foreseeable future . . . but as the ROC Constitution is a one-China constitution, it does not rule out the option of eventual reunification between Taiwan and Mainland China if the overall conditions across the Taiwan Strait are ripe. That it to say, the developments in Mainland China reach a stage when its political democracy, economic prosperity and social well-being become congruent with those of Taiwan. . . . Therefore, as of now, there is no timetable for reunification; nor is there any urgency for such a move on either side of the Taiwan Strait.[40]

The KMT has also emphasized that no deal with China would be possible without the approval of the people of Taiwan. In the same February 2006 speech, Ma said, "Since Taiwan has become a full-fledged democracy, reunification with Mainland China cannot proceed without the consent of the Taiwanese people."[41] Some KMT politicians have also indicated that more specific preconditions would need to be met prior to unification talks with China. In November 2005, for example, Ma stated that unification talks would be possible only if Beijing revisits its verdict on the Tiananmen Square incident: "If Beijing doesn't redress June 4, we can't talk about reunification."[42] More recently, Ma stated that China would have to withdraw the short-range ballistic missiles deployed opposite Taiwan before the two sides could enter into a meaningful cross-Strait dialogue.[43] Moreover, as mentioned above, the KMT has even suggested that independence is a possible option in the long term. In February 2006 the KMT ran a newspaper advertisement titled "Taiwan's Pragmatic Path," which stated that the only acceptable short-term option was maintaining the status quo; the advertisement also stated, however, that there were several options for Taiwan's future status, including unification, independence, or maintaining the status quo indefinitely.[44]

The DPP and the Pan-Green camp have faced tremendous problems since President Chen's election in March 2000, in part because the DPP grew up as an opposition movement and DPP politicians had very few opportunities to learn executive-branch governance skills. According to one DPP official, "The DPP knows how to function in opposition; it was born to oppose, not to rule."[45] The lack of administrative experience is one of several challenges that derive from the DPP's origins in the *dangwai* ("outside the party") movement. Another is that the party is composed of numerous and diverse groupings of activists and politicians, many of whom joined together even though they had little in common other than opposition to the KMT and support for democratization and expanded political and civil rights. The DPP's origins as a "catchall party for KMT opponents" limit its ability to articulate a comprehensive and consistent policy program.[46] Gaining widespread support among voters was another critical challenge for the DPP. Before the 2004 presidential election, the DPP had never won a majority of the vote in a major national election, and had rarely carried more than 40 percent of the vote even in local elections. The party was most successful in contests where the opposition was internally split or otherwise poorly coordinated, as was the case in the 2000 presidential election.

Since capturing the presidency, the Chen administration has faced an uncooperative, opposition-controlled legislature that has blocked many of its key policy initiatives and personnel appointments. Chen has also faced sharp divisions within the Pan-Green camp, principally in the form of factional struggles within the DPP. Beyond challenges from factions within his own party, Chen also must contend with a sometimes rocky relationship with the other member of the Pan-Green camp, the Taiwan Solidarity Union, which was founded by ardent independence supporters and views former KMT president Lee Teng-hui as its "spiritual leader." Lee emphasizes the importance of forging a uniquely Taiwanese national identity and supports changing the island's formal name from "Republic of China" to "Republic of Taiwan." Even though the TSU is a small party, its support is of considerable importance to the DPP and its strong support for independence sometimes constrains President Chen's options. The electoral reforms that took effect in January 2008, however, diminished the TSU's influence and may even force its leadership to consider merging with the DPP.

Given these political dynamics, the DPP presidential candidate in 2008, Hsieh Chang-ting, faced the challenge of solidifying the "deep-Green" base while also appealing to more moderate voters. In 1991, the DPP added support for an independent Republic of Taiwan to its party platform. The DPP has moderated its position over time, however, as part of a strategy designed to attract more moderate voters. Although the DPP has softened its stance on independence and sought to portray itself as the party that is most serious about Taiwan's national security, it still faces the challenge of assuring moderate voters that it will not risk sparking an unnecessary conflict with China. The KMT has sought to capitalize on this vulnerability and turn the threat from China into an electoral advantage by portraying the DPP as a risky choice when it comes to handling cross-Strait relations.

To counter the Pan-Blue camp's charges of recklessness and allay US concerns, the DPP has adopted the position that there is no need to declare independence, since Taiwan is already an independent country. The DPP states that its goal is preserving the status quo, which it defines as two independent countries. President Chen stated on 17 May 2006 that Taiwan was committed to safeguarding the cross-Strait status quo, which he defined as follows: "Neither of the two countries are subordinate to each other, because they are two independent sovereignties. Both sides have their own national flag, national anthem, legislature, judicial system and military."[47] President Chen's position is that China is attempting to change the status quo, in part through its ongoing military buildup. According to Chen, "With regard to relations between Taiwan and China, we feel that it is necessary to maintain the status quo. . . . [H]owever, we feel that China is already changing the status quo in the Taiwan Strait."[48]

The DPP clearly rejects unification as a short-term option. Moreover, President Chen has dismissed Beijing's "one country, two systems" approach as "totally unattractive to the Taiwan people" and blasted its implementation in Hong Kong as a "total failure."[49] Chen has also decried the peace agreement that KMT chairman Ma Ying-jeou has proposed as an interim measure to stabilize cross-Strait relations. According to Chen, "The so-called peace agreement based on the principle of 'no Taiwan independence, no use of force by China' proposed by Chairman Ma is nothing short of an agreement to surrender. It means capitulating. Everyone knows that such a peace agreement would change rather than maintain the status quo."[50] At the same time, however, President Chen has indicated that he would not rule out reunification if that option gained the support of the people of Taiwan. According to Chen, "We do not exclude any possibility for the future of Taiwan and any possible form the development of cross-Strait relations may take. We should not exclude independence as one of the options nor should we exclude unification as a possible choice."[51] In addition, in late 2005, Chen suggested that the European Union could serve as a potential model for the future of cross-Strait relations, provided that China would be willing to accept Taiwan as an independent sovereign state. Nonetheless, President Chen continues to favor pursuing greater independence and reducing Taiwan's economic reliance on the mainland.

President Chen's shifting position on cross-Strait relations reflects a difficult political balancing act, which is further complicated by the Pan-Green camp's internal divisions on cross-Strait policy. Some Pan-Green politicians, such as 2008 DPP presidential candidate Hsieh Chang-ting and former Legislative Yuan member Lee Wen-chung, are urging the DPP to adopt a new China policy that emphasizes a more liberal approach to economic exchanges. At the same time, however, many TSU politicians and some within the DPP are continuing to pressure the Chen administration to push toward independence and resist any moves toward cross-Strait economic or political integration.[52]

In the area of defense policy, the DPP has pushed for increased defense spending and acquisition of maritime patrol aircraft, missile defense systems, and diesel submarines from the United States. According to a former Chen administration official, these systems are required to support Taiwan's short-term and long-term national security goals.[53] The DPP's current position stands in marked contrast to its opposition to high levels of military spending and expensive arms acquisitions when the KMT was in power. President Chen has also changed his position on defense spending since his days as an opposition-party legislator. Since his victory in the 2000 presidential election, Chen has repeatedly emphasized the importance of modernizing Taiwan's military. In a January 2005 speech, for example, President Chen said, "Beijing has continued to suppress Taiwan's space in the international community and even attempts to create a legal basis for the use of force against Taiwan in the so-called anti-secession law. Therefore, A-Bian [Chen, referring to himself] urges the public to support the policy of strengthening self-defense capabilities."[54] President Chen has also suggested that enhancing Taiwan's military power is important not only for deterrence and defense, but also to improve the island's bargaining leverage in any future cross-Strait negotiations. In July 2005, following the visits of several opposition-party delegations to the mainland, Chen said: "China has continued its arms build-up and increased the deployment of ballistic missiles aimed at Taiwan. Only by enhancing our self-defense capabilities can we have dignity and bargaining chips in any negotiations with China."[55] Within this context, Pan-Green politicians argue that the Pan-Blue camp's opposition to the special budget and increased defense spending is little more than a tactical effort to deny Chen a political victory.[56] Although the Pan-Green coalition supports increased defense spending to counter the growing Chinese military threat, Pan-Green politicians also suggest that the greatest threats to Taiwan's security are excessive economic dependence on China and collusion between Beijing and the Pan-Blue opposition.

Divided Government and Political Gridlock

The consequences of separation of power and purpose for domestic politics in Taiwan have been severe since 2000, when the election of President Chen Shui-bian ended more than fifty years of uninterrupted KMT rule over the island. Since taking office in 2000, President Chen has faced an uncooperative, opposition-controlled legislature.[57] The Pan-Blue coalition has adopted an obstructionist approach, attempting to unseat Chen several times, blocking many key bills proposed by the Executive Yuan, and refusing to vote on a number of personnel appointments that require legislative approval. In short, since the DPP's victory in the 2000 presidential election, the combination of separation of power and separation of purpose has resulted in severe political gridlock and a highly partisan atmosphere in Taiwan, as exemplified by the controversy over the fourth nuclear power plant, the dispute over the 2004 presidential election, protracted struggles over budget bills and Control Yuan nominations, and multiple attempts by the opposition to recall President Chen.

Although divided government is often a problematic arrangement in many democratic countries, Taiwan's political troubles represent more than a simple case of "democracy inaction."[58] The legislative-executive stalemate and intensely partisan political atmosphere that have gripped Taiwan since 2000 reflect underlying institutional weaknesses. Many in Taiwan recognize that solving these systemic problems will require further adjustments to the island's political and electoral systems. Indeed, Taiwan recently enacted legislative and electoral reforms designed to address some of these problems, and President Chen pushed for further changes to the ROC constitution, but was unable to win approval for these amendments prior to the end of his second and final term in 2008.

Constitutional Reforms

Several reforms to Taiwan's political and electoral systems have been recently approved, and further changes were debated as part of President Chen's proposed "constitutional reengineering" project. The reforms are likely to have a major effect particularly because of the changes they will bring about in the legislative election system. Although reforming an electoral system is usually a difficult and time-consuming process, and the intended effects of many changes may take a considerable amount of time to materialize, much broader alterations in the pattern of politics and policymaking often occur. Indeed, in Giovanni Sartori's words, electoral systems are "the most manipulative instrument of politics."[59] Some of the proposals for further changes to Taiwan's current system of government could have even larger implications if they are approved, despite the very high bar that has been set for amending the constitution. The specific content of the proposed reforms is still under debate, however, and the fate of the broader "constitutional reengineering" project remains highly uncertain.

Taiwan's legislative and electoral reforms. The approval of Taiwan's recently enacted legislative and electoral reforms was a remarkable political achievement, especially considering the island's problems with political gridlock, the extreme contentiousness of partisan politics, and the fact that legislators approved a reform package that was likely to cause many of them to lose their jobs. Notwithstanding these considerable obstacles, on 23 August 2004 the Legislative Yuan overwhelmingly approved the reform package, and on 7 June 2005 the National Assembly officially adopted these constitutional changes by an overwhelming majority.[60] Under the reforms, which took effect with the January 2008 legislative election, the number of seats in the Legislative Yuan was reduced from 225 to 113, and the SNTV multimember-district electoral system was replaced by a single-member-district, dual-vote system. The downsized Legislative Yuan consists of seventy-three single-member geographical constituency–based seats, thirty-four at-large seats, and six seats reserved for representatives of the island's indigenous population. The at-large seats are distributed according to the proportion of votes each party obtains, and a party must obtain at least 5 percent of the total vote to win at-large seats. In addition, the term of office for members of the Legislative Yuan has been increased from three to four years.

All of these changes are supposed to address problems with the old system, which was associated with incompetent legislators, extremist views, money politics and vote-buying, and pork barrel politics. The new system is supposed to favor candidates with moderate views, diminish the influence of local special interests, and increase the salience of broader public policy issues.

For many proponents of the reforms, one of the intended outcomes is the election of more competent and capable legislators. In particular, the shift from multimember to single-member legislative districts is expected to raise the bar for candidates seeking election to the legislature. Under the multimember-district system, it was possible to win a seat in the Legislative Yuan with a relatively small percentage of the vote in a district. Candidates who catered to a small group of voters or powerful local interests often won seats under this system. The new system may result in improved quality of elected officials, at least in competitive races where parties have the incentive to field the best candidate, but it is not likely to yield such benefits in "safe" districts where the dominant party can effectively put forth any candidate and still have a high probability of winning.

The reforms may also create incentives for candidates and legislators to devote greater attention to broader policy issues. Many commentators in Taiwan viewed the SNTV system as a factor that contributed to a circuslike atmosphere in the legislature, in which members aggressively pursued local interests and tended to ignore national issues. In contrast, the new single-member-district system requires candidates to appeal to a broader range of voters, potentially shifting the focus of legislative elections from personalities and pork barrel politics to broader and more substantive policy issues. According to former DPP Legislative Yuan member Lee Wen-chung, adopting single-member districts compel candidates "to seek the support of the majority of voters, just as candidates do in elections for city mayors and county commissioners." Accordingly, Lee argues, under the new system candidates have strong incentives to "promote issues that are popular with a majority of the people."[61] It is also possible that the pressure on legislators to broaden their voter appeal and win the support of their own party to run as the only nominee in a district will also pressure them to make foreign affairs and national security a major policy priority. In addition, lengthening the period of time between election campaigns may allow legislators to devote more time to working on policy issues, since they will not need to turn to campaigning for reelection quite as quickly after taking office as they did under the old system.

The reforms may also reduce the prevalence of corruption, in part by giving political parties strong incentives to field more competent and professional candidates. The reforms should also help to reduce corruption by making vote-buying a less effective and more costly way to try to win elections. The final and perhaps most important expected outcome of the reforms is that they are likely to result in a shift toward the development of a two-party system. The change to single-member districts in which a plurality will be required to win elections is likely to reduce the influence of the smaller political parties.[62] Finishing second, third, or fourth in a geographical constituency will no longer be sufficient to win legislative seats; the shift from multimember to winner-take-all districts is likely to contribute to a consolidation in the number of parties. Indeed, the TSU and PFP opposed the shift to single-member districts for exactly this reason. At the same time, however, the new system grants voters a second ballot to choose the thirty-four at-large legislators, which should allow smaller parties to win some seats. But the requirement that a party must win at least 5 percent of the total vote to qualify for these at-large seats may make it difficult for the smaller parties to maintain their influence in the Legislative Yuan. As for the larger parties, the long-term impact of the changes on the balance of power between the DPP and the KMT remains to be seen, but KMT politicians have suggested they believe the new system is likely to favor their party.[63] The KMT's overwhelming victory in the January 2008 legislative election, the first held under the revised rules, appeared to confirm this belief that the new system would work to the party's advantage.

Finally, the change to Taiwan's method of amending the constitution that was included in the reform package will have major implications for future constitutional changes, especially those that touch on controversial issues. Under the former system, the Legislative Yuan proposed amendments, which then had to be ratified by an ad hoc meeting of the National Assembly. Under the new system, the National Assembly has voted itself out of existence, and constitutional amendments must clear very high hurdles to be approved. Proposed amendments must first be passed by a supermajority of three-quarters of the Legislative Yuan (85 of 113 legislators) and then must be ratified by winning the approval of a majority of all eligible voters (not merely a majority of all voters who cast ballots) in an islandwide referendum. The changes will make it difficult—though not impossible—for Taiwan to amend its constitution to redefine its national territory, change its official name, or otherwise redefine sovereignty—all of which are potential "red lines" for Beijing.

In early 2006, some Legislative Yuan members, apparently fearing for their jobs, mounted a brief attempt to roll back the amendments by raising the number of legislative seats from 113 to 168. The move earned the scorn of political commentators, as reflected by the withering criticism of a *Taipei Times* editorial titled "Lawmakers Fear for Their Snouts," which accused the measure's proponents of engaging in a thinly veiled attempt to save their jobs at the expense of long-sought political reforms:

> Do these legislators think that this appears to be anything other than pure self-interest? Doubtless the lawmakers backing the new amendment have been doing some quiet number crunching on their own, and don't like the picture that the results of their calculations paint. The legislators who have got cold feet about legislative reform probably believe that they stand to lose their jobs, their cushy livelihood earning payoffs from corrupt business-people and bureaucrats and—perhaps just as importantly in a few cases— their immunity from prosecution.[64]

The move to reverse the amendments failed quickly, in large part due to widespread public support for downsizing the legislature and reforming the electoral system.

Opinion polls indicated that the majority of citizens in Taiwan were dissatisfied with the performance of the legislature, leading most politicians to support the reforms. According to a December 2004 poll sponsored by the Taiwan Think Tank, for example, about 63 percent of people in Taiwan were dissatisfied with the performance of the Legislative Yuan. In particular, respondents cited their displeasure with the efficiency of the Legislative Yuan, the qualifications of its members, corruption, and political posturing.[65] Given the widespread disgust with the Legislative Yuan, it is hardly surprising that the overwhelming majority of respondents to a 2005 survey approved of the legislative and electoral reforms.[66]

Although Pan-Green and Pan-Blue supporters are at odds on many issues, the need for legislative and electoral reform was one area in which members of both political camps were united. There was clearly a broad consensus in favor of reform that transcended the boundaries of party lines. Although the breadth of public support for the amendments was striking, and although the reforms hold out the promise of some dramatic changes, many politicians, pundits, and scholars argue that further constitutional reforms are still needed to improve the functioning of Taiwan's political system.

Calls for further "constitutional reengineering." The current ROC constitution dates back to the period when the KMT was still in power on the mainland. The ROC constitution was adopted in Nanjing, China, on 25 December 1946. It was promulgated by the ROC government on 1 January 1947 and took effect on 25 December 1947. The document enshrined many of the core principles of the KMT, established a government composed of five branches, and guaranteed a variety of civil and political rights. As the Chinese Communist Party began to gain ground, however, the ROC government acted to enhance the power of the president and curtail many of these rights. On 18 April 1948, the ROC National Assembly passed the "temporary provisions for suppression of the communist rebellion," which granted broad emergency powers to the ROC president and effectively suspended many of the rights guaranteed by the constitution. But the "temporary provisions" were hardly temporary. Indeed, they remained in force for more than forty years. When the National Assembly finally voted to abolish them, on 22 April 1991, it marked a major milestone in the process of Taiwan's democratization.

Many more changes were required as Taiwan continued to liberalize and democratize, however, and these changes required extensive revisions to the 1947 ROC constitution. Indeed, the ROC constitution has been revised seven times since 1991.

In the first of these revisions to the ROC constitution, the National Assembly adopted ten amendments, the most important of which provided for regular elections for members of the Legislative Yuan and National Assembly. The second revision took place in 1992, when the National Assembly adopted eight more amendments, notably providing for the direct election of the president and vice president, provincial governor, and municipal mayors. This revision also allowed the president to nominate members of the Control Yuan, Examination Yuan, and Judicial Yuan, and to appoint them subject to the consent of the National Assembly. The third revision, which was adopted in 1997, comprised ten new amendments, including a procedure for the recall of the president and vice president to be initiated by the National Assembly.

The fourth revision, which was adopted in 1997, consisted of eleven additional amendments. Perhaps the most important of these gave the president of the ROC the power to select the premier, without legislative approval for the appointment. Another key amendment gave the president the power to dissolve the Legislative Yuan following a vote of no-confidence against the premier. Still another gave the Executive Yuan the right to request that the Legislative Yuan "reconsider" passage of bills that the latter deemed "difficult to execute," but stipulated that a majority vote of the Legislative Yuan was sufficient to uphold the original bill.

The fifth revision, adopted in 1999, included provisions related to the composition of the National Assembly, social welfare services, and benefits for retired military personel. The sixth revision, adopted in 2000, comprised eleven articles, perhaps most notably transferring the right to initiate the recall of the president and vice president to the Legislative Yuan.

The seventh revision, discussed in greater detail above, was adopted in 2005. It provided for a 50 percent reduction in the number of seats in the Legislative Yuan, extended the term of its members from three to four years, and replaced the SNTV, multimember-district system for legislative elections with a single-member-district, two-vote system. It also abolished the National Assembly and stipulated that future amendments to the ROC constitution were to be approved by the Legislative Yuan and then submitted for a nationwide referendum.

Even after these seven constitutional changes, many key issues remain to be addressed. According to DPP Legislative Yuan member Lin Cho-shui, "The seven constitutional amendments over the past few years have only solved some of the constitutional problems. It is crucial that another round of constitutional reforms are launched to further revamp the constitutional framework and the sooner this is done, the better."[67] President Chen, for his part, appeared to regard the enactment of further reforms as a critical element of his historical legacy. Indeed, Chen stated that he viewed the seventh revision as the "first phase" of a two-part reform process, and that he hoped to complete the second part during his presidency. In accordance with Chen's emphasis on further reforms, the DPP in June 2005 established a commission to begin drafting proposals for the "second phase" of the reforms. The presidential office also established a "constitutional reengineering" office. In April 2006, however, the opposition-controlled legislature dissolved it, along with several other organizations under the presidential office.

It is clear that President Chen regarded this set of reforms as one of the top priorities for his second term, but the content of this second phase sparked a heated debate in Taiwan. In his 2004 inaugural speech, Chen indicated that the constitutional-reengineering project would not touch on sovereignty issues. In several subsequent public statements, he reaffirmed the earlier promise that the reengineering effort would focus not on sovereignty issues, but on enhancing governance, strengthening competitiveness, and deepening and consolidating democracy. Subsequently, however, President Chen suggested that the proposed constitutional overhaul should address not only issues related to Taiwan's system of government, but also much more sensitive issues related to the island's sovereignty and its relationship with China. Although there was fairly broad agreement that future modifications to the constitution should address improving Taiwan's system of government, the sovereignty issues were highly controversial.

Many academics in Taiwan argued that the second phase of the reengineering process should address systemic problems that have their roots in the seemingly haphazard and piecemeal constitutional changes that were enacted during the period of democratization. Many changes were made simply because they seemed like expedient solutions at the time, or because they promised to grant a short-term advantage to one of the political parties. Indeed, the KMT made several changes that favored its interests, and the DPP tended to support changes that seemed to improve its prospects of gaining greater political power. In a few cases, major changes were made to serve the immediate interests of one or two powerful politicians, with little thought given to how the changes would play out in the longer term. For example, many observers argue that the amendment that gave the president the right to appoint the premier without the consent of the legislature was made with individual, short-term interests in mind. Specifically, they assert that this change was enacted primarily to help President Lee Teng-hui reduce the influence of some of his rivals within the KMT. Some of the current systemic problems also reflect the legacy of one-party rule, when institutional arrangements and separation of power didn't really matter, since the KMT controlled everything. According to several prominent scholars and current and former government officials, Taiwan needs to change the system to one that is a better match for its current and future political needs.

President Chen, for his part, stated that, "to better facilitate governance as well as to enhance our national competitiveness, we need to review those parts of our Constitution that are not timely, relevant, or viable."[68] To this end, Chen indicated that the constitutional revisions should replace Taiwan's semipresidential political system with either a parliamentary system or a presidential system.[69] Chen did not express a clear preference for a particular type of system, but he stated that the new system should be "clear and specific, unlike the one we have now."[70] Chen elaborated on his views while addressing a September 2005 constitutional reform forum:

> If Taiwan chooses a parliamentary system it should have a complete parliamentary system (*quantao de neige zhi*) in which the leader of the majority party forms a cabinet and establishes a government, and there would be no need for a directly elected president. If Taiwan chooses a presidential system, it should establish a complete presidential system (*quantao dou shi zongtong zhi*) in which the president is not only the head of state, but also the highest administrative official, and in which the president has the power to veto any bill passed by the legislature.[71]

Although President Chen asserted no preference for either a presidential or a parliamentary system, the DPP traditionally has favored presidentialism.

Indeed, the DPP has long supported strengthening the role of the president. It is opposed to giving the legislature the power to approve or reject the president's appointment of the premier. Some DPP lawmakers have even suggested giving the president the power to dissolve an uncooperative legislature.[72] According to DPP lawmakers, the party's long-term goal remains consolidating the government into three branches and changing the system of government to a presidential system. This preference for a presidential system stems in part from the DPP's origins as a prodemocratization movement that advocated direct election of the president. It also derives from more pragmatic considerations, namely the DPP's long-standing belief that victory in executive elections is the fastest route to political power, especially given the KMT's traditional strength in legislative contests.[73]

In contrast to the DPP, the other major parties do not support adopting a presidential system. Ma Ying-jeou, the KMT's 2008 presidential candidate, has suggested that he does not favor a pure presidential system. For example, Ma has indicated that the president's appointment of the premier should require legislative confirmation, which would weaken the power of the president and strengthen the role of the legislature.[74] The Taiwan Solidarity Union, for its part, favors a parliamentary system, according to TSU legislators. This is unsurprising, given that a parliamentary system would likely give greater influence to small parties like the TSU, since they would potentially play an important role in the formation of coalitions.

Constitutional reforms related to sovereignty issues are even more controversial than proposed amendments designed to improve Taiwan's system of government. The Pan-Blue camp is adamantly opposed to any such amendments. Moreover, constitutional changes that touch on sovereignty are controversial even within the Pan-Green camp. Indeed, the DPP's inability to forge a consensus on the inclusion of sovereignty issues reportedly forced the party leadership to delay the release of its draft constitutional revisions.[75] Some DPP heavyweights supported the inclusion of controversial sovereignty issues in the draft to energize proindependence voters, but other key figures in the party opposed pushing for controversial amendments that were sure to be shot down by the opposition-controlled legislature and risked undermining US-Taiwan relations.[76]

President Chen was well aware that the Pan-Blue camp's control of the Legislative Yuan doomed any proposed sovereignty changes to failure. In a March 2006 interview with the *Washington Post,* Chen acknowledged that sovereignty-related changes would not be able to meet the "high threshold" required for approval of amendments under the new system:

> If proposed constitutional changes do not have the support of all political parties, both ruling and opposition, they will not possibly be passed by the Legislative Yuan. . . . [A]ny reform must be able to transcend the differences

between the Pan-Blue and Pan-Green camps and between political parties.
... [C]onsequently, we must wait until society is mature enough, with sufficient support from the people and the approval of the legislature. Only then
can we possibly deal with these sensitive issues regarding sovereignty.[77]

Given that there was virtually no chance of success with an opposition-
controlled Legislative Yuan, many analysts argued that Chen was probably
using the sovereignty issue as part of an attempt to regain the political initiative in the wake of the presidential-office corruption scandal, and to put
the Pan-Blue camp on the defensive in the run-up to the 2008 elections. In
addition, many analysts concluded that President Chen's discussion of including sovereignty issues in the constitutional reengineering project was
meant to show his commitment to the DPP's "deep-Green" supporters and
energize Pan-Green voters.[78]

The prospects for further constitutional reform in the next couple years
are uncertain at best, especially given the Pan-Blue camp's control of the
legislature and the divisions within the Pan-Green camp on the appropriate
scope and content of the next phase of the reforms. If the Pan-Green camp
reaches a consensus on further constitutional changes, the outcome will
turn in large part on the Pan-Blue camp's willingness to support the proposed reforms. One potential complicating factor is that the KMT itself appears to be divided on the question of further constitutional changes.[79] KMT
presidential candidate Ma Ying-jeou has indicated that he does not favor
pushing for further changes in the near future given that major changes were
approved in 2005. Some prominent KMT politicians, however, have indicated that they are not opposed to pursuing another round of reforms in the
near term. Most notably, Legislative Yuan speaker Wang Jin-ping has indicated that further constitutional amendments would be acceptable as long as
they are intended to improve governance and do not touch on potentially
sensitive sovereignty issues.

Conclusion

Prior to democratization, the president and head of the KMT party apparatus
functioned as a supreme leader who dominated the political process, particularly in the areas of foreign policy and national defense affairs. Martial law
and emergency decrees augmented the strong personal authority of the president. The Legislative Yuan was almost completely under the president's
control. It exercised little independent authority, especially in sensitive areas
such as national security, foreign policy, and defense policy. Accordingly,
prior to 1996, the government allocated whatever level of resources it
deemed appropriate to national defense, with little or no regard to legislative
opinion.

Since Taiwan's democratization, however, the island's political institutions and extremely contentious political environment have emerged as the most important factors shaping its response to Chinese military modernization. Taiwan's semipresidential system of government is based on an authoritarian-era constitution that was amended somewhat haphazardly during the democratization process. The island's political system does not offer mechanisms to resolve stalemates between the legislative and executive branches. As Shelley Rigger puts it, "It has become clear that constitutional reform is the great unfinished task of Taiwan's democratization."[80] The consequences of these problems have become especially severe in recent years, because the island faces deep domestic political divisions and the major parties disagree about how to protect Taiwan's interests. Because the political system makes it so difficult to reach compromises under these circumstances, and does not provide the tools to resolve impasses between the legislative and executive branches, divided government has resulted in severe political gridlock and impeded Taiwan's ability to respond adequately to the increasing threat posed by the modernization of the Chinese military.

The shortcomings of Taiwan's political institutions and the contentiousness of the island's domestic politics offer a persuasive explanation for its response to Chinese military modernization, but it is important to keep in mind that US security assurances, threat perceptions, and domestic politics all influence Taiwan's response to Chinese military modernization. Moreover, these three factors interact in a way that contributes greatly to explaining Taiwan's security policy. In particular, the perception that the United States is likely to intervene in the event of a cross-Strait conflict, and the assumption that China is unlikely to use its growing military capabilities to attack Taiwan, interact in a way that reduces the perceived costs of domestic political conflicts over defense spending and military modernization. For politicians in Taiwan who think the United States would intervene in a cross-Strait conflict under practically any conceivable circumstances, and that any such conflict is highly unlikely to erupt in the near term, inaction on defense issues seems less risky than it would if there were stronger doubts about US willingness or capability to intervene, or greater concerns about the possibility that China might actually use force against Taiwan. Given the dubious validity of these assumptions about US support and Chinese willingness to use force, however, the costs of political gridlock could actually turn out to be very high indeed.

PART 3
Conclusion

CHAPTER 9

Implications for Regional Security and US-Taiwan Relations

In the 1980s and early 1990s, most analysts assessed that the cross-Strait military balance favored Taiwan, mainly because of its superior equipment and training. The relative backwardness of the People's Liberation Army (PLA) left it with few credible options to use force against Taiwan. Even in 1995 and 1996, when China conducted major military exercises and launched several short-range ballistic missiles into the waters off Taiwan, the PLA had little capability to do more than put on such symbolic displays. Since the late 1990s, however, China has increased its defense spending substantially and fielded an impressive array of modern military hardware. The PLA has also revised its doctrine, implemented a series of wide-ranging software reforms, and embarked on several major organizational and institutional changes. Chinese military modernization has accelerated and become much more comprehensive, constituting an intensifying threat to Taiwan's national security.

Despite China's improving military capabilities and the growing threat they represent to Taiwan's security, Taiwan's own defense budget declined for about a decade. This seemingly puzzling response to PLA modernization resulted in a widening capabilities gap between the two sides of the Taiwan Strait. Taiwan has lost its traditional qualitative edge over the PLA and appears to be falling further behind. This growing gap in military capability is giving China's military the ability to undertake a variety of potential courses of action against Taiwan, should the civilian leadership order it to use force. China's growing military power is also making third-party intervention in a Taiwan Strait conflict an extremely challenging operational problem. In particular, the Chinese military's emerging antiaccess capabilities—such as long-range surface-to-air missiles, modern submarines, advanced antiship cruise missiles, and a growing arsenal of increasingly accurate and lethal cruise and ballistic missiles—would pose serious challenges for the United States.[1] In short, defending Taiwan has become a much more difficult mission than it was five to ten years ago. Consequently, the shifting cross-Strait military balance has given rise to a considerable amount of concern, with some analysts envisioning a worst-case scenario in which the PLA achieves a rapid victory over Taiwan's armed forces before the United States has time to intervene in the conflict.[2] Even as the military threat has become more severe and Taiwan's defense modernization efforts have lagged behind advances in Chinese capabilities, the island's leaders have made a number of statements and policy changes that Beijing has seen as provocative moves toward formal independence. This in particular has prompted serious concerns in Washington, leading even some of Taiwan's most ardent supporters to question the wisdom of intervening militarily in any future conflict.

Taiwan's response to this growing security threat defies the predictions of traditional approaches to the study of international relations, which predict that states respond to growing security threats through some combination of internal and external balancing behavior. In other words, according to these approaches, Taiwan should respond through some combination of increasing the resources it devotes to defense and strengthening its relationship with the United States, but Taiwan's defense modernization has not been as rapid or comprehensive as might be expected given the growing threat to its security, and the island's leaders have taken a number of actions that risk provoking China and thus potentially undermining US political and military support. What explains this puzzle? The key conclusion of this study is that US security assurances, threat perceptions, and domestic politics and political institutions are the main factors that influence Taiwan's security policy. Indeed, security ties, threat perceptions, and domestic politics have interacted to make Taiwan's response to PLA modernization since the late 1990s much more modest than many observers would have anticipated. These same factors have also contributed to Taipei's propensity to risk angering Beijing and alienating Washington.

These findings underscore the importance of using analytic frameworks that encompass both international and domestic political factors. Taiwan currently faces deep domestic divisions, and the major political parties disagree very strongly about how best to protect Taiwan's interests. Since 2000, these disagreements have been combined with divided government, resulting in severe political gridlock. This political stalemate has impeded Taiwan's ability to respond adequately to the increasing threat posed by Chinese military modernization. Moreover, the perception that US intervention is reasonably likely in the event of a cross-Strait conflict, and the assumption that China is unlikely to use its growing military capabilities to attack Taiwan in any case, interact with these domestic political factors to reduce the perceived costs of gridlock on issues related to defense spending and military modernization. In addition, domestic political incentives sometimes encourage provocative behavior toward China, while US security assurances and doubts about China's willingness to use force make the risks of such actions seem more acceptable to some politicians in Taiwan.

Implications for Cross-Strait Relations and Regional Security

Taiwan's modest response to Chinese military modernization since the late 1990s raises serious doubts about the island's ability to defend itself in the event of a conflict with China. Moreover, the shifting cross-Strait military balance has the potential to produce greater instability in the China-Taiwan security relationship. Although any Chinese use of force would still involve tremendous risks and uncertainties, the shifting cross-Strait military balance is increasing the chances that China could successfully utilize force to achieve its political objectives and reducing the likely costs of Chinese military action. Taiwan's military weakness thus has the potential to increase the possibility of a cross-Strait conflict, especially if coupled with political and diplomatic decisions that appear provocative to leaders in Beijing. Indeed, this combination of increasing military vulnerability and political decisions that Beijing perceives as further movement toward permanent separation from the mainland has disturbing implications for stability in the cross-Strait relationship.

This situation is dangerous for the United States as well as for Taiwan, especially considering that US involvement in a cross-Strait conflict would entail particularly grave risks and consequences. First of all, US intervention in a cross-Strait conflict would mean war with an emerging great power that has nuclear weapons and sees the interests at stake in such a conflict as critical to regime survival. This would create potentially serious escalation control problems. Second, a war between the United States and China would place enormous pressure on US alliances in the region and subject other bilateral relationships to severe stress. This would compel traditional US security partners and other countries in the region to choose between two highly unpalatable options: becoming embroiled in a conflict with China or jeopardizing their long-standing ties with the United States. Leaders in these countries would certainly prefer to avoid facing such a stark choice, and Washington might not like the decisions some of those countries would make if they were compelled to do so. To be sure, a US-China conflict over Taiwan would have numerous potentially serious consequences. Such a conflict could spark a regional arms race, exacerbate already serious problems in Sino-Japanese relations, and contribute to tremendous political, military, and economic instability in the region. Finally, war termination would pose severe challenges, because a durable settlement would require resolution of the fundamental political issues on terms acceptable to Beijing, Taipei, and Washington. Failure to reach a political outcome acceptable to all parties would likely result in a protracted US-China confrontation and perhaps even a series of regional conflicts.

Implications for Taiwan's Defense

Taiwan's quickly eroding security position not only increases the possibility of instability in the cross-Strait security relationship, but also decreases the chances that Taiwan could successfully defend itself without rapid, large-scale US military intervention. Although the tremendous power asymmetry between China and Taiwan means that Taiwan probably cannot realistically hope to develop the capabilities that it would need to defeat a determined PLA invasion attempt absent significant US intervention, this does not diminish the importance of moving forward with its defense reform and modernization programs. Even though Taiwan probably cannot win on its own, the island should continue to strengthen its defense posture. Indeed, Taiwan should raise the priority accorded to enhancing its military capabilities.

Further efforts at strengthening Taiwan's defense posture should focus on the achievement of several major objectives. First and foremost, Taiwan should ensure that its armed forces have the ability to hold out at least long enough to allow substantial US forces to arrive in the region. The United States would need time to move its forces across the considerable distances that separate their peacetime locations from the Taiwan Strait, unless key military assets had already been deployed to the area around Taiwan due to heightened tensions in the region. This means that Taipei should assume that the US military, which is also overstretched because of the "war on terror" and the occupation of Iraq, would probably need several weeks to prepare and deploy sufficient capabilities to defend Taiwan following the eruption of cross-Strait hostilities. Accordingly, Taipei's defense strategy should focus on staying in the fight at least long enough to allow the US military to intervene decisively. Even if US intervention was not forthcoming, the ability to endure a Chinese assault for several weeks or more would enhance deterrence by denying China the prospect of a quick and easy military victory.

Implementing a strategy based on endurance entails dealing with several difficult operational challenges. One of the most difficult military problems for Taiwan in this respect is preserving the operational capability of its air force. Taiwan must ensure that its air force can survive initial Chinese cruise and ballistic missile attacks. It must also protect its air bases against attacks by special operations units and other PLA ground forces. Importantly, Taiwan's strategy should also focus on denying China any prospect of achieving victory at minimal cost. Taiwan cannot realistically hope to deter China from using force under all circumstances. Nonetheless, by demonstrating that an invasion campaign would be neither quick nor easy, the island can at least prevent Beijing from lowering its threshold for military action. Moreover, achieving these objectives would help to ensure that if Taiwan eventually engages in dialogue with the People's Republic of China (PRC), it would not have to do so from a position of weakness and vulnerability.[3]

Attempting to achieve these objectives will involve dealing with several domestic political issues. First, given Taiwan's budgetary situation, dramatically increasing the defense budget most likely means facing "guns versus butter" trade-offs. The government would have to make potentially painful choices, either raising taxes or reducing spending on other government programs. Second, even if the government overcomes these challenges and raises the defense budget to 3 percent of gross domestic product, this will not provide sufficient funding for Taiwan to address all of its defense problems. Consequently, Taiwan's leaders will need to make difficult decisions to ensure that their limited defense resources are used in the most critical areas. These include command, control, communications, computers, intelligence, surveillance, and reconnaissance (C4ISR), joint operations, air and missile defense, and homeland defense. Taiwan must allocate resources efficiently rather than simply emphasizing the balance of interests between the three services and their favored programs when making budget decisions. This in turn requires reaching a consensus on national military strategy and defense priorities.

Implications for US-Taiwan Relations

Taiwan's security policy also has important implications for the island's relationship with the United States, its only major source of political and military support. In many respects, the US-Taiwan security relationship is closer today than at any time since 1979, when Washington informed Taipei of its intent to withdraw from the 1954 US-ROC mutual defense treaty and established diplomatic relations with China. Nevertheless, US policymakers have expressed frustration that Taiwan is not doing enough about its defense and at the same time making political moves that have the potential to provoke China and draw the United States into an otherwise avoidable conflict. Washington is emphasizing the urgency of the need for Taiwan to move forward with its military modernization and defense reform efforts. The relatively slow pace at which Taiwan is making decisions and committing resources, however, is falling far short of Washington's expectations. Declining defense budgets and delays in weapons procurement have caused tremendous frustration in Washington, prompting some policymakers to question the strength of Taiwan's commitment to its own defense. At the same time, US criticism has led to consternation in Taipei. Indeed, many Ministry of National Defense officials in Taiwan bristle at suggestions that delays in the procurement process reflect a lack of commitment to the island's defense. They also resent what they perceive as the tendency of US officials to publicly chastise Taiwan about the need to increase its defense budget and quicken the pace of arms purchases from the United States.

The impasse also has the potential to undermine US support for Taiwan. It has already diminished Washington's willingness to approve additional major arms sales requests from Taiwan. For example, the George W. Bush administration is reportedly reluctant to consider some of Taiwan's requests due to misgivings about the Chen Shui-bian administration's inability to win legislative approval for the special budget it proposed to fund arms sales that Washington approved in April 2001. US policymakers are clearly reluctant to approve any more major arms packages if Taiwan's willingness and ability to secure funding for acquisition of major weapon systems remains in doubt. Making the trade-offs required to boost defense spending and develop the capabilities required to resist a determined Chinese attack, at least for an amount of time sufficient to allow the United States to intervene decisively, would help ameliorate US concerns that the island is not doing enough to guarantee its own security.

As for the United States, even though its relationship with Taiwan is no longer a formal alliance, it still entails several difficult alliance management challenges. Perhaps the most central aspect is that the United States must strike an appropriate balance between two extremes: unintentionally leading Taiwan to believe that US support is unconditional, and unnecessarily stoking Taiwan's fears of abandonment. The dilemma for the United States is that the tension between these two objectives means that actions intended to deal with either one run the risk of exacerbating problems in the other. On the one hand, attempts to reassure Taiwan may inadvertently contribute to the impression that the United States would intervene on Taiwan's behalf under virtually any conceivable circumstances, which could lead to provocative behavior toward China and failure to devote required resources to defense modernization. On the other, attempts to disabuse Taiwan of the notion that it has a "blank check" may heighten fears of abandonment in ways that could have very negative unintended consequences.

Taiwan has nowhere else to turn for anything approaching a comparable level of assistance. Simply put, no other country is willing to risk Beijing's ire by selling advanced weapons to Taiwan, and no other country has the capability to intervene decisively on Taiwan's behalf in the event of a cross-Strait conflict.[4] Given these circumstances, if Taipei became gravely concerned about US abandonment, it probably would not be long before the island's leaders would face a difficult choice between accepting some sort of political accommodation on Beijing's terms and developing a potentially destabilizing capability to deter the PRC from using force against Taiwan through threat of unacceptable punishment.

One possible unintended consequence is that heightened concerns about US abandonment could drive Taipei to pursue an independent and possibly nonconventional capability to deter China. Perhaps the most worrisome possibility in this regard is that it could motivate Taiwan to pursue the development of a nuclear capability as a deterrent against a Chinese attack. Developing a nuclear weapons capability to deter a potential adversary is one way that some states have hedged against the possibility of abandonment, especially when deploying conventional capabilities sufficient to defeat the adversary without external assistance would be prohibitively expensive. The Chen administration has declared that it will not develop nuclear weapons.[5] The Kuomintang's "hard ROC" defense strategy also explicitly rules out the development of weapons of mass destruction.[6] Nonetheless, it would be imprudent to dismiss this possibility completely, especially given Taipei's attempts to develop nuclear weapons in the 1970s and 1980s, which were rolled back under heavy US pressure.

An alternative response to heightened fears of US abandonment would be a decision to accede to unification on China's terms. This outcome would be inconsistent with US interests if Taiwan was forced to accept a deal that did not protect its hard-won freedom and democracy. Eventual cross-Strait unification is perfectly acceptable from the perspective of US policy, so long as it takes place through a peaceful process and results in an agreement that is acceptable to the people of Taiwan.[7] If the deteriorating cross-Strait military balance and acute fears of US abandonment compel Taiwan's leaders to negotiate from a position of weakness, however, these critical conditions are unlikely to be met.

Another important challenge with potentially serious implications for US-Taiwan relations is the growing gap in threat perceptions between Washington and Taipei. If Taiwan doubts China's resolve, even the recognition of increasing PLA capabilities is unlikely to motivate a determined balancing response or lead to a more moderate approach to cross-Strait relations. Moreover, doubts about China's willingness to use force may also lead to miscalculation about China's likely responses to potentially provocative political moves on Taiwan's part. The worst possible combination would be military weakness and provocative political behavior that runs the risk of sparking an otherwise avoidable cross-Strait war. Consequently, Washington should not only encourage Taiwan to enhance its defense capabilities, but also caution Taiwan not to dismiss Chinese statements that appear intended to signal Beijing's determination to prevent independence no matter what the costs.

Still another crucial challenge for US policymakers is dealing with the domestic political factors and constraints that shape the incentives of politicians in Taiwan. The United States has relatively little ability to influence domestic politics in Taiwan. Nonetheless, greater sensitivity to domestic political factors in Taiwan would likely increase the effectiveness of US policy. For example, Washington should consider finding ways to provide greater incentives in areas such as industrial cooperation. Taiwan's new defense laws mandate industrial cooperation and technology transfer to enhance its military capacities, including in the shipbuilding, aerospace, and information technology industries. Moreover, elected officials in Taiwan are keenly aware that pork wins votes in democracies. Legislators tend to respond to incentives that will get them reelected, which means that Washington will likely need to find ways to give a larger role to Taiwanese companies if it wants legislators to support expensive arms purchases from the United States. In short, as one former US official observes, "If legislators had greater confidence that more defense spending would translate into more jobs and more profit for home-grown businesses . . . they would naturally be more inclined to spend taxpayer money on defense."[8]

The United States also must be more sensitive to the possibility that some of its statements and actions may influence the political debate in Taiwan in counterproductive ways. In particular, Washington should refrain from questioning Taiwan's commitment to its own security. This approach appears to have proven counterproductive, particularly with regard to the protracted debate over the arms sales approved in April 2001. US diplomats and other US officials repeatedly emphasized the importance that the Bush administration attached to approval of the special budget that was proposed to fund major arms purchases from the United States, describing it as "a litmus test of Taiwan's commitment to its self-defense."[9] Washington's frustration is understandable for a number of reasons, but publicly chastising Taiwan by arguing that it simply is "not serious" about its own defense only worsens the problem. Suggesting that the island risks losing US support because of the failure to resolve the debate over the arms purchases has not helped either.

Finally, the US-Taiwan security relationship must move beyond the arms procurement debate, which has diverted much-needed attention from equally pressing national security and defense reform issues, such as the ongoing efforts to civilianize the defense bureaucracy, enhance training and exercises, improve the military's ability to conduct joint operations, upgrade the military's communications networks, harden critical infrastructure to withstand a Chinese attack, and address the recruitment and retention challenges associated with the movement toward an all-volunteer military.

Conclusion

The China-Taiwan issue is fundamentally a political problem. As such, it will ultimately require a political solution. Nonetheless, Taiwan's ability to defend itself is critical to maintaining stability in cross-Strait relations. In short, deterrence will have an important role to play in cross-Strait relations until a political solution that is acceptable to both sides becomes a more realistic possibility. At the same time, however, encouraging Taiwan to refrain from any unnecessarily provocative political moves that risk an otherwise avoidable cross-Strait conflict is just as important as ensuring that Taiwan's military capabilities are sufficient to deny China the prospect of a quick and easy victory. Balancing these imperatives is no easy task for US policymakers.

Taiwan's security requires a formidable defense posture, strong ties with the United States, and a stable and constructive relationship with China. Consequently, the United States and Taiwan must work together to ensure peace and stability in the Taiwan Strait. This does not mean giving Taiwan a blank check by promising to defend it under any and all circumstances, but it is in the interests of the United States to help Taiwan protect its democracy and prosperity. Washington must continue encouraging Taiwan's leaders to make the hard choices required to enhance the island's defenses. Washington must also continue cautioning them to refrain from further substantive or symbolic moves that would risk sparking a conflict with China. Although the United States has an important role to play in promoting stability, it is Taiwan's leaders who are ultimately responsible for achieving a strong defense and adopting a prudent approach to dealing with the mainland. Despite the domestic political challenges, nothing less than this can reduce the chances of a conflict that would very likely destroy much of what Taiwan has achieved through its remarkable economic and political transformation.

Notes

The views expressed in this book are the author's own and do not necessarily reflect the views of the Naval War College, Department of the Navy, or Department of Defense.

Chapter 1

1. There are a number of recent studies that focus on PLA modernization. See, for example, Dennis J. Blasko, *The Chinese Army Today: Tradition and Transformation for the 21st Century,* New York: Routledge, 2006; Keith Crane, Roger Cliff, Evan S. Medeiros, James C. Mulvenon, and William H. Overholt, *Modernizing China's Military,* Santa Monica: RAND, 2005; David M. Finkelstein, "The Chinese People's Liberation Army in 2020," paper presented at the National Intelligence Council's "2020 Project" workshop, Washington, DC, 26 May 2004; James C. Mulvenon and Andrew N. D. Yang, eds., *A Poverty of Riches: New Challenges and Opportunities in PLA Research,* Santa Monica: RAND, 2003; Harold Brown, Joseph W. Prueher, and Adam Segal, eds., *Chinese Military Power,* New York: Council on Foreign Relations, May 2003; and David Shambaugh, *Modernizing China's Military: Progress, Problems, and Prospects,* Berkeley: University of California Press, 2002.

2. The downward trend is evident whether the budget is viewed as a share of government expenditure, a percentage of the island's gross domestic product, or in absolute terms.

3. See Bernard D. Cole, *Taiwan's Security: History and Prospects,* New York: Routledge, 2006; Mark A. Stokes, "Taiwan's Security: Beyond the Special Budget," *Asian Outlook* no. 2 (27 March 2006); Michael D. Swaine and Roy D. Kamphausen, "Military Modernization in Taiwan," in Ashley J. Tellis and Michael Wills, eds., *Strategic Asia 2005–06: Military Modernization in*

an Era of Uncertainty, Seattle: National Bureau for Asian Research, September 2005; Kharis Ali Templeman and Thomas Edward Flores, "Threats, Alliances, and Electorates: The Empirical Puzzle of Taiwanese Military Spending," paper presented at the annual Midwest Political Science Association conference, Chicago, 8 April 2005; and Martin Edmonds and Michael M. Tsai, eds., *Defending Taiwan: The Future Vision of Taiwan's Defense Policy and Military Strategy,* London: Routledge, 2003.

4. See Mancur Olson and Richard Zeckhauser, "An Economic Theory of Alliances," *Review of Economics and Statistics* 48:3 (August 1966).

5. "Premier Defends Special U.S. Arms Purchase Proposal," *Taipei Times,* 6 August 2004.

6. On the implications of Chinese nuclear force modernization, see Xie Zhi-peng, "Cong zhonggong hewu xiandaihua fazhan yanxi jian lun dui quyu anquan zhi yingxiang" (Investigation into the PRC's Nuclear Weapons Modernization and Its Influence on the Asia-Pacific Region), *Guofang zazhi* (National Defense Magazine) 21:4 (August 2006). On Taiwanese concerns about the January 2007 Chinese antisatellite weapon test, see Stephen Che, "MND Concerned over Satellite Blast," *China Post,* 24 January 2007.

7. Threat perceptions derive not only from assessments of military capabilities, but also from expectations about intentions. See Stephen M. Walt, *The Origins of Alliances,* Ithaca: Cornell University Press, 1987.

8. See National Security Council, *2006 National Security Report,* Taipei: Government Information Office, 20 May 2006.

9. Ministry of National Defense, *2006 National Defense Report,* Taipei: Government Information Office, 2006, pp. 82–85. According to the report, "intimidation warfare" consists of military pressure or show-of-force actions short of full-scale war, such as large-scale military exercises, computer network attacks, psychological operations, provocative naval and air activity in Taiwan Strait, and partial or full blockade. "Paralysis warfare" would involve surprise attack, cyber warfare, missile strikes, long-range precision strikes, special operations, and sabotage. It would aim at achieving a quick, decisive victory by "rapidly paralyzing Taiwan's command and control system and political and military nerve centers and disintegrating Taiwan's organized military operations." Finally, "invasion warfare" would entail occupation of the offshore islands, the Penghu islands, or Taiwan itself.

10. Ministry of National Defense, *2006 National Defense Report,* Taipei: Government Information Office, 2006, pp. 82–85. The report warns that if the cross-Strait military balance continues to shift toward China, however, paralysis warfare and invasion will become much more serious threats to Taiwan's security in a few years.

11. Denny Roy, "Taiwan's Threat Perceptions: The Enemy Within," Asia-Pacific Center for Security Studies, March 2003, p. 1, www.apcss.org/publications/ocasional%20papers/optaiwanthreat.pdf.

12. Cole, *Taiwan's Security*, p. 172.

13. Ministry of National Defense, *2004 National Defense Report*, Taipei: Government Information Office, 2005, p. 53.

14. For an assessment of the ways in which domestic political factors may prevent states from responding adequately to external security challenges, see Randall L. Schweller, "Unanswered Threats: A Neoclassical Realist Theory of Underbalancing," *International Security* 29:2 (Fall 2004).

15. Shelley Rigger, "Taiwan's Best-Case Democratization," *Orbis* (Spring 2004).

16. Shelley Rigger, "The Unfinished Business of Taiwan's Democratization," in Nancy Benkopf Tucker, ed., *Dangerous Strait: The U.S.-Taiwan-China Crisis*, New York: Columbia University Press, 2005, p. 33.

17. Stokes, "Taiwan's Security," p. 1.

18. For a detailed analysis of this phenomenon in the context of the US political system, see Giovanni Sartori, *Comparative Constitutional Engineering: An Inquiry into Structures, Incentives, and Outcomes*, New York: New York University Press, 1997, pp. 86–91.

19. I thank an anonymous reviewer for raising this point about the ways in which provocation is a winning campaign strategy.

Chapter 2

1. See Michael S. Chase, Kevin L. Pollpeter, and James C. Mulvenon, *Shanghaied? The Economic and Political Implications of the Flow of Information Technology and Investment Across the Taiwan Strait*, Santa Monica: RAND, 2003, pp. 3–9.

2. Some Pan-Green politicians in Taipei argue that no such understanding was ever reached, but China and the Kuomintang continue to maintain that negotiators from both sides agreed to uphold the "one China" principle, even though they have acknowledged their differing interpretations of its meaning and significance.

3. Alan Romberg, *Rein in at the Brink of the Precipice: American Policy Toward Taiwan and U.S.-PRC Relations*, Washington, DC: Stimson Center, 2003, pp. 155–157.

4. See Robert Ross, "The 1995–96 Taiwan Strait Confrontation: Coercion, Credibility, and the Use of Force," *International Security* 25:2 (Fall 2000).

5. John Garver, *Face Off: China, the United States, and Taiwan's Democratization*, Seattle: University of Washington Press, 1997, pp. 74–88. It was the first time in seventeen years that a US aircraft carrier had passed through the Taiwan Strait.

6. Office of Naval Intelligence, "Chinese Exercise Strait 961: 8–25 March 1996," Suitland, MD, n.d., p. 11, www.gwu.edu/~nsarchiv/nsaebb/nsaebb19/14-01.htm.

7. Ibid.

8. Dennis J. Blasko, Philip T. Klapakis, and John F. Corbett Jr., "Training Tomorrow's PLA: A Mixed Bag of Tricks," in David Shambaugh and Richard H. Yang, eds., *China's Military in Transition,* Oxford: Oxford University Press, 1997, p. 259. As Blasko, Klapakis, and Corbett observe, the exercises "were first and foremost conducted in support of the political goal to affect the presidential election in Taiwan. Any military training that was accomplished was of secondary importance."

9. For a firsthand account of these events, see Ashton B. Carter and William J. Perry, *Preventive Defense,* Washington, DC: Brookings Institution, 1999, pp. 92–122.

10. For more on this debate, see David M. Finkelstein, *China Reconsiders Its National Security: The Great Peace and Development Debate of 1999,* Alexandria, VA: Center for Naval Analysis, December 2000.

11. For a detailed analysis of the embassy bombing and its aftermath, see Robert L. Suettinger, *Beyond Tiananmen: The Politics of U.S.-China Relations, 1989–2000,* Washington, DC: Brookings Institution, 2003, pp. 369–377. According to Suettinger, the incident was "the most damaging blow" to US-China relations since the June 1989 Tiananmen crackdown.

12. See Romberg, *Rein in at the Brink of the Precipice,* pp. 187–188.

13. Office of the Secretary of Defense, *The Military Power of the People's Republic of China, 2000,* annual report to Congress, Washington, DC: US Department of Defense, June 2000, p. 23. The ground, naval, air, and missile exercises were previously scheduled, but "probably were tailored to intimidate Taipei," according to the report.

14. Among the studies that address various aspects of Chinese military capabilities during this period are Ellis Joffe, *The Chinese Army After Mao,* London: Weidefeld and Nicolson, 1987; Paul H. B. Godwin, *The Chinese Communist Armed Forces,* Maxwell Air Force Base, AL: Air University Press, 1988; David Shambaugh and Richard H. Yang, eds., *China's Military in Transition,* Oxford: Oxford University Press, 1997; Larry M. Wortzel, ed., *The Chinese Armed Forces in the 21st Century,* Carlisle, PA: US Army War College, 1999; and James R. Lilley and David Shambaugh, eds., *China's Military Faces the Future,* Washington, DC: American Enterprise Institute, 1999.

15. For an overview of the 1979 conflict, see Harlan W. Jencks, "China's 'Punitive' War on Vietnam: A Military Assessment," *Asian Survey* 19 (August 1979). For an assessment of Hanoi's views on the conflict that draws on a number of participant interviews, see Henry J. Kenny, "Vietnamese Perceptions of the 1979 War with China," in Mark A. Ryan, David M. Finkelstein, and Michael A. McDevitt, eds., *Chinese Warfighting: The PLA Experience Since 1949,* Armonk, NY: Sharpe, 2003. For a recent assessment based on official Chinese military sources and participant memoirs that emphasizes the PLA's shortcomings in intelligence, combined arms

coordination, command and control, and logistics, see Xiaoming Zhang, "China's 1979 War with Vietnam: A Reassessment," *China Quarterly* 184 (December 2005).

16. David Shambaugh, *Modernizing China's Military: Progress, Problems, and Prospects,* Berkeley: University of California Press, 2002, p. 15.

17. Paul H. B. Godwin, "From Continent to Periphery: PLA Doctrine, Strategy and Capabilities Toward 2000," in Shambaugh and Yang, *China's Military in Transition.*

18. Shambaugh, *Modernizing China's Military,* pp. 1–3.

19. Godwin, "From Continent to Periphery," pp. 209–210. As Godwin put it, "The PLA's needs had been very clear before the Gulf War, but were accentuated by the shattering effects of advanced weaponry and equipment during the campaign."

20. See Finkelstein, *China Reconsiders Its National Security.*

21. Richard Fisher, "Defense Policy and Posture I," in Hans Binnendijk and Ronald Montaperto, *Strategic Trends in China,* Washington, DC: National Defense University Press, 1998, www.ndu.edu/inss/books/books%20-%201998/strategic%20trends%20in%20china%20-%20june%2098/chinasess4.html.

22. Wu Qingcai, "Xiaoping's Birth Centenary: Chief Architect of the Path of Building Fewer but Better Troops with Chinese Characteristics," *Zhongguo xinwen she* (China News Service), 13 August 2004 (also appeared as "Military Expert Discusses Deng Xiaoping's Decision to Downsize PLA in 1985," *Foreign Broadcast Information Service,* 13 August 2004).

23. Ibid. "Genuine modernization of military equipment is possible only when the national economy has built a relatively good foundation," Deng said. "Therefore, we should exercise patience for a few years. I think that by the end of this century we will definitely be able to exceed the objective of quadrupling the [gross domestic product]. At that time we shall be economically powerful and can afford to spend more money on the renewal of our equipment."

24. US General Accounting Office, *Impact of China's Military Modernization in the Pacific Region,* Washington, DC: Government Printing Office, 1995, p. 16.

25. The PLA divides its modernization efforts into three broad categories. PLA authors use the term "modernization" *(xiandaihua)* to refer to hardware upgrades. They use the term "regularization" *(zhengguihua)* to refer to the software reforms that are intended to professionalize the armed forces. Finally, the term "revolutionization" *(geminghua)* encompasses all aspects of the PLA's efforts to enhance political work.

26. Lin Chong-pin, "The Military Balance in the Taiwan Straits," in Shambaugh and Yang, *China's Military in Transition,* p. 324.

27. David Shambaugh, "China's Military in Transition: Politics, Professionalism, Procurement and Power Projection," in Shambaugh and Yang, *China's Military in Transition,* p. 27.

28. Godwin, "From Continent to Periphery," pp. 210–214.

29. Office of the Secretary of Defense, *The Security Situation in the Taiwan Strait,* Washington, DC: US Department of Defense, 26 February 1999, p. 7.

30. Godwin, "From Continent to Periphery," p. 214. "In many ways," as Godwin observed, "the [navy's] progress reflects the weakness of the other services in that it is slow and dependent upon imported technologies."

31. Kenneth W. Allen, Glenn Krumel, and Johnathan D. Pollack, *China's Air Force Enters the 21st Century,* Santa Monica: RAND, 1995.

32. Ibid., pp. 127–134. PLA air force pilots reportedly flew only about 100–110 hours per year, compared to a minimum of 180 hours for pilots from NATO countries.

33. US General Accounting Office, *Impact of China's Military Modernization in the Pacific Region,* p. 16.

34. On the rising importance of conventional missiles in the Second Artillery, see Kenneth Allen and Maryanne Kivlehan-Wise, "Implementing the Second Artillery's Doctrinal Reforms," in James Mulvenon and David Finkelstein, eds., *China's Revolution in Doctrinal Affairs: Emerging Trends in the Operational Art of the Chinese People's Liberation Army,* Alexandria, VA: Center for Naval Analysis, 2006.

35. Bates Gill and Michael O'Hanlon, "China's Hollow Military," *National Interest* 56 (Summer 1999).

36. See James Mulvenon and Thomas J. Bickford, "The PLA and the Telecommunications Industry in China," in James C. Mulvenon and Richard H. Yang, eds., *The People's Liberation Army in the Information Age,* Santa Monica: RAND, 1999, p. 245.

37. Office of the Secretary of Defense, *Military Power of the People's Republic of China, 2000,* pp. 12–14.

38. Ibid., p. 21. The report described the PLA's ability to command its forces in a joint service environment as "practically non-existent."

39. John Frankenstein and Bates Gill, "Current and Future Challenges Facing Chinese Defense Industries," in Shambaugh and Yang, *China's Military in Transition,* p. 163. Some of the defense industry's problems dated back to the Maoist-era "Third Front" project, which relocated large portions of the defense-industrial complex to remote areas in China to reduce its vulnerability to a Soviet or US attack.

40. For early assessments of the 1998 reforms, see Harlan W. Jencks, "COSTIND Is Dead, Long Live COSTIND! Restructuring China's Defense Scientific, Technical, and Industrial Sector," and John Frankenstein, "China's Defense Industries: A New Course?" both in Mulvenon and Yang, *The People's Liberation Army in the Information Age.*

41. Deng Xiaoping, "Speech at the Plenary Meeting of the Military Commission of the Central Committee of the CPC," in *Selected Works of Deng Xiaoping, Volume II (1975–1982)*, Beijing: Foreign Languages Press, 1984. As Deng put it in this March 1980 speech, "Our policy is to reduce manpower and use the money thus saved to renew equipment."

42. Yitzhak Shichor, "Demobilization: The Dialectics of PLA Troop Reduction," in Shambaugh and Yang, *China's Military in Transition*.

43. In 1955 there were thirteen military regions. The number was further reduced to eleven in 1969.

44. Godwin, "From Continent to Periphery," p. 202.

45. Lonnie Henley, "PLA Logistics and Doctrine Reform," in Susan M. Puska, ed., *People's Liberation Army After Next*, Carlisle, PA: Strategic Studies Institute, US Army War College, 2000.

46. James Mulvenon, *Professionalization of the Senior Chinese Officer Corps*, Santa Monica: RAND, 1997.

47. Officers could be distinguished from enlisted personnel because their uniforms had four pockets, whereas the uniforms of enlisted personnel had only two pockets.

48. Thomas J. Bickford, "Professional Military Education in the Chinese People's Liberation Army: A Preliminary Assessment of Problems and Prospects," in James C. Mulvenon and Andrew N. D. Yang, eds., *A Poverty of Riches: New Challenges and Opportunities in PLA Research*, Santa Monica: RAND, 2003.

49. The National Defense University was established in December 1985 by merging three major professional military education institutions previously associated with the general departments. Other changes included the establishment of an officer training school for civilian university graduates, creation of a national defense scholarship program, and increased opportunities for military officers to receive training at civilian universities.

50. See Kenneth W. Allen and Eric A. McVadon, *China's Foreign Military Relations*, Washington, DC: Stimson Center, 1999.

51. See Blasko, Klapakis, and Corbett, "Training Tomorrow's PLA."

52. Opposing-force training refers to exercises in which some troops play the role of enemy units, a common practice in the US military. This was a particularly important development for China because opposing-force training is more realistic and challenging, encourages officers to take the initiative in response to changing situations, and exposes troops to possible adversary tactics.

53. Lin, "Military Balance in the Taiwan Straits," p. 326.

54. John Culver, "Defense Policy and Posture II," in Binnendijk and Montaperto, *Strategic Trends in China*, www.ndu.edu/inss/books/books%20-%201998/strategic%20trends%20in%20china%20-%20june%2098/chinasess5.html.

55. Office of the Secretary of Defense, *Security Situation in the Taiwan Strait*, p. 13.

56. M. Taylor Fravel, "The Evolution of China's Military Strategy: Comparing the 1987 and 1999 Editions of *Zhanluexue*," in Mulvenon and Finkelstein, *China's Revolution in Doctrinal Affairs*.

57. David Finkelstein, "Thinking About the PLA's 'Revolution in Doctrinal Affairs,'" in Mulvenon and Finkelstein, *China's Revolution in Doctrinal Affairs*, pp. 1–4.

58. Among a number of early volumes on "high-tech local warfare" are Lu Senshan, ed., *Gao jishu jubu zhanzheng tiaojian xia de zuozhan* (Fighting Under High-Technology Local Warfare Conditions), Beijing: Academy of Military Science Press, 1994; Liu Yichang, *Gao jishu zhanzheng lun* (On High-Technology Warfare), Beijing: Academy of Military Science Press, 1993; and National Defense University, Scientific Research Department, ed., *Gao jishu jubu zhanzheng yu zhanyi zhanfa* (High-Tech Local War and Campaign Tactics), Beijing, 1993.

59. Nan Li, "The PLA's Evolving Campaign Doctrine and Strategies," pp. 146–174.

60. On early PLA information warfare writings, see James C. Mulvenon, "The PLA and Information Warfare," in James C. Mulvenon and Richard H. Yang, ed., *The People's Liberation Army in the Information Age*, Santa Monica, CA: RAND, 1999, pp. 175–186.

61. For more on Chinese views on information warfare in the mid-to-late 1990s, see Dai Qingmin, *Xinxi zuozhan gailun* (Introduction to Information Warfare), Beijing: People's Liberation Army Press, 1999; Cui Yonggui, *Zhanyi xinxi zuozhan yanjiu* (Research on Campaign Information Operations), Beijing: National Defense University Press, 2000; Wang Pufeng, *Xinxi zuozhan yu xin junshi geming* (Information Warfare and the Revolution in Military Affairs), Beijing: Academy of Military Science Press, 1995; and Shen Weiguang, *Xin zhanzheng lun* (On New War), Beijing: People's Press, 1997.

62. Nan Li, "The PLA's Evolving Warfighting Doctrine, Strategy, and Tactics," in Shambaugh and Yang, *China's Military in Transition*, p. 190.

63. Office of the Secretary of Defense, *Security Situation in the Taiwan Strait*, p. 13.

64. Michael O'Hanlon, "Why China Cannot Conquer Taiwan," *International Security* 25:2 (Fall 2000).

65. David A. Shlapak, David T. Orletsky, and Barry A. Wilson, *Dire Strait? Military Aspects of the China-Taiwan Confrontation*, Santa Monica: RAND, 2000, p. xvi.

Chapter 3

1. Particularly important in this regard was the 1979 Taiwan Relations Act, which declared that the use of nonpeaceful means to resolve the

China-Taiwan issue would be a matter of "grave concern" to the United States. The act also stated that Washington would continue to provide arms and military equipment to the Republic of China, but Washington was intentionally vague about the conditions under which it would intervene in the event of a cross-Strait crisis or conflict, favoring a policy of "strategic ambiguity."

2. Specifically, Washington agreed that it would not increase the quantity or quality of arms sold to Taiwan, and that it would "reduce gradually" its arms sales to the island, so long as China adopted a peaceful approach to the resolution of the Taiwan issue.

3. For more on the democratization process in Taiwan, see Shelley Rigger, *Politics in Taiwan: Voting for Democracy,* London: Routledge, 1999; Linda Chao and Ramon H. Myers, *The First Chinese Democracy: Political Life in the Republic of China on Taiwan,* Baltimore: Johns Hopkins University Press, 1998; Bruce J. Dickson, *Democratization in China and Taiwan: The Adaptability of Leninist Parties,* New York: Oxford, 1998; Alan M. Wachman, *Taiwan: National Identity and Democratization,* Armonk, NY: Sharpe, 1997; and Tien Hung-mao, ed., *Taiwan's Electoral Politics and Democratic Transition: Riding the Third Wave,* Armonk, NY: Sharpe, 1996.

4. On the emergence of the Democratic Progressive Party, see Shelley Rigger, *From Opposition to Power: Taiwan's Democratic Progressive Party,* Boulder: Lynne Rienner, 2001.

5. The "go south" policy, which Lee initiated in 1994, provided a boost to Taiwanese investment in Southeast Asia, but it did little to stanch the flow of investment to the mainland. In September 1996, Lee announced the "no haste, be patient" policy, which required case-by-case approvals for Taiwanese investments in high-technology and infrastructure development projects in China. The policy also imposed limits on investments by companies listed on Taiwan's stock exchange and capped individual investments in the People's Republic of China at US$50 million.

6. Barry Naughton, ed., *The China Circle: Economics and Electronics in the PRC, Taiwan, and Hong Kong,* Washington, DC: Brookings Institution, 1997.

7. See Alan Romberg, *Rein in at the Brink of the Precipice: American Policy Toward Taiwan and U.S.-PRC Relations,* Washington, DC: Stimson Center, 2003, pp. 185–189.

8. Office of the Secretary of Defense, *The Military Power of the People's Republic of China, 2000,* annual report to Congress, Washington, DC: US Department of Defense, June 2000, p. 23. The ground, naval, air, and missile exercises were previously scheduled, but "probably were tailored to intimidate Taipei," according to the report.

9. Office of the Secretary of Defense, *The Security Situation in the Taiwan Strait,* Washington, DC: US Department of Defense, 26 February 1999, pp. 3–4.

10. Lin Chong-pin, "The Military Balance in the Taiwan Straits," in David Shambaugh and Richard H. Yang, eds., *China's Military in Transition,* Oxford: Oxford University, 1997, p. 314.

11. "A Call to Arms," *Taiwan Business Topics* 34:11 (2004), www.amcham .com.tw/publication_topics_view.php?volume=34&vol_num=11&topics_id= 561.

12. Ministry of National Defense, *2004 National Defense Report,* Taipei: Government Information Office, 2004, pp. 141–145.

13. Government Information Office, *The Republic of China Yearbook, 1997,* Taipei, 1997, pp. 123–124.

14. Dennis Van Vranken Hickey, *The Armies of East Asia: China, Taiwan, Japan, and the Koreas,* Boulder: Lynne Rienner, p. 143.

15. Dennis Van Vranken Hickey, *United States–Taiwan Security Ties: From Cold War to Beyond Containment,* Westport: Praeger, 1994, pp. 47–48. In addition, Hickey points out that Washington's 1982 decision not to sell Taiwan advanced fighter aircraft to replace the island's aging Cold War–era fighters "was an especially bitter pill for Taipei."

16. Hickey, *United States–Taiwan Security Ties,* pp. 42–44.

17. The special budget mechanism was also used to pay for pensions and to fund the construction of military housing.

18. For detailed accounts of the 1992 F-16 sale to Taiwan, see Hickey, *United States–Taiwan Security Ties,* pp. 77–93; and Romberg, *Rein in at the Brink of the Precipice,* pp. 150–154.

19. Mark A. Stokes, "Taiwan's Security: Beyond the Special Budget," *Asian Outlook* no. 2 (27 March 2006), p. 4.

20. Damon Bristow, "Taiwan's Defense Modernization: The Challenges Ahead," in Martin Edmonds and Michael M. Tsai, eds., *Defending Taiwan: The Future Vision of Taiwan's Defense Policy and Military Strategy,* London: Routledge, 2003, p. 82. Bristow cites Taiwan's purchase of 450 M-60A3 tanks, which he argues are poorly suited for operations in Taiwan's mountainous terrain, as an example of this problem. He argues that the procurement of the tanks was "pushed through by the Army" for bureaucratic and institutional reasons.

21. In 2006, the Democratic Progressive Party revived some of the corruption charges surrounding the Lafayette procurement, and investigators questioned several high-profile former Kuomintang politicians and retired senior military officers.

22. Office of the Secretary of Defense, *Security Situation in the Taiwan Strait,* p. 6.

23. Lin, "Military Balance in the Taiwan Straits."

24. Office of the Secretary of Defense, *Security Situation in the Taiwan Strait,* p. 9.

25. Lin, "Military Balance in the Taiwan Straits."

26. Dennis Van Vranken Hickey, *Taiwan's Security in the Changing International System,* Boulder: Lynne Rienner, pp. 23–25.

27. Office of the Secretary of Defense, *Security Situation in the Taiwan Strait,* p. 15.

28. Ibid., p. 4.

29. See, for example, David A. Shlapak, David T. Orletsky, and Barry A. Wilson, *Dire Strait? Military Aspects of the China-Taiwan Confrontation,* Santa Monica: RAND, 2000.

30. *Republic of China Yearbook, 1997,* p. 123.

31. Ibid. The government's 1997 yearbook summarized the objective of Republic of China defense policy as follows: "The primary objective of the ROC's defense policy is to defend the area currently under ROC control, which includes Taiwan, the Pescadores, Kinmen, and Matsu."

32. Government Information Office, *Republic of China Yearbook, 2001,* p. 126. According to the yearbook, "The changes to the ROC's Armed Forces over the past few years reflect a shift from balancing offensive and defensive capabilities to simply assuring defense."

33. Stokes, "Taiwan's Security," p. 5. According to Mark Stokes, "Prior to the Chen administration, Taiwan's defense strategy was largely army-centric. It was believed that the PRC would not be able to claim a decisive victory without controlling the entire territory of Taiwan, and therefore the army would be the primary defensive force."

34. Liu Jung-chuan Liu (colonel, ROC army), "Planning the Army's Modernization," in Edmonds and Tsai, *Defending Taiwan,* p. 97.

35. Michael Swaine, *Taiwan's National Security, Defense Policy, and Weapons Procurement Processes,* Santa Monica: RAND, 1999.

36. For example, Tang Fei was influential as minister of national defense because of the personal stature derived from his military career.

37. Swaine, *Taiwan's National Security.*

38. Tzeng Jang-ruey, "Revolutionary Trends in the ROC's Professional Military Education," in Edmonds and Tsai, *Defending Taiwan,* pp. 209–228.

39. Government Information Office, *Republic of China Yearbook, 2001,* p. 129.

40. Ibid.

41. This program is usually referred to as the "Jingjian Project."

42. Government Information Office, *Republic of China Yearbook, 1997,* p. 123.

43. Government Information Office, *Republic of China Yearbook, 1995,* p. 157.

44. Government Information Office, *Republic of China, 1988: A Reference Book,* Taipei, 1988, p. 157.

45. See Office of the Secretary of Defense, *Security Situation in the Taiwan Strait,* www.dod.mil/pubs/twstrait_02261999.html.

46. David Shambaugh, "China's Military in Transition: Politics, Professionalism, Procurement, and Power Projection," in Shambaugh and Yang, *China's Military in Transition,* p. 2.

47. Ibid., p. 21. As David Shambaugh put it, "Certain 'pockets of excellence' exist and the PLA's fighting spirit is by no means slack, but overall it remains an antiquated force."

48. Dennis J. Blasko, Philip T. Klapakis, and John F. Corbett Jr., "Training Tomorrow's PLA: A Mixed Bag of Tricks," in Shambaugh and Yang, *China's Military in Transition,* p. 258.

49. Office of the Secretary of Defense, *Security Situation in the Taiwan Strait,* pp. 15–18.

50. John Culver, "Defense Policy and Posture II," in Hans Binnendijk and Ronald N. Montaperto, *Strategic Trends in China,* Washington, DC: National Defense University Press, 1998, www.ndu.edu/inss/books/books %20-%201998/strategic%20trends%20in%20china%20-%20june% 2098/chinasess5.html.

51. Lin, "Military Balance in the Taiwan Straits," p. 321.

52. US General Accounting Office, *Impact of China's Military Modernization in the Pacific Region,* p. 19.

53. Bates Gill and Michael O'Hanlon, "China's Hollow Military," *National Interest,* 56 (Summer 1999), p. 55. Gill and O'Hanlon assessed that the Chinese military lagged behind the US military by about two decades in many key areas. Their overall conclusion was that the Chinese military was "not very good, and not getting better very fast."

54. Shlapak, Orletsky, and Wilson, *Dire Strait?* pp. 47–49. This RAND study found that two aircraft carrier battle groups, a single land-based fighter wing, and perhaps a dozen heavy bombers would be more than enough to thwart a Chinese invasion attempt.

55. Culver, "Defense Policy and Posture II." As Culver pointed out, "Taiwan has been the locus of Chinese threat perceptions since at least 1993, when procurement from the former–Soviet Union began to be directed to the Nanjing Military Region (opposite Taiwan) and military training activity near the Taiwan Strait increased." Nonetheless, at the end of the 1990s, the future direction of the PLA was unclear. According to Culver, "In the course of examining the spectrum of development possibilities for the Chinese military in the next 10 to 20 years, two possibilities at the extreme ends of that spectrum stand out: China could continue to make halting progress, without major breakthroughs, excepting the evolution of a few pockets of modernity in the military; or, China's development pattern could break completely with the past and exhibit unprecedented abilities to integrate a new level of technology into its military."

56. David Finkelstein, "Thinking About the PLA's 'Revolution in Doctrinal Affairs,'" in James Mulvenon and David Finkelstein, eds., *China's*

Revolution in Doctrinal Affairs: Emerging Trends in the Operational Art of the Chinese People's Liberation Army, Alexandria, VA: Center for Naval Analysis, 2006, p. 6.

57. Thomas Christensen, "Posing Problems Without Catching Up," *International Security* 25:4 (Spring 2001).

58. Office of the Secretary of Defense, *Military Power of the People's Republic of China, 2000,* pp. 21–22.

59. Ibid., p. 22.

Chapter 4

1. Office of the Secretary of Defense, *The Military Power of the People's Republic of China, 2005,* annual report to Congress, Washington, DC: Department of Defense, July 2005, p. 37. According to the Defense Department's assessment, "Beijing views unification as a long-term goal. Its immediate strategy is focused on deterring Taiwan from moving toward *de jure* 'independence.'"

2. David M. Finkelstein, *China Reconsiders Its National Security: "The Great Peace and Development Debate of 1999,"* Alexandria, VA: Center for Naval Analysis, December 2000.

3. State Council Information Office, *The One China Principle and the Taiwan Issue,* Beijing, 21 February 2000.

4. Alan Romberg, *Rein in at the Brink of the Precipice: American Policy Toward Taiwan and U.S.-PRC Relations,* Washington, DC: Stimson Center, 2003, pp. 189–190.

5. Ibid.

6. Thomas J. Christensen, "Tracking China's Security Relations: Causes for Optimism and Pessimism," *China Leadership Monitor* no. 1 (Winter 2002), p. 4.

7. See Thomas J. Christensen, "Beijing's Views of Taiwan and the United States in Early 2002: The Renaissance of Pessimism," *China Leadership Monitor* no. 3 (Summer 2002), media.hoover.org/documents/clm3_tc.pdf.

8. See "China Ups Pressure on Taiwan," *BBC News,* 15 March 2000.

9. Larry Diamond, "Anatomy of an Electoral Earthquake: How the KMT Lost and the DPP Won the 2000 Presidential Election," in Muthiah Alagappa, ed., *Taiwan's Presidential Politics,* Armonk, NY: Sharpe, 2001.

10. Romberg, *Rein in at the Brink of the Precipice,* p. 193.

11. See Christensen, "Beijing's Views of Taiwan and the United States."

12. Romberg, *Rein in at the Brink of the Precipice,* pp. 199–202.

13. The Democratic Progressive Party gained seventeen seats, and the newly formed Taiwan Solidarity Union, which was led by former president Lee Teng-hui and was even more ardently proindependence than the DPP, won thirteen seats.

14. Christensen, "Beijing's Views of Taiwan and the United States."

15. Ibid. Christensen points out that Chinese Taiwan-watchers were still less pessimistic than they had been in 2000.

16. The Chen administration released a formal clarification ten days after Chen's speech. See Government Information Office, "Explanation of President Chen Shui-bian's Remarks of August 3, 2002," Taipei, 12 August 2002.

17. Since 1949, there have been no direct transportation links between China and Taiwan. In the absence of direct links, most cross-Strait trade is composed of goods shipped indirectly through Hong Kong or third-country ports. In addition, travelers flying between Taiwan and cities on the mainland must stop over in another location, usually Hong Kong, before continuing on to their destination.

18. "Mainland Offers Taiwan Goodwill Gesture," *China Daily,* 18 October 2002.

19. See "Taiwanese Passport Move Denounced," *China Daily,* 14 June 2003.

20. "Separatist Law Bound to Draw Strong Response," *China Daily,* 27 November 2003.

21. For the full text of the Taiwan Affairs Office statement, see "Curbing 'Taiwan Independence' Most Urgent Task," *People's Daily,* 17 May 2004.

22. Thomas Christensen, "Taiwan's Legislative Yuan Elections and Cross-Strait Security Relations: Reduced Tensions and Remaining Challenges," *China Leadership Monitor* no. 13 (Winter 2005), p. 1.

23. "Anti-Secession Law Adopted by NPC (Full Text)," *China Daily,* 14 March 2005. See also "Full Text of Explanations on Draft Anti-Secession Law," *People's Daily,* 8 March 2005, which provides commentary from Wang Zhaoguo, vice chairman of the Standing Committee of the National People's Congress, and includes a brief discussion of the drafting process.

24. See Philip P. Pan, "China Reaches Out to Taiwanese Opposition Party," *Washington Post,* 1 April 2005; and Mure Dickie and Kathrin Hille, "Beijing Fetes KMT in Attempt to Squeeze Taipei," *Financial Times,* 1 April 2005.

25. See Shelley Rigger, "Two Visits, Many Interpretations," *Far Eastern Economic Review* (May 2005); and Keith Bradsher, "Nationalist Chairman's Visit to Mainland Spurs Taiwanese Interest in Accords," *New York Times,* 1 May 2005.

26. Tung Chen-yuan, "An Assessment of China's Taiwan Policy Under the Third Generation Leadership," *Asian Survey* 45:3 (May–June 2005), p. 349. As Tung observes, China's overall Taiwan strategy is focused more on "preventing independence" than on "promoting unification." The wording, and even the title, of antisecession law reflected this emphasis on preventing what China would consider a worst-case outcome. President Hu Jintao's

new Taiwan policy formulation ("strive for talks, prepare to fight, don't fear delay") reflects this approach.

27. Author interviews, United States, 2007.

28. Edward Cody, "China Easing Its Stance on Taiwan," *Washington Post,* 15 June 2006.

29. See John Pomfret and Philip P. Pan, "Chinese Premier Presses U.S. on Taiwan, Trade," *Washington Post,* 23 November 2003; and "Junshi zhuanjia tan fan 'taidu' zhanzheng: liu tiao daijia zhanfan bicheng" (Military Experts Discuss Opposing 'Taiwan Independence' with War: Six Costs, War Criminals Will Be Penalized), *Liaowang xinwen zhoukan* (Outlook Weekly), 27 November 2003.

30. See Peter Hays Gries, *China's New Nationalism: Pride, Politics, and Diplomacy,* Berkeley: University of California Press, 2004.

31. Christensen, "Taiwan's Legislative Yuan Elections and Cross-Strait Security Relations," p. 8.

32. Ibid., p. 3.

33. Finkelstein, *China Reconsiders Its National Security.*

34. Edward Cody, "With Taiwan in Mind, China Focuses Military Expansion on Navy," *Washington Post,* 20 March 2004, p. A12.

35. Office of the Secretary of Defense, *The Military Power of the People's Republic of China, 2006,* pp. 10–12. Longer-term objectives of PLA modernization may include regional contingencies beyond Taiwan. According to the report, "Current trends in China's military modernization could provide China with a force capable of prosecuting a range of military operations in Asia—well beyond Taiwan—potentially posing a credible threat to modern militaries operating in the region."

36. The PLA itself divides this ambitious program into three categories: "modernization" refers to hardware improvements; "regularization" encompasses software issues, such as personnel, training, educational, legal, and organizational reforms; and "revolutionization" refers to changes in political work.

37. According to China's 2004 defense white paper, "The current international situation continues to undergo profound and complex changes. Peace and development remain the dominating themes of the times. Although the international situation as a whole tends to be stable, factors of uncertainty, instability, and insecurity are on the increase." See State Council Information Office, *China's National Defense in 2004,* Beijing, December 2004, p. 2.

38. State Council Information Office, *China's National Defense in 2004,* p. 2.

39. Ibid.

40. As a recent RAND study points out, "PLA military strategists perceive the United States as posing both an immediate and long-term challenge

to Chinese national security interests." Specifically, according to this study, "Chinese military planners and political leaders are decidedly uncomfortable with the U.S. military presence in the world; they fear that the United States can and will use military force whenever and wherever it wants, including in scenarios involving Chinese security interests." See Keith Crane, Roger Cliff, Evan Medeiros, James Mulvenon, and William Overholt, *Modernizing China's Military: Opportunities and Constraints,* Santa Monica: RAND, 2005, p. xxii.

41. "Chinese Leaders Urge Armed Forces to Push Modernization," *People's Daily,* 12 March 2004. Jiang was speaking at a meeting of military representatives during the annual session of the National People's Congress.

42. Author interviews, United States and China, 2001–2007.

43. State Council Information Office, *China's National Defense in 2004,* p. 2.

44. Thomas J. Christensen, "China, the U.S.-Japan Alliance, and the Security Dilemma in East Asia," *International Security* 23:4 (Spring 1999).

45. Thomas J. Christensen, "The Contemporary Security Dilemma: Deterring a Taiwan Conflict," *Washington Quarterly* 25:4 (Autumn 2002), p. 15.

46. Official media characterized the increase as being in line with economic growth, and stated that China did not have the capacity to pursue a large-scale military buildup. See, for example, "China's Defense Budget Up 14.7% in 2006," *People's Daily,* 4 March 2006.

47. Office of the Secretary of Defense, *Military Power of the People's Republic of China, 2006,* p. 20.

48. International Institute for Strategic Studies, *The Military Balance 2006,* London, 2006.

49. Crane et al., *Modernizing China's Military.*

50. Office of the Secretary of Defense, *Military Power of the People's Republic of China, 2006,* p. 20.

51. See, for example, Dwight Perkins, "China's Economic Growth: Implications for the Defense Budget," in Ashley J. Tellis and Michael Wills, eds., *Strategic Asia 2005–06: Military Modernization in an Era of Uncertainty,* Seattle: National Bureau of Asian Research, 2006.

52. Office of the Secretary of Defense, *Military Power of the People's Republic of China, 2005,* pp. 21–22.

53. Crane et al., *Modernizing China's Military.*

54. See "Chinese President Calls for Reviving Up Army Building to Safeguard National Sovereignty," *PLA Daily,* 12 March 2006.

55. "Remarks by NPC Deputies and CPPCC Members from PLA During Discussion on State Affairs," *PLA Daily,* 13 March 2006.

56. "Academic Urges China to Spend More on Military," *Reuters,* 6 June 2006.

57. Shen Dingli, "Compete with the United States in a Justifiable Way," *Shanghai dongfang zaobao* (Oriental Morning Post), 7 February

2006. In particular, Shen argues, China needs a larger military budget "to avoid being bullied."

58. On these growing problems, see State Environmental Protection Administration, *Environmental Protection in China, 1996–2005,* Beijing: State Council Information Office, June 2006; Philip Bowring, "China's Rise, Revised," *International Herald Tribune,* 26 December 2005; Murray Scot Tanner, "Chinese Government Responses to Rising Social Unrest," testimony presented to the US-China Economic and Security Review Commission, 14 April 2005; and Elizabeth Economy, *The River Runs Black: The Environmental Challenge to China's Future,* Ithaca: Cornell University Press, 2004.

59. Cao Gangchuan, minister of national defense, highlighted these constraints during an October 2005 press conference with US defense secretary Donald Rumsfeld. According to Cao: "The top priority of the Chinese government today is to develop the country's economy and improve the livelihood of its people. . . . [G]iven the duties and obligations of the government, it is simply impossible for us to massively increase the investment into defense capabilities building." Although Cao's comments were likely intended to defuse US concerns about the growth of the Chinese defense budget and the potential implications of Chinese military modernization for regional security, they probably also reflected a realistic appraisal of Beijing's policy priorities and the limitations domestic challenges are likely to impose on further dramatic increases in military spending. For the full transcript of the press conference, see US Department of Defense, "News Transcript: Joint Media Availability with Secretary Donald Rumsfeld and General Cao Gangchuan," Washington, DC, 19 October 2005, http://dod.mil/transcripts/2005/tr20051019-secdef4121.html.

60. For an example of Chinese views on the defense-industrial reforms, see Sun Guangyun, *Zhongguo guofang keji gongye de gaige he fazhan wenti* (Reforms and Problems in the Development of China's National Defense Science and Technology Industry), Beijing: Aviation Industry Press, 2003.

61. Evan S. Medeiros, Roger Cliff, Keith Crane, and James C. Mulvenon, *A New Direction for China's Defense Industry,* Santa Monica: RAND, 2005, pp. xv–xvi.

62. Ibid., p. xviii.

63. Ibid., p. xvi.

64. Office of the Secretary of Defense, *Military Power of the People's Republic of China, 2006,* p. 22.

65. "China Military to Open Site to Private Bidders," *Bloomberg,* 25 October 2005.

66. Office of the Secretary of Defense, *Military Power of the People's Republic of China, 2007,* p. 3.

67. Ibid.

68. Office of the Secretary of Defense, *Military Power of the People's Republic of China, 2004,* p. 23.

69. See Rich Chang, "Missile Buildup Is Accelerating: MND," *Taipei Times,* 8 March 2006; and "Taiwan Says It Now Faces 784 Chinese Missiles," *Agence France Presse,* 8 March 2006.

70. Office of the Secretary of Defense, *Military Power of the People's Republic of China, 2004,* p. 37.

71. Ronald O'Rourke, *China Naval Modernization: Implications for U.S. Navy Capabilities,* Washington, DC: Congressional Research Service, 18 November 2002, p. 5.

72. Office of the Secretary of Defense, *Military Power of the People's Republic of China, 2004,* p. 23.

73. "China Tests New Land-Attack Cruise Missile," *Jane's Missiles and Rockets* (October 2004).

74. Lin Chieh-yu, "China a Threat by 2015, Defense Minister Says," *Taipei Times,* 5 October 2004.

75. Office of the Secretary of Defense, *Military Power of the People's Republic of China, 2005,* p. 29.

76. Lowell E. Jacoby (vice admiral, US Navy; director, Defense Intelligence Agency), "Current and Projected National Security Threats to the United States," statement for the record before the Senate Select Committee on Intelligence, Washington, DC, 16 February 2005, p. 13.

77. According to a recent Congressional Research Service report, "China is modernizing its extensive inventory of anti-ship cruise missiles (ASCMs), which can be launched from land-based strike fighters and bombers, surface combatants, submarines and possibly shore-based launchers. Among the most capable of the new ASCMs being acquired by the PLA Navy is the Russian-made SS-N-27 Sizzler, a highly dangerous ASCM that is to be carried by eight new Kilo-class submarines that China has purchased from Russia." See O'Rourke, *China Naval Modernization,* p. 5.

78. O'Rourke, *China Naval Modernization,* p. 29.

79. See Robert M. Walpole, "Foreign Missile Developments and the Ballistic Missile Threat to the United States Through 2015," statement before the Senate Subcommittee on International Security, Nonproliferation, and Federal Services, Washington, DC, 11 March 2002; Bates Gill, James C. Mulvenon, and Mark Stokes, "The Chinese Second Artillery Corps: Transition to Credible Deterrence," in James C. Mulvenon and Andrew N. D. Yang, eds., *The People's Liberation Army as Organization: Reference Volume v1.0,* Santa Monica: RAND, 2002; and Michael S. Chase and Evan Medeiros, "China's Evolving Nuclear Doctrine," in James Mulvenon and David Finkelstein, eds., *China's Revolution in Doctrinal Affairs: Emerging Trends in the Operational Art of the Chinese People's Liberation Army,* Alexandria, VA: Center for Naval Analysis, 2006.

80. Office of the Secretary of Defense, *Military Power of the People's Republic of China, 2005*, p. 28.

81. Ibid., p. 29.

82. Zheng Dacheng, "Lun zhonggong haijun zhi 094 xing hedongli dandao feidan qianjian" (The Chinese PLA Navy's Type-094 Nuclear-Powered Ballistic Missile Submarine), *Haijun xueshu yuekan* (Naval Science Monthly) 41:1 (February 2007), www.mnd.gov.tw/publication/subject.aspx?topicid= 2642. According to Zheng, the overall capability of China's second-generation nuclear-powered ballistic missile submarine will represent a considerable improvement over its first-generation version, the Xia, and it will constitute a strategic deterrent that could influence the United States if it were considering intervening in a China-Taiwan conflict.

83. Walpole, "Foreign Missile Developments," p. 4.

84. Office of the Secretary of Defense, *Military Power of the People's Republic of China, 2005*, p. 28. The CSS-5 medium-range ballistic missiles are solid-propellant road-mobile missiles.

85. You Ji, "Adding Offensive Teeth to a Defensive Air Force: The New Thinking of the PLAAF," *Issues and Studies* 35:2 (March–April 1999).

86. Office of the Secretary of Defense, *Military Power of the People's Republic of China, 2006*, p. 4.

87. Ibid., p. 6.

88. Edward Cody, "China Now Test-Flying Homemade AWACS," *Washington Post*, 13 November 2004. China tried to purchase four Phalcon radar systems from Israel, but Washington employed diplomatic pressure to persuade Israel to cancel the proposed deal, which would have been worth about US$1 billion.

89. Office of the Secretary of Defense, *Military Power of the People's Republic of China, 2006*, p. 4.

90. O'Rourke, *China Naval Modernization*, p. 5. Also according to this report, "China is deploying modern surface-to-air missile systems across from Taiwan, including long-range and high-altitude systems that have an advertised range sufficient to cover the entire Taiwan Strait."

91. See Medeiros et al., *New Direction for China's Defense Industry*, pp. 109–154. Evan Medeiros and his colleagues found that these improvements in the Chinese shipbuilding constitute a major contribution to the modernization of Chinese naval power. According to the study, "China's shipyards are now producing more advanced naval vessels more quickly and efficiently than in the past. These improvements are best reflected in the serial output of several new classes of military ships in recent years" (p. xxii).

92. O'Rourke, *China Naval Modernization*, p. 11.

93. Office of the Secretary of Defense, *Military Power of the People's Republic of China, 2006*, p. 5.

94. Ibid., p. 30.

95. O'Rourke, *China Naval Modernization,* p. 10.

96. Ibid.

97. Lyle Goldstein and William Murray, "Undersea Dragons: China's Maturing Submarine Force," *International Security* (Spring 2004).

98. Ibid., p. 4.

99. O'Rourke, *China Naval Modernization,* p. 6.

100. See Goldstein and Murray, "Undersea Dragons."

101. O'Rourke, *China Naval Modernization,* p. 26.

102. Ibid., pp. 16–17.

103. For a highly detailed account of the modernization of Chinese ground forces, see Dennis J. Blasko, *The Chinese Army Today: Tradition and Transformation for the 21st Century,* London: Routledge, 2006.

104. Office of the Secretary of Defense, *Military Power of the People's Republic of China, 2006,* p. 5.

105. O'Rourke, *China Naval Modernization,* p. 13.

106. Ibid.

107. Chinese authors have published numerous books on information warfare in recent years. Some of the more interesting volumes include Chi Yajun, ed., *Xinxihua zhanzheng yu xinxi zuozhan lilun jingyao* (Essentials of Informationized War and Information Operations Theory), Beijing: Academy of Military Science Press, 2005; Shen Weiguang, Jie Xizhang, and Li Jijun, *Zhongguo xinxi zhan* (Chinese Information Warfare), Beijing: Xinhua Press, 2004; Li Naiguo, *Xinxi zhan xin lun* (A New Theory of Information Warfare), Beijing: Academy of Military Science Press, 2004; Li Niu, *Xinxi zuozhan zhihui kongzhi* (Information Warfare Command and Control), Beijing: People's Liberation Army Press, 2002; Zhang Tianping, *Zhanlue xinxi zhan yanjiu* (Strategic Information Warfare Research), Beijing: National Defense University Press, 2001; Qing Yonggui, *Zhanyi xinxi zuozhan yanjiu* (Campaign Information Operations Research), Beijing: National Defense University Press, 2000; and Dai Qingmin, ed., *Xinxi zuozhan gailun* (Introduction to Information Warfare), Beijing: People's Liberation Army Press, 1999. In addition, for examples of recent articles, see Wang Baocun, "Zhimian junshi biange: jingzhu xinxi zhan 'gaodi'" (Facing Military Transformation: Competing for the "High Ground" in Information Warfare), *Liaowang xinwen zhoukan* (Outlook Weekly), 25 July 2003; and Li Zhiwei, "Junshi gao jishuhua de wu da qushi: fang junshi kexueyuan zhanlue yanjiubu Chen Bojiang daxiao" (Five Major Trends in the High-Tech Transformation of Military Affairs: An Interview with Senior Colonel Chen Bojiang of the Academy of Military Science's Strategic Research Department), *Guangming ribao* (Guangming Daily), 20 September 2000.

108. Office of the Secretary of Defense, *Military Power of the People's Republic of China, 2006,* p. 35.

109. Dean Cheng, *"Zhanyixue* and Joint Campaigns," in Mulvenon and Finkelstein, *China's Revolution in Doctrinal Affairs,* p. 114.

110. Office of the Secretary of Defense, *Military Power of the People's Republic of China, 2006,* p. 31.

111. Richard P. Lawless, "Statement Before the Senate Foreign Relations Committee, Subcomittee on East Asian and Pacific Affairs," Washington, DC, 23 April 2004.

112. Office of the Secretary of Defense, *Military Power of the People's Republic of China, 2006,* p. 33.

113. Medeiros et al., *New Direction for China's Defense Industry,* p. xxiii.

114. Kevin Pollpeter, "The Chinese Vision of Space Military Operations," in Mulvenon and Finkelstein, *China's Revolution in Doctrinal Affairs.* Types of capabilities discussed in Chinese writings include antisatellite satellites, laser antisatellite weapons, kinetic-energy weapons, and computer network attacks. Chinese analysts also emphasize passive countermeasures like camouflage, concealment, denial, and deception. Some writers mention taking into account the timing of satellite overflights to schedule sensitive activities.

115. Office of the Secretary of Defense, *Military Power of the People's Republic of China, 2006,* p. 35.

116. Two of the most important and informative volumes that address the PLA's evolving approach to warfare are Wang Houqing and Zhang Xingye, eds., *Zhanyixue* (The Science of Campaigns), Beijing: National Defense University Press, May 2000; and Peng Guangqian and Yao Youzhi, eds., *The Science of Military Strategy,* Beijing: Military Science Publishing House, 2005. The latter volume is the official PLA Academy of Military Science translation of the Chinese version of *The Science of Strategy,* which was published in 2001. These volumes deal with the strategic and operational levels of warfare. For PLA views on the tactical level of warfare, see Yao Jiangning, *Hetong jingong zhanshu jiaocheng* (Combined Offensive Tactics Teaching Materials), Beijing: Academy of Military Science Press, 2005; and Jing Jisheng, *Hetong fangyu zhanshu jiaocheng* (Combined Defensive Tactics Teaching Materials), Beijing: Academy of Military Science Press, 2005.

117. State Council Information Office, *China's National Defense in 2004.* See also Academy of Military Science, Operations Theory and Regulations Research Department, *Xinxihua zuozhan lilun xuexi zhinan: xinxihua zuozhan 400 ti* (Informationized Operations Theory Study Guide: 400 Informationized Operations Questions), Beijing, 2005.

118. See, for example, Xiong Guangkai, "On World Revolution in Military Affairs and the Chinese Army Building: Speech by Gen. Xiong Guangkai, Deputy Chief of the General Staff, Chinese People's Liberation Army, at the 5th International Symposium Course in the National Defense University, CPLA, October 17, 2003," *International Strategic Studies* no. 4 (2003).

119. Wang and Zhang, *Science of Campaigns.*

120. Xiong, "On World Revolution in Military Affairs," pp. 4–5.

121. On the PLA's evolving concepts of operations, see Mulvenon and Finkelstein, *China's Revolution in Doctrinal Affairs.* The term *gangyao* has no precise English-language equivalent, but it translates roughly as "guidelines," "outline," "essentials," or "compendium."

122. David Finkelstein, "Thinking About the PLA's 'Revolution in Doctrinal Affairs,'" in Mulvenon and Finkelstein, *China's Revolution in Doctrinal Affairs,* pp. 10–11.

123. Ibid., p. 19. At the same time, however, David Finkelstein cautions that there are differences between "basic theory" and "applied theory" in Chinese military science, and that this must be taken into account when assessing the available primary sources. In short: "Studying such volumes as *Zhanyixue* provides tremendous and much needed insights into the theoretical framework of operational theory at the campaign level of warfare, but it would be analytically dangerous to assume *prima facie* that its contents reflect the specifics of the various newly published series of *gangyao.*"

124. David M. Finkelstein, "The Chinese People's Liberation Army in 2020," paper presented at the National Intelligence Council conference "The Changing Nature of Warfare: Global Trends 2020," 26 May 2004, p. 21.

125. See Wang and Zhang, *Science of Campaigns.*

126. Some PLA strategists make the counterargument that the complexity and speed of modern, "informationalized" warfare favors decentralized command systems with greater flexibility.

127. See, for example, Lu Lihua, *Jundui zhihui lilun xuexi zhinan* (Military Command Theory Study Guide), Beijing: National Defense University Press, 2005.

128. Wen Han, "A Vice Admiral of the Navy and a Lieutenant General of the Air Force Have Been Promoted As Deputy Chiefs of General Staff," *Wen wei po,* 17 July 2004.

129. Ibid.

130. Recent Chinese-language publications on joint operations include Ceng Sunan, ed., *Yitihua lianhe zuozhan zhuanti yanjiu* (Research on Integrated Joint Operations), Beijing: Academy of Military Science Press, 2004; Jiang Fangran, ed., *Lianhe zuozhan silingbu gongzuo* (Joint Operations Headquarters Work), Beijing: Academy of Military Science Press, 2004; Zhou Dewang, *Lianhe zuozhan zhihui jigou yamjiu* (Joint Operations Command Structure Research), Beijing: National Defense University Press, 2002; Gao Yubiao, *Lianhe zhanyixue jiaocheng* (Joint Campaign Teaching Materials), Beijing: Academy of Military Science Press, 2001; Zhang Peigao, *Lianhe zhanyi zhihui jiaocheng* (Joint Campaign Command Teaching Materials), Beijing: Academy of Military Science Press, 2001; An Weiping, ed., *Lianhe zuozhan xinlun* (New Theory of Joint Warfare), Beijing: National Defense University Press, 2000; Chen Anran, *Lianhe zuozhan zhengzhi gongzuo* (Political Work in Joint Operations), Beijing: National Defense University

Press, 1999; and Wang Zhiyuan, ed., *Lianhe xinxi zuozhan* (Joint Information Warfare), Beijing: Academy of Military Arts and Literature Press, 1999.

131. Cheng, *"Zhanyixue* and Joint Campaigns," in Mulvenon and Finkelstein, *China's Revolution in Doctrinal Affairs,* p. 101.

132. Ibid., p. 102.

133. Ibid., p. 107.

134. Ibid., p. 115.

135. Joint campaigns involve the participation of forces from more than one service, while combined arms campaigns involve the participation of multiple branches from a single service. For full definitions of these terms, see US Department of Defense, *Department of Defense Dictionary of Military and Associated Terms,* Joint Publication no. 1-02, Washington, DC, 12 April 2001 (as amended through 17 September 2006), www.dtic.mil/doctrine/jel/doddict/index.html.

136. Office of the Secretary of Defense, *Military Power of the People's Republic of China, 2006,* p. 16.

137. Ibid., p. 17.

138. See, for example, Wang Jingfa, *Zhongguo junshi houqin biange da zhanlue* (Strategy of Chinese Military Logistics Transformation), Beijing: National Defense University Press, 2005; and Shao Hua and Yan Hui, *Xinxi shidai yu junshi houqin* (The Information Age and Military Logistics), Beijing: Contemporary China Press, 2004.

139. Office of the Secretary of Defense, *Military Power of the People's Republic of China, 2006,* p. 30.

140. Ze Dongsheng, "War Mobilization," in Qian Shugen, ed., *Zhongguo zhanzheng dongyuan baike quanshu* (China War Mobilization Encyclopedia), Beijing: Academy of Military Science Press, 2003, p. 4. Depending on the scale of the conflict, a state may undertake either a general mobilization or a local mobilization. The *China War Mobilization Encyclopedia* also indicates that mobilization may be carried out either openly or clandestinely. The more traditional option is open mobilization, which entails publicly issuing a mobilization order and announcing that the nation is shifting to a wartime footing. Chinese strategists, however, also envision the possibility of clandestine mobilization, which is conducted secretly and employs various types of cover and deception techniques to prevent adversaries from detecting Chinese preparations.

141. Ze, "War Mobilization," p. 8.

142. Chen Zhao, "Zhanzheng dongyuanxue" (Science of Mobilization), in Qian, *Zhongguo zhanzheng dongyuan baike quanshu,* p. 3.

143. Antoaneta Bezlova, "China's Army Leaner and Meaner," *Asia Times,* 25 January 2006.

144. Finkelstein, "Chinese People's Liberation Army in 2020," p. 3.

145. Kenneth Allen and Maryanne Kivlehan-Wise, "Implementing PLA Second Artillery Doctrinal Reforms," in Mulvenon and Finkelstein, *China's*

228 NOTES

Revolution in Doctrinal Affairs, pp. 183–184. The PLA still relies heavily on conscripts, however, and faces several associated problems. Many conscripts have only a middle-school education. In addition, corruption and abuse of conscription systems remain widespread problems.

146. Studies that focus on professional military education and defense education include Liu Zhihui, *Jundui yuanxiao jiaoyu gaige* (Military School and University Educational Reform), Beijing: National Defense University Press, 2004; Wang Xinguo, ed., *Guofang jiaoyu* (National Defense Education), Beijing: Machine Industry Press, 2004; Fu Jingyun and Gao Hongqing, eds., *Guofang jiaoyu gailun* (Introduction to National Defense Education), Beijing: Academy of Military Science Press, 2003; Yuan Wei and Zhang Zhuo, *Zhongguo junxiao fazhan shi* (History of the Development of China's Military Schools), Beijing: National Defense University Press, 2001; and Qiu Shulin, *Jundui yuanxiao tizhi yanjiu* (Military School and University System Research), Beijing: National Defense University Press, 2000.

147. Thomas J. Bickford, "Professional Military Education in the Chinese People's Liberation Army," in James C. Mulvenon and Andrew N. D. Yang, eds., *A Poverty of Riches: New Challenges and Opportunities in PLA Research,* Santa Monica: RAND, 2003, p. 1.

148. Qian Haihao, *Jundui zuzhi bianzhixue jiaocheng* (Military Organizational Studies Teaching Materials), Beijing: Academy of Military Science Press, 2001, p. 121.

149. Bickford, "Professional Military Education." Nevertheless, by 1998, only about half of the PLA's academies and schools had their own campus computer networks.

150. David Shambaugh, *Modernizing China's Military: Progress, Problems, and Prospects,* Berkeley: University of California Press, 2002. See also Academy of Military Science, World Military Affairs Research Department, *Yilake zhanzheng: zhanlue, zhanshuji junshi shang de jingyan jiaoxun* (The Iraq War: Strategic and Tactical Experience and Lessons), Beijing, 2005; and Zhan Xuexi, *Yilake zhanzheng* (The Iraq War), Beijing: People's Press, 2004.

151. Ministry of National Defense, *2004 National Defense Report,* Taipei: Government Information Office, 2005, p. 32.

152. Ibid.

153. Office of the Secretary of Defense, *Military Power of the People's Republic of China, 2006,* p. 16.

154. Ministry of National Defense, *2004 National Defense Report,* p. 32.

155. Ko Shu-ling, "Lu Urges Legislature to Counter Beijing's Build-Up," *Taipei Times,* 13 March 2006.

156. Office of the Secretary of Defense, *Military Power of the People's Republic of China, 2005,* p. 3.

157. Office of the Secretary of Defense, *Military Power of the People's Republic of China, 2006*, p. 3.

158. Ibid., p. 2.

159. "PLA to Conduct Maneuver at Dongshan Island This Month," *People's Daily*, 8 July 2004.

160. See Office of the Secretary of Defense, *Military Power of the People's Republic of China, 2006*, pp. 38–41; and Andrew Scobell, "China's Military Threat to Taiwan in the 21st Century: Coercion or Capture?" *Taiwan Defense Affairs* 4:2 (Winter 2003–2004). These potential courses of action are not mutually exclusive. For example, Beijing might choose to combine air and missile strikes with a blockade to maximize pressure on Taiwan. In addition, it is of course possible that Beijing might move through two or more of the potential courses of action sequentially, progressing from lower to higher levels of intensity. For instance, Beijing might progress from persuasion and coercion to limited-force options and ultimately decide to escalate to an amphibious invasion if lower levels of violence failed to achieve China's political objectives. Nonetheless, it is useful to consider these courses of action as distinct for the purpose of assessing the options available to Chinese leaders should they make the fateful decision to use force against Taiwan.

161. Wang Wenrong, ed., *Zhanluexue* (The Science of Strategy), Beijing: National Defense University Press, 1999, p. 252.

162. See Lee Jui-kuang, "Year 2005–2010: Evaluation of China's Implementation of Decapitation Warfare Against Taiwan," *Taiwan Defense Affairs* 4:3 (Spring 2004).

163. Mark A. Stokes, "The Chinese Joint Aerospace Campaign: Strategy, Doctrine, and Force Modernization," in Mulvenon and Finkelstein, *China's Revolution in Doctrinal Affairs*. For a skeptical take on the PLA's prospects for success, see Robert A. Pape, "Why a Chinese Preemptive Strike Against Taiwan Would Fail," *Taiwan Defense Affairs* 3:2 (Winter 2002–2003).

164. PLA writings on topics related to this type of scenario include Academy of Military Science, World Military Affairs Research Department, ed., *Kuaisu juedingxing zuozhan gouxiang* (Rapid and Decisive Operations Concepts), Beijing, 2005; and Fan Chengbin, *Gao jishu tiaojian xia zhanyi tanhuan zhan yanjiu* (Research on Campaign Paralysis Warfare Under High-Tech Conditions), Beijing: National Defense University Press, 2003. On psychological warfare, see Wen Lanchang, ed., *Gao jishu tiaojian xia xinlizhan gailun* (An Introduction to Psychological Warfare Under High-Tech Conditions), Beijing: Academy of Military Science Press, 2001.

165. For a detailed analysis of "noncontact warfare," see Liu Yuejun, Zhang Liming, and Xin Xilu, *Fei jiechu zhan* (Noncontact Warfare), Beijing: Academy of Military Science Press, 2004. For a brief discussion of the

roles of information warfare, firepower, and psychological operations in noncontact warfare, see "Xiandai junshi pinglun: 'fei jiechu' zuozhan de qianti shie jiechu" (Contemporary Military Affairs Commentary: Contact Is the Prerequisite for 'Noncontact' War), *Xinhua,* June 27, 2005.

166. Shi Yinhong, "Several Grand Strategy Issues Concerning Taiwan Require Facing Up To," *Zhanlue yu guanli* (Strategy and Management) (April 2000).

167. Stokes, "Chinese Joint Aerospace Campaign," p. 236.

168. Ibid., p. 301.

169. Office of the Secretary of Defense, *Military Power of the People's Republic of China, 2006,* p. 39.

170. For Taiwanese views, see Wu Chia-shin, "The Assessment of Communist China's Threat to Launch Amphibious (or Sea-Air-Land) Invasion Against Taiwan During 2005–2010 and the Improvements for Taiwanese Ground Forces," *Taiwan Defense Affairs* 4:3 (Spring 2004).

171. This discussion draws on Richard L. Russell, "What If . . . 'China Attacks Taiwan!'" *Parameters* 31:3 (Autumn 2001).

172. Wang and Zhang, *Science of Campaigns.*

173. Office of the Secretary of Defense, *Military Power of the People's Republic of China, 2006.*

174. On operational challenges that antiaccess strategies could pose for US forces, see Christopher Bowie, *The Anti-Access Threat and Theater Air Bases,* Washington, DC: Center for Strategic and Budgetary Assessments, 2002.

175. O'Rourke, *China Naval Modernization,* p. 24.

176. Office of the Secretary of Defense, *Military Power of the People's Republic of China, 2006,* pp. 25–26.

177. Roger Cliff, Mark Burles, Michael Chase, Derek Eaton, and Kevin Pollpeter, *Entering the Dragon's Lair: Chinese Military Anti-Access Strategies and Potential U.S. Responses,* Santa Monica: RAND, 2007.

178. Office of the Secretary of Defense, *Military Power of the People's Republic of China, 2006,* p. 30.

179. Ibid.

180. Edward Cody, "China Builds a Smaller, Stronger Military," *Washington Post,* 12 April 2005.

181. Office of the Secretary of Defense, *Military Power of the People's Republic of China, 2006,* pp. 40–41.

182. See Lonnie D. Henley, "War Control: Chinese Concepts of Escalation Management," in Andrew Scobell and Larry M. Wortzel, eds., *Shaping China's Security Environment: The Role of the People's Liberation Army,* Carlisle, PA: Strategic Studies Institute, US Army War College, 2006. For Chinese views, see Xiao Tianliang, *Zhanzheng kongzhi wenti yanjiu* (Research on Problems of War Control), Beijing: National Defense University Press, 2002.

183. Office of the Secretary of Defense, *Military Power of the People's Republic of China, 2006,* p. 13. Furthermore, according to this report, "The lack of operational experience hampers outside assessments of the extent to which PLA reformers have produced a force capable of meeting the aspirations of its doctrine. The same applies to internal PLA assessments as well, giving rise to the potential for false confidence or other miscalculations in crises."

184. David Shambaugh, "China's Military Making Steady and Surprising Progress," in Tellis and Wills, *Strategic Asia 2005–06.*

185. Jim Yardley and Thom Shanker, "Chinese Naval Buildup Gives Pentagon New Worries," *New York Times,* 8 April 2005.

Chapter 5

1. National Security Council, *2006 National Security Report,* Taipei: Government Information Office, 20 May 2006.

2. Office of the President, "President Chen Shui-bian's Inauguration Speech," Taipei, 20 May 2000, p. 5.

3. In 2005, Nauru shifted recognition back to Taipei, apparently after Taiwan offered a better deal than the tiny island was receiving from the PRC. See Ministry of Foreign Affairs, "The Republic of China (Taiwan) and the Republic of Nauru Restored Full Diplomatic Relations on May 14, 2005," Taipei, 7 October 2002.

4. Office of the President, "President Chen's Opening Address to the 29th Annual Meeting of the World Federation of Taiwanese Associations," Taipei, 3 August 2002.

5. The Chen administration released a formal clarification about ten days after Chen's speech. See Government Information Office, "Explanation of President Chen Shui-bian's Remarks of August 3, 2002," Taipei, 12 August 2002.

6. See White House, Office of the Press Secretary, "Remarks by President Bush and Premier Wen Jiabao in Photo Opportunity," Washington, DC, 9 December 2003.

7. The reformulated questions contained less controversial wording. One question asked voters if they would support the procurement of missile defense systems to counter China's missile buildup. The other question asked voters to express their support for negotiations with China on the establishment of a peaceful framework for the management of cross-Strait relations.

8. Alice Hung, "President Chen Seen Walking Tightrope on PRC," *Reuters,* 18 May 2004.

9. Vice President Lu added fuel to the fire by comparing the National Unification Council and national unification guidelines to "spoiled food in a freezer" left behind by the Kuomintang when it was the ruling

party. She said they should have been discarded long ago, since they were well past their "expiration dates." See Han Nai-kuo, "NUC Is Like 'Spoiled Food in a Freezer': Vice President," *Central News Agency,* 28 February 2006.

10. See Mark Magnier and Tsai Ting-i, "Taiwan Name-Change Campaign Annoys China," *Los Angeles Times,* 14 February 2007.

11. President Chen made the statement in a 4 March 2007 speech marking the twenty-fifth anniversary of the Formosan Association for Public Affairs, an influential proindependence lobbying group. For the full text of Chen's remarks, see "Zongtong chuxi Taiwanren gonggong shiwuhui 25 zhounian qingzhu wanyan" (President Chen Attends the Formosan Association for Public Affairs 25th Anniversary Banquet), 4 March 2007, www.president.gov.tw/php-bin/prez/shownews.php4?rid=12655.

12. See "DPP, KMT Rally for UN Referendums," *Taipei Times,* 16 September 2007.

13. See "Mainland Official Lambastes Taiwan Leader's New Secessionist Remarks," *Xinhua,* 16 September 2007, http://news.xinhuanet.com/english/2007-09/16/content_6734679.htm; and "China Condemns Taiwan Pro-UN Membership Rally, Prepares for 'Serious Situation,'" *International Herald Tribune,* 16 September 2007, www.iht.com/articles/ap/2007/09/17/asia/as-gen-china-taiwan.php.

14. Author interviews, United States, 2007.

15. Thomas J. Christensen, "A Strong and Moderate Taiwan," speech to US-Taiwan Business Council defense industry conference, Annapolis, MD, 11 September 2007, www.state.gov/p/eap/rls/rm/2007/91979.htm.

16. Chen dismissed US criticism as well-meaning, but misguided: "The United States has its interest, while we have ours. Sometimes the two do not correspond and sometimes they even clash. We will do our best to find common ground and reach a consensus." See "Chen Rebuts US' Referendum Criticism," *Taipei Times,* 14 September 2007.

17. Office of the Secretary of Defense, *Military Power of the People's Republic of China, 2006,* annual report to Congress, Washington, DC: Department of Defense, 2006, p. 37.

18. "Arms Procurement Necessary for the Nation's Survival," *Taipei Times,* 24 April 2005.

19. Chen Chien-hsun, "Taiwan's Burgeoning Budget Deficit," *Asian Survey* 45:3 (May–June 2005).

20. Defense spending also declined in absolute terms, falling from about US$8.09 billion in 2002 to US$7.84 billion in 2006. See Ministry of National Defense, *2006 National Defense Report,* p. 211.

21. Ministry of National Defense, *2006 National Defense Report,* p. 145.

22. Chinmei Sung and Perris Lee, "Taiwan Approves $50 Billion Budget, Military Spending," *Bloomberg,* 16 June 2007.

23. Chen, "Taiwan's Burgeoning Budget Deficit." Tax revenue has been declining for many years, with the sharpest drop seen in the period from 1996—the year of Taiwan's first-ever democratic presidential election—to the present.

24. Chen, "Taiwan's Burgeoning Budget Deficit," p. 393.

25. The submarine acquisition in particular has been bogged down by concerns about high program costs and a considerable amount of uncertainty over who would actually build the boats, since the United States no longer manufactures diesel submarines and none of the countries that do are willing to risk offending China by selling submarines to Taiwan.

26. All government bills are initially sent to the Procedure Committee, which must list a bill on the legislative agenda before it can be read and referred to the appropriate standing committee or committees. The Procedure Committee is thus a very important player, since it has the power to prevent the other relevant committees from even considering the Executive Yuan's proposals.

27. Ministry of National Defense, *2004 National Defense Report,* p. 145.

28. Author interview with a US analyst, Washington, DC, March 2004.

29. Michael D. Swaine, *Taiwan's National Security, Defense Policy, and Weapons Procurement Processes,* Santa Monica: RAND, 1999, p. 46.

30. Li Wenzhong, He Minhao, Lin Zhuoshui, Duan Yikang, Chen Zhongxin, Tang Huosheng, and Xiao Meiqin, *Taiwan bingli guimo yanjiu baogao* (Research Report on the Scale of Taiwan's Armed Forces), Democratic Progressive Party, Policy Committee Research Report Series, Taipei, March 2003, p. 30.

31. Ku Ch'ung-lien, "My Views on the National Defense Report and the Future Development of the Military," *Jianduan keji* (Defense Technology Monthly) (September 2002).

32. See, for example, Chen Chao-min (vice minister of armament and acquisition, Taiwan Ministry of National Defense) in "Remarks to the U.S.-Taiwan Defense Industry Conference," San Antonio, TX, 13 February 2003.

33. National Security Council, *2006 National Security Report,* p. 88.

34. Author interview with an international relations scholar, Taipei, 2002.

35. Luor Ching-jyuhn, Wang Huei-huang, and Yeh Jun-hsiu, "Reinventing National Defense Organization in Taiwan," *Taiwan Defense Affairs* 2:1 (Fall 2001), p. 147.

36. Mark Stokes, "Taiwan's Security: Beyond the Special Budget," *Asian Outlook* no. 2 (27 March 2006), p. 2.

37. Ibid., p. 4.

38. Loh I-cheng, "Behind Taiwan's Debate over the $18.3 Billion US Arms Deal," National Policy Foundation Backgrounder no. 094-001 (26 January 2005).

39. Author interview with a US researcher, Washington, DC, January 2006.

40. See Li Lu-t'ai, "Jilong ji jian jiaru zhan zhandou xulie hou: zaitan jiandui fanking zuozhan" (Adding Kidd-Class Destroyers to the Force: A Reexamination of ROC Navy Air Defense Operations), *Haijun xueshu yuekan* (Naval Science Monthly) 40:4 (July 2006); and Chang Kuo-hua (lieutenant commander, ROC navy), "Haijun jiandui fangkong zuozhan nengli zhi tantao: yi jilong ji jian wei li" (Discussion of the ROC Navy's Fleet Air Defense Capability: The Example of the Kidd-Class Destroyers), *Haijun xueshu yuekan* 40:4 (July 2006).

41. "Arms Procurement Necessary for the Nation's Survival."

42. "Lawmakers Plan to Shift Funding to Buy Weapons," *Taiwan News*, 24 August 2005.

43. Mark Magnier, "Taiwan's Logjam on Weapons Bill Frustrates U.S.," *Los Angeles Times*, 8 October 2005.

44. The Kuomintang had submitted requests for submarines, PC-3 aircraft, and Patriot antimissile batteries under Lee Teng-hui. Many of the critics of the arms procurement plan supported the same proposals when the KMT was in power.

45. "A Call to Arms," *Taiwan Business Topics* 34:11 (2004).

46. Su Chi, "Soft Power + Defensive Defense = National Security," *United Daily News*, 24 January 2006.

47. "Parties Spar over Pentagon Report," *Taipei Times*, 21 July 2005.

48. Author interview with a Taipei-based researcher, Washington, DC, February 2006.

49. Ko Shu-ling, "KMT Willing to Review Arms Plan," *Taipei Times*, 24 August 2005, p. 3. Lin maintained that it was a bad deal regardless of whether it was funded with a special budget bill or as part of the annual defense budget.

50. Ko Shu-ling, "Pan-Blues Kill Arms Bill Again," *Taipei Times*, 23 March 2005.

51. Specifically, about 92 percent of those who cast valid ballots voted yes, but only about 45 percent of eligible voters participated, and the result was thus declared invalid.

52. I thank an anonymous reviewer for pointing out that the boycott of the referendum implied opposition.

53. "KMT, PFP Debate Tsai's Logic on 2004 Referendum," *Central News Agency*, 30 September 2005.

54. Ministry of National Defense, Military Spokesman's Office, "Evaluation of Factors Limiting Domestic Submarine-Building," Taipei, 22 March 2005.

55. Ibid. US deputy defense secretary Paul Wolfowitz conveyed this message to Legislative Yuan speaker Wang Jin-ping in June 2004. The following

month, Richard Lawless, US deputy assistant secretary of defense for East Asia, sent a letter to Taiwan in which the Defense Department formally declared that it did not support the proposal because it would not be cost-effective and would probably delay the timetable for delivery of the submarines.

56. Ministry of National Defense, Military Spokesman's Office, "Evaluation of Factors Limiting Domestic Submarine-Building."

57. Ibid. As the spokesman for the Ministry of National Defense put it in his statement: "It is absolutely not the case that the Americans have taken the whole bowl of rice for themselves."

58. Author interview, United States, 2007.

59. I thank an anonymous reviewer for raising this important point about the reasons for the Pan-Blue camp's opposition to the arms sales proposal.

60. "KMT Lawmakers Back a Strong National Defense," *Central News Agency,* 1 May 2005. For example, KMT Legislative Yuan member Shuai Hua-min, a retired ROC army general, said he supported maintaining sufficient defense capabilities to ensure that Taipei would have at least some leverage in future negotiations with China, but opposed the special budget because he regarded some of the proposed arms purchases as a waste of scarce resources.

61. See Ministry of National Defense, Military Spokesman's Office, "Clarifications Concerning the ROC Three-Part Major Military Procurement," Taipei, 18 March 2005.

62. Ministry of National Defense, Military Spokesman's Office, "Speech of Minister Lee Jye, Ministry of National Defense," Taipei, 22 February 2005.

63. For more on this comical publicity campaign, see Lin Chieh-yu, "Give Up Milk Tea, Save Up for Weapons, MND Urges," *Taipei Times,* 22 September 2004, p. 4.

64. Rich Chang, "High Success Rate Claimed for Patriots," *Taipei Times,* 22 March 2005.

65. Ministry of National Defense, Military Spokesman's Office, "Clarifications."

66. Ibid.

67. Ibid.

68. Ibid.

69. "Taiwan Says U.S. Arms Deal Will Fend Off China," *Reuters,* 28 June 2005.

70. Lilian Wu, "President Offers Leadership Advice to New Generals," *Central News Agency,* 29 December 2005. Chen also stated that Taiwan should not rely too heavily on foreign intervention in the event of a conflict, and that increasing the defense budget would not squeeze out spending on social welfare programs.

71. Lai I-chung, "Can Opposing Weapons Purchases Bring Peace?" *Taiwan Daily,* 28 September 2004.

72. "Taiwan Says U.S. Arms Deal Will Fend Off China."

73. See Office of the President, "News Release: President Chen Promotes General Peng Sheng-chu," Taipei, 31 March 2006. President Chen criticized the opposition for blocking the budget "for no reason" other than partisan rivalry and the desire to jockey for electoral position.

74. Jane Rickards, "Defense Minister Urges Support for Weapons Purchase," *China Post,* 22 September 2004.

75. Changes in the foreign exchange rate also contributed to the reductions in the total amount of funding that were announced in March and September 2005. When the budget was originally submitted in June 2004, the exchange rate was NT$34.5 = US$1, but the March 2005 special budget used an exchange rate of NT$33.0 = US$1, and the September 2005 special budget used a rate of NT$32.0 = US$1.

76. "Changes in Defense Budget Seen As a 'Grueling Decision,'" *Taiwan News,* 31 August 2005.

77. Ministry of National Defense, "Press Conference Reference Material," Taipei, 7 March 2006.

78. Rich Chang, "MND Gives Up on Special Budget," *Taipei Times,* 22 February 2006.

79. "Taiwan Opposition Looks for Accord on Arms Deal," *Reuters,* 24 March 2006.

80. See for example "Taiwan Opposition Can't Agree on US Arms Deal," *Reuters,* 15 March 2006. This and other media reports suggested that many lawmakers were willing to approve the purchase of the twelve P-3 Orion antisubmarine warfare aircraft, but wanted to shelve the Ministry of National Defense's request for six Patriot missile batteries and could not reach an agreement over the diesel electric submarines.

81. Rich Chang, "Defense Minister Determined to Fight On," *Taipei Times,* 20 March 2006.

82. "President Chen Promotes General Peng Sheng-chu."

83. Office of the Secretary of Defense, *Military Power of the People's Republic of China, 2006,* p. 6.

84. Ko Shu-ling, "Lee Links Budget to China Threat," *Taipei Times,* 18 March 2005, p. 3.

85. National Security Council, *2006 National Security Report,* p. 89. The report also proposes the creation of a Taiwanese advanced defense research agency "to provide a platform for integrating defense technological needs and setting development goals for critical defense technologies."

86. Richard A. Bitzinger, "The Eclipse of Taiwan's Defense Industry and Growing Dependencies on the United States for Advanced Armaments: Implications for U.S.-Taiwan-Chinese Relations," *Issues and Studies* 38:1 (March 2002).

87. Rich Chang, "Missile Buildup Is Accelerating: MND," *Taipei Times,* 8 March 2006.

88. Chu Ming, "Wan Chien Missile Can Attack China's Ballistic Missile Bases from Long Distances; Successful Test Places Hong Kong, Shanghai, Fujian, Zhejiang, and Guangdong Within Range," *P'ing-kuo jih-pao* (Apple Daily), 20 April 2006. The report states that the Chungshan Institute of Science and Technology initiated work on the program in 1999.

89. Stokes, "Taiwan's Security," p. 8.

90. "Taiwan Made 3 Cruise Missile Prototypes: Jane's," *Agence France Presse,* 9 January 2006.

91. "Taiwan to Improve Long-Range Strike Capability," *Ch'uan-chiu fang-wei tsa-chih* (Defense International) (February 2005).

92. Chu, "Wan Chien Missile."

93. Ibid.

94. Hsu Shao-hsuan, "Lee Jye Confirms That 'Wan Chien' Project Targets Enemy Airports," *Tzu-yu shih-pao* (Liberty Times), 9 March 2006; and Lu The-yun, "Lee Jye Furious at the Charge of Arms Sale Scoundrel in the Legislative Yuan," *United Daily News,* 9 March 2006.

95. "Taiwan Made 3 Cruise Missile Prototypes."

96. See Tseng Shiang-yin, "The Enhancement of Taiwan's Missile Defense," *Taiwan Defense Affairs* 5:3 (Spring 2005); and Liu Yuan-chung, "The Threat Evaluation of PLA Tactical Guided Missiles to Taiwan Between 2005 and 2010," *Taiwan Defense Affairs* 4:3 (Spring 2004).

97. Michael D. Swaine and Roy D. Kamphausen, "Military Modernization in Taiwan," in Ashley J. Tellis and Michael Wills, eds., *Strategic Asia 2005–06: Military Modernization in an Era of Uncertainty,* Seattle, National Bureau of Asian Research, September 2005, pp. 406–407.

98. Richard Lawless (US deputy assistant secretary of defense for Asian and Pacific affairs) in "Remarks to US-Taiwan Business Council Defense Industry Conference," San Antonio, TX, 13 February 2003. Lawless urged Taiwan to improve its missile defense capabilities, stating that, "without defenses, the PRC's growing arsenal of increasingly accurate and lethal ballistic missiles may have devastating strategic and operational-level effects on Taiwan's critical infrastructure, air defenses, and naval operations."

99. Kurt M. Campbell, Jeremiah Gertler, Derek Mitchell, and Clark Murdock, *The Paths Ahead: Missile Defense in Asia,* Washington, DC: Center for Strategic and International Studies, March 2006, p. 21.

100. Chang King-yuh, Tseng Yung-hsieng, and Chiu Kuan-hsuan, eds., *Quadrennial National Security Estimate Report,* Taipei: Foundation on International and Cross-Strait Studies, 2004, p. 45.

101. Rich Chang, "Defense Officials Losing Faith in Missile Defense Potential," *Taipei Times,* 10 April 2006.

102. See "Arms Procurement Necessary for the Nation's Survival." According to Stokes: "Development of a comprehensive, leak-proof missile

defense architecture that would defend against a full-scale attack associated with an invasion is economically infeasible. However, a limited architecture . . . would provide an effective defense against limited strikes against Taiwan's main urban areas and key military facilities" (p. 11).

103. Chen Pi-chao, "The American RMA, JFO, and Lessons for the Defense of Taiwan," *Taiwan Defense Affairs* 4:4 (Summer 2004). In Chen's words, "The combined active and passive missile defense will better enable Taiwan to practice deterrence by denial. That our air power can largely survive intact initial surprise, saturation missile attacks will by itself deter the attacker from taking the plunge."

104. Swaine and Kamphausen, "Military Modernization in Taiwan," p. 405. The long-range early-warning radars would enhance Taiwan's ability to detect Chinese missiles and aircraft, and could be used to cue missile defense systems. Some analysts have suggested, however, that the systems would be of limited utility in a conflict scenario, since they would likely be disabled or destroyed during the initial wave of Chinese attacks.

105. First-generation jet fighters were initially deployed in the late 1940s and early 1950s and included aircraft such as the US F-86 Sabre and the Soviet Mig-15; second-generation fighters, such as the US F-100 Super Sabre and Soviet Mig-19 and Mig-21, entered service beginning in the early 1950s; third-generation fighters, such as the Northrup F-5, were first deployed in the 1960s; fourth-generation fighters, such as the US F-14, F-15, and F-16 and the Soviet Su-27, entered service in the 1970s and 1980s; fifth-generation fighters, the most modern, include the US F-22 Raptor and F-35 joint-strike fighter. The F-22 achieved initial operating capability in December 2005, and the F-35 is expected to enter service by 2010.

106. See, for example, Chuang Chi-ting, "Military to Study Cause of Crash," *Taipei Times,* 16 November 2001, p. 2. For a detailed analysis of training crashes from 1978 to 2000, see Li Wen-chin (lieutenant colonel, ROC air force), Li Tzung-hsien (captain, ROC air force), and Don Harris, "A Study of the Application of the Human Factor Analysis and Classification Sytem (HFACS) to Aviation Accident Investigations," *Kongjun xueshu yuekan* (Air Force Science Monthly) 592 (July 2006). The article appears in English, with Chinese translation.

107. "Call for Purchase of F-16s Rises After F-5 Fighter Jet Crashes in Taiwan," *Defense News,* 19 June 2006. DPP legislator Hsueh Ling said, "It is ridiculous to continue operating such aircraft, risking the lives of pilots."

108. "Taiwan Works on Defense Strategy in the Event of Attack from China," *Cable News Network,* 6 November 2000, www.taiwansecurity.org/news/cnn-110600.htm.

109. "Improved Version of Indigenous Defense Fighter to Be Tested," *Taipei Times,* 17 April 2006.

110. Swaine and Kamphausen, "Military Modernization in Taiwan," p. 406.

111. "Nations Defenses Strengthened with New US Missiles," *Taipei Times*, 23 September 2004. In September 2000, the United States agreed to sell 200 beyond-visual-range Aim-120 advanced medium-range air-to-air missiles to Taiwan for its F-16s, on the condition that they would not be delivered until China acquired a similar capability. The United States delivered them to Taiwan in September 2004, after the PLA air force had deployed the AA-12, a comparable beyond-visual-range missile, on its Russian-made fighters.

112. The F-16 C/D fighters that Taiwan is considering purchasing from the United States, however, have much greater ground-attack capabilities. See US Air Force, "F-16 Fighting Falcon," www.af.mil/factsheets/factsheet .asp?fsid=103.

113. Wu Taijing, "Taiwan Could Buy HARM, Says Lawmaker," *Taiwan News,* 10 October 2006.

114. Swaine and Kamphausen, "Military Modernization in Taiwan," pp. 405–406.

115. Rich Chang, "Air Force Planned to Buy Jets that Need Shorter Runway," *Taipei Times,* 23 January 2006.

116. See, for example, Lo Chih-cheng, "The Operational Requirements for the ROCAF's Next Generation Fighters," *Taiwan Defense Affairs* 5:2 (Winter 2004–2005).

117. Rich Chang, "MND Eyes Purchase of Fighter Jets," *Taipei Times,* 17 May 2006, p. 2.

118. "Taiwan Military Plans to Buy New Fighter Planes," *Central News Agency,* 19 May 2006. In May 2006 testimony before the Legislative Yuan's Defense Committee, Lieutenant-General Cheng Shih-yu, deputy chief of the General Staff for operations and planning, confirmed that Ministry of National Defense's assessments indicate that Taiwan may face a shortage of advanced fighter aircraft around 2010. He said the military is planning to purchase new fighter planes to fill this anticipated gap. In addition, he said that Taiwan would retire its obsolete F-5s in 2010.

119. Tyan Ding-jong, "Analysis of PLA Air Force Strategy in a Future Cross-Strait War and Improvements for Taiwanese Self-Defense," *Taiwan Defense Affairs* 4:1 (Fall 2003); Yu Chih-kung, "The Strategy of Air Combat in Taiwan Defense Operations," *Taiwan Defense Affairs* 3:2 (Winter 2002–2003); and York W. Chen, "The Shifting Balance of Air Superiority Across the Taiwan Strait and Its Implications for Taiwan's Defense Planning," *Taiwan Defense Affairs* 3:2 (Winter 2002–03).

120. Swaine and Kamphausen, "Military Modernization in Taiwan," pp. 405–406.

121. See Yang Chih-heng, "The Contents and Goals of the ROC's Navy Modernization," *Taiwan Defense Affairs* 2:2 (Winter 2001–2002); Martin Edmonds and York W. Chen, "Assessment of the ROC's Navy Modernization: Strategic and Operational Considerations," *Taiwan Defense Affairs* 2:2 (Winter 2001–02); Wong Ming-hsien and Wu Tung-lin, "Taiwan's Maritime Strategy in the New Security Environment," *Taiwan Defense Affairs* 2:2 (Winter 2001–2002); Chen Te-men, "Assessment of PLA Navy's Blockade Capability Against Taiwan from 2005–2010 and Suggestions to Cope with the Threat," *Taiwan Defense Affairs* 4:1 (Fall 2003); and Eric Grove, "Taiwan's Seapower: A Comprehensive Assessment," *Taiwan Defense Affairs* 2:2 (Winter 2001–2002).

122. See Li, "Adding Kidd-Class Destroyers to the Force"; and Chang "Discussion of the ROC Navy's Fleet Air Defense Capability."

123. Brian Hsu, "Navy Seeking to Replace Aging Knox Frigate Class," *Taipei Times,* 17 April 2004. According to the report, "These frigates, built in the early 1970s, were already approaching their service ceiling of 20 to 30 years when the US delivered them to the navy between 1992 and 1998. Though useable for a few more years, the Knox-class frigates are already spending much more time in port than at sea."

124. "A Call to Arms," *Taiwan Business Topics* 34:11 (2004).

125. On the procurement and potential future employment of submarines by the ROC navy, see T'ang Te-ch'eng (commander, ROC navy) and Yuen Mei-chun (commander, ROC navy), "Taiwan zhoubian haiyang zuozhan huanjing fenxi" (Analysis of the Ocean Operational Environment in the Area Surrounding Taiwan), *Haijun xueshu yuekan* (Naval Science Monthly) 40:5 (October 2006); Yang Zhung-wei (lieutenant commander, ROC navy), "Weilai fan qian zuozhan zhong wo qianjian bingli yunyong zhi tantao" (An Investigation into the Employment of the ROC Submarine Force in Future ASW Operations), *Haijun xueshu yuekan* 40:5 (October 2006); Simon Fu Hsu-sheng (captain, ROC navy), "On the Effect of the PLA Navy's Han-Class SSN Intrusion into Japanese Waters: Discussing the Future ROC Navy's ASW," *Haijun xueshu yuekan* 40:5 (October 2006); Wang Jyh-perng, "What Type of Submarine Meets Taiwan's Requirements?" *Taiwan Defense Affairs* 4:4 (Summer 2004); and Michael M. Tsai, "Submarines and Taiwan's Security," *Taiwan Defense Affairs* 4:4 (Summer 2004).

126. Bernard Cole, "Shifting Balance of Power in the Taiwan Strait," *China Brief* 4:7 (1 April 2004).

127. "Military Sees China Sea Dominance in Taiwan Strait by 2015," *China Post,* 21 March 2005. The Ministry of National Defense report indicated that the acquisition of P-3C antisubmarine warfare aircraft would provide at least a tenfold increase in capability over the military's aging S-2T planes.

128. Ministry of National Defense, Military Spokesman's Office, "Clarifications."

129. See Chai Wen-chung and Mei Fu-shin, "A Case for the ROC Marine Corps," *Taiwan Defense Affairs* 3:1 (Fall 2002). As Chai and Mei note, "Those advocating elimination of the Marine Corps believe that the continued existence of amphibious forces in the absence of the strategic mission of liberating the Chinese mainland would be a poor investment of national defense resources that would disrupt budget programming for the other military services."

130. Chai and Mei, "A Case for the ROC Marine Corps," p. 103.

131. Ibid., p. 103. According to Chai and Mei, "Through assuming such a potentially offensive role, the [ROC marine corps], by its mere existence, would increase the amount of forces the enemy would need to conduct a viable amphibious invasion and inject uncertainty into the enemy's operational planning."

132. Chai and Mei, "A Case for the ROC Marine Corps," pp. 413–414.

133. Wan Jiren (lieutenant colonel, ROC air force), "Lianhe zuozhan zidian youshi: dianzi zhan yunyong yu weilai fazhan" (Information and Electronic Superiority in Joint Warfare: The Use of Electronic Warfare and Its Future Development Trends), *Guofang zazhi* (Defense Journal) 20:8 (2005), p. 50. See also Liu Yi-chung (captain, ROC navy), "Ruhe tisheng benjun dianzizhan zhanli, yi fu taihai zuozhan xuqiu" (How to Enhance the ROC Military's Electronic Warfare Capabilities to Meet the Requirements of a Cross-Strait War), *Haijun xueshu yuekan* (Naval Science Monthly) 40:3 (June 2006).

134. "The First Line of Hyper Warfare: Conversation with Lt. General Abe C. Lin," *Taiwan Defense Affairs* 1:4 (Summer 2001).

135. "'Task Force Tiger' Put to the Test," *Taipei Times,* 27 April 2002, p. 3. According to the article, the unit is named "Task Force Tiger" *(laohu xiaozu).*

136. For more on the potential contributions of Taiwan's information technology and electronics companies, see James C. Mulvenon, "Taiwan and the RMA," in Emily O. Goldman and Thomas G. Mahnken, eds., *The Information Revolution in Military Affairs in Asia,* London: Palgrave Macmillan, 2004.

137. For the ROC military's perspective, see Fan Ch'uan-sheng (colonel, ROC marine corps), "Ruhe youxiao yunyong C4ISR nengliang tisheng zhanchang guanli zhi lianhe zuozhan xiaoneng" (How to Effectively Employ C4ISR Capabilities to Enhance the Effectiveness of Joint Operations Battlefield Management), *Haijun xueshu yuekan* (Naval Science Monthly) 40:3 (June 2006).

138. Peter B. de Selding, "Taiwan Planning to Sell ROCSAT-2 Satellite Imagery," *Space News,* 15 June 2004; and "Satellite Prepares for Business," *Taipei Times,* 21 July 2004.

139. See Michael M. Tsai and Jason C. Lin, "Funding for Taiwan's Defense Reform," *Taiwan Defense Affairs* 4:2 (Winter 2003–2004); Michael M. Tsai, "Funding Taiwan's Defense Reform," *Taiwan Defense Affairs* 4:1 (Fall 2003); Dennis Van Vranken Hickey, "China's Military Modernization and Taiwan's Defense Reforms: Programs, Problems, and Prospects," *Taiwan Defense Affairs* 4:2 (Winter 2003–2004); and York W. Chen and Martin Edmonds, "Taiwan Defense Reform: An Overview Perspective," *Taiwan Defense Affairs* 4:2 (Winter 2003–2004).

140. Michael D. Swaine and James C. Mulvenon, *Taiwan's Foreign and Defense Policies: Features and Determinants,* Santa Monica: RAND, 2001.

141. For an analysis of Taiwan's deterrence strategy, see Shih Chi-hsiung, "The Reality and Feasibility of Deterring China: Reexamining the Meaning of Deterrence in Taiwan's Defense," *Taiwan Defense Affairs* 5:1 (Fall 2004).

142. Ministry of National Defense, *2004 National Defense Report,* p. 84.

143. Ibid., p. 83.

144. Ibid.

145. Ibid.

146. Chen Shui-bian, *Xin shiji xin chulu: Chen Shui-bian guojia lantu—diyice: guojia anquan* (New Century, New Future: Chen Shui-bian's Blueprint for the Nation—Volume 1: National Security), Taipei: Chen Shui-bian Campaign Headquarters, 1999, pp. 50–51.

147. Su Tzu-yun, "The Evolution of Taiwan's Defense Strategy and Defense Concept of Taiwan's New Administration," *Taiwan Defense Affairs* 1:1 (October 2000), pp. 124–125.

148. Ministry of National Defense, *2004 National Defense Report,* p. 84.

149. For the full text of President Chen's speech at the Army Academy, see Presidential Office News Release, "Zongtong zhuchi lujun guanxiao qishiliu zhounian xiaoqing dianli" (President Chen Attends the Army Academy's Seventy-sixth Anniversary Celebration), 16 June 2000. Subsequently in his speech, President Chen discussed the importance of improving training, moving forward with the *Jingshi* military restructuring program, and enhancing the military's ability to conduct joint operations.

150. For a Taiwanese analysis of the PRC's views on this debate, see Parris Chang, "China's Analysis of Taiwan's New Strategic Thinking: Decisive Battle Outside the Territory," *Taiwan Defense Affairs* 4:1 (Fall 2003).

151. Chang, "Defense Officials Losing Faith in Missile Defense Potential."

152. Chang, Tseng, and Chiu, *Quadrennial National Security Estimate Report,* p. 55.

153. Glenn Kessler, "Ex-President Says Taiwan Needs Missiles," *Washington Post,* 19 October 2005. Lee has stated that the missiles are important because of the "psychological effect" they would have on Chinese leaders.

154. Brian Hsu, "Offense Best Defense, Officer Says," *Taipei Times*, 10 January 2003, p. 3. Lieutenant-general Fu Wei-ku, deputy commander of the ROC air force at that time, said, "According to calculations by the US military, the cost-effectiveness of offensive operations against defensive ones is one to nine. It means that if the enemy spends US$100 million on developing missiles to attack us, we have to spend nine times the money on building defensive measures. . . . Given these conditions, I suggest that the military should develop the capability of launching counter operations against the enemy."

155. Even many of those senior military officers and civilian policymakers who support the new strategy and the corresponding shift in emphasis from "resolute defense" to "effective deterrence" acknowledge that the island's armed forces currently lack the capabilities necessary to support the "decisive offshore battle" concept.

156. Lilian Wu, "'Balance of Terror' Not Part of Defense Concept: Defense Minister," *Central News Agency*, 30 September 2004. Lee was responding to a question about Premier Yu's comments the previous week, in which he suggested that Taiwan would attack civilian targets if China launched missiles at Taiwan.

157. Ministry of National Defense, *2004 National Defense Report*, p. 65.

158. Wu, "'Balance of Terror' Not Part of Defense Concept."

159. "Military Balance Could Shift Toward Beijing: MND," *China Post*, 15 December 2004. Lieutenant-General Hu Chen-pu of the ROC army stated that the Three Gorges Dam would not be included on the target list.

160. Joe Hung, "Do We Need Nuclear Weapons?" National Policy Foundation Commentary no. 093-169 (15 October 2004), www.npf.org.tw/publication/ns/093/ns-c-093-169.htm. Hung, an analyst at the National Policy Foundation, a Pan-Blue think tank, argues that Taiwan should develop nuclear weapons to deter China from using force to resolve the Taiwan issue. Another benefit, according to Hung, is that nuclear weapons are less expensive than conventional defense.

161. "Taiwan Will Never Develop Nukes, Vows Chen," *Taiwan News*, 11 November 2004. Chen stated: "For reasons of humanitarianism and international principles of conduct, we believe that nuclear, biological, and chemical weapons and other weapons of mass destruction should be banned from use in the Taiwan Strait. We are willing to openly promise that we will absolutely never develop such weapons of mass destruction."

162. Edward Cody, "Taiwan Sets Self-Defense Objectives," *Washington Post*, 21 May 2006, p. A19.

163. Chen, "The American RMA," p. 12.

164. Author interview with KMT politician, United States, September 2006.

165. Philip P. Pan and David E. Hoffman, "Taiwan's President Maintains Hard Line; Chen Rebukes China in Interview," *Washington Post*, 29 March 2004.

166. US Department of State, "Preview of the Bush-Abe Meeting," Foreign Press Center, Washington, DC, 26 April 2007, http://hongkong.us consulate.gov/ustw_wh_2007042601.html.

167. See Luor, Wang, and Yeh, "Reinventing National Defense Organization in Taiwan," p. 153; and Michael M. Tsai, "Organizational Reinvention and Defense Reform," *Taiwan Defense Affairs* 2:3 (Spring 2002), pp. 2–3.

168. Richard H. Kohn, "An Essay on Civilian Control of the Military," *American Diplomacy* 3 (1997), www.unc.edu/depts/diplomat/ad_issues/am dipl_3/kohn.html.

169. Arthur S. Ding, "The Meanings and Future Prospects to Implement the Two Defense Laws," *Taiwan Defense Affairs* 2:3 (Spring 2002), pp. 9–10.

170. The democratization process also necessitated the reform of the intelligence and security services. See Steven E. Phillips, "Identity and Security in Taiwan," *Journal of Democracy* 17:3 (July 2006).

171. In addition, in the past few years, Taiwan has passed, revised, or amended more than a dozen other defense-related laws. Among the most important of these are the various organization acts regarding the General Staff, the Political Warfare Bureau, and the Armaments Bureau, and the various organization regulations regarding the ROC army, navy, air force, joint logistics command, and reserve command.

172. Stokes, "Taiwan's Security," p. 3.

173. See Ministry of National Defense, *2002 National Defense Report.*

174. Ding, "Meanings and Future Prospects to Implement the Two Defense Laws," p. 12.

175. Luor, Wang, and Yeh, "Reinventing National Defense Organization in Taiwan," p. 142.

176. For more on this topic, see Cheng Ta-chen, "The Establishment of Taiwan's Bureau of Armament and Acquisition," *Taiwan Defense Affairs* 3:3 (Spring 2003).

177. Chen Chao-min in "Remarks to the U.S.-Taiwan Business Council Defense Industry Conference," San Antonio, TX, 13 February 2003.

178. Luor, Wang, and Yeh, "Reinventing National Defense Organization in Taiwan," p. 150.

179. Widely regarded as the most notorious case of corruption in the arms procurement process, the acquisition of the Lafayette frigates touched off a major political controversy involving charges of kickbacks and illegal commissions, and the murder of a procurement officer in the ROC navy. More than a decade later, the case remains unresolved.

180. Ministry of National Defense, *2004 National Defense Report,* pp. 133–134.

181. For more on the role of civilians in defense policy, see Chen Ching-pu, "Defense Policy-Making and Civilian Roles," *Taiwan Defense*

Affairs 4:2 (Winter 2003–2004); and Michael M. Tsai, "Civilian-Based Think Tanks and Defense Affairs," *Taiwan Defense Affairs* 3:1 (Fall 2002).

182. Li Wenzhong, He Minhao, Lin Zhuoshui, Duan Yikang, Chen Zhongxin, Tang Huosheng, and Xiao Meiqin, *Taiwan bingli guimo yanjiu baogao* (Research Report on the Scale of Taiwan's Armed Forces), Democratic Progressive Party, Policy Committee Research Report Series, Taipei, March 2003, p. 17.

183. US Department of Defense, *The Security Situation in the Taiwan Strait,* Washington, DC, February 1999, www.dod.mil/pubs/twstrait_02261999.html.

184. Li et al., *Research Report on the Scale of Taiwan's Armed Forces.*

185. Lee Wen-chung, "The Development of Taiwan's RMA After Implementation of the National Defense Act," *Taiwan Defense Affairs* (January 2004).

186. Luor, Wang, and Yeh, "Reinventing National Defense Organization in Taiwan."

187. Ministry of National Defense, *2004 National Defense Report,* p. 95. Its three missions are "suppression of invasion at the origin, ballistic missile defense, and joint interdiction operations."

188. See, for example, Lo Ping-hsiung, "Human Resource Policy of the ROC Military," *Taiwan Defense Affairs* 4:2 (Winter 2003–2004).

189. Yu Sen-lun, "Draft Dodgers," *Taipei Times,* 22 October 2000.

190. See, for example, Brian Hsu, "Air Force Plans Reforms to Tackle Pilot Shortage," *Taipei Times,* 31 January 2001.

191. "Volunteer Military Will Replace Mandatory System, Yu Reports," *Central News Agency,* 7 October 2003.

192. Ministry of National Defense, *2004 National Defense Report,* pp. 130–131.

193. Mure Dickie, "Taipei Tests Alternatives to Military Conscription," *Financial Times,* 3 May 2002.

194. Debby Wu, "All Volunteer Force Unlikely: DPP," *Taipei Times,* 25 February 2004.

195. Wan Ch'uan-chao (colonel, ROC army), "Lun quanmin guofang de bingyi zhidu" (The Military Service System Under All-Out National Defense), *Guofang zazhi* (National Defense Magazine) 21:1 (March 2006).

196. See Michael M. Tsai, "Jointness and Taiwan's Security," *Taiwan Defense Affairs* 2:4 (Summer 2002); Chen Kuo-ming and Kim Huang, "Joint Operations of the Armed Forces," *Taiwan Defense Affairs* 2:4 (Summer 2002); Zen I-ming, "The Air Force's View on Improving Joint Operations Capabilities for the ROC Armed Forces," *Taiwan Defense Affairs* 2:4 (Summer 2002); Lang Ning-li, "Joint Operations to Command the Sea for Taiwan's Defense," *Taiwan Defense Affairs* 2:4 (Summer 2002); Teng Hsin-yun, "Joint Operations: Views from the ROC Army," *Taiwan Defense Affairs* 2:4 (Summer 2002); and Wang Kun-yi, Cai Yuh-ming, and Chai Wen-chung,

"Joint Operations and Taiwan's Armed Forces Transformation," *Taiwan Defense Affairs* 5:1 (Fall 2004).

197. Xie Taixi (major-general, ROC army reserve), "Jingjin guojun lianhe zuozhan yanxun zhi yanjiu" (Research on Joint Warfare Training and Exercises Under the Military's *Jingjin* Program), *Kongjun xueshu yuekan* (Air Force Science Monthly) 592 (July 2006).

198. Swaine and Kamphausen, "Military Modernization in Taiwan," p. 394.

199. "Taiwan Works on Defense Strategy in the Event of an Attack from China," *Cable News Network,* 6 November 2000, www.taiwansecurity .org/news/cnn-110600.htm.

200. See, for example, Office of the Secretary of Defense, *Military Power of the People's Republic of China, 2003,* p. 50. According to the report, "Navy operations are not well integrated with those of either the army or the air force and joint training is infrequent and rudimentary."

201. Ministry of National Defense, *2004 National Defense Report,* p. 211. The report defines joint operations as "combining two or more services or branches to achieve a common objective."

202. Ministry of National Defense, *2004 National Defense Report,* pp. 65–66.

203. Ibid., p. 90.

204. Ibid., p. 225. From 2000 to 2003, the ROC armed forces published a series of documents related to joint operations, including one titled "Joint Operations Guidelines."

205. See Ministry of National Defense, "Hanguang yanxi" (Han Kuang Exercise), Taipei, 20 July 2006; and Ministry of National Defense, "Zongtong shidao hanguang yanxi chang jungou kending guanbing nuli" (President Observes Han Kuang Exercise, Emphasizes Arms Purchase, and Affirms Hard Work of Officers and Men), Taipei, 20 July 2006.

206. Sofia Wu, "Taiwan Advances in Combined Services Operations: Ex-U.S. Commander," *Central News Agency,* April 29, 2006.

207. Xie, *Research on Joint Warfare and Training Exercises.* Xie recommends strengthening joint staff organizations at all levels, standardizing joint training, improving the planning of joint exercises, using more rigorous evaluative mechanisms, expanding joint training facilities, and employing computer modeling and simulation capabilities.

208. Xie, *Research on Joint Warfare and Training Exercises.*

209. For more on the debate over Taiwan's efforts to enhance the military's joint operations capabilities, see Shu Hsiao-ming, "Advancing to Joint Operations: A Forum on Amending the National Defense Act," *Ch'uan-ch'iu fang-wei tsa-chih* (Defense International) (June 2006); Shu Hsiao-huang, "Taiwan Legislators Call for Continued Military Reform," *Ch'uan-ch'iu fang-wei tsa-chih* (May 2006); Chen Pi-chao, "The American

RMA, Joint Forces Operations and Lessons for the Defense of Taiwan," *Taiwan Defense Affairs* (July 2005); and Lee Wen-chung, "The Development of Taiwan's RMA After Implementation of the National Defense Act," *Taiwan Defense Affairs* (January 2004).

210. See Michael M. Tsai, "The Importance of Military Education," *Taiwan Defense Affairs* 3:4 (Summer 2003); Sun Min-hwa, "Research on the Viewpoint and Suggestions of Military Academy Graduates Regarding Military Education," *Taiwan Defense Affairs* 5:3 (Spring 2005); Liu Kuang-hua, "Tentative Proposals for the Reform of Strategic Education in the NDU, ROC," *Taiwan Defense Affairs* 5:2 (Winter 2004–2005); Chai Wen-chung and Su Tzu-yun, "Military Education and Defense Reform," *Taiwan Defense Affairs* 4:2 (Winter 2003–2004); and Chen Te-man, "Challenges Faced by the ROC National Defense University in the Rapid Changing Age," *Taiwan Defense Affairs* 5:2 (Winter 2004–2005).

211. Ministry of National Defense, *2004 National Defense Report*, pp. 211–220.

212. See Ministry of National Defense, "Guofangbu 'Han kuang 23 hao yanxi' diannao bingqi tuiyan shuoming" (The MND's Explanation of the 'Han Kuang 23 Exercise' Computer War Game)," Taipei, 24 April 2007, www.mnd.gov.tw/publish.aspx?cnid=69&p=8646; and Ministry of National Defense, "Guojun 'Han kuang 23 hao yanxi' diannao bingqi tuiyan zhixing gaikuang" (General Situation of the ROC Military's 'Han Kuang 23 Exercise' Computer Wargame), Taipei, 24 April 2007, www.mnd.gov.tw/publish.aspx?cnid=69&p=8645.

213. Rich Chang, "War Simulations Underway," *Taipei Times,* 25 April 2006.

214. Ministry of National Defense, "Major Military Exercise Schedule for 2005," Taipei, n.d.

215. For more details on the "Han Kuang 21" exercise, see Office of the President, "President Chen Inspects Anti-Special Forces and Anti-Airborne Attack Drills in Taichung," Taipei, 27 July 2007; Ministry of National Defense, Military Spokesman's Office, "Explanation of Hanguang no. 21 Military Exercise Computer Wargames," 26 April 2005; and Mac William Bishop, "MND Pulls Off Intricate Military Drill," *Taipei Times,* 28 July 2005.

216. Huang Tai-lin, "Chen Won't Use Helicoptor in Terror Drill: Officials," *Taipei Times,* 13 April 2005.

217. Ministry of National Defense, "Major Military Exercise Schedule for 2005."

218. Chang, "War Simulations Underway."

219. Ministry of National Defense, *2004 National Defense Report*, pp. 211–212. The scenario for the 2004 "Han Kuang 20" exercise featured a Chinese surprise attack involving ballistic missile and air strikes, special

operations attacks, sabotage, information operations and electronic warfare, and airborne landings.

220. On the process of establishing civilian supremacy over the military, see M. Taylor Fravel, "Towards Civilian Supremacy: Civil-Military Relations in Taiwan's Democratization," *Armed Forces and Society* 29:1 (Fall 2002).

221. Stokes, "Taiwan's Security," p. 4.

222. Office of the President, "Financial Times Interview with President Chen," Taipei, 3 November 2006.

223. Steven Kosiak and Andrew Krepinevich, "The Amended FY 2002 Defense Budget Request," Washington, DC: Center for Strategic and Budgetary Assessments, 28 June 2001.

224. Denny Roy, *Taiwan's Threat Perceptions: The Enemy Within,* Honolulu: Asia-Pacific Center for Security Studies, March 2003, p. 4.

225. Author interviews, United States, 2006–2007.

226. Author interview, United States, 2006.

227. Denny Roy, *Taiwan's Threat Perceptions,* p. 8.

228. Office of the Secretary of Defense, *Military Power of the People's Republic of China, 2006,* p. 6.

229. Bernard D. Cole, *Taiwan's Security: History and Prospects,* New York: Routledge, 2006, pp. 176–177.

230. Ibid., p. 89.

231. Office of the Secretary of Defense, *Military Power of the People's Republic of China, 2006,* p. 37.

232. Ibid., p. 6. For Taiwanese views, see Liu Chien-hung, "China's Growing Military Power and Its Implications," *Taiwan Defense Affairs* 5:3 (Spring 2005).

233. "Arms Procurement Necessary for the Nation's Survival," *Taipei Times,* 24 April 2005.

Chapter 6

1. Yang Chih-heng, "The Evolution and Adaptation of Taiwan's Military Strategy," in Martin Edmonds and Michael M. Tsai, eds., *Defending Taiwan: The Future Vision of Taiwan's Defense Policy and Military Strategy,* London: Routledge, 2003, p. 57.

2. Michael Swaine, *Taiwan's National Security, Defense Policy, and Weapons Procurement Processes,* Santa Monica: RAND, 1999. Policymakers in Taiwan may have overestimated the willingness and ability of the United States to intervene on Taiwan's behalf, especially early in a conflict with China.

3. Shih Hsiu-chuan, "Lee Says China Dare Not Attack," *Taipei Times,* 8 August 2005. Lee also suggested that an amphibious assault would

be an extremely difficult mission for the PLA: "It would take at least an army of ten divisions for China to attack Taiwan, which is an impossible mission."

4. Shih, "Lee Says China Dare Not Attack." Although this particular statement is relatively recent, it appears to reflect long-standing views that Lee held when he was president of the ROC.

5. Denny Roy, "U.S.-Taiwan Arms Sales: The Perils of Doing Business with Friends," *Asia-Pacific Security Studies* 3:3 (April 2004), p. 2.

6. Deborah Kuo, "Chen Shui-bian Tells Military Taiwan Cannot Afford 'Illusions' About Beijing," *Central News Agency,* 20 September 2004.

7. Chen Shui-bian, "President Chen's Address to the National Day Rally," Taipei: Government Information Office, 10 October 2005.

8. Martin Walker, "Can Taiwan Truly Rely on the US?" *United Press International,* 8 February 2006.

9. "Highlights: Taiwan Legislative Yuan," Washington, DC: Open Source Center, 14 December 2005.

10. Pi Yuan-t'ing, Chang Li-the, and Ch'en Wei-hao, "An Interview with Admiral Ting Chien-ching, Former Submarine Fleet Commander," *Chien-tuan k'o-chi* (Defense Technology International), February 2006 (translated by the Open Source Center and released as "Taiwan: Interview with Former Submarine Fleet Commander," Washington, DC, March 26, 2006).

11. Jane Rickards, "Defense Minister Urges Support for Weapons Purchase," *China Post,* 22 September 2004.

12. "Parris Chang Says the US, Japan Will Defend Taiwan," *Central News Agency,* 14 August 2005.

13. Floor Wang, "U.S. Poised to Help Taiwan in Case of China Invasion: DPP Lawmaker," *Central News Agency,* 10 April 2005.

14. Bernard D. Cole, *Taiwan's Security: History and Prospects,* New York: Routledge, 2006, p. 30.

15. For the full text of Deputy Secretary Zoellick's remarks, see "Hearing of the House International Relations Committee, Subject: China's Resurgence," Washington, DC, 10 May 2006. See also "U.S. Official Says Taiwan's Independence Means War for America," *Agence France Presse,* 11 May 2006.

16. Daniel Sneider, "Taiwan Official Wary of China," *Mercury News,* 22 June 2005.

17. Max Hirsch, "Joseph Wu Slams China's Invasion Plans," *Taipei Times,* 10 November 2006. Wu said: "China's acquisition of long-range bombers and mid-air refuelers from Russia means that it seeks to project its military power beyond Taiwan, because Chinese fighter jets wouldn't need to refuel mid-air in a cross-Strait attack. Taiwan is so close that it doesn't need such resources."

18. Rich Chang, "Analyst Says US Could Consider Taiwan a Lost Cause," *Taipei Times,* 15 August 2005.

19. Roger Milton, "Expect Sino-US War over Taiwan in Next 10 Years: Expert," *Straits Times,* 9 January 2006. For the full version of the argument summarized in this article, see Ted Galen Carpenter, *America's Coming War with China: A Collision Course over Taiwan,* New York: Palgrave Macmillan, 2006.

20. Walker, "Can Taiwan Truly Rely on the US?"

21. Shaheen was certainly not the only source of conflicting remarks about US policy toward Taiwan, but her comments created a controversy that ultimately resulted in her resignation. See Susan V. Lawrence, "U.S.-Taiwan Relations: The Guardian Angel Finally Had Enough," *Far Eastern Economic Review* (April 2004).

22. Author interview with a former ROC government official, United States, 2006.

23. For a detailed account, see Nancy Bernkopf Tucker, *Taiwan, Hong Kong, and the United States, 1945–1992: Uncertain Friendships,* New York: Twayne, 1994, pp. 125–159.

24. Ibid., pp. 146–147.

25. Thomas J. Christensen (deputy assistant secretary for East Asian and Pacific affairs), "A Strong and Moderate Taiwan," speech to the US-Taiwan Business Council's annual defense industry conference, Annapolis, MD, 11 September 2007, www.state.gov/p/eap/rls/rm/2007/91979.htm.

26. "U.S. Official Warns of 'Repercussions' If Taiwan Fails to Approve Weapons Deal," *Associated Press,* 6 October 2004. Pan-Blue politicians accused Lawless of attempting to bully Taiwan into approving the budget by threatening to abandon the island. One opposition lawmaker, Sun Ta-chien, even derided the United States as a "mafia leader" that was demanding "protection money" from Taiwan.

27. Bill Gertz, "Taiwan Slammed on Lax Defense," *Washington Times,* 20 September 2005, p. 7. "In the end," Ross said, "the US ability to contribute to Taiwan's defense in a crisis is going to be measured against Taiwan's ability to resist, defend and survive on its own capabilities."

28. Eugene Low, "US Losing Patience as Taiwan Dithers Over Weapons Deal," *Straits Times,* 17 September 2005.

29. Rob Simmons in "Hearing on China's Military Modernization and the Cross-Strait Balance," US-China Economic and Security Review Commission, Washington, DC, 15 September 2005.

30. C. Richard D'Amato in "Hearing on China's Military Modernization and the Cross-Strait Balance." See also Eugene Low, "US Losing Patience as Taiwan Dithers Over Weapons Deal," *Straits Times,* 17 September 2005.

31. "Arms Bill Has to Pass Eventually, President Says," *Central News Agency,* 29 September 2005.

32. Eugene Low, "US Defense of Taiwan Is 'Not a Given,'" *Taipei Times,* March 9, 2006. Senator Warner's remarks were made in the context of a discussion about President Chen's decision to "cease the operations" of the National Unification Council.

33. Mark A. Stokes, "Taiwan's Security: Beyond the Special Budget," *Asian Outlook* no. 2 (27 March 2006), p. 2.

34. Lai I-chung, "Taiwan-US Controversy," *Taiwan Daily,* 27 December 2004.

35. Daniel Sneider, "Taiwan Official Wary of China," *Mercury News,* 22 June 2005.

36. Chang, "Analyst Says US Could Consider Taiwan a Lost Cause."

37. Chicago Council on Global Affairs, Global Views 2006 Team, *The United States and the Rise of China and India: Results of a 2006 Multination Survey of Public Opinion,* Chicago, 2006, p. 22.

38. Ibid., p. 60.

39. Huang Kwang-chun, "Vice Defense Minister Warns Against China's Military Buildup," *Central News Agency,* 23 June 2005. Consequently, he argued that Taiwan should acquire advanced arms to bolster its self-defense capabilities.

40. Xie Zhi-peng (colonel, ROC air force), "Cong zhonggong hewu xiandaihua fazhan yanxi jian lun dui quyu anquan zhi yingxiang" (An Investigation into the Development of the PRC's Nuclear Weapons Modernization and Its Influence on the Asia-Pacific Region), *Guofang zazhi* (National Defense Magazine) 21:4 (August 2006).

41. David A. Shlapak, David T. Orletsky, and Barry Wilson, *Dire Strait? Military Aspects of the China-Taiwan Confrontation and Options for U.S. Policy,* Santa Monica: RAND, 2000.

42. See, for example, General Peter J. Schoomaker (chief of staff, US Army), "The Army's Preparedness for Current and Future Missions," statement before the House Armed Services Committee, Washington, DC, 23 January 2007; and General James T. Conway (commandant, US Marine Corps), "Implications of Iraq Policy on Total Force Readiness," statement before the House Armed Services Committee, Washington, DC, 23 January 2007.

43. Michael O'Hanlon, "U.S. Military Modernization: Implications for U.S. Policy in Asia," in Ashley J. Tellis and Michael Wills, eds., *Strategic Asia 2005–06: Military Modernization in an Era of Uncertainty,* Seattle: National Bureau of Asian Research, 2006, pp. 41–66.

44. See, for example, Office of the Undersecretary of Defense (Policy), *Quadrennial Defense Review 2006,* Washington, DC: US Department of Defense, 2006, p. 29.

45. At the same time, however, at least one ROC military officer assesses that the strengthening of the US presence on Guam may also have negative implications for Taiwan's security. According to Colonel Li Kuo-jung of the

ROC army, although the enhancement of the US base on Guam will strengthen Washington's military presence in the Western Pacific and increase the US military's ability to defend Taiwan, it may ultimately reduce Taiwan's geostrategic importance to the United States. See Li Kuo-jung, "Meijun qianghua guandao jidi dui woguo zhi yingxiang" (An Investigation into the Enhancement of the US Military Base on Guam and Its Impact on the ROC), *Guofang zazhi* (National Defense Magazine) 21:2 (July 2006).

46. Peter Rodman (assistant secretary of defense for international security affairs, Department of Defense) in "Hearing on China's Military Modernization and US Export Controls," US-China Economic and Security Review Commission, Washington, DC, 16–17 March 2006, p. 32.

47. See Stephen Che, "MND Concerned Over Satellite Blast," *China Post,* 24 January 2007.

48. Ong Hwee Hwee, "Taiwan Worries About US Ability to Come to its Rescue," *Straits Times,* 22 January 2007.

49. Cole, *Taiwan's Security,* p. 180.

50. Chicago Council on Global Affairs, Global Views 2006 Team, *The United States and the Rise of China and India,* p. 60.

51. Lynn Davis, J. Michael Polich, William H. Mix, Michael D. Greenberg, Stephen Brady, and Ronald E. Sortor, *Stretched Thin: Army Forces for Sustained Operations,* Santa Monica: RAND, 2006.

52. Cole, *Taiwan's Security,* pp. 179–180.

Chapter 7

1. See Stephen M. Walt, *The Origins of Alliances,* Ithaca: Cornell, 1987. Walt's principal argument is that states balance against "threat" rather than power alone. In contrast to traditional balance of power approaches, Walt's definition of threat encompasses not only military power, but also perceived aggressive intentions.

2. Chen Fu-cheng, "An Assessment of the Chinese Communist Military Forces' Capability to Invade Taiwan," in *Chung-kung wu-li fan tai yen-chiu* (Research on the Use of Chinese Communist Military Power Against Taiwan), n.p., July 1995 (also appeared as "PRC Capability to Invade Taiwan Assessed," *Foreign Broadcast Information Service,* 3 March 1999). Chen is a colonel in the ROC armed forces, but his specific service affiliation is unknown.

3. Chen Fu-cheng, "A Comparison of Military Strength on Both Sides of the Taiwan Strait," in *Research on the Use of Chinese Communist Military Power* (also appeared as "Book Compares Cross-Strait Forces," *Foreign Broadcast Information Service,* 25 February 1999).

4. Chen, "Assessment of the Chinese Communist Military." Interestingly, despite the deficiencies in equipment and transportation Chen identifies in his study, Chen indicates that he was one of those who concluded that the PLA may very well have been capable of invading Taiwan in the mid-1990s if Chinese leaders were willing to accept heavy costs.

5. Chen, "Comparison of Military Strength."

6. Government Information Office, *Republic of China, 1988: A Reference Book,* Taipei, 1988, p. 160.

7. Chen, "Assessment of the Chinese Communist Military."

8. Ministry of National Defense, *2002 National Defense Report,* Taipei: Government Information Office, 2002.

9. Ministry of National Defense, *2004 National Defense Report,* p. 23.

10. "China Targets Taiwan in White Paper, MND Says," *Central News Agency,* 29 December 2004. The official quoted is Wang Shih-chien, deputy director of the Information Center, Office of the Deputy Chief, General Staff for Intelligence.

11. National Security Council, *2006 National Security Report,* Taipei, 20 May 2006, p. 39.

12. Ibid., p. 2.

13. Yu Yongzhang (colonel, ROC army), "Cong zhonggong junli chengzhang lunshu taihai buduicheng zhanzheng dui wo zhi weixie" (Reflections on China's Increasing Military Power and the Cross-Strait Asymmetric Warfare Threat to Taiwan), *Guofang zazhi* (National Defense Magazine) 20:1 (2005).

14. Deborah Kuo, "China Pulling Wool Over Taiwan Public's Eyes: MND," *Central News Agency,* 22 September 2005.

15. Daniel Sneider, "Taiwan Official Wary of China," *Mercury News,* 22 June 2005.

16. Author interviews with ROC think tank analysts and former ROC government officials, United States, 2006.

17. Ministry of National Defense, *2004 National Defense Report,* p. 53. See also "MND Estimates China's Future Military Stance," *China Post,* 8 February 2006.

18. "Military Balance Could Shift Toward Beijing: MND," *China Post,* 15 December 2004.

19. Simon Tisdall, "The Writing's on the Wall for Wary Taiwan," *The Guardian,* 2 April 2005.

20. Author interviews, United States, September–October 2006.

21. National Security Council, *2006 National Security Report,* pp. 39–40.

22. Ibid.

23. Ibid., p. 39.

24. Lin Chieh-yu, "China a Threat by 2015, Defense Minister Says," *Taipei Times,* 5 October 2004.

25. Benjamin Kang Lim, "Taiwan Sees Military Balance Tipping to China by Next Year," *Reuters,* 11 January 2003.

26. National Security Council, *2006 National Security Report,* p. 41.

27. Author interviews with ROC officials, United States, 2006.

28. Liu Yi-you (colonel, ROC army), "Diyici bowan zhanzheng hou de zhonggong goujian tezhong budui tantao: jianlun wo yinying duice" (An Investigation into the Development of the PRC's Special Forces Since the First Gulf War and ROC Countermeasures), *Guofang zazhi* (National Defense Magazine) 21:4 (August 2006). According to Liu, PLA special operations forces would carry out direct action, special reconnaissance, and information warfare operations.

29. "Military Balance Could Shift Toward Beijing." According to the article, "Based on the increasing number of illegal immigrants from mainland China in recent years, there are already quite a number of people with special combat skills embedded on the island for possible sabotage and other subversive actions."

30. "Defense Chief Sees Mainland Attack in 5 to 10 Years' Time," *China Post,* 10 March 2005.

31. Chen Chia-chen, *Taiwan zuihou 72 xiaoshi* (Taiwan's Final 72 Hours), Taipei: Hsing-kuang Publishing, 2004. The author states that he is a former officer in the ROC marine corps and an editor at the monthly magazine *Defense International.*

32. Lin Chu-chin, *Taiwan dangdezhu gongjun san tian ma?* (Can Taiwan Hold Off the PLA for Three Days?), Taipei: Ch'i-p'in Wen-hua Publishing, 2000. The author states that he is a former officer in the ROC army and presents the book as a nonfiction analysis of Taiwan's ability to resist a PLA invasion.

33. Ministry of National Defense, *2004 National Defense Report,* p. 53.

34. Hsueh identified four variables as influences on the stability of cross-Strait relations: the cross-Strait military balance; the deterrent value of US support for Taiwan; nationalism and the political situation in China; and domestic politics in Taiwan.

35. Author interviews, United States, 2006.

36. "NSB Head Doubts That a Cross-Strait War Is Likely Soon," *Taipei Times,* 23 March 2003.

37. "Parris Chang Says the US, Japan Will Defend Taiwan," *Central News Agency,* 14 August 2005.

38. Ko Shu-ling, "Beijing Is Unlikely to Wage War: Koo," *Tapei Times,* 31 March 2006. Koo said Beijing would not risk conflict over Taiwan because a war would scare off foreign investors and could precipitate an economic collapse.

39. Author interviews, United States and Taiwan, 2001–2004.

40. Lim, "Taiwan Sees Military Balance Tipping."

41. Ibid. "The highest ideal of Beijing leaders is to achieve unification without fighting," Lin said. At the same time, however, he warned that Taiwan could not completely dismiss the possibility of war: "We cannot afford to be so complacent."

42. "PRC Would Most Likely Invade Taiwan in 2012, MND Warns," *Taiwan News,* 23 September 2004.

43. Author interviews, United States and Taiwan, 2003–2007.

44. "China 'Likely' to Use Force, Mac Head Says," *Central News Agency,* 7 November 2004.

45. National Security Council, *2006 National Security Report,* p. 77. The report calls this the "greatest hidden risk" of China's rise.

46. National Security Council, *2006 National Security Report,* p. 32.

47. "Taiwan President Warns of China's Invasion Time Frame, Snubs Call for Talks," *Agence France Presse,* 3 April 2006. Vice President Annette Lu has made similar statements. In March 2006, Lu stated that Beijing intended to establish contingency-response combat capabilities by 2007, prepare for a large-scale military engagement by 2010, and develop superiority that would allow the PLA to ensure victory in a decisive battle by 2015. See Ko Shu-ling, "Lu Urges Legislature to Counter Beijing's Build-Up," *Taipei Times,* 13 March 2006.

48. "China 'Likely' to Use Force, Mac Head Says." Wu emphasized the importance of US and Japanese support.

49. Shu Chin-chiang, "Taiwan Has To Bolster Its Defenses and Resolve," *Taipei Times,* 11 August 2005. What is most concerning from Shu's point of view is that the Pan-Blue parties, which he refers to as the "pro-Beijing parties," are playing into China's hands. According to Shu: "In the face of the ever-increasing military threat from China, the pro-Beijing parties are holding up the passage of the budget which will enable Taiwan to buy US weapons. This is little short of encouraging China to invade Taiwan, and then to expand into the Asia-Pacific region."

50. "Parties Spar over Pentagon Report," *Taipei Times,* 21 July 2005.

Chapter 8

1. Randall L. Schweller, "Unanswered Threats: A Neoclassical Realist Theory of Underbalancing," *International Security* 29:2 (Fall 2004).

2. It is important to note, however, that this did not ensure an appropriate response to the Chinese military threat when the ROC was a one-party state ruled by the Kuomintang. On the contrary, the KMT regime may very well have chosen an overactive response to the Chinese military

threat, to mobilize domestic and international support and justify continued one-party rule and often severe political repression.

3. "Editorial: Taiwan Still Needs a Good Offense," *Taipei Times,* 14 January 2006.

4. "Analysts Wondering If Ma Will Support Arms Budget," *Taipei Times,* 21 August 2005, p. 3.

5. Office of the President, *A-bian zongtong dianzi bao* (A-Bian's E-Newsletter) no. 219 (Taipei, 22 December 2005), www.president.gov.tw/1_epaper/periodical/219yjyahb/ch000022/main.htm.

6. See, for example, Shelley Rigger, "The Education of Chen Shui-bian: Taiwan's Experience of Divided Government," *Journal of Contemporary China* 11:33 (2002).

7. Craig Meer, "Taiwan, a Divided Island," *Asia Times,* 8 November 2006.

8. Shelley Rigger, "The Unfinished Business of Taiwan's Democratization," in Nancy Benkopf Tucker, ed., *Dangerous Strait: The U.S.-Taiwan-China Crisis,* New York: Columbia University Press, 2005, p. 34.

9. Ibid., p. 43.

10. Ibid.

11. Chu Yun-han, "Taiwan's Year of Stress," *Journal of Democracy* 16:2 (April 2005), p. 48.

12. Shelley Rigger, "Political Science and Taiwan's Domestic Politics: The State of the Field," *Issues and Studies* 4:39 (December 2002–March 2003), p. 73.

13. Rigger, "Education of Chen Shui-bian," p. 615.

14. Ibid., p. 614.

15. Rigger, "Political Science and Taiwan's Domestic Politics," p. 73.

16. Rigger, "Education of Chen Shui-bian," p. 615.

17. Liao Ta-chi, "How Does a Rubber Stamp Become a Roaring Lion? The Transformation of the Role of Taiwan's Legislative Yuan During the Process of Democratization (1950–2000)," *Issues and Studies* 41:3 (September 2005).

18. Prior to reforms that took effect in January 2008, the Legislative Yuan had 225 members. Of these, 168 were elected in multimember districts and 41 were chosen through proportional representation among political parties to represent an islandwide constituency. In addition, 8 seats were reserved for members of the aboriginal population and another 8 were set aside to represent ROC citizens residing overseas. The members who represented overseas constituents were also chosen through proportional representation.

19. "A Call to Arms," *Taiwan Business Topics* 34:11 (2004).

20. Ibid.

21. Rigger, "Unfinished Business of Taiwan's Democratization."

22. Ibid., p. 21.

23. Larry Diamond, *Developing Democracy: Toward Consolidation,* Baltimore: Johns Hopkins University Press, 1999.

24. Rigger, "Unfinished Business of Taiwan's Democratization," pp. 23–25.

25. Diamond, *Developing Democracy,* p. 75.

26. Rigger, "Unfinished Business of Taiwan's Democratization," p. 26.

27. Ibid., p. 29.

28. For more on the SNTV system and its implications for politics, see Eric P. Moon, "Single Non-Transferable Vote Methods in Taiwan in 1996: Effects of an Electoral System," *Asian Survey* 37:7 (July 1997); Wang Yeh-lih, "The Political Consequences of the Electoral System: Single Nontransferable Voting in Taiwan," *Issues and Studies* 32:8 (1996); and John Hsieh Fuh-sheng, "The SNTV System and Its Political Implications," in Tien Hung-mao, ed., *Taiwan's Politics and Democratic Transition: Riding the Third Wave,* Armonk, NY: Sharpe, 1996.

29. Moon, "Single Non-Transferable Vote Methods," p. 661.

30. Rigger, "Unfinished Business of Taiwan's Democratization," p. 31.

31. Ibid., pp. 31–32.

32. Ibid.

33. See Lin Jih-wen, "The Politics of Reform in Japan and Taiwan," *Journal of Democracy* 17:2 (April 2006).

34. Shelley Rigger, "Party Politics and Taiwan's External Relations," *Orbis* 49:3 (Summer 2005).

35. "DPP Rejects Soong's Warnings of War," *Taiwan News,* 8 November 2004.

36. Su Chi, "The Need for a Peace Accord," *China Times,* 27 October 2006.

37. Su Chi, "Taiwan's Security: A KMT Perspective," presentation to the US-Taiwan Business Council's annual defense industry conference, Denver, 11 September 2006.

38. Su Chi, "Soft Power + Defensive Defense = National Security," *United Daily News,* 24 January 2006.

39. For more on the KMT's defense policy, see Su Chi, "Taiwan's National Security: A KMT View," speech at the US-Taiwan Business Council's annual defense industry conference, Annapolis, MD, 10 September 2007; and "Defense White Paper of the KMT: A New Military for a Secure and Peaceful Taiwan (Summary)," Taipei, 2 September 2007.

40. Ma Ying-jeou, "Bridging the Divide: A Vision for Peace in East Asia," speech at the London School of Economics and Political Science, 13 February 2006.

41. Ibid.

42. See "KMT Chief Ma on Issue of Reunification," *Associated Press,* 2 November 2005.

43. "Ma Says Missiles Must Go for China Talks," *Taiwan News,* 17 June 2007.

44. Mo Yan-chih and Jewel Huang, "Sparks Fly Over KMT's Controversial Ad," *Taipei Times,* 16 February 2006. The ad originally appeared in the *Liberty Times,* which is generally considered a proindependence newspaper.

45. Author interview, Taiwan, 2003.

46. Shelley Rigger, *From Opposition to Power: Taiwan's Democratic Progressive Party,* Boulder: Lynne Rienner, 2001. Rigger argues that this internal diversity is not always a weakness, however, and that the party's factions, though prone to squabbling, actually play an informal negotiating role that holds the DPP together. She also concludes that the party's policy positions are fairly moderate.

47. See Office of the President, "President Chen Meets with UK Parliament Members," Taipei, 17 May 2006; and Ko Shu-ling, "'Status Quo' is Two Independent Countries: Chen," *Taipei Times,* 18 May 2006. Chen made the comments in a meeting with a delegation from the British House of Commons' Foreign Affairs Committee.

48. Office of the President, "*Financial Times* Interview with President Chen," Taipei, 3 November 2006, p. 3.

49. Philip P. Pan and David E. Hoffman, "Taiwan President Pushes Independence from China," *Washington Post,* March 29, 2004.

50. Office of the President, "*Financial Times* Interview with President Chen," Taipei, 3 November 2006, p. 4.

51. Edward Cody and Anthony Faiola, "Taiwan's President Set to Open Debate on New Constitution," *Washington Post,* 14 March 2006, p. A13.

52. Keith Bradsher, "Small Pro-Independence Party Gaining in Taiwan," *New York Times,* 9 December 2004. According to DPP politician Hsiao Bi-khim, "The fundamentalists are a bit disappointed in our administration." Moreover, she said that the TSU in particular was putting President Chen in a position that has "made him feel compelled to consolidate our traditional supporters."

53. Author interview, United States, October 2006. According to the former official, the short-term goal is building up enough defense capability to hold out until US forces have time to intervene decisively. The long-term goal is enhancing defense capability to allow Taiwan to negotiate with China from a position of strength.

54. "Taiwan Unveils New Armored Vehicle and Stresses Need to Build Defenses," *Agence France Presse,* 11 January 2005.

55. Peter Harmsen, "New Party Team Arrives in China As Chen Urges Better Defense," *Agence France Press,* 7 July 2005.

56. Author interviews, United States, September–October 2006. According to one former Chen administration official, it is irrational for the KMT to oppose acquisition of the weapon systems that they themselves

requested when they were in power. As this former official put it, "If they think they will win the 2008 presidential election, it is also very short-sighted for them to risk leaving themselves in a weak position. They are placing all of their bets on their ability to manage Taiwan's relationship with China, but they will be in a weak position and China will have considerable leverage."

57. The Kuomintang not only refused to cooperate with President Chen when he offered to appoint several KMT politicians to cabinet posts, but also punished KMT members who agreed to serve in Chen's administration by expelling them from the party.

58. This term is borrowed from the irreverent yet incisive analysis of democratic politics in the United States offered in *The Daily Show with John Stewart Presents America (The Book): A Citizen's Guide to Democracy Inaction,* New York: Warner, 2004.

59. Giovanni Sartori, *Comparative Constitutional Engineering: An Inquiry into Structures, Incentives, and Outcomes,* New York: New York University Press, 1997, p. ix.

60. The reform package passed with 249 votes in the 300-member National Assembly. See Edward Cody, "Taiwan Revises Constitution, Revamps Political System," *Washington Post,* 7 June 2005.

61. Debby Wu, "Consensus Elusive on Legislative Reform," *Taipei Times,* 6 June 2004.

62. See Giovanni Sartori, *Comparative Constitutional Engineering: An Inquiry into Structures, Incentives, and Outcomes,* New York: New York University Press, 1997, pp. 44–45. According to Sartori's analysis of the consequences of electoral systems, if the supporters of small parties are dispersed fairly evenly across constituencies, the new system is likely to lead to two-party politics. However, if supporters of small parties are geographically concentrated, the system may permit more than two parties.

63. Author interviews, United States, 2007.

64. "Editorial: Lawmakers Fear for Their Snouts," *Taipei Times,* 28 April 2006, p. 8. The editorialist also stated that such actions explained why many people describe politicians with terms like "liar," "hypocrite," "egomaniac," "spineless guttersnipe," "opportunistic parasite," and "self-serving slime-ball."

65. Taiwan Think Tank, "Taiwanese People's Impression of the Legislative Yuan," Taipei, 5 January 2005. Focus Survey Research conducted the telephone poll on behalf of Taiwan Think Tank from 21 December to 23 December 2004. The sample size was 1,084.

66. Chi Huang, "Taiwan's Election and Democratization Study, 2005: The National Assembly Election," Taiwan: National Chengchi University, Election Study Center.

67. Ko Shu-ling, "Constitutional Reform to Solve Turmoil: Lawmaker," *Taipei Times,* 9 September 2005, p. 3.

68. Cody and Faiola, "Taiwan's President Set to Open Debate."

69. Ko Shu-ling and Flora Wang, "DPP Promises Not to Break 'Four Noes,'" *Taipei Times,* 4 October 2006.

70. Ko Shu-Ling, "Chen Proposes Change of Constitution," *Taipei Times,* 25 September 2006.

71. Office of the President, *Zongtong canjia minzhu jinbu dang 2006 xianzheng gaizao xilie yantaohui* (President Chen Participates in the DPP's 2006 Constitutional Reform Forum), Taipei, 24 September 2006, www .president.gov.tw/php-bin/prez/shownews.php4?rid=12192.

72. The president can currently do this only in response to a no-confidence vote against the government.

73. See Rigger, "Education of Chen Shui-bian," p. 616.

74. Ko, "Constitutional Reform to Solve Turmoil."

75. Ong Hwee Hwee, "DPP Delays Release of Carter Draft," *Straits Times,* 5 October 2006. President Chen's weakened political position and US pressure were also seen as factors that led the DPP to delay the release of the draft constitutional amendments.

76. Proposed constitutional amendments must be approved by a three-quarters vote in the Legislative Yuan and then submitted to an islandwide referendum. Given that the Pan-Blue parties control the legislature, a draft constitution that includes a change in the national title or adjustments to the island's territorial boundaries would be doomed to failure.

77. Cody and Faiola, "Taiwan's President Set to Open Debate."

78. According to one source, President Chen recognizes that the bar is too high to include sovereignty issues in the constitutional reforms. His strategy is to secure the "deep-Green" base by promoting sovereignty-related changes that he knows are destined to fail, and then moving forward with less controversial proposals.

79. Shih Hsiu-chuan, "Ma and Wang Diverge on Constitutional Tinkering," *Taipei Times,* 7 March 2006.

80. Rigger, "Political Science and Taiwan's Domestic Politics," p. 72.

Chapter 9

1. Roger Cliff, Mark Burles, Michael S. Chase, Derek Eaton, and Kevin L. Pollpeter, *Entering the Dragon's Lair: Chinese Anti-Access Strategies and Their Implications for the United States,* Santa Monica: RAND, 2007.

2. There are two reasons that being largely knocked out of the fight before the United States could intervene militarily is the worst-case scenario for Taiwan. First, if China could crush Taiwan's willingness or ability to resist before the United States could intervene, and the PLA managed to

land and sustain substantial ground forces on Taiwan, this would compel Washington to decide between accepting the action as a fait accompli or attempting to reverse the outcome by engaging Chinese troops on the island, which could require the deployment of substantial US ground forces. Second, even if Washington became involved under such circumstances, which seems somewhat doubtful, a Taiwan that was effectively out of the fight would probably have little if any influence in war-termination negotiations.

3. Ideally, Taiwan would be able to negotiate from a more comprehensive position of national strength, which would mean economic vibrancy and sociopolitical cohesion as well as a formidable defense posture.

4. Taiwan could also turn to Japan for assistance, but it seems unlikely that Tokyo would become involved if Washington chose to sit on the sidelines. Moreover, it seems doubtful that unilateral Japanese intervention would be enough to prevent a Chinese victory.

5. Ministry of National Defense, *2006 National Defense Report,* Taipei: Government Information Office, 2006.

6. "Defense White Paper of the KMT: A New Military for a Secure and Peaceful Taiwan (Summary)," Taipei, 2 September 2007, p. 5.

7. For a detailed assessment of how Washington should respond if Taiwan decides to unify with the mainland, see Nancy Bernkopf Tucker, "If Taiwan Chooses Unification, Should the United States Care?" *Washington Quarterly* 25:3 (Summer 2002).

8. Randall Schriver, "Defense: Time to Take Ownership," *Taipei Times,* 4 April 2007.

9. Edward Cody, "Politics Puts Hold on Taiwan Arms Purchase," *Washington Post,* 10 October 2004.

Selected Bibliography

Academy of Military Science, Military History Research Department, *Haiwan zhanzheng quanshi* (The Complete History of The Gulf War), Beijing, 2001.

——, Operations Theory and Regulations Research Department, *Xinxihua zuozhan lilun xuexi zhinan: xinxihua zuozhan 400 ti* (Informationized Operations Theory Study Guide: 400 Informationized Operations Questions), Beijing, 2005.

——, World Military Affairs Research Department, *Yilake zhanzheng: zhanlue, zhanshuji junshi shang de jingyan jiaoxun* (The Iraq War: Strategic and Tactical Experience and Lessons), Beijing, 2005.

——, World Military Affairs Research Department, ed., *Kuaisu juedingxing zuozhan gouxiang* (Rapid and Decisive Operations Concepts), Beijing, 2005.

Alagappa, Muthiah, ed., *Taiwan's Presidential Politics,* Armonk, NY: Sharpe, 2001.

Allen, Kenneth W., Glenn Krumel, and Johnathan D. Pollack, *China's Air Force Enters the 21st Century,* Santa Monica: RAND, 1995.

An Weiping, ed., *Lianhe zuozhan xinlun* (New Theory of Joint Warfare), Beijing: National Defense University Press, 2000.

"Anti-Secession Law Adopted by NPC (Full Text)," *China Daily,* 14 March 2005.

Bezlova, Antoaneta, "China's Army Leaner and Meaner," *Asia Times,* 25 January 2006.

Binnendijk, Hans, and Ronald N. Montaperto, *Strategic Trends in China,* Washington, DC: National Defense University Press, 1998.

Blasko, Dennis J., *The Chinese Army Today: Tradition and Transformation for the 21st Century,* New York: Routledge, 2006.

Bowie, Christopher, *The Anti-Access Threat and Theater Air Bases,* Washington, DC: Center for Strategic and Budgetary Assessments, 2002.

Brown, Harold, Joseph W. Prueher, and Adam Segal, eds., *Chinese Military Power,* New York: Council on Foreign Relations, May 2003.

Carpenter, Ted Galen, *America's Coming War with China: A Collision Course over Taiwan,* New York: Palgrave Macmillan, 2006.

Ceng Sunan, ed., *Yitihua lianhe zuozhan zhuanti yanjiu* (Research on Integrated Joint Operations), Beijing: Academy of Military Science Press, 2004.

Chang Kuo-hua (lieutenant commander, ROC navy), "Haijun jiandui fang-kong zuozhan nengli zhi tantao: yi jilong ji jian wei li" (Discussion of the ROC Navy's Fleet Air Defense Capability: The Example of the Kidd-Class Destroyers), *Haijun xueshu yuekan* (Naval Science Monthly) 40:4 (July 2006).

Chang, Rich, "Analyst Says US Could Consider Taiwan a Lost Cause," *Taipei Times,* 15 August 2005.

Chao, Linda, and Ramon H. Myers, *The First Chinese Democracy: Political Life in the Republic of China on Taiwan,* Baltimore: Johns Hopkins University Press, 1998.

Chase, Michael S., Kevin L. Pollpeter, and James C. Mulvenon, *Shanghaied? The Economic and Political Implications of the Flow of Information Technology and Investment Across the Taiwan Strait,* Santa Monica: RAND, 2003.

Che, Stephen, "MND Concerned over Satellite Blast," *China Post,* 24 January 2007.

Chen Anran, *Lianhe zuozhan zhengzhi gongzuo* (Political Work in Joint Operations), Beijing: National Defense University Press, 1999.

Chen Chia-chen, *Taiwan zuihou 72 xiaoshi* (Taiwan's Final 72 Hours), Taipei: Hsing-kuang Publishing, 2004.

Chen Kuo-ming and Kim Huang, "Joint Operations of the Armed Forces," *Taiwan Defense Affairs* 2:4 (Summer 2002).

Chi Yajun, ed., *Xinxihua zhanzheng yu xinxi zuozhan lilun jingyao* (Essentials of Informationized War and Information Operations Theory), Beijing: Academy of Military Science Press, 2005.

Chicago Council on Global Affairs, Global Views 2006 Team, *The United States and the Rise of China and India: Results of a 2006 Multination Survey of Public Opinion,* Chicago, 2006.

Christensen, Thomas J., "Beijing's Views of Taiwan and the United States in Early 2002: The Renaissance of Pessimism," *China Leadership Monitor* no. 3 (Summer 2002).

———, "China, the U.S.-Japan Alliance, and the Security Dilemma in East Asia," *International Security* 23:4 (Spring 1999).

———, "Posing Problems Without Catching Up," *International Security* 25:4 (Spring 2001).

———, "Taiwan's Legislative Yuan Elections and Cross-Strait Security Relations: Reduced Tensions and Remaining Challenges," *China Leadership Monitor* no. 13 (Winter 2005).

———, "Tracking China's Security Relations: Causes for Optimism and Pessimism," *China Leadership Monitor* no. 1 (Winter 2002).

Chu Yun-han, "Taiwan's Year of Stress," *Journal of Democracy* 16:2 (April 2005).

Cliff, Roger, Mark Burles, Michael Chase, Derek Eaton, and Kevin Pollpeter, *Entering the Dragon's Lair: Chinese Military Anti-Access Strategies and Potential U.S. Responses,* Santa Monica: RAND, 2007.

Cody, Edward, "China Easing Its Stance on Taiwan," *Washington Post,* 15 June 2006.

———, "Politics Puts Hold on Taiwan Arms Purchase," *Washington Post,* 10 October 2004.

———, "Taiwan Revises Constitution, Revamps Political System," *Washington Post,* 7 June 2005.

Cole, Bernard D., *Taiwan's Security: History and Prospects,* New York: Routledge, 2006.

Crane, Keith, Roger Cliff, Evan S. Medeiros, James C. Mulvenon, and William H. Overholt, *Modernizing China's Military,* Santa Monica: RAND, 2005.

Cui Yonggui, *Zhanyi xinxi zuozhan yanjiu* (Research on Campaign Information Operations), Beijing: National Defense University Press, 2000.

Culver, John, "Defense Policy and Posture II," in Hans Binnendijk and Ronald N. Montaperto, *Strategic Trends in China,* Washington, DC: National Defense University Press, 1998.

"Curbing 'Taiwan Independence' Most Urgent Task," *People's Daily,* 17 May 2004.

Dai Fengxiu, *Guofang dongyuan zhanlue yu duice* (National Defense Mobilization Strategy and Countermeasures), Beijing: Academy of Military Science Press, 2004.

Dai Qingmin, *Xinxi zuozhan gailun* (Introduction to Information Warfare), Beijing: People's Liberation Army Press, 1999.

Davis, Lynn, J. Michael Polich, William H. Mix, Michael D. Greenberg, Stephen Brady, and Ronald E. Sortor, *Stretched Thin: Army Forces for Sustained Operations,* Santa Monica: RAND, 2006.

Dickie, Mure, and Kathrin Hille, "Beijing Fetes KMT in Attempt to Squeeze Taipei," *Financial Times,* 1 April 2005.

Dickson, Bruce J., *Democratization in China and Taiwan: The Adaptability of Leninist Parties,* New York: Oxford, 1998.

Edmonds, Martin, and Michael M. Tsai, eds., *Defending Taiwan: The Future Vision of Taiwan's Defense Policy and Military Strategy,* London: Routledge, 2003.

Fan Chengbin, *Gao jishu tiaojian xia zhanyi tanhuan zhan yanjiu* (Research on Campaign Paralysis Warfare Under High-Tech Conditions), Beijing: National Defense University Press, 2003.

Finkelstein, David M., *China Reconsiders Its National Security: The Great "Peace and Development" Debate of 1999,* Alexandria, VA: Center for Naval Analysis, December 2000.

————, "The Chinese People's Liberation Army in 2020," paper presented at the National Intelligence Council conference "The Changing Nature of Warfare: Global Trends 2020," Washington, DC, 26 May 2004.

Fravel, M. Taylor, "Towards Civilian Supremacy: Civil-Military Relations in Taiwan's Democratization," *Armed Forces and Society* 29:1 (Fall 2002).

Fu Jingyun and Gao Hongqing, eds., *Guofang jiaoyu gailun* (Introduction to National Defense Education), Beijing: Academy of Military Science Press, 2003.

"Full Text of Explanations on Draft Anti-Secession Law," *People's Daily,* 8 March 2005.

Gao Yubiao, *Lianhe zhanyixue jiaocheng* (Joint Campaign Teaching Materials), Beijing: Academy of Military Science Press, 2001.

Gill, Bates, and Michael O'Hanlon, "China's Hollow Military," *National Interest* 56 (Summer 1999).

Gries, Peter Hays, *China's New Nationalism: Pride, Politics, and Diplomacy,* Berkeley: University of California Press, 2004.

Hickey, Dennis Van Vranken, *United States–Taiwan Security Ties: From Cold War to Beyond Containment,* Westport: Praeger, 1994.

Jiang Fangran, ed., *Lianhe zuozhan silingbu gongzuo* (Joint Operations Headquarters Work), Beijing: Academy of Military Science Press, 2004.

Jing Jisheng, *Hetong fangyu zhanshu jiaocheng* (Combined Defensive Tactics Teaching Materials), Beijing: Academy of Military Science Press, 2005.

Joffe, Ellis, *The Chinese Army After Mao,* London: Weidefeld and Nicolson, 1987.

"Junshi zhuanjia tan fan 'taidu' zhanzheng: liu tiao daijia zhanfan bicheng" (Military Experts Discuss Opposing 'Taiwan Independence' with War: Six Costs, War Criminals Will Be Penalized), *Liaowang xinwen zhoukan* (Outlook Weekly), 27 November 2003.

Ko Shu-ling, "Lu Urges Legislature to Counter Beijing's Build-Up," *Taipei Times,* 13 March 2006.

————, "Pan-Blues Bring Legislature to Standstill," *Taipei Times,* 13 April 2005.

Lang Ning-li, "Joint Operations to Command the Sea for Taiwan's Defense," *Taiwan Defense Affairs* 2:4 (Summer 2002), pp. 78–109.

Lee Jui-kuang, "Year 2005–2010: Evaluation of China's Implementation of Decapitation Warfare Against Taiwan," *Taiwan Defense Affairs* 4:3 (Spring 2004).

Li Kuo-jung, "Meijun qianghua guandao jidi dui woguo zhi yingxiang" (An Investigation into the Enhancement of the US Military Base on Guam and Its Impact on the ROC), *Guofang zazhi* (National Defense Magazine) 21:2 (July 2006).

Li Lu-t'ai, "Jilong ji jian jiaru zhan zhandou xulie hou: zaitan jiandui fank-ing zuozhan" (Adding Kidd-Class Destroyers to the Force: A Reexam-ination of ROC Navy Air Defense Operations), *Haijun xueshu yuekan* (Naval Science Monthly) 40:4 (July 2006).

Li Naiguo, *Xinxi zhan xin lun* (A New Theory of Information Warfare), Bei-jing: Academy of Military Science Press, 2004.

Li Wenzhong, He Minhao, Lin Zhuoshui, Duan Yikang, Chen Zhongxin, Tang Huosheng, and Xiao Meiqin, *Taiwan bingli guimo yanjiu baogao* (Research Report on the Scale of Taiwan's Armed Forces), Democratic Progressive Party, Policy Committee Research Report Series, Taipei, March 2003.

Li Zhiwei, "Junshi gao jishuhua de wu da qushi: fang junshi kexueyuan zhanlue yanjiubu Chen Bojiang daxiao" (Five Major Trends in the High-Tech Transformation of Military Affairs: An Interview with Senior Colonel Chen Bojiang of the Academy of Military Science's Strategic Research Department), *Guangming ribao* (Guangming Daily), 20 Sep-tember 2000.

Liao Ta-chi, "How Does a Rubber Stamp Become a Roaring Lion? The Transformation of the Role of Taiwan's Legislative Yuan During the Process of Democratization (1950–2000)," *Issues and Studies* 41:3 (September 2005).

Lin Chieh-yu, "China a Threat by 2015, Defense Minister Says," *Taipei Times,* 5 October 2004.

Lin Chu-chin, *Taiwan dangdezhu gongjun san tian ma?* (Can Taiwan Hold Off the PLA for Three Days?), Taipei: Ch'i-p'in Wen-hua Publishing, 2000.

Liu Yichang, *Gao jishu zhanzheng lun* (On High-Technology Warfare), Bei-jing: Academy of Military Science Press, 1993.

Liu Yi-you (colonel, ROC army), "Diyici bowan zhanzheng hou de zhong-gong goujian tezhong budui tantao: jianlun wo yinying duice" (An In-vestigation into the Development of the PRC's Special Forces Since the First Gulf War and ROC Countermeasures), *Guofang zazhi* (Na-tional Defense Magazine) 21:4 (August 2006).

Liu Yuejun, Zhang Liming, and Xin Xilu, *Fei jiechu zhan* (Noncontact Warfare), Beijing: Academy of Military Science Press, 2004.

Liu Zhihui, *Jundui yuanxiao jiaoyu gaige* (Military School and University Educational Reform), Beijing: National Defense University Press, 2004.

Lu Lihua, *Jundui zhihui lilun xuexi zhinan* (Military Command Theory Study Guide), Beijing: National Defense University Press, 2005.

Lu Senshan, ed., *Gao jishu jubu zhanzheng tiaojian xia de zuozhan* (Fight-ing Under High-Technology Local Warfare Conditions), Beijing: Acad-emy of Military Science Press, 1994.

Ma Ying-jeou, "Bridging the Divide: A Vision for Peace in East Asia," speech at the London School of Economics and Political Science, 13 February 2006.

Maples, Michael D., "Current and Projected National Security Threats to the United States," statement for the record, Senate Armed Services Committee, Washington, DC, 27 February 2007.

McConnell, J. Michael, "Annual Threat Assessment of the Director of National Intelligence for the Senate Armed Services Committee," statement for the record, Senate Armed Services Committee, Washington, DC, 27 February 2007.

Ministry of National Defense (Republic of China), *National Defense Report,* Taipei: Government Information Office, 2002, 2004, 2006.

Mulvenon, James C., *Soldiers of Fortune: The Rise and Fall of the Chinese Military-Business Complex, 1978–1998,* Armonk, NY: Sharpe, 2001.

Mulvenon, James, and David Finkelstein, eds., *China's Revolution in Doctrinal Affairs: Emerging Trends in the Operational Art of the Chinese People's Liberation Army,* Alexandria, VA: Center for Naval Analysis, 2006.

Mulvenon, James C., and Andrew N. D. Yang, eds., *A Poverty of Riches: New Challenges and Opportunities in PLA Research,* Santa Monica: RAND, 2003.

Mulvenon, James C., and Richard H. Yang, eds., *The People's Liberation Army in the Information Age,* Santa Monica: RAND, 1999.

National Defense University, Scientific Research Department (People's Republic of China), ed., *Gao jishu jubu zhanzheng yu zhanyi zhanfa* (High-Tech Local War and Campaign Tactics), Beijing, 1993.

National Security Council (Taiwan), *2006 National Security Report,* Taipei: Government Information Office, 20 May 2006.

Naughton, Barry, ed., *The China Circle: Economics and Electronics in the PRC, Taiwan, and Hong Kong,* Washington, DC: Brookings Institution.

Niu Li, *Xinxi zuozhan zhihui kongzhi* (Information Warfare Command and Control), Beijing: People's Liberation Army Press, 2002.

Office of Naval Intelligence (United States), "Chinese Exercise Strait 961: 8–25 March 1996," Suitland, MD, n.d., www.gwu.edu/~nsarchiv/nsaebb/nsaebb19/14-01.htm.

Office of the President (Republic of China), *A-bian zongtong dianzi bao* (A-Bian's E-Newsletter) no. 219 (Taipei, 22 December 2005).

———, "President Chen's Televised Address to the Nation Concerning the 'Discretionary State Affairs Fund,'" Taipei, 5 November 2006.

———, "Zongtong canjia minzhu jinbu dang 2006 xianzheng gaizao xilie yantaohui" (President Chen Participates in the 2006 Constitutional Reform Forum of the Democratic Progressive Party), Taipei, 24 September 2006.

Office of the Secretary of Defense (United States), *The Military Power of the People's Republic of China,* annual report to Congress, Washington, DC: US Department of Defense, 2000–2006.

————, *The Security Situation in the Taiwan Strait,* Washington, DC: US Department of Defense, February 1999.

O'Hanlon, Michael, "Why China Cannot Conquer Taiwan," *International Security* 25:2 (Fall 2000).

Olson, Mancur, and Richard Zeckhauser, "An Economic Theory of Alliances," *Review of Economics and Statistics* 48:3 (August 1966).

Ong Hwee Hwee, "Taiwan Worries About US Ability to Come to Its Rescue," *Straits Times,* 22 January 2007.

Pan, Philip P., "China Reaches Out to Taiwanese Opposition Party," *Washington Post,* 1 April 2005.

Pan, Philip P., and David E. Hoffman, "Taiwan President Pushes Independence from China," *Washington Post,* 29 March 2004.

Pape, Robert A., "Why a Chinese Preemptive Strike Against Taiwan Would Fail," *Taiwan Defense Affairs* 3:2 (Winter 2002–2003).

Peng Guangqian and Yao Youzhi, eds., *The Science of Military Strategy,* Beijing: Military Science Publishing House, 2005.

Puska, Susan M., ed., *People's Liberation Army After Next,* Carlisle, PA: Strategic Studies Institute, US Army War College, 2000.

Qian Haihao, *Jundui zuzhi bianzhixue jiaocheng* (Military Organizational Studies Teaching Materials), Beijing: Academy of Military Science Press, 2001.

Qian Shugen, ed., *Zhongguo zhanzheng dongyuan baike quanshu* (China War Mobilization Encyclopedia), Beijing: Academy of Military Science Press, 2003.

Qing Yonggui, *Zhanyi xinxi zuozhan yanjiu* (Campaign Information Operations Research), Beijing: National Defense University Press, 2000.

Qiu Shulin, *Jundui yuanxiao tizhi yanjiu* (Military School and University System Research), Beijing: National Defense University Press, 2000.

Rigger, Shelley, "The Education of Chen Shui-bian: Taiwan's Experience of Divided Government," *Journal of Contemporary China* 11:33 (2002).

————, *From Opposition to Power: Taiwan's Democratic Progressive Party,* Boulder: Lynne Rienner, 2001.

————, "Political Science and Taiwan's Domestic Politics: The State of the Field," *Issues and Studies* 4:39 (December 2002–March 2003).

————, *Politics in Taiwan: Voting for Democracy,* London: Routledge, 1999.

————, "Taiwan's Best-Case Democratization," *Orbis* (Spring 2004).

————, "The Unfinished Business of Taiwan's Democratization," in Nancy Benkopf Tucker, ed., *Dangerous Strait: The U.S.-Taiwan-China Crisis,* New York: Columbia University Press, 2005.

Romberg, Alan, *Rein in at the Brink of the Precipice: American Policy Toward Taiwan and U.S.-PRC Relations,* Washington, DC: Stimson Center, 2003.

Ross, Robert, "The 1995–96 Taiwan Strait Confrontation: Coercion, Credibility, and the Use of Force," *International Security* 25:2 (Fall 2000).

Roy, Denny, "U.S.-Taiwan Arms Sales: The Perils of Doing Business with Friends," *Asia-Pacific Security Studies* 3:3 (April 2004).

Russell, Richard L., "What If . . . 'China Attacks Taiwan!'" *Parameters* 31:3 (Autumn 2001).

Ryan, Mark A., David M. Finkelstein, and Michael A. McDevitt, eds., *Chinese Warfighting: The PLA Experience Since 1949,* Armonk, NY: Sharpe, 2003.

Sartori, Giovanni, *Comparative Constitutional Engineering: An Inquiry into Structures, Incentives, and Outcomes,* New York: New York University Press, 1997.

Schweller, Randall L., "Unanswered Threats: A Neoclassical Realist Theory of Underbalancing," *International Security* 29:2 (Fall 2004).

Scobell, Andrew, "China's Military Threat to Taiwan in the 21st Century: Coercion or Capture?" *Taiwan Defense Affairs* 4:2 (Winter 2003–2004).

Scobell, Andrew, and Larry M. Wortzel, ed., *Shaping China's Security Environment: The Role of the People's Liberation Army,* Carlisle, PA: Strategic Studies Institute, US Army War College, 2006.

Shambaugh, David, *Modernizing China's Military: Progress, Problems, and Prospects,* Berkeley: University of California Press, 2002.

Shambaugh, David, and Richard H. Yang, eds., *China's Military in Transition,* Oxford: Oxford University Press, 1997.

Shao Hua and Yan Hui, *Xinxi shidai yu junshi houqin* (The Information Age and Military Logistics), Beijing: Contemporary China Press, 2004.

Shen Weiguang, *Xin zhanzheng lun* (On New War), Beijing: People's Press, 1997.

Shen Weiguang, Jie Xizhang, and Li Jijun, *Zhongguo xinxi zhan* (Chinese Information Warfare), Beijing: Xinhua Press, 2004.

Shih Hsiu-chuan, "Lee Says China Dare Not Attack," *Taipei Times,* 8 August 2005.

———, "Ma and Wang Diverge on Constitutional Tinkering," *Taipei Times,* 7 March 2006.

Shlapak, David A., David T. Orletsky, and Barry A. Wilson, *Dire Strait? Military Aspects of the China-Taiwan Confrontation,* Santa Monica: RAND, 2000.

State Environmental Protection Administration (People's Republic of China), *Environmental Protection in China, 1996–2005,* Beijing: State Council Information Office, June 2006.

Stokes, Mark A., "Taiwan's Security: Beyond the Special Budget," *Asian Outlook* no. 2 (27 March 2006).

Su Chi, "The Need for a Peace Accord," *China Times,* 27 October 2006.

———, "Soft Power + Defensive Defense = National Security," *United Daily News,* 24 January 2006.

————, "Taiwan's Security: A KMT Perspective," presentation to the US-Taiwan Business Council's annual defense industry conference, Denver, 11 September 2006.

Sun Guangyun, *Zhongguo guofang keji gongye de gaige he fazhan wenti* (Reforms and Problems in the Development of China's National Defense Science and Technology Industry), Beijing: Aviation Industry Press, 2003.

Swaine, Michael, *Taiwan's National Security, Defense Policy, and Weapons Procurement Processes,* Santa Monica: RAND, 1999.

Swaine, Michael D., and Roy D. Kamphausen, "Military Modernization in Taiwan," in Ashley J. Tellis and Michael Wills, eds., *Strategic Asia 2005–06: Military Modernization in an Era of Uncertainty,* Seattle: National Bureau for Asian Research, September 2005.

Tanner, Murray Scot, *Chinese Economic Coercion Against Taiwan: A Tricky Weapon to Use,* Santa Monica: RAND, 2007.

Templeman, Kharis Ali, and Thomas Edward Flores, "Threats, Alliances, and Electorates: The Empirical Puzzle of Taiwanese Military Spending," paper presented at the annual Midwest Political Science Association conference, Chicago, 8 April 2005.

Tellis, Ashley J., and Michael Wills, eds., *Strategic Asia 2005–06: Military Modernization in an Era of Uncertainty,* Seattle: National Bureau of Asian Research, 2006.

Teng Hsin-yun, "Joint Operations: Views from the ROC Army," *Taiwan Defense Affairs* 2:4 (Summer 2002).

Tien Hung-mao, ed., *Taiwan's Electoral Politics and Democratic Transition: Riding the Third Wave,* Armonk, NY: Sharpe, 1996.

Tsai, Michael M., "Jointness and Taiwan's Security," *Taiwan Defense Affairs* 2:4 (Summer 2002).

Tucker, Nancy Benkopf, ed., *Dangerous Strait: The U.S.-Taiwan-China Crisis,* New York: Columbia University Press, 2005.

————, "If Taiwan Chooses Unification, Should the United States Care?" *Washington Quarterly* 25:3 (Summer 2002).

————, *Taiwan, Hong Kong, and the United States, 1945–1992: Uncertain Friendships,* New York: Twayne, 1994.

Wachman, Alan M., *Taiwan: National Identity and Democratization,* Armonk, NY: Sharpe, 1997.

Walt, Stephen M., *The Origins of Alliances,* Ithaca: Cornell University Press, 1987.

Wang Baocun, "Zhimian junshi biange: jingzhu xinxi zhan 'gaodi'" (Facing Military Transformation: Competing for the "High Ground" in Information Warfare), *Liaowang xinwen zhoukan* (Outlook Weekly), 25 July 2003.

Wang Fuchen, ed., *Jiaotong dongyuanxue* (Transportation Mobilization Studies), Beijing: Academy of Military Science Press, 2004.

Wang Houqing and Zhang Xingye, eds., *Zhanyixue* (The Science of Campaigns), Beijing: National Defense University Press, May 2000.

Wang Jingfa, *Zhongguo junshi houqin biange da zhanlue* (Strategy of Chinese Military Logistics Transformation), Beijing: National Defense University Press, 2005.

Wang Kun-yi, Cai Yuh-ming, and Chai Wen-chung, "Joint Operations and Taiwan's Armed Forces Transformation," *Taiwan Defense Affairs* 5:1 (Fall 2004).

Wang Pufeng, *Xinxi zuozhan yu xin junshi geming* (Information Warfare and the Revolution in Military Affairs), Beijing: Academy of Military Science Press, 1995.

Wang Wenrong, ed., *Zhanluexue* (The Science of Strategy), Beijing: National Defense University Press, 1999.

Wang Xinguo, ed., *Guofang jiaoyu* (National Defense Education), Beijing: Machine Industry Press, 2004.

Wang Zhiyuan, ed., *Lianhe xinxi zuozhan* (Joint Information Warfare), Beijing: Academy of Military Arts and Literature Press, 1999.

Wen Lanchang, ed., *Gao jishu tiaojian xia xinlizhan gailun* (An Introduction to Psychological Warfare Under High-Tech Conditions), Beijing: Academy of Military Science Press, 2001.

Wu Chia-shin, "The Assessment of Communist China's Threat to Launch Amphibious (or Sea-Air-Land) Invasion Against Taiwan During 2005–2010 and the Improvements for Taiwanese Ground Forces," *Taiwan Defense Affairs* 4:3 (Spring 2004).

Wu Yu-shan, "The ROC's Semi-Presidentialism at Work: Unstable Compromise, Not Cohabitation," *Issues and Studies* 36:5 (September–October 2000).

Wu Zhaoyan and Xu Guirui, "Cong Taihai zhanchang huanjing tantao wojun gou zhi biyaoxing" (Examining the Necessity of the Military Procurements from the Perspective of the Taiwan Strait Battlefield Environment), *Haijun xueshu yuekan* (Naval Science Monthly) 41:1 (February 2007).

Wu Ziyong, *Zhanzheng dongyuanxue jiaocheng* (War Mobilization Teaching Materials), Beijing: Academy of Military Science Press, 2001.

Xia Liping, "China: A Responsible Great Power," *Journal of Contemporary China* 10:26 (2001).

Xiao Tianliang, *Zhanzheng kongzhi wenti yanjiu* (Research on Problems of War Control), Beijing: National Defense University Press, 2002.

Xie Taixi (major-general, ROC army reserve), "Jingjin guojun lianhe zuozhan yanxun zhi yanjiu" (Research on the Jingjin Program Military's Joint Warfare Training and Exercises), *Kongjun xueshu yuekan* (Air Force Science Monthly) 592 (July 2006).

Xie Zhi-peng, "Cong zhonggong hewu xiandaihua fazhan yanxi jian lun dui quyu anquan zhi yingxiang" (Investigation into the PRC's Nuclear Weapons Modernization and Its Influence on the Asia-Pacific Region), *Guofang zazhi* (National Defense Magazine) 21:4 (August 2006).

Xiong Guangkai, "On World Revolution in Military Affairs and the Chinese Army Building: Speech by Gen. Xiong Guangkai, Deputy Chief of the General Staff, Chinese People's Liberation Army, at the 5th International Symposium Course in the National Defense University, CPLA, October 17, 2003," *International Strategic Studies* no. 4 (2003).

Yao Jiangning, *Hetong jingong zhanshu jiaocheng* (Combined Offensive Tactics Teaching Materials), Beijing: Academy of Military Science Press, 2005.

Yardley, Jim, "Taiwan's Young Democracy Tested in Comic-Opera Battle," *New York Times,* 23 November 2006.

Yu Yongzhang (colonel, ROC army), "Cong zhonggong junli chengzhang lunshu taihai buduicheng zhanzheng dui wo zhi weixie" (Reflections on China's Increasing Military Power and the Cross-Strait Asymmetric Warfare Threat to Taiwan), *Guofang zazhi* (National Defense Magazine) 20:1 (2005).

Yuan Wei and Zhang Zhuo, *Zhongguo junxiao fazhan shi* (History of the Development of China's Military Schools), Beijing: National Defense University Press, 2001.

Zen I-ming, "The Air Force's View on Improving Joint Operations Capabilities for the ROC Armed Forces," *Taiwan Defense Affairs* 2:4 (Summer 2002).

Zhan Xuexi, *Yilake zhanzheng* (The Iraq War), Beijing: People's Press, 2004.

Zhang Peigao, *Lianhe zhanyi zhihui jiaocheng* (Joint Campaign Command Teaching Materials), Beijing: Academy of Military Science Press, 2001.

Zhang Tianping, *Zhanlue xinxi zhan yanjiu* (Strategic Information Warfare Research), Beijing: National Defense University Press, 2001.

Zhang Xiaoming, "China's 1979 War with Vietnam: A Reassessment," *China Quarterly,* no. 184 (December 2005).

Zheng Dacheng, "Lun zhonggong haijun zhi 094 xing hedongli dandao feidan qianjian" (The Chinese PLA Navy's Type-094 Nuclear-Powered Ballistic Missile Submarine), *Haijun xueshu yuekan* (Naval Science Monthly) 41:1 (February 2007).

Zhou Dewang, *Lianhe zuozhan zhihui jigou yamjiu* (Joint Operations Command Structure Research), Beijing: National Defense University Press, 2002.

Index

professionalization, 65–67;
professional military education,
27, 70–71; reorganization,
25–26; Second Artillery Corps,
23; software reforms, 65–67;
space operations, 64–65; "Strait
961" exercise, 17; strategy and
doctrine, 28–29; training and
exercises, 27, 71–73; "Two
Transformations" defense policy,
20, 25
Christensen, Thomas, 86
Chungshan Institute of Science and
Technology, 98
Clinton, Bill, 4, 16, 93;
administration of, 140
Conflict scenarios: air and missile
campaign, 74–76; amphibious
invasion, 76–78; limited use of
force, 74; naval blockade, 76;
persuasion and coercion, 73–74
Cornell University, 17
Cross-Strait: conflict, 87; economic
links, 15, 16; military balance,
159; 1992 Consensus, 16;
relations, 81, 82, 197–198;
tensions, 157; trade, 159; travel,
16

D'Amato, Richard, 148–149
Defense Journal (Guofang zazhi),
11
Democratic Progressive Party
(DPP), 7–9, 32, 46–50, 83,
85–86, 89, 95, 128, 140, 176;
affiliated analysts, 149; "decisive
offshore battle" concept,
117–121; defense policy, 181;
independence, support for,
179–180; officials, 163; since
2000 presidential election, 179
Deng Xiaoping, 20, 21
"De-Sinification," 48

"Eight-Point Proposal," 16
Executive Yuan, 98, 122, 167, 186

Falklands War, 20, 28
France, 35–37, 124
Fuzhou (city), 82

Guam, 152
Gulf War, 19, 20, 28, 51
Guofang zazhi (Defense Journal),
11
Guofang zhengce pinglun (Taiwan
Defense Affairs), 11

Haijun xueshu yuekan (Naval
Science Monthly), 11
Holdridge, John, 32
Hsiao Bi-khim, 167
Hsieh Chang-ting, 179
Hsueh Shih-min, 162
Hu Chen-pu, 101–102, 141
Hu Jintao, 55

Institute for Taiwan Defense and
Strategic Studies, 11
Iraq War, 152–153

Japan, 53–54, 81, 82, 151
Jiang Zemin, 16–17, 20, 52

Kaohsiung (port), 18
Keelung (port), 18
Keith, James, 148
Kinmen (island), 74, 82, 160
KMT. See Kuomintang
Koo Chen-foo, 16
Kosovo, 18, 21, 28, 46
Kuomintang (KMT), 7, 11, 32, 34,
36, 47, 50, 85, 89, 95–97,
99–100, 104, 119, 122, 124, 126,
128, 133, 164, 165, 174,
176–177; control of ROC
government and, 167–169

Lafayette frigates, 36
Lee, David, 142
Lee Jye, 100, 103–105, 119, 131, 161
Lee Teng-hui, 8, 17–19, 21, 32, 33, 46, 88, 140
Lee Wen-chung, 183–184
Legislative Yuan, 8, 34, 83, 89, 91, 98, 101, 104, 142, 162, 167, 183, 185, 189; National Defense Committee, 105, 119, 129, 171; Procedure Committee, 95; role in government, 170–171
Li Ao, 105
Lin Chong-pin, 162
Lin Yu-fang, 97, 165
Lu, Annette, 132–133

Matsu (island), 74, 82, 160
Ma Ying-jeou, 164, 178
"Message to Compatriots in Taiwan," 15
Ministry of National Defense (ROC), 6, 11, 40, 42, 89, 98, 100, 124–127, 156–159; Bureau of Armaments and Acquisition, 124; General Political Warfare Bureau, 101, 102, 141; Integrated Assessment Office, 124; Organization Act, 122–124, 134–135; Strategic Planning Department, 124

National Security Council, Taiwan, 6
Nauru, Netherlands, 35, 83
Naval Science Monthly *(Haijun xueshu yuekan),* 11
"Nine-Point Proposal," 15

"One China" principle, 16, 17, 47

P-3C antisubmarine warfare planes, 103

PAC-3 missile defense system, 97, 103
PACOM. *See* United States, Pacific Command
Pan-Blue parties, 7, 8, 11, 49, 89, 92, 165, 171; opposition to special budget, 95–100, 102–104; policy positions, 177–178, 181–182, 189–190; relationship between KMT and PFP, 176; supporters, 185
Pan-Green parties, 8, 11, 47, 102, 159, 164–165, 171, 175; since 2000 presidential election, 179; supporters, 185
People's First Party, 7, 89, 96–97, 99, 165
People's Liberation Army. *See* Chinese People's Liberation Army
People's Republic of China: defense industry, 24–25, 56–57; domestic economic development, 21; nationalism, 51; Taiwan Affairs Office, 48, 49; 2000 Taiwan white paper, 46; 2004 national defense white paper, 53; 2008 Olympics, 51, 162–163
Philippines, 152
PLA. *See* Chinese People's Liberation Army

Qian Qichen, 47, 48
Quadrennial Defense Review, 151

RAND, 30
Reagan, Ronald, 4
Republic of China: Chinese military, assessment of, 155–157; companies, 16, 33; constitutional reforms, 182; domestic politics, 7–9, 32, 167; electoral system, 172–175; investment in China,

About the Book

Confounding expectations, Taiwan reduced its military spending for many years, even as its sole adversary, the People's Republic of China, modernized its military and significantly increased its defense budget. Michael Chase examines the key factors that have shaped Taiwan's security policy over a span of three decades.

Chase explores both the role of US security assurances in formulating Taiwan's defense policy and the profound influence that domestic politics has played. He also considers the context of cross-Strait relations and the implications of Taiwan's security choices for potential instability and conflict in the region and beyond. Relying on extensive Chinese-language sources and interviews, he offers the most definitive treatment of Taiwan's security policy to date.

Michael S. Chase is assistant professor in the Strategy and Policy Department at the US Naval War College.